# LOST
# GENERATIONS

D1604296

# LOST GENERATIONS

## A Boy, a School, a Princess

J. Arthur Rath

A Latitude 20 Book
University of Hawai'i Press
Honolulu

**Library of Congress Cataloging-in-Publication Data**

Rath, J. Arthur
Lost generations : a boy, a school, a princess / J. Arthur Rath.
p.  cm.
"A Latitude 20 book."
Includes index.
ISBN-13: 978-0-8248-2949-0 (hardcover : alk. paper)
ISBN-10: 0-8248-2949-2 (hardcover : alk. paper)
ISBN-13: 978-0-8248-3010-6 (pbk. : alk. paper)
ISBN-10: 0-8248-3010-5 (pbk. : alk. paper)
1. Kamehameha Schools.  2. Kamehameha Schools /
Bernice Pauahi Bishop Estate—Finance.
3. Kamehameha Schools—Alumni and alumnae.
4. Rath, J. Arthur.  I. Title.
LD7501.H423R38 2006
371'.009969'31—dc22
2005013950

Designed by Trina Stahl Design

Printed by The Maple-Vail Book Manufacturing Group

*Fading away like the stars in the morning,*
*Losing their light in the glorious sun,*
*Thus shall we pass from this earth and its toiling,*
*Only remembered for what we have done.*

Princess Bernice Pauahi Bishop,
1831–1884. *Bishop Museum photo.*

Charles Reed Bishop, 1822–1915.
*Bishop Museum photo.*

"Only Remembered," words by Dr. Horatius Bonar.

# Contents

Prelude · 1

PART ONE: *Only One Who Didn't Know* · 5
1. High School Reunion · 5
2. Alumni Offer Help · 8
3. Facts about My Father · 11
4. Recollections · 18

PART TWO: *Homeless* · 20
5. Youthful Nomad · 20
6. Big Island Days · 35

PART THREE: *Chinese Connection* · 48
7. Brief History of Hawai'i · 48
8. Being Hawaiian · 58

PART FOUR: *School That Saves Lives* · 64
9. Art and Oz · 64
10. Kamehameha Schools · 75
11. Auntie Nona · 80
12. Charting a New Direction · 85
13. War Years on Campus · 88

PART FIVE: Hawai'i Changes · 125
14. Off to College · 125
15. Hawaiian Culture · 131
16. The Lei · 135
17. Oz Becomes a Trustee · 139
18. Educational Vision · 148

PART SIX: Abandoned Children · 153
19. Dickie and Lokelani Appointed · 153
20. Fear and Intimidation · 168
21. Determining Hawaiian Children's Future · 175

PART SEVEN: Third Revolution · 182
22. Help the Children · 182
23. Colbert, the Court Master · 184
24. Randie, the Music Maestro · 187
25. The Student and the Trustee Bully · 190
26. Nona Writes a Letter · 195
27. The Integrity of the Trust · 200
28. The Alumni Meet—and March · 202
29. "Broken Trust" Appears · 214
30. Reactions · 219
31. Margery, the Attorney General · 223
32. Bobby Harmon Loses His Job · 226
33. Judge Yim Releases His Report · 230
34. The Court Master Releases His Report · 234
35. Lokelani Begins Damage Control · 239
36. Why Can't the Trustees Behave? · 245
37. Letting the Genie Out of the Bottle · 257

Interlude · 262

38. The Court Master's Consolidated Report · 266
39. Lawyers Crank Out a Response · 272
40. The Attorney General's Preliminary Report · 274
41. Fattening Local Bank Accounts · 276
42. Lokelani Goes to Trial · 283
43. Personal Profiteering · 292
44. Oz and His Attorneys · 300
45. Influence Peddling · 303

46. Trustees the Nail, IRS the Hammer · 309
47. At Last They Go! · 314
48. A Four-Year Yo-Yo Contest · 317

PART EIGHT: *Aftermath* · 324
49. Oz and I Reflect · 324
50. Classmates · 331
51. Same Old, Same Old · 342
52. Instant Replay · 350

Postlude · 356

Index · 363

# LOST
# GENERATIONS

# Prelude

THIS BOOK'S first half describes my disconnected life before becoming one of Princess Bernice Pauahi Bishop's spiritual children and introduces schoolmate Oswald Stender, an orphan raised as an old-time Hawaiian. In chapter 7 are my family's stories of early plantation days, a perspective on why America overthrew Hawai'i's kingdom, and the "good and industrious" maxim that helped save the Hawaiian race.

The second half is about corruption and revolution: rising socialism, turmoil within the Bishop Estate, and how "a disguised champion" strove to make things *pono*—moral and proper.

I've organized this book into eight parts for reading in its entirety or selectively, telling everything through "talk stories," each sufficient unto itself. A large capital letter indicates the beginning of a talk story; one transitions into another, creating the cumulative drama of *Lost Generations*.

Talk stories occur when a group gathers, and everyone from the littlest child to the oldest adult has a chance to be listened to courteously.

Islanders also use the term "talk story" for a one-on-one conversation.

A storyteller may adopt another persona, as does an actor, and sometimes applies the present tense. Explanatory material and genealogy are added in subordinate clauses; these become parenthetical phrases or side excursions, similar to my footnotes. When describing personal exploits, the storyteller includes underlying themes, as do I.

To heal strife, a form of talk story called *"ho'oponopono"* (described in chapter 28) may be invoked. The opportunity this offered for resolution is the cusp within this book—a potential point for change.

I attended court hearings, collected legal papers, reviewed archived documents, studied press reports, and interviewed people. While walking to the state attorney general's office in downtown Honolulu one afternoon, I glanced at buildings set within spacious dark-green lawns surrounded by flowering trees and thought: "Hawai'i is a beautiful cover for corruption."

Answering my ringing cell phone, I heard an excited voice screech, "*Stop!*"

I immediately stopped right in place.

It was an attorney who'd given me court documents. Lowering her voice, speaking slowly, she said: "The other side knows what you're doing," drawing out the word "k-n-o-ws."

Pausing as I absorbed that, she finished curtly: "You are in grave danger," and she hung up.

My total conversation had been, "Hello."

She wouldn't return phone calls.

Lono Lyman, a younger male cousin, asked around and didn't find my name on any Honolulu "hit list"—this is *not* a top-ten music list.

Realizing "the other side" uses intimidation, I continued collecting information. But as time passed, doubts rose, and I grew increasingly concerned:

- Was I out of synch with contemporary hedonism?
- Would this book's theme—struggles of good people within a Godless environment—be relevant to readers weaned on modern media saturated with violence, sex and sexuality, glamorous living, material possessions, self-importance, lifestyles of the rich and famous?

For messages to breathe, I must enrich pages by living within the book; I had to stop centering on personal materialism that offered only glittering images of self. Such was the society in which I spent most of my adult life while reaching for worldly gains and images, seeking and squandering riches, striving to rise above others' anger and abuse.

So I stopped.

Spirituality fostered in a Hawaiian Princess's safe harbor surfaced. I became less complicated, more open, able to learn from good people within this book. You and I meet people like them everywhere; they live with dignity, joy, confidence, peace, and kindness. They teach us about courage, overcoming evil, healing the spirit, making love endure, and keeping promises.

For over a thousand years, talk stories of various forms have been traditional within Hawaiian culture. I chose this vernacular as a way of evoking others to talk their own stories.

J. Arthur Rath
Fall 2005

PART ONE

# ONLY ONE WHO DIDN'T KNOW

>—◆>—○—<◆—<

CHAPTER 1

## High School Reunion

### 1994

I LEARNED *who* I was in the eighth through twelfth grades at Kamehameha School for Boys during the years 1944 to 1949. I found out *what* I was from my forty-fifth class reunion. It began with a casual remark.

At the welcoming reception, classmate Tom Hugo said, "I'm pleased at how things turned out for you. My dad would have felt the same."

Huh? I hadn't known Tom Hugo Sr., his dad. Uncomprehending, I smiled quickly, nodded my head while saying "thanks," and went to the next event—an orientation on the new directions for Kamehameha Schools.

We sat in the auditorium containing so many fond memories as the speaker said, "Kamehameha wants early achievers. We're enrolling those who've proved to be outstanding students by the sixth grade."

Older alumni looked uneasily at each other.

Many of us wouldn't have been admitted under such criteria. Erratic early school records would certainly have kept me out; I shuffled through five schools in two states and on two islands during my first six grades.

A few seats away sat Joe Pokini, one of three pure-blooded Hawaiian men in our class. Joe grinned and winked at me, realizing he'd no longer be welcomed; he took vocational courses and retired from the U.S. Corps of Engineers. Pure-Hawaiian brothers Rex and David Pahoa, sports stars and outstanding students in the vocational program, might also be left out as well; both had successful technical careers.

This happened in June 1994 during Kamehameha Schools new "alumni week." It was my first association with class members in forty-five years. Students were gone, we had the run of the place, and it was like returning to our home. That year classes graduating during years ending in 9 and 4 had reunions, and my class of 1949 was included with alumni from 1944, 1954, 1959, and so forth.

We attended lectures, workshops, tours, social events, and a *lū'au* (a Hawaiian feast). Those of us from outside of Honolulu stayed in dormitories on the former girls school campus. A classmate from Kaua'i brought two boxes filled with fish for frying, two coolers with raw fish for snacking, poi made from her family's own taro, *limu kohu* (edible seaweed), a bag of rice, a rice cooker, and pots and pans. Someone brought Chinese crack seed. Chipping in for beverages, we ate, drank, sang with guitar and *'ukulele* accompaniment, and talked story until late in the night.

We older male alumni had attended a diversified Kamehameha that offered precollege, general studies, and vocational education paths. All boys took some vocational courses, starting in the schools vegetable gardens. Girls chose precollege or general education, and all learned home nursing. Young women boarders acquired social graces within a finishing school environment.

Only a college preparatory program remained.

I walked around the lower campus where vocational students had learned automobile repair, carpentry, drafting, electrical work, metal lathing and machining, welding, and other trades. Empty buildings were tomblike.[1]

Princess Bernice Pauahi Bishop willed her wealth to educate Hawaiians, to help them meet challenges from an encroaching Western civilization. Kamehameha Schools purpose was to produce "industrious men and women."

I had an idea: Our class represented the diversified educational tracks Kamehameha once offered. During our fiftieth reunion we could present trustees with a summary of our career outcomes. Maybe this would help make the schools more inclusive again. After all, Oz Stender, vocational student from the class of 1950, became an important businessman and is now a Bishop Estate trustee. I'd do the research and find out if classmates wanted me to draft such a letter.

After enjoying each other's company so much, classmates decided to hold yearly reunions in Las Vegas, Nevada, between the on-campus alumni weeks now available every five years.

---

[1] Kamehameha was modeled originally after Hilo Boarding School, developed in 1836 by David and Sarah Lyman, my maternal missionary ancestors; I'm their 125th descendant. They combined vocational training with academic instruction to help Hawaiians and other minorities meet a changing society's challenges. After the Civil War opened opportunities to all, the Lyman's approach was used with freed American blacks at Hampton Institute, Virginia, 1868, and at Tuskegee Institute, Alabama, 1881. The latter is where George Washington Carver devoted most of his life to teaching and product innovation.

The five-tiered campus of Kamehameha Schools sprawls across 600 acres on Kāpalama Heights, Oʻahu. Other campuses are on the islands of Hawaiʻi and Maui. Honolulu Advertiser *photo by Cory Lum.*

## CHAPTER 2
# *Alumni Offer Help*
### 1994

Don Ho invited classmates to his evening show at Waikīkī's Polynesian Palace Hotel; our drinks were "on the house." Don's voice is still of superior quality, but that didn't stop us from "improving" his show by joining in whenever we knew the song.

While he sang "Down by the Shack by the Sea," we practically drowned him out with different words to the melody: We sang "Down by the Barns on Alapai Street," the old Hawaiian Rapid Transit radio-show theme song. Bowing to the inevitable, Don called us to the stage where we gave his audience a taste of true local music—fun for us and the audience.

Sitting grouped in a circle in his apartment-sized dressing room, we were enjoying the lingering good feeling his shows create when Don asked, "What can we do to help the Bishop Estate?"

We'd toured Bishop Estate headquarters at Kawaiahaʻo Plaza that afternoon. An investment department official told us how rich the estate was becoming and encouraged us to bring any good deals to his attention. While the crowd moved on to an outdoor party, I asked what was considered "a good deal."

"Anything yielding the equivalent of a 25 percent annual return," he replied.

It didn't appear that the Bishop Estate needed help.

Don explained that the state legislature enacted a law forcing the Bishop Estate to sell land leased to homeowners at a fraction of its value.

Those of us living on the mainland were hearing this for the first time and expressed the fear that Kamehameha would lose its financial base.

"Why not organize a political action committee?" suggested one.

"Yes: 20 percent of Islanders are Hawaiians who can help influence political opinion," responded another.

"Let's talk with Oz Stender about it," urged a third.

Classmate William Fernandez, a retired California federal judge, said he'd talk with Oz and offered to lead our efforts in developing a plan. Pat Gandall promised research assistance. In the U.S. Air Force for twenty-one years as an intelligence officer, Pat spent several years as a special agent in civilian clothes for the inspector general in the Office of Special Investigation. After retiring, he supervised clerks in the court system for the Superior Court of California in Orange County.

I was familiar with a "Practical Politics" program General Electric used to advance its local interests in Syracuse, New York, where it once employed 16,000 persons. Politically nonpartisan, the program taught employees ways to influence decision making. I drew on that and other experiences when Pat and I developed a plan to help Hawaiians become politically active. It was organized around small neighborhood cells reaching districts throughout the Hawaiian Islands. Full of zeal, we completed it within six weeks.

Judge Fernandez said our schema looked like a Viet Cong organizational chart: tightly structured, localized, manageable by a small cadre—very workable.

He forwarded it to Oz, who liked it a lot. Oz said he was intrigued by how so few could network with so many—and this was before e-mail became ubiquitous.

Oz hosted a lunch at the Oʻahu Country Club and invited representatives from other classes, a member of the estate's legal staff, and its government relations manager. He'd checked with estate lawyers before arranging the luncheon; they reviewed our plans and didn't think they posed any problems. As far as Oz was concerned, we had a green light and could start the plan after the meeting. That's why I flew in from New York for the luncheon.

Oz ate with us but left before discussions, explaining, "What you have to cover is outside my area of responsibility. The staff here can help you."

The meeting went well. The lawyer was very positive, but the government relations manager said virtually nothing and just looked sour and annoyed. Judge Fernandez met privately with her after the meeting while I paced excitedly in the country club lobby.

Bill Fernandez appeared about an hour later. He had a long expression and shook his head. The government relations manager told him our plan was impossible because, in her words, "Political activity puts the estate's tax-exempt status in jeopardy."

"I explained it again to her," Bill said; he was trying to reassure me that he did his best. "I promised her that we'll implement the program ourselves, raise outside contributions for political education, and distribute money fairly in a nonpartisan way to candidates interested in helping Hawaiian children. I told her about your plans to teach political training in communities having large concentrations of Hawaiians. I explained that we wouldn't identity ourselves with the Bishop Estate.

"She looked me straight in the eyes when she said, 'The estate has a completely hands-off policy on any political activity. It does not encourage participation by groups connected with the estate in any way.'

"I reminded her, 'We, not the Bishop Estate, will be doing this.'

"She answered, 'Alumni will be linked implicitly with the Bishop Estate.'"

Bill and I said nothing as he drove me to my mother's apartment in Nu'uanu. Before leaving his car I said, "There are things I have to do before talking with Don. Let's see him tomorrow night."

The next day I went to the trustees' headquarters to talk with the government relations manager.

"Alumni just want to be helpful," I explained. "Hawaiians are vastly outnumbered in the legislature. They have little political clout with elected representatives because not enough of them vote. Encouraging Hawaiians to be part of the political process is the crux for our plan."

Unaware that I was talking with "Madame Svengali," I thought her answer was incredibly naive: "The estate can muster support in front of the legislators. I arrange for alumni to show up and carry signs."

She just doesn't get it, I thought, attempting to depart graciously.

Don, Bill, and I ate chow mien in a small restaurant after Don's late show that night. I told Don the estate couldn't accept our help because it had to avoid political activity. Bill repeated what he had been told and concluded with this observation: "Trustees are going to extreme lengths to be proper."

The Bishop Estate's government relations manager had perfected the art of political misdirection.

# CHAPTER 3

## Facts about My Father

### 1996

Two years later I was stretching my long, cramped legs on the *lānai* of cousin Kea's suburban condominium after a twelve-hour flight from New York.

Rows of airline seats were closer together than they are now. The person in front of me had kept wiggling and leaning back, banging my knees. I finally tapped his shoulder and whispered, "Please, sir."

He stopped momentarily but soon resumed fidgeting; probably had an itchy butt.

No other seats were available and the stewardess wouldn't let me move into the first-class section. Instead of acting irritated, I scrunched up and concentrated on what I'd tell Kea. She would be the first contemporary to hear my dark secret—I wondered how she would regard me then. I was very apprehensive about this during the entire flight.

⊶⊙⊷

Just before sunset, I was enjoying views of a golf course and the ocean, drinking Long Island ice tea, believing it was iced tea flavored with cola. Kea became a cordon bleu chef in France. You don't question what she serves.

After several sips I was somewhat relaxed and revealed what I had rehearsed during the flight:

"Kea, at an early age I stopped asking about my missing father because my mother gave me vague answers and quickly changed the subject."

"Hualani is controlling," Kea acknowledged.

I obliquely began to tell my tale:

"I spent time with Molly Lyman while in Honolulu two years ago. She was interested in the research I was doing on Kamehameha Schools vocational programs and reminisced about living on the old campus while her father, Ernest Webster, was principal from 1914 to 1923.

"'Our family had its meals in the boys' dining room,' Molly told me. 'I was treated as a fair-haired little princess. Young men in West Point–style military uniforms smiled, nodded, and often waved to me.'

"Molly continued to be regal all her life, Kea. For a change of pace, Uncle Belden would take me with him to seedy bars where we'd speak pidgin English and joke with sassy Korean barmaids—lots of laughs."

"I hope you didn't tell your mother," Kea grinned.

Shaking my head, I continued:

"Molly was in late stages of cancer; she was being assisted at home by hospice volunteers. It was my last chance for information neither Mother nor anyone else provided.

"She lay on the bed wearing a *muʻumuʻu* in what had been 'my room' when I stayed with Molly and Belden. It always had a nice breeze wafting down from Mānoa Valley. Pulling my chair close, I gently asked her to tell me of my father.

"'You said you were friends with his brother and sister when attending Punahou.'"

"'I guess you're old enough,' Molly answered." I would think so; I was then sixty-two years of age.

"Molly began: 'Your father hung around with a rough crowd in Pālama's slums. He and friends played Hawaiian music on guitars and *ʻukulele* in bars; your father was admired for his silvery falsetto singing. I know only he was in a fight and was arrested for murder.'"

As an aside, I told Kea that when returning to the mainland I visited Bob Lyman, my mother's brother, who lives in Florida. I asked Uncle Bob about the fight, and since Molly had told me something about it, he gave me more details.

"'It was one of those instances when men who are drinking start arguing, and tempers rise,' Bob began. 'Someone throws a punch at your father, his being a haole. Junior makes a punching bag of the guy who hit him. The guy's head slams against the bar rail and he falls to the floor dead from a concussion. Your dad was a trained boxer from Springfield College; the guy he beat up was just a rowdy. Junior was jailed for murder.'"

I told Kea, "Bob didn't know more about it than that."

I continued describing my discussion with Molly. "She told about a second death involving my father: 'He let a young Hawaiian woman drive his car; both of them had been drinking. She went too fast around a curve on the

Pali, crashed the car, and was killed. Police arrested your father because the woman was an unlicensed driver. Junior was charged once again with murder. Because a judge reduced both charges to manslaughter, he wasn't castrated at Pālama Settlement's male sterilization clinic.'"

I had learned of this practice from reading Pālama's history. Castration was the fate of Hawai'i's men in the 1930s who were charged with multiple and serious offenses.[1]

"'Alcohol was also probably to blame for his other problem,' Molly said.

"I felt as though Pandora's box was open. Molly continued:

"'Your father raped your mother while out on bail. Your mother was twenty-two years old and shared a house with other young working women. Junior Rath was also twenty-two. He knew one of your mother's housemates and later claimed he had crawled into your mother's bed by mistake. He muffled Hualani's cries while overpowering her.

"'So naive. She didn't realize she was pregnant until a doctor told her during a routine medical check up.'

"Molly finished the story abruptly:

"'Belden and his two brothers ordered Junior to make things right so you'd have a father's surname. Junior left after a courtroom wedding ceremony. He wasn't charged with rape and a judge banished Junior from the Islands instead of jailing him for manslaughter.'

"Molly's words, delivered in a matter-of-fact voice, made me feel frailer than she appeared—and she was dying!

"I know the rest of the story. My father boarded a boat to the mainland and never became part of my life nor contributed money. According to my Territory of Hawai'i birth certificate, I was born a child of Caucasian-Hawaiian ancestry and named James Arthur Rath III. To his family, I didn't exist.

"After my talks with Molly, I asked my mother for more information." I shook my head, indicating "more" wasn't forthcoming.

"Hualani's sharp and as spunky as ever," said Kea.

"True. This is how she reacted once I started asking questions: 'Can't understand you. My hearing aid isn't working.' It was working a few sentences earlier," I explained to Kea.

"'O.K., MOTHER,' I answered loudly. 'I WILL WRITE MY QUES-

---

[1] When the twentieth century ended, the *Honolulu Advertiser* newspaper honored James and Ragna Rath as among Hawai'i's influential persons of the past hundred years. James died before Junior's misdeeds and was described in his obituary as "The Saint of Pālama Settlement" because of all the lives that he, through the settlement, had helped save. Ragna helped mothers learn health and child care and got them milk to drink.

TIONS ON THIS NOTEPAD.' I planned to lead into each question by reinforcing her answer to the previous one so she couldn't misdirect the sequence. She studied what I wrote and, assuming her social worker role, she delivered curt answers in a flat, emotionless voice.

"My first question was: 'Did you and Junior Rath live together before I was born?'

"Shaking her head haughtily, she retorted, 'No.'

"My second question was: 'Did you live together after I was born?'

"'No.'"

"The next question was: 'Did he ever see me?'

"'No.'

"My last question was: 'Did his mother, brothers, or sisters express interest in me?'

"'No.'

"I stopped writing. Hualani wouldn't reveal feelings unless she was angry; she just withdrew, making me feel insecure. I realize now she was worried I'd become a 'junior' Junior. I had to do everything just so. She made criticisms, didn't give compliments, controlled what was said by monopolizing conversations.

"She'd spent part of her girlhood with her mother's relatives in Vancouver, British Columbia; the manners she forced on me probably came to her in Vancouver from Victorian England. She was that 'proper.' Living with her a total of only three years cumulatively allowed me to escape growing up to be 'perfect.'

"The rest of my early life was spent in foster homes and with relatives and family friends. I had five years of stability as a Kamehameha School for Boys boarding student—it was my only real boyhood home."

So much was built up within me that my talk story had become a monologue; I had an urgency to expunge everything. Unwittingly, I had reverted to my mother's behavior. Kea sat calmly and showed no emotions as I rambled, without verbal give and take.

"Seeing Tom Hugo after talking with Molly, I thanked him for inserting the first piece to a jigsaw puzzle now seemingly completed. Tom explained, 'My father worked with your mother in the Department of Social Services in the early 1930s. He asked her if he could raise you.'

"Speechless, I put my right arm on one of Tom's broad shoulders, giving him a slight hug. His late father probably saw me in the 1940s; he drove a Honolulu Rapid Transit bus route to Kaimukī where my grandparents lived."

At this point, I digressed from talking about myself, excitedly interjecting surprising things I'd learned about young Hualani. "She was quite striking and outgoing. Her hair hung below her waist. She was a fearless swimmer in even the roughest ocean. She made social work rounds on horseback in the country. She'd gallop up to people who used land they confiscated from persons sent to Moloka'i's leper colony and scold them. She initiated court cases forcing land grabbers to relinquish or pay for lepers' land. . . ."

Kea interrupted my ramblings by casually saying, "We all knew about your father."

"*What?*" I was stunned. "Why didn't anyone tell me?"

"There was no reason. What happened wasn't your fault."

Trying to comprehend, I told Kea that Duke Kahanamoku was the only person to mention my father to me. Duke told me Junior was an outstanding swimming coach. He took a pre-Olympics team of four Hawaiian boys on a mainland tour and they won every meet. Duke commented that I looked like him. This must have made my mother edgy. Duke had finished by saying, "Too bad what happened." Not knowing what this meant, I was too awed by this towering hero to ask questions.

Kea and I talked a bit about Duke Kahanamoku, standard bearer for the qualities of nobility that Kamehameha boys were urged to emulate. He was in the class of 1910 at Kamehameha, popularized the native Hawaiian crawl stroke, won five Olympic medals in swimming over a twelve-year period, and is known as "the father of surfing."

Kea is a trustee for Nadine Kahanamoku's scholarship at the John Burns School of Medicine, University of Hawai'i. It gives medical students financial aid. Duke and Nadine had no children of their own and gave their estates to help young people, as did Princess Pauahi.

The sun had sunk and the afterglow in the sky and on the ocean was blood red. My second goblet of Long Island ice tea was empty. The stoicism I use to sublimate life's pains drained as I drank.

I was overwhelmed by Kea's words: "*We all knew about your father.*" Suddenly I was racked with sobs, thinking of those who knew and said nothing. Yet I was grateful to all who protected my psyche—soul, spirit, and mind—when I was young and so vulnerable. Appreciation for silence and kindnesses made me weep.

How could I not know *anything* from *anyone* through *all* those years? Once able to control my voice, I blurted, "Love from Hawaiians, indifference from others."

Kea replied soothingly, as Hawaiian women do so easily: "It was not unusual for haole families to shun children of mixed marriages. Women carried the burden and bore the blame for misfortune. Males escaped responsibility. The hush-hush you experienced is the Hawaiian tradition of not laying the problems of adults on children."

Kea rose to bring me a mug of coffee and returned to the kitchen to prepare one of her outstanding meals.

Remaining on the *lānai,* I studied the heavens, thinking about the words *"not laying the problems of adults on children."*

Stars shine brighter nowhere than in Hawaiian skies. But instead of stars, I saw the smiling faces of people in Kona where I lived before going to Kamehameha: cowboys, fishermen, musicians, the elephant man. Images shifted kaleidoscopically, then lingered on these scenes that are as vivid today:

- Mr. Hua teaching me to play the *'ukulele* I carry most everywhere except to school. . . .

This first graduating class at Kamehameha School for Girls (1897) began the tradition of seniors making their own white graduation gowns. First on the left in the back row is the author's aunt, Kalei Ewaliko; she became a water colorist and schoolteacher. Second from the right is Lydia Aholo, Queen Lili'uokalani's adopted daughter. Principal Ida Pope paid Lydia's tuition at her alma mater, Oberlin College in Ohio. *Reprinted with permission of Kamehameha Schools.*

- Auntie Kalei Lyman, who was in Kamehameha School for Girls first class and became a well-known art teacher, showing me how to "paint on the run." We'd stop during car trips on the Big Island so I could make a quick pencil sketch of a scene. She is telling me: "Concentrate, absorb the impression and emotions it gives you. Write down which colors to add later. . . ."
- A Christmas party where other children receive presents. I am about to leave empty-handed. Santa Claus calls out my name, steps behind the tree, and grandly hands me the last package; it is big and wrapped in newspaper. Eagerly I tear the paper off and hold a long, well-oiled leather rope with a running noose at one end. Moses probably braided it from the hide that made me tough. . . .

The images are from long ago, but *never* far away.

I now know *what* I am: I am a person protected from ill will, given a chance in life.

CHAPTER 4

## Recollections

1996

$\mathrm{V}$ICKIE LYMAN and I hiked up the mountains behind Kamehameha Schools the next day. I couldn't maintain her pace; she scurried over high rocks, I pulled myself up, stopped to pick and munch strawberry guavas, study blooming wild orchids, and pray while gazing down on miles of trees. At one point I stood above rain clouds forming over a valley. Vickie waited wherever the trail forked off so I wouldn't be lost while perambulating.

After three hours I joined her in the parking lot. She was going to drive me to her home on the other side of the island, my favorite retreat. Passing world-famous surfing beaches on O'ahu's North Shore, we continued until the road ended. Time stopped here as well.

Cousins Kimo and Vickie's house was hidden from the road and guarded by geese. If they didn't recognize you as "family," their sudden gaggling would scare you out of your wits as they rushed from behind brush, sharp beaks aimed at your ankles. Noisy geese started the dogs barking and roosters began crowing—strangers did not arrive unannounced.

This home, in the family for almost eighty years, looked even older than that; it was built of lumber from the old 'Ewa sugar plantation. There was electricity and indoor plumbing, but water still came from the pipe stuck in a mountain behind the house. A banyan tree's branches covered the outdoor "living room," providing shade and rain shelter. A porch outside an upstairs bedroom was home to two male and three female peacocks that would scold me if I slept late in the morning.

Vickie returned to town, leaving me alone for a couple of days. "Radar," the small dog with long ears and sharp hearing, kept me company and calmed the geese.

We headed for the beach. Coral reefs are close to shore here and swimming is not good; that and remoteness isolate this cove. I hung my shirt and a water bottle in a heliotrope tree; although roots were uncovered by high winter surf, it remained firmly anchored on shore. I sensed a message.

Snuggling between two sandbanks, I breathed deeply before meditating. Radar started whining, his ears pointing straight up. Hearing screams, I scrambled to the top of the bank.

Sounds came from a flaming figure 400 yards away running toward the ocean. He dropped at the shoreline, silent, not moving.

I ran to the house and phoned the fire station, and rescue team members arrived seemingly instantly. Firemen deduced that the victim drove here for immolation. He poured a can of gasoline over himself and ignited a cigarette lighter. Did he change his mind? People knowing about such things said he probably expected to die immediately by inhaling the burning fumes. It hadn't worked. Experiencing instant hell, he tried dousing the flames.

I walked to the death scene the next morning; high tides washing in made the white sand pristine. Something about the size of a ping-pong ball tossed in the water. I swam out and brought back a round, waxy, translucent yellowish substance; it was wrinkled like a miniature human brain. A friend identified it as spermaceti from a whale and mounted it on a *koa* pedestal for me—another symbol from the cove at the end of the road.

Back in Honolulu, I walked and walked throughout parts of downtown Honolulu I knew as a boy. The second-floor balcony at 'Iolani Palace is where child movie star Shirley Temple waved to me when I was about three years old—well, she actually waved to the entire crowd, but small children *do* tend to personalize experiences.

I savored the sights, sounds, and smells of Chinatown before entering nearby Foster Botanical Garden; we picnicked within this 14-acre living museum when I was a child. I listened carefully as birds sang within the rare and unusual setting. Remembering Auntie Kalei's urgings, I concentrated on visual and emotional impressions—colors seemed brighter, shadows contained intricate details; watchfulness produced a cornucopia of visual stimuli during my self-guided tour.

Events within the past forty-eight hours had sharpened my cognizance and comprehension; having nothing to hide, I could participate more fully in life. I thought, *Realizing what I am will guide me into grateful living if I open my mind, see objectively, listen carefully, and respond humanely.*

Youthful experiences, often meandering, are routes to wisdom and lifetime values. Only youth's physical surfaces leave; all else lingers.

PART TWO

# HOMELESS

&gt;━◆━○━◆━&lt;

CHAPTER 5

## *Youthful Nomad*

### 1932–1939

$\mathbf{M}$Y MOTHER decided to keep me, so I spent my first four years with her parents in Honolulu instead of with Tom Hugo's family. A goldfish in a bowl on a table near our front doorway is my earliest recollection of a possession. I remember a Hawaiian man, probably Mr. Hugo, giving it to me.

Hualani traveled between the islands of Oʻahu and Molokaʻi helping poor people whom she called "clients."

Grandfather Lyman had a black piglet that followed me like a puppy; it snuffed with its round nose and tickled my ear when I hugged it. When he grew too big for me to hold, Grandfather put "Piggy" into his car's trunk and made me sit in the back seat. Piggy squealed and I screamed as Grandfather drove him to a farm to grow fat and become like other pigs.

Uncle Sam taught me to read when I was three. We shared a prank: When teenage friends were at the house, Sam placed the evening newspaper in front of me. To no one in particular, he'd say: "I wonder what the governor did today?" That was my cue to read a story out loud about Governor Poindexter.

$\mathbf{I}$ was four when mother and I boarded the *Matsonia* ocean liner to travel to the mainland. It was in 1935, during the depths of the Depression; the Territory of Hawaiʻi's social work budget was cut, and mother lost her job. She qualified for one in the State of Washington, having been born there while her parents served in the Salvation Army.

Aunt Maile, thirteen years old, cried angrily when told to leave our cabin because it was time for the ocean liner to leave. While passengers threw streamers from the *Matsonia*, Maile ran to the pier's highest point. Music of the Royal Hawaiian Band playing "Aloha 'Oe" and Maile jumping and waving her arms frantically at me were my last memories of Hawai'i.

Standing at the boat rail, I threw my carnation lei into the ocean. If it floated ashore, I would return to Hawai'i some day. Grandfather said so.

Diagnosed with schizophrenia as a young woman, Maile was given a lobotomy and spent the rest of her long life in an institution. Pictures show her always smiling. In today's world, her brain would be intact, she would be medicated instead of institutionalized, and probably would smile less. Grandfather created a life annuity for Maile by selling his share of Lyman royal lands to his nephew Richard Lyman. The land in Puna on the Big Island had ancient fishponds, a black sand beach, and a blue lake having a waterfall used as a setting for Hollywood movies.

Mother and I had a room at the Salvation Army Girls Home in Seattle, Washington. A number of prostitutes made it their winter residence while few ships and sailors were in Seattle's harbor. We were admitted because mother's parents were Salvation Army officers. When a pretty young woman moved in across the hall, I lined up my stuffed animals outside our door so she'd know there was a kid in the house.

After dinner the girls sat in the living room where the piano was and sang hymns. Mother couldn't sing a note, but my new friend from across the hall could and she helped me. I remember the girls' voices singing: *"On a hill far away, there's an old rugged cross, the emblem of suffering and shame . . ."* ("Old Rugged Cross," by George Bennard); *"And He walks with me and He talks with me, and tells me I am his own . . ."* ("In the Garden," by C. Austin Miles); *"This is my story, this is my song,*

Arthur Rath is second from left in this photo from Castle Kindergarten, Honolulu (1935). *Photo courtesy of the author.*

*praising my Savior all the day long . . .*" ("Blessed Assurance," 1837, music by Phoebe B. Knapp, words by Fannie Jane Crosby). These were among the favorite hymns of the twentieth century. The poetry as well as the melodies had great emotional power as Americans coped with World Wars and the Depression.

I benefited throughout my life from exposure to music such as this. During a time of religious revival, blind composer Jane van Alstyne (pen name Fannie Jane Crosby), while in her forties, began to write words for the 8,000 hymns that she completed before dying in 1915 at age 94. She met three presidents, performed at President Grant's funeral (1915), and read one of her gospel poems before the U.S. Congress.

My friend across the hall had me convinced that Dentyne gum grew on trees. She probably hid it for me to find in the big willow in front of the home because gum stopped growing there after she left.

W hen we moved out of the home into a second-floor apartment, I attended school in the morning and spent afternoons at a child care center. On Saturdays mother took me to violin lessons, after which we went to museums or concerts. Late in the day we rode the bus to the farmer's market, hanging around until closing time when vegetable and fruit prices were really cheap.

Books became my best friends. A librarian let me have a card, but she wouldn't give one to my mother because she couldn't write her name in a cursive style. The woman at the counter scolded her: "What do you mean you can only print your name? You have to be able to write in order to take out library books."

Born left-handed, mother's school teachers forced her to do everything right-handed. She wrote easy-to-read printing.

I spoke up: "I will sign her name." The librarian studied us both: I was tow-headed and blue-eyed, and mother's skin was seemingly darker in afternoon shadows.

"No. She must do it herself."

On my own I figured out how to beat the system. Mother pointed to books she wanted to read. I took my card and the books to the checkout counter. Should the librarian question me about suitability of my selection, I'd recite something about the author or subject from the book jacket. Maybe she thought I was a prodigy.

Discovering that I had taken change from her purse to buy candy, Mother gave me the fire cure. Turning on a gas burner, she held my "stealing hands" over it. "Doing this hurts me more than it hurts you," she said. How could that be possible? But I never stole again.

There was little food we could afford except for produce from the farmer's market and baked beans she sometimes refried—tasting awful to a child's palate. One evening she had tears in her eyes while reading a newspaper's grocery advertisement.

This State of Hawai'i identification photo of Ruth Hualani Lyman Rath was taken while in her fifties, when she assisted patients of Hansen's disease and their families. The disease once was called leprosy. *Courtesy of the author.*

"What's wrong?" I asked.

"There is a wonderful special on hams. But you won't eat any." Ham made me think of Piggy.

Feeling guilty, I answered, "Oh, I will now." She bought and baked a small ham. It was good. I loved "crackling," its crisp roasted skin, and nibbled on it after dinner listening to the radio as Orson Welles told us about the world ending. Crackling soothed my fears.

Never did I express a negative opinion about food after that. Being willing to try anything others ate yielded many pleasant surprises.

The State of Washington ran out of money; social workers and other government employees weren't paid, and we were evicted from our apartment. A girl in my class lived across the street and I asked if her parents would allow mother and me to sleep in their basement room where the two of us played. Her family welcomed us, always fed me oatmeal with brown sugar in the morning, and made sure I swallowed a teaspoon of ghastly tasting cod-liver oil.

Mother went almost immediately to California for work, and the state sent me to live with foster parents Mother and Daddy Holzclaw in a rural area near Seattle. I called her "Mother Holzclaw" because I had a mother but called him just "Daddy" because I didn't have one.

The Holzclaws grew their own fruit and vegetables and raised poultry—bantam hens, chickens, ducks, and turkeys. Mother Holzclaw cooked on a big wood-burning stove and made pancakes right on the iron stove top without using a frying pan.

Sunday afternoons, Daddy and I walked to a store to buy a quart of ice cream. He cut the ice cream into squares on the kitchen table; we took our plates to the living room and ate ice cream "the proper way," slowly, carefully, maintaining the square shape as it became smaller and smaller.

I wasn't supposed to finish before the Holzclaws. I closed my eyes and made a wish before eating that last square. I'd wish some ice cream was left in the box. The wish usually came true.

Sometimes Mother Holzclaw and I were "day laborers" on a farm. I'd offer to give the few cents I received for each quart of berries I picked. "No. You buy the ice cream this week," she'd tell me.

I always thought the ice cream tasted especially good when I paid. I associated the words "ice cream sundaes" with cutting ice cream into squares on Sundays with the Holzclaws.

My fondest memory of rural Washington is of sitting on outdoor furniture under a cherry tree and singing with Daddy. He enjoyed Stephen Foster's songs and taught me "Old Folks at Home," "Laura Lee," and "Old Black Joe." He especially liked the way I could sing "Beautiful Dreamer"—my tessitura at the time was probably matched for it. Hum this song; you'll sense what I suggest about its youthful lyricism.

His favorite song was written by a woman named Carrie Jacobs-Bond. He "knew it from the war," he said, but didn't explain what that meant. It was the last song in the little repertoire he was helping me develop. He closed his eyes while I sang it.

> *When you come to the end of a perfect day*
> *And you sit alone with your thought,*
> *While the chimes ring out with a carol gay*
> *For the joy that the day has brought.*
> *Do you think what the end of a perfect day*
> *Can mean to a tired heart*
> *When the sun goes down with a flaming ray*
> *And the dear friends have to part?*

When cherries were ripe, Daddy put some in a bowl for a pit-spitting contest. He always lost and raked up the pits. His false teeth slept every night in a glass of water by his bed. "They don't allow me to spit pits far," he said, pretending to lisp.

Mother Holzclaw gave me singing lessons in the living room next to the piano. "Natural singing is controlling air flow and keeping the voice free," she explained. Her commands became instinctive to me:

- Breathe in by pushing your tummy out. Don't move your chest at all.
- Let air out in a steady stream. Pretend you are blowing out all the candles on a cake using one breath.
- As you sing this scale, keep your throat and lips relaxed. No tightness anywhere. Do not contort your face. Keep moving your tummy out as you take in a breath, move it slowly in for vocal support as you sing.
- Pretend the sound comes from your eyes, not out of your mouth.

Doing all this was supposed to make my five-year-old voice "ring" so as to be heard from a distance. Electronic loudspeaker systems weren't in use, and she had plans. One day she announced that I was ready to go on stage for "Ham and Eggs."[1]

All performances were similar to the first: We entered a large tent filled with old people sitting on folding chairs on both sides of a center aisle. Mother Holzclaw held my left hand as we walked down the aisle up to a stage with a piano on stage right and a speaker's podium in the center. She motioned for me to sit on a chair placed on stage left. I couldn't readily tell my right hand from my left, let alone figure out "stage left"—I just went where she pointed.

I sat and stared down at bald heads and white and blue hair. When it was time, she walked to the piano, my signal to stand near but not behind the podium. As she started playing, I sang Daddy's favorites. I stood straight, arms at my side, and applied everything she taught me.

The nostalgic music was to help the audience recall better times. No one clapped when a song ended; it was like being in church. I sang one Stephen Foster song after another, Mother Holzclaw playing an introduction to each song. The next to the last in our song cycle began, *"There is an old spinning wheel in the parlor, spinning dreams of the long, long ago"* (lyrics by Victor Young, music by William J. Hill, 1930).

---

[1] Backers of the "Ham and Eggs" program wanted a general welfare payment of $30 every Thursday. This name was chosen because having regular income would allow recipients to enjoy a "real meal" of ham and eggs. This was in 1936 and few of America's large and growing elderly population had pensions. Social Security—one of Franklin D. Roosevelt's "planks" in his 1935 presidential race—was not yet fully operational. The Great Depression was raging and it was a good milieu for proponents of an old-age benefit panacea—greater distribution and velocity of money. "Ham and Eggs" was a version of the Townsend Plan nurtured with many emotional and political appeals by Francis W. Townsend of Long Beach, California. It was based on the right of every retired U.S. citizen over sixty years of age to receive a monthly income, provided the sum be spent domestically within a month. The money would come from federal sales or gross income taxes. The Townsend Plan was defeated in the U.S. House of Representatives in 1939.

Then it was time for "A Perfect Day." When it was finished, Mother Holzclaw stopped playing, the audience started clapping, and cheers rose as the main speaker came down the aisle.

I heard lots of revival-style speaking during the year I sang for "Ham and Eggs." The fiery preacher played by Burt Lancaster in the movie *Elmer Gantry* waved his hands and shouted like a "Ham and Egger."

The most fervent speaker wasn't much larger than I because he had no legs. A tall man rolled him to the stage in a wheelchair, then lifted him carefully into a big living room chair with arms on it so he wouldn't fall out. "He lost his legs in a factory accident," Mother Holzclaw whispered. "Ham and Eggs will pay injured workers."

The speaker began quietly at first, then began yelling in the loudest voice I'd heard. Maybe it was because he had a huge head in which to "ring" his sounds. I don't remember what he said, except that he repeated: "America's elderly deserve a fair deal—we must have pensions!" When he finished, the audience stood, clapped, and hollered. He wiped his brow with a blue and white bandanna as the tall man wheeled him down the aisle and out of the tent.

During trips to the ocean, while the Holzclaws raked for clams at low tide, I'd lie on my stomach in the shallow water and crawl around on my hands, truly believing I was swimming.

Wandering off during a Ham and Eggs picnic at a lake, I decided to swim off a dock having a diving board. I ran across the dock, jumped out as far as possible, and sank immediately in deep water. I couldn't touch the bottom to crawl and "swim!"

Before leaving for California, my mother gave me *A Boy's Book of King Arthur*, by Sidney Lanier. The artwork was by America's greatest illustrator, N. C. Wyeth. My favorite picture showed Lady Nimue, the Lady of the Lake, reaching her arm up from the water to hand King Arthur his sword; the king and his companion were on horseback. The words said, "And when they came to the sword the hand held, King Arthur took it up."

Visualizing Lady Nimue, I stretched my arm to the bright surface and calmly watched bubbles rise from my mouth. Someone drifting by on a raft grabbed my hand and pulled me to the surface.

A six-year-old neighbor girl and I were playing hide and seek near the Holzclaw's barn. I found her naked in a stall inside the barn. Giggling, she encouraged me to strip and she'd show me "what her daddy does." Terrified, I ordered her to dress quickly before Daddy Holzclaw came and spanked us both.

I had hoped the State of Washington would allow the Holzclaws to adopt me, but they were probably too old. When I was almost six they put a tag on me; written on it was the name and address of my Aunt Eva in Los Angeles. We went to a train station, where Daddy handed money to a redcap porter and asked him to look after me.

This was the first black man I'd ever met. He took me to the dining car, helped me order, fixed a Pullman bed for me, told me to say my prayers, and closed the curtains in the train car. He shined my shoes during the night and in the morning found a window seat for me in the observation car.

He made certain my hand was in Aunt Eva's before leaving me at the Los Angeles train station. I gave him two dollars of my "traveling money."

Mother worked for the State of California in its southwest farm belt at a time when many Oklahoma families traveled there to escape the dust bowl of the 1930s. I once visited mother in Atascadero, an artichoke-growing area, and stayed in the hotel where she had a room. She told me that John Steinbeck's book, *The Grapes of Wrath*, was very realistic and that some "Okies" thought she was associated with the book because her name was Rath.

Aunt Eva had a job in a department store and couldn't take care of me; my mother traveled throughout the state and I couldn't stay with her; so the State of California placed me with the Gulbranson family. Living with them was eleven-year-old Jimmy, another foster child.

Across the street was Jerry, a young painter in his twenties, who became my close friend. A polio victim, he spent his days in a wheelchair working with oils on canvas. I visited him after school and on weekends, and he encouraged me to practice my violin there. He liked to draw my hands and taught me the rudiments of drawing and oil painting. Jerry was calm and interesting to talk with—in contrast to mean, angry Jimmy.

Jerry's father, who had been gassed by the Germans during World War I, told me stories about "over there." Once he put on his U.S. Army uniform, including wrapped leggings, medals, and hat. He saluted and said, "Thank you for the time you spend with my son." He taught me to sing a war song: "Inky Dinky Parlez-Vous."

I surprised him by singing "A Perfect Day." Then he told me a story: "American soldiers sang that song both after victories and after days when there was no fighting; it was almost a second national anthem over there. The day peace was declared, the song passed from one trench to another on the war front—and it came from German trenches as well. The Germans knew the words. This experience was similar to

Christmas Eve when Americans sang 'Silent Night' from their trenches and Germans sang 'Stille Nacht' back from theirs."

It took me about thirty minutes to reach the Episcopal cathedral if I raced fast on roller skates. Each member of the boys choir was paid a nickel on Saturdays to rehearse and a nickel on Sundays to sing in church. I bought World War I–style lead soldiers for five cents each, and it didn't take long until I had a good-sized army to hide from Jimmy.

We watched the director carefully because we never knew who he'd pick to sing. His favorite trick was to point to one soloist to sing part of a passage, then point to another to continue, then point again to the first soloist to finish it. He grinned when we "nailed it" and scowled if any of us was a beat late.

I was riding in the back of a bus to a violin lesson when a man seated across the aisle asked if I knew "The Blue Bells of Scotland." I nodded—it was in the music book I had with me.

"Please play it," he said.

I stood up, opened the violin case, and he held the music. Other passengers remained quiet. He sniffed and had watery eyes when I finished, so I played it again.

He gave me a dime, enough to buy two soldiers and a motorized machine gun; one soldier drove the motorcycle and the other was in the side car behind the machine gun.

The Gulbransons favored Jimmy and generally ignored me. I was careful not to say or do something to annoy them—especially if Mr. Gulbranson smelled of whiskey. Jimmy liked to hit me on the arms and in the stomach; I learned to be wary of sudden attacks.

We did the evening dishes together; Jimmy washed, I wiped. He'd wait until I held a dinner plate, then slug me on the arm hoping I would drop the plate and be punished for breaking it. I dropped a plate only the first time because I saw how to anticipate his blow. He'd move his foot forward and lower his head. That was my signal to hold tightly and take it. He'd hit me more if I tried to duck or move away.

Movie actor Jack Haley sometimes came to the house to see Jimmy. I have no idea what the connection was. Haley was being filmed in the role of the Tin Man in the *Wizard of Oz*. It was released in 1939 and I had a chance to see the movie before leaving Los Angeles.

Jimmy bragged about the Tin Man being a friend of his. I wished I could brag that the Cowardly Lion was my friend.

Jimmy and his gang were trying to make me steal. I resisted because it would disappoint Jerry—and I remembered my hands being burned. They shoved me inside a novelty store while waiting outside; I was supposed to go to a counter and grab and stuff pocket knives in my overalls. They'd cut the pockets so that many knives would drop down the lining without making my pocket bulge.

Seeing me scuttering around, looking terrified, the store manager came over to ask if he could help. I confessed immediately.

Grabbing me by the shoulder, he took me outside and scolded the boys. He took me inside until they were gone. He didn't punish me, but I was to tell the boys he spanked me hard. "Come see me if they ever try again to make you steal," he advised.

Mother arrived soon afterwards to tell the Gulbransons we were returning to Hawai'i. My lei had made it to shore!

I was seven years old, Jimmy was about to turn thirteen, and I was lucky to leave before he did anything worse than hit me. He'd threatened to kill me if I ever left. Before my mother showed up with her good news, I was taking my violin to bed with me in case he was in a bad mood. The night before we left I asked the Gulbransons if my mother could sleep in the room Jimmy and I shared. Jimmy slept on the couch and didn't hang around to give a good-bye punch.

Mother went to work on Moloka'i and I lived in Honolulu with my grandparents Major David and Major Charlotte Lyman, Salvation Army, retired. Expected to go to school barefoot, like other kids, I had to get ready fast. Trudging up and down my grandparent's stony driveway calloused my feet so I could walk on pebbles and hot asphalt without wincing.

Uncle Belden brought boxing gloves to prepare me for fights awaiting the "new kid in school." He taught me to turn my hand to hit with a wide fist, to block blows and counterpunch, to make myself steady by placing my feet on an angle, and to move back and forth and sideways while in this position. He taught me to explode my breath loudly as I breathed. Most important, he showed me how to feint, or to fake a punch—he explained that word—and then to step forward so my body weight followed a blow.

I entered Punahou's third grade barefooted, wearing khaki shorts and an aloha shirt as did all boys. Jane Burroughs was in the seat next to me. Her grandfather, Edgar Rice Burroughs, was living in Honolulu at that time. He wrote books about Tarzan, King of the Apes. The class tough guy, an ape called "George," sat behind me.

I was the only student in the class who was not living with parents; George used that as a taunt: "How come you have no mother and father Attah Rat? You're a bastard, aren't you?"

He'd nudge past me in the school hallway snarling, "Move, little bastard." I had done him no harm. He was another Jimmy.

During recess I avoided him and his pals. Except for Jane, I wasn't making friends. No one wanted anything to do with me if I avoided George's ritualistic beating.

After about a week of this, I agreed to meet George after school. The word quickly got around. Jane looked concerned—it was me, little Cheetah, up against George, King Kong.

After school ended, boys surrounded me in the schoolyard. George stepped in and rushed toward me.

I held my fists up, stood still with feet angled, and at the last fraction of a second side-stepped to the left, nicking him over the eyes as he passed me. He was startled.

George turned and rushed again. Instead of moving aside, I jabbed quickly with both hands, stepped back, feinted with my left hand, stepped in and hit him flat in the face with my right fist, using the full weight of my 57 pounds. I followed up with a swinging left.

It was over. George was crying and had a black eye forming.

I didn't have to fight anyone after that. Never again did I hear the word "bastard." No one even teased me about playing the violin. Ken Nakagawa, the only Japanese boy in my class, immediately became my closest pal.

Ken was in my corner for my fight against a bigger and older neighborhood tough who would stand on a corner calling us "Punahou sissies" as we got off the Kaimukī bus. After a few days of this, I agreed to fight.

I was hit a lot, but this tough guy didn't step into his punches. I kept shuffling back and forth, as Belden taught me. I punched only his arms, as Jimmy did to me.

He was not used to long fights, and this one dragged on. I refused to quit because I was used to being hit and would not cower.

After a while, he had trouble raising his arms. Then, confused and hurt by my quick jabs to his unprotected face, he suddenly hugged me and said, "Enough. You're no sissy."

Ken was ecstatic. This meant he wasn't a sissy either.

Near the end of 1941, life was in a regular groove at my grandparent's home in Honolulu; I felt secure. My mother was promoted from Moloka'i to Kona on the island of Hawai'i.

I was in the fifth grade and rode to school in a red Ford convertible driven by Patty Zane, a happy, attractive Punahou high school coed. Her father was a doctor, she planned to go to the University of California–Berkeley, and they welcomed me into their home. I took violin lessons at a music school on the Punahou campus, sang in the school's chorus, rode an electric trolley home from school, and had nearly earned my third Cub Scout badge.

Grandfather raised nearly a hundred anthuriums of many colors and had a hothouse—a glass shed—where he grew orchids. He'd given me a six-days-a-week job watering the plants. His property was arranged in three terraced levels, with differing varieties of tropical flowers on each terrace and an arbor with a magnificent *mauna loa* vine on the top level. He introduced me to the word "initiative" after I failed to sweep up poinciana blossoms fallen on the driveway from his huge tree. It means "don't wait to be told."

I felt secure here, as I was when living at the Holzclaws.

I went to a community church on Sunday mornings and usually sneaked out to play tackle football while my grandparents attended a Salvation Army afternoon service. One Sunday I came home with a chipped front tooth and bleeding mouth; I was very frightened because I had been told, "You don't play on the Lord's day." Grandfather whipped my bare legs with a branch from a bamboo bush growing in the backyard. It stung and left telltale stripes. He did it just that one time. Uncles later warned me: "Don't ever try smoking—he'll give you a big cigar and make you smoke and get sick." None of my uncles smoked because that's what happened to them.

On Thursday evenings, Grandfather and I went to the Salvation Army mission hall. The "revival" service before the soup kitchen meal was tame stuff after Ham and Eggs meetings. I beat the bass drum quietly during singing and saving. New people were supposed to be redeemed every week, but some of the same men always came forward. Grandfather called them "our regular dinner guests."

Our neighborhood church gave certificates as "Fishers of Men" for every person Sunday school students brought for three weeks in a row. I wanted to set a fishing record; my first catch included the neighborhood boy I fought and his friends.

I kept a straight face as they solemnly stood and loudly sang, "Make Me a Sunbeam . . . out of my life, may Jesus shine." We were learning from Sunday school that God works wonders.

I had lured Kathleen Nakagawa to Sunday school three times; this coming Sunday—December 7—would be her brother's third attendance. Ken was my ninth catch. I was proud of my school of fish.

The U.S. Navy's fleet was in and in the afternoon, Sunday school students would visit some of the ships lined up in Pearl Harbor. Sailors were always friendly to us "locals," giving a tour, a peek at the *Esquire* magazine "Vargas Girls" pinned up over their hammocks, and free ice cream cones in the ship's dining room.

Responding to radio announcements starting at about 7:00 A.M., Uncle Belden and Uncle Sam dressed in army uniforms and left for Schofield Barracks. Wearing navy whites, Uncle Bob returned to 'Aiea Naval Station. Grandfather put on a helmet and prepared to drive to a Red Cross first aid center where he was a volunteer.

I heard one explosion after another and saw big puffs of smoke in the air. The military simulated attacks during periodic war maneuvers, but the radio announcer kept saying, "This is the real McCoy."

"Japs are attacking!" Grandfather said. "Stay in the house with your grand-mother."

Ken was waiting on the front steps, where I told him, "There's no Sunday school because Japs are attacking." He looked anguished and ran home. Realizing I used the insulting "J" word to my best friend, I almost cried. I should not have repeated what Grandfather said. I was more upset over this than "the Real McCoy."

My grandparents lived about 7 miles from Pearl Harbor on a hillside by Dia-mond Head where the army stored ammunition. Planes with big red circles on their wings and fuselage flew over our house, so from my grandfather's room I took colored chalk he used for Sunday school "chalkboard" lectures. I sketched a huge U.S. Army P-40 fighter plane on our big outdoor cement patio. Art lessons from Jerry in Los Angeles and lots of practice when I was supposed to be doing schoolwork enabled me to draw a very realistic looking warplane. I colored it with lots of chalk to frighten away Japanese planes.

With our house thus protected, I went to the military observation post on the hill next to our backyard. It was a single-room tin shack mounted on tall metal legs manned by soldiers who climbed a ladder to enter it. Looking through mounted telescopes gave them clear views of Pearl Harbor and approaches to Diamond Head. The two soldiers welcomed the oatmeal and raisin cookies I brought and let me use a telescope. I watched bombing and strafing until smoke from burning ships clouded the view.

I told Grandmother I hid in the dirt basement. Busy praying, she hadn't come looking for me. So upset, she forgot to ask about her newly baked cookies. She prob-ably thought Grandfather took them to the Red Cross.

Changes came quickly. Martial law was in effect and the military took charge. Curfew meant civilians had to be inside their houses before dark; they'd be arrested if a block warden saw lights shining from a house.

Families built air-raid shelters in their yards, the army strung barbed wire along beaches, and the U.S. Army Corps of Engineers took over Punahou School. Its fourth and other elementary grades relocated into an Episcopal church's Sunday school building.

The worst thing about the war for me was that Grandfather forbade me from associating with Kenneth Nakagawa. There was no reason, except that Ken was Japanese. How could a man who led us in daily prayer sessions at home demand this? It was the first time I doubted him.

In later years, I realized that old-timers had deeply ingrained fears of Hawai'i being taken over by Japanese. They worked harder than anyone else, kept to themselves, and seemed to be successful in any enterprise. Ken's grandfather, a doctor, was among upper-class Japanese who came to Hawai'i. Ken's father went to the University of Nebraska, became a dentist, was active in civic affairs, and lived in a very nice house at the end of our block.

Even though Ken couldn't come to my grandparents' house, I did my watering and went to his house or the Zane's. My grandparents thought I was always at the Zane's, "who are such nice people."

Grandfather and other Islanders mellowed as they realized Hawai'i's Japanese were fervent American patriots. But Ken wouldn't return to our church; he was afraid of Grandfather.

I went to his new church in downtown Honolulu and asked its minister to write a letter to me stating Ken was attending there. I wanted to show it to our minister so he'd give me another "Fishers of Men" certificate. It didn't work. Our minister wanted what I caught in his pool.

Not long after the attack, I took a bomb to school for "show-and-tell." About three feet long, painted blue and silver, it was a dud—a practice airplane bomb given my uncles years earlier when Uncle Albert was stationed at Schofield Barracks. It was kept in our red-dirt basement.

I put the bomb in the trunk of Patty's car and she drove me to school. It caused excitement when kids helped me carry it into class. I hadn't thought of how difficult it would be to take it home on the bus. Although hollow, it was heavy and the bus stop was quite a distance away. I'd put it down to rest my arms. Brakes shrieked and a car stopped when an excited driver saw me picking it up.

Honolulu Rapid Transit didn't use open electric street cars on the bus route up the hill to the church where we now attended school. I had to walk past the bus driver to enter the passenger section. Drivers of two buses wouldn't let me on. The third driver, who was very friendly to me, said I could ride. With big letters, he wrote "FAKE" on a piece of paper and taped it to the bomb. He had me sit in the front seat so everyone saw this sign while boarding the bus. I realize now that he was probably Mr. Hugo.

Our class became smaller as children with mainland relatives left the Hawaiian Islands. I said farewell to my classmate. "Goodbye Jane. I'll think of you when reading about Tarzan."

Islanders believed a Japanese invasion was imminent. Our teacher taped a map of the Pacific on our blackboard, labeled new areas the Japanese occupied, and drew arrows pointing to Hawai'i. Our Islands looked small, isolated, and vulnerable.

Years later I heard that pharmacies ran out of diaphragms during the war's early months. Island women stocked up to avoid having Japanese soldiers' babies.

We children carried gas masks and practiced using them in a room filled with tear gas. Twice, while coming home from school, I had to leave a bus and ask to enter a family's air-raid shelter while sirens wailed.

My grandparents felt I would be safer living with my mother on the Big Island. O'ahu was in a war zone; Kona was spread out, isolated, and primitive—and not a military target.

As for my mother, I was beginning to show independence and would now need to learn how to become emotionally safe from her.

CHAPTER 6

# Big Island Days

### 1942–1945

$A$s with everyone else in Kona, our source of fresh water was rain caught on the roof. The rainy season is nature's symphony time. Since Mother didn't come home until after 7:00 P.M., I'd sit next to a window, engrossed.

*The sky grows gray at about 4:00 P.M.;*
*Initial sounds are pianissimo,*
*The crescendo begins with a hush,*
*Drops falling on distant forests slowly approach.*
*Winds drive them from hills*
*And the volume rises.*
*Rhythms become faster, intenser,*
*Surrounding me with percussion.*
*Rain HAMMERS the tin roof—*
*Forte, double forte, triple forte!*
*The cacophony slows and abates,*
*Other sounds are becoming prominent:*
*Water gushing from the roof into gutters,*
*Overflow splashing onto lava rocks.*
*Dissonance transforms into a smooth melody:*
*Water flow adjusts and runs through drain pipes*
*Into the holding tank, steadily,*
*Methodically, reassuringly.*

During the hour or so that rain fell, adults enjoyed "cocktail hour." Mother sometimes came home earlier to take me so I could have *pūpū*s for dinner—island-style snacks: spare ribs, sushi, teriyaki steak on sticks. One hostess filled cherry tomatoes with lomi salmon—delicious!

I asked mother why she drank whiskey "neat"—out of a shot glass—instead of having a cocktail as others did. "So I know exactly how much alcohol I consume," she answered. "I never drink more than one shot an hour. People might 'load up' my mixed drink."

Months with little or no rainfall were called the "dry season." People cautiously watched the water level in the storage tank; running out of water was disastrous. It was also "dry" because of limited entertaining. During dry season, Mother and I took turns bathing out of one bucket of water. We used a two-hole outhouse in the backyard. In it were a Sears and Roebuck catalog for "wipes" and a bag of lime with a rice scoop in it—you were supposed to drop lime down the hole to deaden odors. A huge guava tree next to the outhouse produced the biggest, juiciest guavas imaginable; we used them for sherbet.

A crew from the University of Hawai'i's extension service drilled endlessly through lava rock near Kailua, hoping to locate an underground vein of water. This happened after I left; Kona now has enough water to keep its golf courses green, and cocktail hours are enjoyed year around.

Except for groves of coffee trees, Kona was mainly barren. Below Mauna Loa, lava fields had signs with dates of the flow. Many Hawaiians lived in fishing villages along the famous Kona Coast, where the ocean is so bountiful.

I attended Konawaena, a combined school with a predominantly Japanese student body. School administrators scheduled vacations when coffee beans were ripe and red so children could join their parents in "picking the cherries," as they were called, one by one.

We ate lunch in classrooms, boys in one and girls in another. Boys carefully opened the Japanese language newspaper in which their lunches were wrapped and propped the newspaper up to hide behind while eating. When leaving to go to the bathroom, I saw their meager fare: a ball of rice, a small pickled plum or pickled daikon for flavor; some boys had a few bits of scrambled egg to go with their rice.

I ate in the back row, facing the wall, hiding my sandwich, a small can of juice, and sometimes a cookie, ashamed it was so lavish.

Having shorter legs, Japanese students crouched on their haunches while watching games or talking. Most Caucasians find this difficult to do; survivors of Japanese prison camps forced to "rest" this way described it as "torture." It was painful to me, so I sat on the ground, and the seat of my khaki pants showed the results. Boys delighted in pointing out that I had a "wet" or "dirty ass."

A tall Portuguese boy named Richard was the class's neatest dresser. He always stood. Each day he wore the same kind of uniform: a crisply starched, white, short-sleeved shirt and clean, well-pressed, long khaki pants. He was barefoot, as were we all.

I told my mother about how neat he always looked and she surprised me by saying, "Richard has just one outfit. I visited his home." This was the first time I realized some classmates might be Mother's clients. "Portuguese families are very proud. Richard washes his shirt and pants every night, he starches them and his mother irons them in the morning."

After learning this, I stood with Richard on the playground, treating my own clothes more carefully.

I realized Mother was doing her best. She could communicate with almost anyone in Hawai'i in English, pidgin English, or Hawaiian, and she used a smattering of Japanese. No one and no thing frightened her—except the possibility of my turning out "bad." Her anxiety caused her to scream, scold, and terrify me.

I found out that her job was dangerous after a demented client threw a cane knife when she approached his shack. Ikua Purdy, Grandfather's friend when both were *paniolo,* made a cat-o'-nine-tails for my mother. It had a handle to which were attached strips of leather, each with good-sized lead weights at the end. She'd tuck it in her briefcase when walking a long trail; some of the weights stuck out.

Her fierce-looking dog "Pat," half pit bull and half Australian heeler, often rode in her car. I once saw Pat hold a coconut against the ground with his paws, tear off the husk with his teeth, carry the nut in his mouth, break it against a rock, and then eat the meat.

I was almost hysterical when Mother disappeared while swimming in Kealakekua Bay. She dove under a big wave, got caught in an undertow, and didn't surface for the longest time. She acted very matter-of-factly when she emerged and walked back up the beach. Tutoring as always, the first thing she did was point to the stone wall behind me by the ruins of a *heiau*. "Prior to the nineteenth century," she informed me, "Hawaiian women buried their placenta there." I realize, retrospectively, that because of circumstances, she buried her feelings somewhere after I was born.

The Department of Health sent a representative to Konawaena with traps and promises to pay us a nickel for each rat tail we brought to a collection area by the school entrance. I wanted a dozen traps, but six was all I got.

I tied a string to each trap, anchored it to a rock, set the traps with cheese in the evening, and checked them first thing in the morning. I hung filled traps on the overhead drain pipe by the string so a mongoose wouldn't devour my catch. Home from school, I cut off the rats' tails, preserved them in a jar filled with kerosene, buried the bodies, lit a newspaper and waved it over the trap to remove any blood odor, and reset the traps in a different location.

On Friday we brought our jars filled with kerosene and tails to school for payday. I had all the hospital buildings as my trapping area and was becoming rich: Weekly earnings sometimes totaled a dollar or more.

During the rare occasions when the local grocery store received a shipment of candy bars, I'd spend my money. I remember reading one of Jack London's stories while eating Milky Ways: "Koolau the Leper" held off the police and army who tried to send him to the leper colony on Molokaʻi. My head ached from the sugar rush, and the tingling from caramel flavoring stayed on the back of my tongue for a long time.

I accompanied my mother on some of her visits to clients and during one of them was startled by seeing a man with elephantiasis sitting in the shadow of a plumeria tree. I thought he was a leper because of his grotesquely large legs and misshapen and discolored bare feet. For some reason, I ignored his looks and sat next to him. Almost immediately he told stories in a sweet, gentle voice. From then on I looked forward to visiting this genuinely kind person. I asked what made his legs so huge. "Mosquitoes," he answered. The elephant man told the truth; they carry the filariae that afflicted him.

Once each month, even during the school year, I rode a commodity truck delivering staples to persons on relief throughout the Kona District. The Territory supplied households with a 100-pound bag of rice, dry beans, flour, condensed milk, and canned vegetables to augment what they grew and caught. Mother's clients waited in groups along the highway; some became friends.

"It is rude to refuse to eat what people you know will eat," Mother admonished.

When first tasting breadfruit poi for lunch at the home of one of my mother's clients, I almost gagged, but I smiled my way through and was invited to lunch the following month. A large starchy fruit grown on a tree, breadfruit is baked and eaten like a squash. It can be mixed with water and made into yellow poi—but it doesn't taste anything like taro poi.

By then I'd discovered the secret of holding my breath while chewing and swallowing distasteful food. Something small and soft could be gulped down whole without gagging, and eventually I ate breadfruit poi while breathing.

$W$e lived in the former nurse's quarters at the old Kona Hospital, a few miles from the new hospital. Government, ranches, plantations, and some branches of territorial government supplied housing to its workers. The old hospital had two main buildings on a high hill with a clear view of the ocean 6 miles away. Because of this vista, the army bivouacked soldiers in tents all around us.

Local police and military police used one building for offices and a temporary jail; Mother's social work office and an area for commodity storage occupied the other. Soldiers put up a shooting range near the former nurses' cottage where we lived, and I became their mascot.[1] They taught me to shoot a rifle, a .45 pistol, and I lay down to use a submachine gun.

The military police took me riding Saturday nights while they collected drunks. Mother allowed this because I'd learn that heavy drinking makes people irresponsible and they end up in jail.

My mother traveled a 4,000-square-mile area and sometimes brought a teenage girl home prior to placement with a family in a "safer" location. Military outposts were along the island's coastline, and Mother was concerned about the proximity of mainland soldiers to attractive and trusting Hawaiian country girls. The age of sexual consent was thirteen. Transplanting girls was her way of avoiding unplanned parenthood.

When she was away for several nights, I sometimes stayed at a Hongwanji Mission about a mile away. Buddhist monks described universal values within religions and, I was astonished to learn, the Bible's "Ten Commandments" paralleled the Buddhists' guiding principles. It was an important discovery and I was eager to share this, but I realized that Grandfather wouldn't be interested in me writing to him about the "pathway to enlightenment" I discovered in a Japanese temple!

$D$uring school vacations I begged to go to McCandless Ranch, eager to be around men instead of subject to mother's discipline. She scolded fiercely for the smallest infraction. I didn't know why she was angry, but I was the sole person on whom she could take out her frustrations.

---

[1] I came to know some servicemen before and after they fought in the Pacific. They gave me many interesting souvenirs, including an entire suit of armor the Japanese use for sword fighting. I put it on the wall over the head of my bed and it almost crushed my skull one night when it dropped during an earthquake. The strongest impression I have from all of this is the change in the personality of one of the most outgoing and nicest persons I knew. He was like a big brother. He went to battles in the Pacific as a Ranger and came back with a haunted look in his eyes. He'd pat me on my head, but he was lost within himself.

Saturdays and vacation mornings she'd leave a list of household chores and some "new" English words for me to look up and use in a sentence that evening. Each week I had to locate trees and plants, paste a leaf from each in a scrapbook, find their botanical, English, and Hawaiian names in reference books, and write them down.

Mother couldn't reach me while I was at the ranch, where there was no telephone, no electricity, and no running water. Unaware of her riding prowess, I felt independent because it took several hours on horseback to get there.

McCandless Ranch's holdings on the slopes of Mauna Kea ran from the mountain (13,796 feet high) to the sea in the ancient Hawaiian way of dividing land. Land was divided this way by early Hawaiians so that families would have a *kuleana* (a small piece of property) to use for growing vegetables on cool slopes and catching fish in the ocean.

Cowboys moved cattle up and down the mountain to graze in valleys holding deep deposits of soil and nutritious grass. The ranch had several small buildings on the slope to house cowboys working the area. I stayed in the main ranch house, near the top of the mountain. It had two bedrooms and a small porch upstairs. One large room downstairs served as kitchen, eating, and communal area; about twelve of us ate together.

Moses cooked over a wood fireplace. Not much bigger than I, he had a hunch on his back. He was of Portuguese ancestry and had a nice musical lilt when speaking.

Cowboys had cots in a separate bunkhouse, twenty or so dogs slept in a barn next to the blacksmith's shop, and my bedroom was over the kitchen. Moses owned the only gun in camp and slept on the upstairs porch, protecting me from ghosts.

When the stew pot hanging in the fireplace contained mostly onions and potatoes, Moses, the dogs, and I went hunting. The dogs' job was to locate wild pigs and sheep. We followed on horseback, listening for excited barking and snarling.

Trained not to attack, the dogs would corner game against a ridge of lava rock so Moses could have a clear shot and not waste ammunition—impossible to buy during the war. Another reason they stayed back was that a wild boar's tusks can quickly rip open a dog's stomach. Moses used a Winchester 25-20 rifle—very powerful. It propelled a bullet about 1.75 inches long.

Moses could roll and light a cigarette with one hand while holding his horse's reins with the other. He shook tobacco from a bag of Bull Durham onto a piece of paper, rolled it, licked it closed, popped it in his mouth, lit a wooden match by snapping it on his thumbnail, and puffed away happily. Before doing this neat trick, he would hand me the rifle and let me shoot wild sheep, trusting I wouldn't hit a dog.

I helped Moses field dress the kill and pack meat on the extra horse we brought along. After Moses shot an unusually large pig, I asked, "Why doesn't this pig have balls?"

"Cowboy rope when baby. Drag him away while modda pig run fo' save other babies. He cut balls off, leave him loose, and him grow mo' big like now. Meat taste real *ono.* You find out when we cook 'em. Same kine thing us do with young bull."

Moses and I skinned the kill at the ranch house. He cut slabs of meat, put them into empty rice bags, and hung the bags above the dogs' reach in the barn. Men going down the mountain that weekend would deliver the bags of meat to cowboys' families. The rest was for ranch house stew.

Moses was right; the big, fat, gelded pig's meat was tender and sweet. The crackling was *ono,* too.

Cowboys tested my mettle as we sat around the dinner table by the light of kerosene lanterns. I pretended to savor "mountain oysters" gelded from the day's newly created steers when they are branded.

The next morning Moses filled the entire frying pan with batter for one pancake he made for me. He added a handful of mountain oysters left over from last night—or maybe saved *especially* from last night. It was testicles for breakfast!

If I held my breath, I could swallow anything. I just had to keep calm so my heart didn't pump hard and turn my face telltale red. The cowboys studied me from the sides of their eyes while sipping tea from a bowl. Cowboys didn't use cups.

Pretending not to notice, I happily picked out the mountain oysters from the pancake and gobbled them down, letting out my breath after each swallow, as though I was expressing gusto.

I put jelly on the remaining doughy mess, munched away, and sipped my bowl of tea. The cowboys seemed grumpy and disappointed that I pulled it off. Moses, chuckling by the fireplace, nodded his head eagerly at me.

Moses coached me into becoming a four-night pepper-contest winner. He made sure I ate lots of bread during dinner. We went outside to rinse my mouth with vinegar before going to the table for the contest. "We pickle you fo' no hurt," he explained.

This is the story of the championship match. Fat Frank sat on one side of the dining table; I sat opposite him on the bench. A mason jar holding a branch of small red chili peppers was in front of us, and saucers of Hawaiian rock sea salt and glasses filled with water were to our right. A water pitcher sat on the table. The first of us to drink water would lose.

Spectators surrounded the table. Fat Frank started. He pulled a pepper from the branch, dipped it in salt, chewed it slowly, looked me in the eyes, swallowed, sneered, and said, "Us goin' see what you is, small boy. These kine peppers mo' hot than hell." Fat Frank undoubtedly was surprised I was still alive after three nights of pepper contests.

I had in mind a quick comeback to his "hotter than hell" statement, but I held my words instead of retorting, "You should know." You didn't fool with Fat Frank. He would have kicked me in the balls.

Nonchalantly, I picked a pepper and popped it into my mouth. Momentarily covering my mouth with a hand as though reflecting, I gulped the whole pepper but pretended to slowly chew. I smiled innocently at Frank.

The scorekeeper called out, "Each got one." I didn't dip the peppers in salt; that would've made me thirsty.

By the time a cowboy called out, "Each got eight," Fat Frank was sweating profusely. I continued to gulp peppers, pretending to chew.

Tears were running from Frank's eyes. He made the terrible mistake of wiping his eyes with fingers he used to pull peppers from the branch. Ouch! That burned!

Fat Frank squinted as if in great pain. He grabbed the pitcher with two hands and gulped water from it. I had won!

Moses put some bread next to me. I gobbled some, then rushed outside to throw up. Better that than experience a chili pepper afterburn, as Fat Frank surely would.

Moses followed me to see if I was okay. I said, "Tomorrow if Fat Frank farts while smoking his cigarette in the outhouse, the place will explode." Moses acted as if that was the funniest thing he'd ever heard.

Testes and hot peppers—these were my passage to manhood.

During a late afternoon fog, a cowboy taught me "drinker's honor." The fog was thick because we were so far up Mauna Kea. I could see no farther than my mule Gypsy's ears.

Cowboys called this afternoon phenomenon *uhiwai*—"water covering." An oil-skin poncho and a wide-brim *lauhala* hat kept me from being drenched. Completely dependent on Gypsy finding the ranch house, I sang encouraging words to her: "The sooner we get there, the sooner we rest," as she plodded forward.

We caught up to the cowboy ahead of us. Stopped under an *'ōhi'a* (a native tree), he was standing on his saddle reaching around in the tree's crotch. "Yee hee!" he screeched, holding a whiskey bottle up for me to see. After two long swigs, he showed it to me again. It was half full. He put it back. "Us guys leave whiskey in trees. Whoevah empty 'em gotta put new one back. Da kine 'drinker's honor,'" he giggled.

By the end of summer I could snap a 10-foot bullwhip, was moderately competent with a lasso, could help herd cattle, plant grass seed, and I knew about hunting for meat. But was that enough for me to claim I was a useful cowboy?

I found out as we drove cattle down the mountain to Kailua for their boat ride to Honolulu. A steer fell, breaking a front leg. Moses didn't have the rifle unless he was hunting or keeping ghosts away, so he pointed to what was hanging from my waist and said, "Attah, use you knife. We finish mo' latah."

My 6-inch switchblade knife had a savage history: It was used in a murder, and my uncle Lofty Cook brought it to me from the Hilo Police Station. A Filipino barber made a leather sheath and I wore it on the ranch, making eleven-year-old me feel pretty tough.

It was one thing for me to use this "death weapon" to gut a dead sheep or turn a free-range chicken into Sunday's dinner—but kill a steer? I had to. I couldn't strut around with the knife on my belt if I didn't.

The process was familiar. Friends and I spent many Saturday mornings at the local butcher shop watching animals be slaughtered, sawed, and sliced. Mr. Ackerman used a club to stun a steer, hitting it behind its horns prior to cutting its throat. He didn't club a pig—he just stuck it in the throat with a long knife. and it screamed as long as it could.

Watching the process in rural Kona was our entertainment equivalent of Honolulu city kids' Saturday movie matinees. It was gruesome, but since three of us boys shared these experiences, none of us acted squeamish in front of another. Eventually we became inured.

An elderly Japanese man always showed up with a sharp paring knife, chopsticks, soy sauce, and a bowl to eat the freshly killed beef heart Mr. Ackerman had for him. He devoured it slice by slice while it was still warm, sitting on a bench outside the butcher shop, wagging his head, as if in deep conversation with an invisible companion.

Moses had given me a far more daunting test than killing a range chicken or merely watching a slaughter.

After tethering Gypsy out of sight, I attached a rope around the downed Hereford steer's neck, tied it to a tree, said some prayers, and slid my knife out of its case. In my nervousness, I forgot what soldiers said about not looking the enemy in the face. I glimpsed at the steer's big brown eyes. It stared unblinkingly at me, informing me of its pain, letting me know it was okay to proceed.

I did remember what soldiers told me about using a bayonet: Lunge with a deep stab and continue with a steady slash to the left, since I am right-handed and have more strength in that arm. I aimed for the throat.

Ugh! I had cut a primary vein, blood gushed out, and the steer fell on all fours, eyes glazed. It was quickly over.

I was wearing my rain poncho, remembering how Mr. Ackerman wore a canvas butchering suit. If my clothes were spattered as the ranch poncho now was, Mother would have been relentless both before and after finding out what I had just done.

Then came the awful, smelly disemboweling process. I left everything in a pile; should Moses want "organ food," he could dig for it. I was unable to move the steer to skin it and couldn't bring myself to try cutting off its head. I hadn't the slightest interest in slicing a piece of warm heart to improve my courage; this is what the Japanese man in the butcher shop explained it would do. Instead, I ran in the bushes to throw up. In a little while I came back and sat by the dead steer, sort of talking to its spirit. I kept Gypsy out of sight of the mess.

Hours later, Moses and two other cowboys returned, leading two extra horses by a rope. They brought two saws. Impassive, they didn't even say "good job," but quickly skinned the steer, sawed it into hunks, and packed meat onto the horses. Moses rolled up the brown-and-white hide, tied it with a rope, and placed it on top of the meat. The men headed to the main ranch house. Gypsy was her usual subdued self as we followed them.

At the ranch house, no one made a big thing of my efforts. From then on I was no longer teased about my knife, or much of anything. Moses put his gun away and slept in the bunkhouse.

The cowboys were unusually cheerful. Beef was an extraordinary treat compared with gamey-tasting wild mutton—ranchers raised cattle to sell, not to eat. For several days we feasted on steak cooked over the coals and meat roasted on spits. We had potatoes baked in the ashes, rice, poi, canned tomatoes, canned beans, sliced onions, and hardtack. Each meal was an extremely happy time; the cowboys were unusually talkative, and even Fat Frank made a point of being complimentary about me in some of his stories. I was one of the gang.

Moses nailed the brown-and-white steer's hide on the exterior bunkhouse wall to cure and later strip and weave. He prepared packages of beef for cowboys to take to families.

What was left became beef jerky—*pipi kaula.* Moses salted chunks of meat and rubbed it with hot peppers and soy sauce. He hung it in the cooking and communal area and built a huge, smoky fire in the fireplace. We ate outside for two days while the meat smoked.

After smoking it, Moses put the meat chunks on a clothesline to dry in the sun for several days. When it was firm, he trimmed the meat into smaller pieces. He said it was important to boil jerky before serving because it attracted flies while drying outdoors. I kept mum about all of this; someone might tell my mother and she'd never let me return.

I brought home some *pipi kaula.* "How come they had beef?" Mother asked. I just shrugged my shoulders like a dumb kid.

I had also brought a 30-caliber machine gun with a twisted barrel home. It was from a U.S. Army plane lost in fog that crashed in a forest on Mauna Kea's slopes. Moses took me to explore the crash site; I wanted to take the 50-caliber gun from the plane's nose, but Moses said no. It looked undamaged and Moses thought I might get in trouble for having it.

Pleased with the *pipi kaula,* Mother let me put the smaller machine gun in my closet. With the souvenirs servicemen brought me back from the Pacific, my small room was beginning to look like an arsenal.

A fter being brought down the mountains and fattened on molasses and mesquite bean slop, cattle were ready for Honolulu slaughterhouses. They would have to swim out to the big boat in Kailua Bay; the ship's crews couldn't load from docks because the submerged lava could rip holes in boat bottoms during low tide.

Getting beef on board was a village spectator event; young women brought leis for the cowboys to wear on their woven *lauhala* hats. Even I had one.

Acting like show *paniolo,* our cowboys added to the excitement with lots of hooting and showing off by twirling their lassos. (I know some of them had beer with their lunch.) They agitated the cattle into bellowing and rushing around the holding pen.

When a cowboy roped a steer, he twisted his end of the rope around the saddle's pommel and headed to the pen gate where a helper tied a blindfold over the steer's eyes. The cowboy urged his horse out the gate toward the water, forcing the steer to follow and start swimming.

Boatmen tied each steer by its horns to the gunwales of a large rowboat and headed for the cattle boat. This big boat was high on either end and low in the middle where the cattle rode. Ropes with harnesses dropped from the poles sticking in the air and men in the rowboat attached a harness around each steer's middle. Hoists on the poles lifted animals into the air. Sometimes a harness loosened and an animal fell and bawled while swimming blindly. Once positioned above the center of the boat, steers were lowered into the hold and crew members removed their blindfolds. They would be in Honolulu the next morning.

This was Hawaiian ranching. Jobs were hard to find, and I'd be grateful to work at McCandless Ranch after finishing Konawaena High School. What was my option— picking coffee beans?

M r. Allen A. Bailey accompanied the Kamehameha School for Boys basketball team to Konawaena in 1943. At an assembly attended by the entire student body, dignified young men in blue-gray uniforms sang Hawaiian songs a cappella in four-part harmony. Inspired to become one of them, I went to the principal's office and asked to be among those Mr. Bailey would interview for admission. The secretary stared at me a little strangely but included me on the list.

Called from seventh-grade gym class, I appeared before Mr. Bailey looking like a skinny plucked chicken—barefoot, no shirt, wearing just blue shorts. Mr. Bailey was encouraging, as though he knew of me. I qualified because of my Hawaiian bloodlines; he said he was willing to let me in as a boarder. I heard later that no one looking like me ever attended Kamehameha Schools.

Astonished to learn I had filled out all of the forms and needed only what passed as her signature, Mother was extremely angry. She did not want me to attend Kamehameha! She was incredulous when I stood up to her. We kept arguing about this for several days, and I would not yield: This was the potential turning point of my life. She knew her father wanted me to ignore my Hawaiian heritage. Because I didn't appear Hawaiian, he thought passing as a pure haole would offer me a better chance in life. He'd be furious if my mother allowed my Hawaiian roots to grow.

My backbone had been stiffened by the fervor of the uniformed young men singing, "Ring, ring Kalihi ring, swell the echo of our name . . . ray, ray Kamehameha." Toughened by McCandless Ranch, I wouldn't back down. I threatened to run away.

"There are other people who care how I grow up," I declared. I knew two families would welcome me as one of their own: Lofty and May Cook and their daughters in Hilo, and my uncle Clarence and Aunt Margery Lyman in Kona—he was Auntie Kalei's son, an agricultural extension worker, and Margery was a teacher. I stayed with Clarence and Margery frequently and felt loved by them.

Then again, I could always go to the Huas. Living in the easygoing, old-time Hawaiian style, they probably wouldn't mind another kid. I played the 'ukulele pretty well and knew Hawaiian songs; he sometimes let me sing with his group. He was my Hawaiian Daddy Holzclaw.

Other people were challenging the way my mother treated me. Aunt Kahiwa, Kea's mother, had recently had an intense verbal fight with my mother while she was visiting us in Kona, and Kahiwa demanded that Hualani ease up on me. Kea was with us in Kona when it happened and told me about it fifty years later, when I "confessed" my beginnings to her.

Kea said, "Kahiwa scolded Hualani: 'Stop dominating and isolating Arthur. He needs to be with young people his age. Let him spend a lot of time with the Cooks and Beamers in Hilo. You will turn Arthur to crime if he becomes resentful and rebellious. He'll go to jail. He'll become a mama's boy if he gives in to you.'"

I had to escape. Kamehameha was the answer. I demanded that my mother allow me this opportunity. Perhaps reflecting on what Kahiwa had said and within the deep recesses of her social worker mind, my mother may have realized this was the chance to save my life. Realizing attending Kamehameha would cause me to be unwelcome at my grandparents' home, she arranged for Aunt Em, a probation officer, and her life companion, Aunt Harriett, to look after me during weekend passes and Thanksgivings.

During vacations I traveled between Oʻahu and Kona on a cattle boat. Going to the Big Island with other students on an empty boat was fun; I had my *ʻukulele* and we sang on the upper decks and slept there.

Returning to Honolulu with the hold full of cattle was not so pleasant. Odors of manure rising from the cattle below made me seasick as the steamboat worked its way across the channel between Molokaʻi and Oʻahu. Open-ocean swells of the Kaiwi Channel are world famous for roughness.

PART THREE

# CHINESE CONNECTION

>–+‹›–0–‹+‹<

CHAPTER 7

## Brief History of Hawai'i

### Prior to 1778 and through 1935

THIS ABBREVIATED history of Hawai'i introduces the role of Kamehameha Schools in saving Hawaiians from extinction.

It also provides the opportunity to clear up my grandfather's lifelong deception. Never did he let his Canadian wife know that he was part Chinese. He wouldn't reveal this because of whites' intense prejudices against Chinese during his time. I learned of this lineage while looking in another direction—for my father's hidden background. By then I was too old to brag of having a Hawaiian heart and a Chinese brain. I now proudly introduce Great-Great Grandfather Chun Hung, a.k.a. "Hungtai." I love his story.

Hawaiians planted and irrigated sugarcane fields long before Captain Cook arrived in 1778, chewing cane for quick energy but growing it to feed to pigs so the meat would have a marvelously rich taste.

Do you enjoy barbecues? Mentally savor what our Hawaiian ancestors experienced: sugar-fed pork, flavored with sea salt and chili peppers, roasting underground for hours in its natural juices; the meat had a subtle, smoky taste and fell off the bones. Those so inclined might drink some *ōkolehao*, a liquor made from ti plant roots. Loosely translated, *ōkolehao* means "knock you on your butt."

English explorers envisioned rum when viewing Hawai'i's cane stalks. Between 1792 and 1794, Captain Vancouver made three visits and brought us new plants, as well as cattle, sheep, and those damned goats. He was investigating economic opportunities should England colonize Hawai'i. Agriculturists on board suggested distilling native sugar into rum for the Chinese market. A daily ration of rum with slices of

Hawaiian pineapple and fresh limes added would also cheer crew members on a slow boat to China.

Chinese passed through Hawai'i as early as 1788, many being carpenters on English ships, and some involved in buying sandalwood from Hawai'i's forests, which were filled with these valuable trees that are known for their exquisitely aromatic wood. Hawaiians were put to work harvesting the trees, and the sandalwood forests were decimated.

Sugarcane was common to south China, where it had been cultivated and made into sugar for centuries. A Chinese is credited with the first attempt to manufacture sugar from Hawaiian native cane. Chun Hung, my Chinese ancestor from Macao, knew the art of sugar making. He was a "tong see"—sugar master. Chun, who became known as "Hungtai," established the first sugar works at Wailuku, Maui, in 1828 in cooperation with Kamehameha III. He sold the white sugar made at his mill in his store, Hungtai, Honolulu's first. It was on the corner of Fort and Merchant Streets, a busy commercial area then and now.[1]

Merican missionaries settled in before the English. When they started arriving from New England in 1820, they saw our men and women dancing bare-breasted and proud. Hawaiians' sense of dignity in the naturalness of their bodies was mistaken by westerners as wanton paganism—lewd and lascivious. Until that time, we had not learned to be ashamed of our bodies.

Missionaries forbade hula dancing, demanded that women wear loose-fitting dresses—called *mu'u-mu'u*—and began replacing the Hawaiian language with English. Inexplicably, we obeyed missionaries' edicts.

Defying dour Calvinists, Winona Beamer's great-grandmother, Isabella Kalili Desha, went underground to a secret *hālau* to study the hula to teach to her descendants. Helen Desha Beamer, her daughter, began teaching it in Hilo in 1902. Hawaiians respect Beamer women for preserving their culture.

Some missionary children, along with shrewd American newcomers, identified Hawaiian-grown sugar as a way to get rich. Hawai'i was perfect for creating a sugar

---

[1] Chinese names are in reverse order from Western names. "Chun" was his surname, but for advertising purposes, my great-great-grandfather used "Hungtai" as his personal name. In addition to the Hungtai Sugar Works and Hungtai Store, he owned the Canton Hotel and the Pagoda Building, a mercantile, meeting, and social center known as "Chinaman's Hall." Natives took kindly to early Chinese entrepreneurs who had education and skill, learned the language with great facility, intermarried with Hawaiians, and had large families. Rufus Lyman, son of missionaries, married Chun's daughter Hualani and had fifteen children who survived to adulthood. David Belden Lyman, my grandfather, was one of them.

Missionaries imposed clothing and behavior standards on Hawaiians. Entrepreneurs pushed them off public land and natives lost their transient way of life—raising crops in the hills, catching fish in the sea, and having climate-idealized, inexpensive grass dwellings both *mauka* and *makai*. *Bishop Museum Archives photo.*

industry for the U.S. market: Its volcanic soil is wonderfully rich in lime, potash, phosphoric acid, and nitrogen; the Islands have a year-round growing season; rain falls frequently on mountains and uplands; streams flow into lowland ponds.

It takes 4,000 tons of water to grow enough cane for 1 ton of sugar, and there was ample water for planters to adopt the Hawaiian custom of irrigating fields. Americans first initiated ventures with the experienced Chinese sugar planters in Hawai'i but went on their own after learning the techniques. Great-Great-Grandfather was not interested in going big time; satisfied in raising sugar to sell to local consumers, he advertised in *The Polynesian* newspaper:

> HUNGTAI have for sale at their plantation, at Wailuku, east side of Maui, a quantity of superior WHITE SUGAR, not inferior to the best imported Loaf Sugar. Also WHITE SYRUP, a superior article for family use. For the information of merchants and others trading to these islands, they would state that they are enlarging their business, having now 150 acres of Sugar Cane under cultivation, and in the course of the next season will have 250 acres. By the 1st of December next, they will have a large lot of BROWN SUGAR for sale, on as reasonable terms as can be offered by any other firm.

His American partners concluded there was not enough profit in sugar unless they went into exporting, for which they needed a lot of land. Foreigners realized the native kingdom was vulnerable to overturn by clever entrepreneurs. If controlled economically and psychologically, its indigenous population would feel weak and inferior; they would be easy to take over.[2]

Americans began operating their first successful sugar plantation before 1840. Sugar is a plantation crop dependent on vast tracts of land and cheap, docile labor. Whites could acquire Hawai'i's land easily through purchase and tricks, but lack of local labor was a problem; our population was badly depleted and declining and many of our working-age men were on whaling ships.[3]

Hawaiian men, not submissive to the near-slave labor conditions of plantation fields, rejected overseer thugs on horseback who intimidated with whips and insults and who were apt to walk past a row of bent-over workers to randomly aim a kick at someone's testicles. Hawaiians preferred going to sea or eking out a living on their own instead of working on plantations where they'd be bullied.

Planters began importing coolies from China as contract laborers. Many saved their money, went into business, and married Hawaiian women who appreciated their industriousness and cooking skills. No one is more ardent than a Chinese man intent on winning a bride, I've been told.

The U.S. Chinese Exclusion Laws, effective in 1898, forced sugar planters to

---

[2] Ships from the British Navy sailed into Honolulu Harbor in March 1843 and militarily occupied Hawai'i. Its government declared this an unlawful colonial occupation, and on July 31, 1843, the ships sailed away after England declared Kamehameha III was the rightful sovereign. Fifty years later American sailors and marines helped a group of businessmen favoring U.S. annexation overthrow the monarchy.

[3] In 1852, whalers brought almost 375,000 gallons of oil into Hawaiian ports. Sperm whale oil was used in lamps, to make soap, paints, and spermaceti candles; whale bone was used in corsets to cinch the waists of ladies, for ribs in umbrellas, and for other purposes. The industry declined after petroleum was discovered by Edwin L. Drake in Titusville, Pennsylvania, in 1859 and kerosene was introduced as a lamp fuel.

Because Hawai'i during whaling days was the crossroads of the Pacific, whaling captains sometimes cast anchor in the quiet waters of almost unknown Hilo Harbor. There were no hotels at that time and wayfarers stayed at the Hilo Boarding School mission house. Uncle Henry Lyman wrote, "One solemn whaling captain I beheld taking his ease in our rocking chair; he made an indelible impression upon my childish imagination, for he was a survivor of the wreck of the Essex—an ill fated whale ship which had been sunk in the South Pacific Ocean by an infuriated sperm whale." Herman Melville, living in the Islands at the time, visited the mission home, as did Robert Louis Stevenson and Jack London. There is no record that Melville turned the survivor of the *Essex* into Captain Ahab, but he heard of the man and of the angry whale.

find other races for labor. They began importing Japanese men, known as a tightly knit cultural group. Planters thought the Japanese workers would return home when their labor contract expired, but "picture brides" began arriving and joining the men in the fields. The Japanese chose to stay.

The growing Japanese population made American businessmen concerned that Hawai'i might be annexed by Japan, especially after ships from the Japanese navy began visiting. The *Honolulu Star* newspaper wrote, "Hawai'i will become the white race against the yellow race."

Trying to achieve racial balance, sugar planters recruited Portuguese from Madeiras and the Azores. Many brought wives, expecting to be treated as other whites. But a haole, or white person, according to the new caste system, meant a Caucasian of northern European or American origin, not Portuguese or Spanish.

"Haole" originally referred to any foreigner, in contrast to indigenous Hawaiians.

$A$fter King Kalākaua went to Washington in 1876 to negotiate a reciprocity treaty, Hawaiian sugar could enter the United States without import taxes. The United States renewed the treaty on a year-to-year basis but wouldn't extend it unless the military was allowed to use Pearl Harbor as a naval station.

King Kalākaua vowed he'd never surrender Pearl Harbor. Retaliating with armed force, island sugar producers made the king sign a new constitution taking away his power. Hawaiians call it "The Bayonet Constitution."

In 1881, less than four years after ratifying the treaty, Congress passed the McKinley Act, allowing all sugar to enter the United States free of import duty. The United States had Pearl Harbor, but Hawaiian sugar no longer had any advantage over foreign sugar, such as that from the Philippine Islands.

$B$y 1883 the Hawaiian race was perilously close to extinction. Our population had been reduced by over 90 percent since being "discovered."[4] Captain Cook's putting Hawai'i on the map made it a popular Pacific Ocean stopping point for sailors from cargo and whaling ships to pick up barrels of drinking water, fresh pineapples, vegetables, and salted meat and enjoy rest and relaxation among our friendly folk.

Our people died by the hundreds of thousands from measles, smallpox, whooping cough, and other diseases carried by visitors, newcomers, and imported field-

---

[4] Some scholars claim Hawai'i's population was around 1 million when Cook arrived. Others use the figure 400,000. Whether the loss was 960,000 or 360,000, it was devastating and made Hawaiians a minority within their own homeland.

workers. Hawaiians, long living in isolation, had no immunity. Hawaiians were also destroyed psychologically; they were treated as a low caste by haole, lost use of their land, and couldn't adjust to the Western culture being forced on them.

At the rate Asians were being imported for plantation labor, they would soon outnumber Hawai'i's native people.

Princess Bernice Pauahi Bishop, fifty-one-years old and dying of cancer, did what she could to save our race. She created the Bishop Estate to establish and maintain Kamehameha Schools—a boarding school for boys and one for girls. She believed education was vital to help Hawaiians survive among encroaching Western and Eastern cultures. Her will states her intentions:

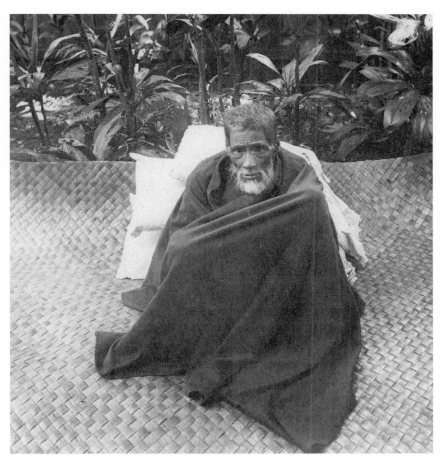

Knowledge of natural medical treatments couldn't save this *kahuna*. Having no immunity, thousands of Hawaiians died from diseases newcomers imported. *Bishop Museum Archives photo, J. J. Williams, photographer.*

I desire my trustees to provide first and chiefly a good education in the common English branches, instruction in morals, and in such useful knowledge as may tend to make good and industrious men and women.

The princess was the great-granddaughter of King Kamehameha I, who had unified the Hawaiian Islands in the eighteenth century. Childless, she made all Hawaiian youngsters her spiritual children. She transferred legal ownership of 437,000 acres of royal lands to five men whom she appointed as her trustees. They and their successors became responsible for preserving and enhancing the value of her assets while following her instructions.

Her trustees are "fiduciaries"—persons to whom property or power is entrusted and who are to act at all times for the sole benefit and interests of the trust with undivided loyalty. Such responsibility calls for persons of great character and experience.

Because her will could be carried out only by her trustees, their selection would always be a crucial decision; ultimately, everything depended on them. Alas—this was the fateful flaw.

King Kalākaua died in 1891 and was succeeded by his sister Liliʻuokalani. Members of the business community plotted to depose our queen so Hawaiʻi could be annexed to the United States. For whereas the McKinley Act let all foreign sugar into the United States free of duty, it also provided a price support of two cents per pound for domestic American sugar.

Should Hawaiʻi become a U.S. Territory, Hawaiian sugar would be "domestic" sugar and could qualify for the two-cents-per-pound price support. By this time, Great-Great-Grandfather Chun Hung's refining secrets were practiced by the haole, who had accumulated vast amounts of sugar lands.

Hawaiʻi's first revolution occurred in 1893, when the monarchy was overthrown by the committee of thirteen. Four of its leaders were descendants of missionaries who believed the Islands were theirs because their parents had given Hawaiians the English language, civilization, and Christianity.

The queen was attempting to restore some of the powers stripped from her brother, King Kalākaua. Her determination to restore some of the monarchical power concerned the plotters; they turned to the might of Americans who were in Honolulu's harbor.

One-hundred sixty-two armed United States Marines and sailors positioned themselves near ʻIolani Palace on January 16, 1893, violating five treaties between the U.S. government and the Hawaiian nation and violating international law. They faced a handful of poorly equipped royal guards and weaponless natives. The white plotters became leaders of the new Republic of Hawaiʻi and imprisoned the queen. A commission of white military officers convicted her of treason for seeking to introduce a new constitution.

Having the support of the U.S. government, American planters and other businessmen proclaimed abrogation of the Hawaiian monarchy. Although President Cleveland later condemned the role of the U.S. government in overthrowing the Hawaiian monarchy and called for Queen Lili'uokalani's restoration, Congress ignored what he said.

In 1898, two months after a resolution to annex Hawai'i was introduced in Congress, it was passed in both houses and signed by America's new president, expansionist-minded William McKinley. Hawai'i was officially annexed by the United States on August 12, 1898, and became the Territory of Hawai'i by the Organic Act of 1900.

The *New York Illustrated Magazine* wrote: "One of the last things ex-queen Liliuokani did before the American flag was hoisted . . . was to give a farewell lua." "*Lua*," which is a common word for "outdoor toilet," was an unfortunate misspelling of *lū'au*. The article continued: "On this occasion the hula dance was given. This dance was made unlawful by authorities of the Hawaiian Republic, but it was practiced secretly."

Hawai'i's property rights were vested to the United States, and Hawaiians felt their birthright had been stolen. We would say the same thing about a hundred years later when the U.S. Supreme Court ruled that Princess Pauahi's royal lands, owned by the Bishop Estate, could be condemned and sold by the government.

Pineapple plantations came along after 1901 when James D. Dole began growing an imported variety of pineapple, bigger and better than our wild pineapples. Hawai'i became a sugar and pineapple plantation society with no significant middle class, one effective political party, Republican, and sharp limitations on opportunity unless you were all-white and part of a "Big Five" business (Alexander & Baldwin Ltd., American Factors, C. Brewer & Co. Ltd., Castle & Cooke Ltd., and Theo. H. Davies & Company). It was known as "The Paradise of the Pacific" to white families who controlled the economy and saw themselves as masters of uneducated, uncultured farm laborers. White families believed it was their right to dominate Hawaiians. These were "their islands"; people on them existed for their pursuit of wealth. The term "white oligarchy" was synonymous with the Big Five, meaning power invested in a few persons in a dominant class or a clique by birth.

Big Five agencies controlled transportation, the steamship lines to and from the mainland and interisland, and island railroads as well; they branched into the hotel business and monopolized the tourist industry; they owned or controlled utilities, principal banks, insurance agencies, other financial institutions, and many small wholesale and retail businesses.

Merchants trying to compete with Big Five business interests found it difficult to get loans. Locals said, "You can start a department store in Honolulu if you have land and money, but the Matson Navigation Company will leave your freight on the wharf at San Francisco by mistake."

Only by subterfuge—using second and third parties to buy parcels of land—were Kress and Sears Roebuck stores able to enter the Hawaiian market.

Some Japanese became prominent in the fishing industry, escaping the Big Five's net with great perseverance and ingenuity, but it was difficult for businesspersons of any ancestry to compete in any endeavor.

Under this kind of control, occupational status and pay became based on ethnic identity. Best jobs went to whites, Hawaiians, Portuguese, Chinese, Japanese, and Filipinos, in that order.

As an example of plantation wage variances, white carpenters from the mainland made one and a half times as much as Hawaiian carpenters, twice as much as Portuguese and Chinese, and more than two and a half times as much as Japanese. Filipinos were assigned to the hardest, most tedious manual work. Under this economy, wives of white semiskilled laborers could have a household servant; their husbands could hire an Oriental yardman.

By 1918, sugar planters had brought in 61,000 adult male immigrants who lived on sugar plantations, and Japanese and Chinese comprised half of Hawai'i's population. In 1935, near the height of Filipino importation, 29,413 single Filipino males were in the Territory of Hawai'i, compared with 366 single female Filipinos. This led to homosexuality and sexual violence. Plantation owners used prostitutes to solve the problem.

Charles Erskine, an Englishman married to my Aunt Becky, was bookkeeper for the Waipahu Plantation Store. The store extended credit for transactions in the barracks as well as for groceries. Putting workers into debt by increasing their store accounts forced them to extend their indenture contracts. (The Waipahu Plantation Village is now a 50-acre historical site depicting the lifestyle of the 400,000 immigrants who came to Hawai'i to work on sugar plantations. It shows how the different ethnic groups lived.) Other plantations did the same thing.

Company stores paid company whores.

Aunt Kahiwa, a beautiful woman with a wonderful sense of humor, was a godchild of Queen Lili'uokalani. She was a public health nurse for the Territory of Hawai'i and was assigned to make a health checkup on men in the Hāmākua Plantation barracks complex. Opening the door into the first building, she was greeted by laughter and cheers from two-dozen Filipino men lying completely naked on their cots. They had prepared for sex on seeing this part-Hawaiian woman drive up.

Aunt Kahiwa stuck each man extra firmly in the buttocks with a hypodermic needle. Given a similar excited greeting by nude men in the next barracks, she vaccinated them all. Brandishing a large hypodermic needle when entering the third barracks, she met dead silence.

The men recognized her car when Kahiwa drove up the next month. They sat quietly, fully clothed, subdued, not the slightest bit pleased to see this attractive woman who was there to keep them healthy.

In concluding this chapter on early plantation days, I report that Great-Great-Grand-father's Chinese business associates did not die peacefully in their beds, as did he.

Atai, Ahung's partner, hung himself after the death of his son from leprosy. He is buried in the Mānoa cemetery, which I will discuss later. His brother, Apung, a scapegrace with a penchant for gambling and high living, became partners with Ahung. He may have been influenced by his partner's name, for Apung, too, hung himself.

In addition to a wife, Apung had a whole nest of mistresses—they were called "houris" in those days. Police threatened to bring him before the court, where proceedings would reflect missionary attitudes about the sin of adultery. In order to avoid this exposure, he committed suicide.

No sooner was his corpse cut down and laid on the floor than bereaved favorites, howling lamentations, endeavored to shampoo him back into life. He was buried the same day in the Protestant cemetery while a dense crowd followed him to the grave with a band. Cheerful music of the pipe, cornet, and drum formed a curious accompaniment to the women's wailing.

## CHAPTER 8

# Being Hawaiian

### Current Times and Retrospective, 1837–1940

LOCAL PEOPLE often make another's racial extraction part of their identity, immediately connoting a stereotype: "She's a haole" may suggest a white person who feels superior; "he's Japanese" suggests hardworking, determined; "she's Chinese-Hawaiian" suggests very smart as well as very pretty; "he's Hawaiian" may suggest undependable and far worse. People of different races get along, but stereotypes don't go away.

Hawai'i's percentage of private schools to population is the highest of any state because of the vast disparity in educational standards between public and private schools. Tuition is as high or higher than many New England preparatory schools. Some parents start children in Hawai'i's private schools as early as prekindergarten.

Schools convey racial, economic, and social class considerations. "What school did you go to?" is one of the first questions asked when meeting another for the first time; a person's high school carries a lifelong impression in Hawai'i.

Public school students commonly communicate in pidgin English, the local polyglot of Chinese, English, Filipino, Hawaiian, and Japanese that many use all their lives. Mainland tourists will sometimes address pidgin-English users slowly, simply, and loudly, as if they are deaf and dumb. But the often-heard patois has a special and apparently permanent place in the social structure of Hawai'i.

With its low tuition and generous financial grants, Kamehameha Schools is the ideal for children of Hawaiian ancestry—and the prestige of being able to say, "I attended Kamehameha" is second to none.

Princess Bernice established Kamehameha Schools to awaken the minds and spirits of her people to their own potential in a world of possibilities; to repair psychological damage caused by their being described as "lazy" and "good for nothing"; to strengthen their self-image and restore their dignity; and to teach them skills for gainful employment so they would be able to raise their families, improve their living standards, and stake out their rightful place in society. With no universal education system in place in 1884, her educational legacy became a lifesaver for Native Hawaiians.

Kamehameha Schools instills a sense of bonding, giving its students racial and individual pride. The school song, written by the first principal, the Reverend Oleson, and by its first song master, Dr. Richards, is sung by students and alumni whenever they assemble. Its first verse begins, "Be strong and ally ye, oh sons of Hawai'i, and nobly stand together hand in hand." The second verse starts, "Be firm and deny ye, oh sons of Hawai'i, allurements that your race will overwhelm." "Allurements" is an unusual word to include in a school song. It refers to seductions that can encroach on and destroy Hawaiians.

The pledge that members of the boys school give at Pauahi's yearly memorial service is equally resolute: "To prepare ourselves to have such homes and conditions as shall tend to keep and develop for our race all those noble traits of character she possessed." Personifying noble traits is a way to repel racism.

It was hard to be Hawaiian and ambitious. Major island firms were run by whites who recruited managerial personnel from the mainland rather than upgrade part-Hawaiians or Orientals they already employed. Locals could be trusted to teach a new manager a job but weren't invited to fill it.

Career women who refer to a "glass ceiling" that limits their potential may have some understanding of the frustration Hawaiian men felt by a "grass ceiling." Many twentieth-century male Hawaiians have stories of reaching their grass ceiling, being knocked to the ground by an authority figure, treated as dirt, as if that's where they belong.

My grandfather experienced the grass ceiling while in the Salvation Army; this affected his attitude about me. As a young man, David Belden Lyman was accustomed to respect. The eighth of fifteen children, he postponed advanced education to become a cowboy and then a surveyor to help educate the rest of the flock.

His brother, Clarence Kumukoa Lyman, was the first Hawaiian admitted to West Point (West Point #4382). Two younger brothers graduated from Kamehameha School for Boys, Class of 1904, and attended West Point: Albert Kualii Lyman (#4764), Class of 1909, and Charles Reed Bishop Lyman (#5188), Class of 1913. Queen Lili'uokalani insisted the younger Lyman boys send their West Point report cards to her, rewarding their good grades with gold coins. Because of the gold he accumulated, rough-and-tough Charles Reed Bishop Lyman was called "Queenie."

Queen Liliʻuokalani had a soft spot for my aunt Nellie Cook, who went to boarding school at St. Andrews Episcopal Priory School, founded by Queen Emma. Queen Liliʻuokalani, who lived next door to the Priory, liked Nellie's fine penmanship and had her prepare social invitations and place cards for formal dinners.

Being a proper Priory girl, Nellie scooted away when King Kalākaua invited her to sit on his lap while he was visiting his sister, Liliʻuokalani. Aunt Nellie was frightened by what the Priory's head sister might think of her associating with the Merry Monarch. Interviewed by a newspaper reporter on her hundredth birthday, Aunt Nellie giggled over this recollection.

Two of the three Lyman "West Pointers" lived through World War I. Shortly before his death in World War II, Albert Kualiʻi became the first Hawaiian to attain the rank of general—General Lyman Airport in Hilo is

Under the umbrella on the left is Queen Emma; under the one on the right is Queen Liliʻuokalani. Charles Reed Bishop Lyman, left, and Albert Kualiʻi Lyman, right, visited the queens shortly after completing Kamehameha School for Boys. Both Lyman boys graduated from the U.S. Military Academy at West Point. An older brother graduated from West Point in 1905. *Photo courtesy of the author.*

named after him. His brother, Charles Reed Bishop, named after Princess Pauahi's husband, led operations in New Guinea, Leyte, and Luzon, and was the second Hawaiian general.

My grandfather David, although a tough Hawaiian cowboy, went to business college in Sacramento, California, and enlisted in the Salvation Army in 1900. Two years later, Captain Lyman was sent to London as a delegate to the Salvation Army's First International Congress. General William Booth, the Salvation Army's founder, asked this first Hawaiian to be a Salvation Army officer to preach throughout the slums of London using the name "Hallelujah Lyman." Grandfather became an attraction: Wearing his military-style Salvation Army uniform, he stood over 6 feet in height, weighed more than 200 pounds, had a bronze complexion, and his big bass voice boomed out joyful praises to the Lord.

Grandfather felt that Hawaiians' problems, created by contrasting and unfamiliar races, increasing slums, poverty and disease, and political intrigue, might be solved by following General Booth's method of simplifying the Gospel and bringing it to the understanding of people who would not otherwise be reached.

"Hallelujah" lived a religion of happiness. In an apparent attempt to break up their romance, the Salvation Army reassigned David to separate him from fellow volunteer, red-headed Charlotte Armstrong of Ontario, Canada. Although Charlotte had personal misgivings about David, whom she referred to as "that dark man," she overcame them and married him in 1907.

Captain Lyman asked General Booth for permission to name his second daughter "Evangeline," after Booth's daughter, who went on to became international leader of the Salvation Army. Booth answered, "Yes, and I will be your daughter's spiritual father." By this he meant he would be her Godfather. This was my Aunt Eva, who settled in Los Angeles. Mainlanders called her "Gypsy" because of her swarthy looks.

Captain David Lyman supported a wife and six children by being a school principal and teacher in Kohala on the Island of Hawai'i. During evenings, he rode his horse to plantation camps to teach laborers to read; he gave them Bibles as textbooks.

An agitator was victimizing his fellow Filipinos—cheating them in gambling, putting them in debt, and practicing usury. He didn't want any Christian influence there. The men waited outside their barracks as "Hallelujah" rode in, joyfully calling, "A-l-o-h-a! Let us all read words of the Lord!"

Screaming, the agitator ran forward, waving a bolo knife in each hand.

Field-workers used bolos to hack sugarcane. He was going to throw the bolos and knock the Salvation Army officer from his horse.

Grandfather uncoiled the rope attached to his saddle. Twirling it around his head, he lassoed the troublemaker. Twisting the rope around his saddle horn, he kicked his heels into his horse's belly, and it trotted forward. He quickened his horse's pace and the agitator fell on his stomach and dropped the bolos. Grandfather yelled "whoa." The horse stopped and then defecated —almost on cue.

"Giddap," Grandfather urged as the horse dragged the offender face first, back and forth through the manure. Captain Lyman tied the shocked, dung-faced villain to a fence. Workers followed grandfather into their barracks to read the words of the Lord.

The wilted agitator was still tied up and dirty the next morning when a law officer arrived to take him away. Never again did he show his face in that camp.

Promoted to major in the early 1920s, Lyman was sent to Honolulu to start a school based on his grandfather's Hilo Boarding School principles. George N. Wilcox of Kaua'i, a close friend, provided 40 acres of rich farmland for the Kaimukī Boys Home and gave the Salvation Army some North Shore beach property for the boys' summer camp. Other Lyman family friends donated money for a gymnasium, swimming pool, dairy, church chapel, school buildings, and dormitories to house a hundred boys. Students at Hilo Boarding School sent coconuts to sprout and greenery to plant.

Most of the Kaimukī Boys Home residents originated from detention homes. In Hilo Boarding School tradition, they raised their own vegetables, milk, meat, and eggs. The school had a brass band, a tumbling team, and a basketball team. Major Lyman invited area schools to use the gym and swimming pool, rarities at that time.

By the fifth year, Lyman was meeting opposition from Hawai'i's Salvation Army officials and he had trouble receiving food and supplies from local headquarters. Apparently the commander envied the prestige the Salvation Army's only Hawaiian officer was gaining in the community.

Invited to speak at a Rotary Club meeting, Major Lyman explained how the "head, hands, and heart" philosophy for Kaimukī Boys School was similar to Hilo Boarding School's, where it had been introduced by his grandparents before being used at Kamehameha School for Boys.

Elated by enthusiastic response to his speech from white businessmen,

Major Lyman said to his commanding officer and role model, "I really like the people at Rotary. I would appreciate being considered for membership."

"Rotary is not for people of your sort," the officer told him.

New Salvation Army personnel demanded management changes at the home. Major Lyman had reached above his grass ceiling. He was not the first Hawaiian to receive greater professional respect in a foreign country and on the mainland United States than in Hawai'i.

Major Lyman retired early from the Salvation Army and became active in what he called "prison reform." No longer in uniform and carrying a Bible, he voluntarily helped O'ahu Prison inmates, most of whom were Hawaiians: people of his sort.

# PART FOUR

# SCHOOL THAT SAVES LIVES

>-+◆>-◯-<◆+-<

CHAPTER 9

## Art and Oz

Early 1940s

Princess Pauahi sought to protect Hawaiian children from problems facing adults of a dying race. Her beneficiaries are known as "Nā Pua a ke Aliʻi Pauahi"—the flowers of Princess Pauahi.

When I was picked as one in 1943, over 10 percent of Hawaiians between the ages of twenty and fifty-four were on "relief," now known as "welfare." Potential Kamehameha students throughout the Islands came from three general environments: the City of Honolulu, a rural setting near the ocean, or a ranching community.

While most of the people in this book were children, over half of all Hawaiians lived in the City of Honolulu in small, single-story frame houses. Kamehameha Schools enrollment figures coincided with that ratio. Over 50 percent of the boys and 62 percent of the girls in my class, representative of the entire student body, came from Honolulu and were day students; they were part of the new day scholars' program.

Nearby pineapple canneries provided seasonal work. Unable to compete with whites and Orientals in business, adult Hawaiians filled semipolitical positions such as policemen and park caretakers; others were stevedores and teamsters; some worked at tourist hotels.

Many chose to be cowboys, as cattle ranches on the neighbor islands were closer to old Hawaiʻi than life in Honolulu, and ranches provided housing for cowboys' families. Some 5 percent of the boys in my class, including me, and 6 percent of girls came from ranching communities on the islands of Hawaiʻi and Maui.

Those graduating from Kamehameha Schools had a trade, a white-collar office job, and perhaps a college degree, but the grass ceiling limited chances of rising into management.

The eastern part of the island of Oʻahu is divided by the Koʻolau Range, with a 1,200-foot pass called the Pali, miles up a beautiful valley festooned with flowers and waterfalls. Over the Pali from Honolulu is rural Oʻahu. A narrow, winding road, frequently wet and slippery, and winds strong enough to push spectators off the precipice, made traveling to the other side of the island challenging. It took strength and skill to drive a car not equipped with power steering around the sharp curves. Before a tunnel—referred to as "the *puka* in the Pali"—was built in the 1950s, the windward side of the island seemed a world away from Honolulu. Students from that area became boarders at Kamehameha Schools.

Hawaiians could be like their ancestors in rural villages and out-of-the-way subsistence communities. Oswald Stender grew up this way, as did 40 percent of the boys and 32 percent of the girls in my class. Scores of small valleys in isolated districts throughout the Islands provided a haven; just a small plot of taro and access to the sea and mountains could satisfy material wants. Medical practices of *kāhuna* prevailed through the use of herbs and vegetable compounds.

View of the Koʻolau Mountains and Nuʻuanu Pali Lookout. *Bishop Museum Archives photo, Werner Stoy, photographer.*

Knowing Oswald, or "Oz" as he came to be known, since we were both thirteen years old, I kept in touch with him throughout most of my life. Oswald Kofoad Stender, a boy with a Danish middle and surname, is exactly the kind of person Hawai'i's richest woman had in mind when writing her will. She directed trustees to use part of her estate's income to support and educate orphans and others in indigent circumstances, giving preference to persons of pure or part-Hawaiian blood.

Oz was orphaned in 1933, at the age of two, when his mother, Emily Kamalolo Stender, died from an illness. Albert Stender, Oz's father, remarried, moved from the Islands, and left Oz and his two sisters with John Kamalolo, his maternal grandfather.

A former whaler then living on Maui, Oz's Danish paternal grandfather disinherited Albert for marrying Emily, who was pure Hawaiian; he had absolutely no interest in half-Hawaiian grandchildren.

John Kamalolo was a groundskeeper at Hau'ula Park on Windward O'ahu. His daughter, whom Oz called "Auntie Aukai," was a housemaid and cook for wealthy white families. She lived with her father, whom Oz called "Tūtū Kāne"—Hawaiian for "grandfather." Kamalolo raised Oz as an old-fashioned Hawaiian boy, teaching him to live off the land and ocean.

Tūtū Kāne's home was in Hau'ula on a parcel of leased Hawaiian Homestead land. He grew fruit and vegetables, raised chickens and pigs, caught fish and other seafood in the ocean, and netted mullet, crayfish, and shrimp in a mountain stream where delicious watercress grew. This was authentic old-style Hawaiian living. Oz explains in the following talk stories.

He and two neighbors diverted water from a stream into a quarter-acre pond about 4 feet deep where they grew taro. They put mullet and shrimp into the pond to fertilize the plants and threw food scraps and worms from the compost pile to feed mullet. The pond was a self-contained ecology system.

When the fishing was bad because the ocean was stormy, mullet fed us. Heart-shaped taro leaves rose on stalks above the pond; when outer leaves were about a foot in size, the taro root was large enough to dig up. Ripe roots, from 5 inches in diameter, grew in mud at the bottom of the pond. Because weeds would strangle taro roots, I always had work to do.

Each week one of the families took its turn harvesting taro roots, making poi, and storing it in a big wooden barrel for all to share. Auntie Aukai trimmed the smaller inner taro leaves and steamed them; they taste similar to spinach.

We added flour and water when poi in the barrel was low. Poi was our daily food, sometimes our only food. I learned the entire process, baking the gray root, peeling off its hairy brown outer layer, pounding it on a board while moistening it with water. Fresh poi is sweet and becomes sourer daily as it ferments, having an angry "bite" by the end of the week.

We grew sweet potatoes, tomatoes, and onions on a hillside. Our home was a bower nestled within green and yellow colors: papaya and lime trees near the house; banana plants and avocado, pomelo, and mango trees in the backyard; guava bushes on the hillside. Hibiscus with red, white, and yellow blooms were in front of the house. Plumeria trees bloomed with white and red blossoms at the side of the house. Sisters Henrietta and Dot always had fresh, colorful flowers to wear.

Rich scents of Tahitian gardenia wafted greetings as you walked into the yard of our happy home. It was a typical 1930s-style beach shack. Because temperature was in the mid-70 degrees all year around, we went inside only to get out of the rain and to sleep. Nature made it a haven of beauty, a gentle, cooling breeze wafted from the mountains rising sharply behind—the reason they call this part of Oʻahu the "windward" side of the island.

I swept the yard with a palm frond, weeded the taro pond, fed chickens and pigs, and helped make poi.

When I was eight, Tūtū Kāne said I was now a "fisher boy." He whittled goggle frames from a *hau* tree branch, cut window glass for lenses which he sealed into frames with wax; he trimmed a strip of rubber from a tire's inner tube and attached this rubber band to the goggles. These he adjusted to fit comfortably over my eyes. He tied rubber strips to both sides of a piece of 8-inch hollow bamboo and joined the ends with a cord to fit over a notch in the back of a metal spear having a barb on its front. This device propelled a spear inserted into the bamboo tube, functioning at close range as a powerful slingshot.

At first I speared small fish in water barely over my head, but Auntie and my sisters made a big thing out of my every catch. Auntie would scrape meat from the bones and mix it with seaweed, salt, and kukui nut into a form of *poki;* my small catches didn't have much meat. We nibbled this as we ate poi.

As I grew bigger and dared to go into deeper water, the *poki* pieces became larger; eventually Auntie Aukai steamed, poached, baked, or broiled what I speared. Occasionally schools of fingerling, baby fish, came close to shore; I'd scoop them with a hand net and Auntie fried them whole for a crispy treat.

I enjoyed the challenge of finding, stalking, and spearing fish, always anticipating a thrilling outcome. Come along with me as I describe an outing.

Swimming carefully within 6 feet of a fish, I would grip the bamboo tube firmly with my left hand and aim the spear tip. Fish and I were close to the bottom in 12 feet of water; I spotted a good-sized one, maybe 6 pounds. The water was so clear that I could see the fish's eyes as I slowly approached; it would blink if uneasy and might dart away; before that happened, I would stop and wait. With my right hand, I pulled the spear back gradually, extending to maximum tension the rubber bands holding it in the sling. I kicked slowly, then opened my right hand; the spear burst forward, piercing and stunning the fish.

I dived, grabbed the falling spear, and surfaced for breath. My heart pounded with excitement. Untying the cord around my waist, I pushed one end through the silvery blue fish's mouth and a gill and retied the cord firmly around me. If the fish was big enough for dinner, as this one was, I would swim toward shore. Otherwise, I would reinsert the spear into the bamboo tube, put the end of the sling in the spear's notch, and dive underwater to locate another target.

That's what happened when my aim was true. Otherwise, the empty spear would drop to the ocean bottom for me to retrieve and reload. A fish over a foot in size might swim away with my spear; I would chase after it fast, knowing it would slow down from blood loss. When my chest burned hard, I surfaced to gulp air, then returned underwater, looking anxiously for a wavering line of blood to follow. Wounded fish hide under ledges and in caves.

When the tide comes in, bigger fish lurk inside the reef to gobble smaller ones washed over by breaking waves. If fishing wasn't good, I would swim back and forth, hoping to find a target, quitting before sunset when sharks feed.

I speared squid, wading in shallow, rocky areas while looking into a box having a glass bottom. Squid about 6 to 12 inches in size hide in cracks between rocks. I would spot one, pierce it, and pull it out with a three-pronged spear, then bite the head to wound it and turn its body inside out so it wouldn't cling with its suction cups or crawl out of the cloth bag tied around my waist.

I picked seaweed from the reefs, each having its own flavor and texture. With a bent piece of coat hanger, I pulled *wana*[1] from underwater rocks and pried *'opihi*[2] with a knife from sides of rocks sticking out of the ocean.

O z described experiences on moonlit nights, when large fish approach shore.

When the tide was low, Tūtū Kāne and I would walk through the shallow water; he held a torch up high, I held a spear ready for action.

---

[1] Sea urchin.

[2] Limpets; they are chewy, similar to abalone.

The moon cast a silvery sheen over the ocean, and the torch's flame reflected on the smooth sea. Large fish moved leisurely, seemingly on a shoreline cruise, following the flickering light.

I raised the trident over a fish, and its colors and markings were as clear as if it were a koi slowly moving in a garden pond. I thrust and impaled the heavy fish, then placed it in the burlap bag Tūtū Kāne held open.

We did this to subsist, not for sport, and we would share the night's bounty with neighbors.

W e were especially adventuresome when a bunch of us boys fished together, daring to swim beyond the reefs where the sea is darker and colder, diving deeper, mindless of perils: sharks, sting rays, man-of-war, eels, barracuda; catching a cramp, current, or an undertow; being smashed against a reef by a big wave. We were carefree youths. Nothing bad could happen—we also were exceptionally strong swimmers.

We floated an inner tube in the area we spearfished. It had a net attached in the tube's center into which we tossed our catch; one end of a rope was tied to the tube, the other had a hanging stone anchor.

We looked for lobsters hanging on sides of a sea cave, grabbed them on the back, and tossed them into the tube.

We all participated in netting fish. The net thrower stood on a ledge over the ocean; the rest of us climbed to a higher level and spread out to spot schools of fish. We called out the direction of schools moving inland to the net thrower.

Spotters sometimes identified fish within the moving school's ripples: "*Pāpio! Pāpio!* To your left." The net thrower scampered over sharp lava rock to where we directed him, crouching with the net over his shoulder.

We called out as the school approached, "Coming in now." Upright, he would spot it. Using both arms he smoothly tossed the tent-shaped net to parachute and drop down over the school; lead weights strung along the net's edges closed it as it sank, trapping the fish. The thrower dived into the ocean to retrieve the net. We would join him to help land what we hoped would be a net heavy with fish.

M any visitors learn to act out "The *Hukilau* Song" (written by Jack Owens in 1948). *Huki* means to pull, as on a rope, *lau* is a seine tied to a rope. Everyone who pulls the net gets some of its contents.

Oz describes a typical *hukilau:* "Paddlers take the attached nets into a bay and drop them in a semicircle; the net's bow faces the sea. They throw cut-up bait inside

*Hukilau* participants pull slowly and steadily, bringing nets heavy with trapped fish to shore. *Bishop Museum Archives photo, Harold T. Stearns, photographer.*

the bow; chumming will help to lure fish. They paddle back later in the day to direct the two ends of the extended net to shore. Community members wade out to pull the fish-filled nets onto the beach."

Most Hawaiian elders knew how to use natural elements as medicine. "We had no car," Oz says, and he goes on to explain:

> The mail deliverer could provide emergency "taxi service" to a hospital. But I never had a medical problem Tūtū Kāne couldn't cure. A cut? He'd put sea salt on it. A stomachache? He picked a *noni* for me to eat; this green and yellow acidic fruit tastes terrible. A cold or fever? I'd take a steam bath with camphor oil in our outdoor shed. A burn? He'd gently rub aloe leaf sap over it and tell me to stay out of the sun.
>
> My urine served as an all-purpose antiseptic: Rub it on to soothe the pain from mumps; soak a foot in it to stop infection from a puncture; apply it to where you scraped against a reef to prevent a speck of coral from growing under your skin.
>
> He'd pick a green *kukui* nut and I rubbed its milky white sap on a canker or other mouth sore. Tūtū Kāne roasted ripe *kukui* nuts in a fire, cracked their shells, removed the meat, cut it into little pieces, and mixed it with sea salt. Called *'inamona,* he encouraged me to eat a small amount as a condiment and to eat a lot whenever I needed a laxative. It works fast.
>
> *Kukui* bark was used for dye, its sap for glue, the nuts for candles.

I sanded two dozen *kukui* nuts until they were smooth, drilled a hole through each, strung them together with fishing cord, and wore it proudly to *lūʻau*.

He rubbed a finger along his nose. I mimicked his gesture and laughed. I'd polished my own black *kukui* nut lei with nose oil to make it shine.

Grouped together, coconut trees provide postcard-perfect beachside scenes with their shades of green, yellow, light brown, and grey. They seem like sentinels watching white sand and ever-expanding golden coral reefs, witnessing clear blue water, crashing waves, and spreading and receding ocean foam.

The coconut tree is the most useful plant in the world; its leaves can provide shelter, hats, mats, and floor covering, and its fruit yields food and drink. You can build a raft with the dried nuts, make bowls of them to hold food or catch water, use husks as fuel for a fire, and braid the clothlike fiber near the top of the tree into rope.

Young coconuts hold a refreshing sugary liquid, and the meat is sweet and puddinglike for scooping with a spoon or piece of shell. They're not like the hard-meat coconuts sold in grocery stores for scraping into flakes for cakes and pies.

Servicemen sometimes asked little country boy Oz how to pick coconuts. "I'd explain and then demonstrate: 'Climbing up a 40- to 100-foot coconut tree is like chin-ups. Hold your arms out straight, and pull with your hands as you run up. While gripping the tree with one hand, take the cane knife from your belt and swing it to cut off the coconuts that'll fall to the ground. Slide down the tree.'" Auntie Aukai taught him to explain things simply, directly, and thoroughly.

"Adults conversed with each other in Hawaiian, but spoke English to us children because that was the language we used in school," Oz explained. "Auntie Aukai learned excellent English while working for white families. She helped improve mine, hoping I'd have the chance to become more than a subsistence fisherman."

Opportunity came one day while Oz was in the seventh grade. His local school was in a simple one-story wooden building; classrooms were filled with barefoot children. The principal's secretary came to Oz's classroom to speak to his teacher, who directed him to follow the secretary.

During the brief walk down the hallway, the secretary confided that Mr. Allen A. Bailey was interviewing potential students for Kamehameha Schools eighth grade. With a bit of awe in her voice, she added, "He asked specifically to see Oswald Kofoad Stender."

Reviewing school records before the meeting, Mr. Bailey knew Oz's background. When Oz walked into the principal's office, Allen Bailey saw an average-sized, healthy-looking thirteen-year-old with a charming smile and a sparkle in his eyes.

Oz saw a bald gentleman wearing glasses, with a kindly look on his face. He never had spoken to anyone wearing a suit. Mr. Bailey stood up to shake hands and invited Oz to sit down. He started the interview by saying, "Tell me what you do to help at home."

Oz loved life with Tūtū Kāne, Auntie Aukai, Henrietta, and Dot. As he listened, Allen Bailey realized this highly enthusiastic boy with the lilting voice exceeded Principal Homer Barnes' criteria. Barnes was fond of saying, "If you enjoy hard work, you'll have a good time at Kamehameha."

*Oz will have a glorious time at Kamehameha,* Mr. Bailey thought to himself, after hearing about fishing, taro patch weeding, and poi making.

"You don't need to take an admittance test and your tuition will be free," Mr. Bailey told Oz. "People recommended you—that's why I am here. The school is new and beautiful, students are proud to be there, and you'll fit in perfectly."

He explained that Oz would wear a school uniform, shoes, and a tie; also a blue work uniform and work boots. Oz didn't own a pair of shoes; his best outfit was a patched pair of blue denim pants and an oversized aloha shirt.

Sensing embarrassment, Mr. Bailey reassured Oz that he would be supplied everything he needed to wear. "You'll do your own laundry free of charge. Books and supplies are provided; there are no expenses on campus. You will perform some kinds of maintenance work for these things. But all boys have campus jobs."

Tūtū Kāne and Auntie Aukai declared the need for a neighborhood *lūʻau* to celebrate this marvelous good fortune.


While sharing these boyhood stories fifty years later, Oz reminded me that the word "*lūʻau*" means young taro leaves baked with coconut cream and chicken or octopus. "These were served at a traditional '*ahaʻaina,*' the word for feast. Somehow '*lūʻau*' became a collective noun for a party. As you realize, a Hawaiian is honored by a *lūʻau* at least two times: There is the first birthday *lūʻau* and then one to comfort mourners after the person's death."

I told him about a *lūʻau* my mother reported to me in a letter.

Her opening sentence was "A *lūʻau* will be held at the Hilo Yacht Club for Uncle Arthur Lyman." Then she went on to describe the jelly and chutney she was making—nothing more about the *lūʻau*.

I wanted details about Uncle Arthur's death. But her letter rambled about the exceptional quality of the guavas and mangoes she was given. In the last sentence of the letter were these words: "The *lūʻau* is to celebrate Uncle Arthur's 75th birthday and the first birthday of his first child, a son."

Uncle Arthur, at age ninety-four at the time of this writing, is still taking care of Lyman family farmland in Puna. He's stopped having children, though.

Because Oz was raised as an "old-time" Hawaiian, I asked about his *lūʻau* technique.

Dig a pit in the ground about 4 feet deep, burn logs in it, add soft, porous rocks, and keep the fires going until rocks are white-hot. Place a freshly killed and cleaned pig, from which all hair is removed, onto chicken wire. Hold the edges of the chicken wire, lower the pig into the pit, and fill the pig's cavity with some of the heated stones. Place dampened ti leaves over the pig. Beforehand, wrap pieces of fish, chicken, and young taro leaves together in a ti leaf packet—these are called *laulau*. Include *laulau* in the pit along with yams, sweet potatoes, and breadfruit. Lay wet burlap over everything and cover the pit with loose earth. The porker steams for hours in the underground *imu* (oven). Aroma rising through the earth stimulates hearty appetites; the aroma becomes very rich when it is time to uncover the pig.

For my Kamehameha Schools acceptance party, Tūtū Kāne prepared two of our pigs and *laulau*. We pounded our own poi. Neighbors brought chicken cooked with coconut milk and long rice, shellfish, *poki, ʻopihi,* dried squid and dried fish, and *lomi* salmon—a chopped mixture of small chunks of salted salmon, sweet onions, and tomatoes. For dessert we had coconut cake—*haupia*—a pudding of arrowroot and coconut cream that is cut into squares. You hold *haupia* in your hands to eat it. In fact, at a Hawaiian *lūʻau* you eat everything with your fingers.

There was no beer or booze; lots of our neighbors were Mormons who don't even drink soft drinks or coffee. A few servicemen showed up with candy bars from their PX for the kids. Our *lūʻau* lasted about six hours. Between food courses, guests played guitars and *ʻukulele,* both men and women danced the hula, and we talked story.

I told Oz of a *lūʻau* described in a book I'd just found entitled *America's New Possessions.* Published in 1898, authorship was attributed to General William R. Shafter, Cuban invasion commander during the Spanish-American War. The book was prepared by a young writer who visited the countries America acquired after winning the Spanish-American War: Cuba, the Philippine Islands, Puerto Rico, and Guam from Spain, American Samoa by treaty with Germany, and the Hawaiian Islands by annexation.

I said to Oz, "I think this book is the source of the fictional 'Missionary Dinner' story. Hawaiians were joking with the gullible young haole writer. In the book's section on Hawai'i appears a photograph with this caption: 'Hawaiians gathering driftwood to prepare a lui. They will cook a pig in an imu. *Their ancestors used to cook missionaries.*' The clue to their foolery is the word 'lui' they gave him for the name of the feast. 'Lui' means 'an imaginary sound.'"

I heard chilling stories at *lū'au* in Kona. Old-timers told of fireballs rising at night from graves to follow you. They talked of long-gone chiefs and warriors who march in procession at certain times of the year, ready to capture someone for a gory human sacrifice ceremony. A storyteller would suddenly say loudly, *"Such as here tonight."*

With a vocal tremor, the storyteller pointed to me and warned: "And *you*, Arthur, be especially careful on moonlight nights. You live in Kealakekua, which means 'pathway of the gods.' The spirits are marching in the moonlight; they are looking for a human sacrifice!"

Grandmothers in our family enjoyed directing Pele stories at men. This volcano goddess hangs out in lava-covered Kona. In one story, Pele appears in her beauteous guise at a bachelor party and seduces the young, drunken bridegroom. He awakens in the morning lying next to her other apparition: a toothless, white-haired hag. Pele declares to him, "I own your soul. You will be impotent forever—except with me."

One of the women would then say sagaciously to no one in particular, "No fool around with red-headed wahine." That's because if she wants to look especially seductive, Pele appears with long, reddish hair.

I think of Pele when reading Sylvia Plath's poem, "Lady Lazarus": "I rise from the ashes with my red hair, and eat men like air!"

After stories about our red-headed goddess, it would be time to sing "Koni Au." King Kalākaua adopted its melody from one of his bandmaster's German drinking songs; the king reputedly wrote the words for his pal Robert Louis Stevenson. "Drys" say the song refers to drinking water; "wets" say it is about drinking gin, Pele's favorite firewater. Ambiguous words reflect the Merry Monarch's delight in pleasing everyone with his songs.

Pacify Pele by leaving a bottle of gin with ti leaves and a lei near a lava flow; she'll reappear to admire her prowess. When the bottle is empty, replace it, because she was thirsty. If thirsty for long, she'll become *huhū* (angry); before you know, lava will flame and flow.

CHAPTER 10

# Kamehameha Schools

## 1836, 1930, and 1943

K AMEHAMEHA SCHOOLS began in 1887 with the approach that the Reverend David Belden and Sarah Joiner Lyman developed for Hilo Boarding School in 1836. The Lymans emphasized manual training and academic work.

Many of the first Hilo Boarding School students arrived in loincloths. All were taken into the Lymans' home to live, work, develop hirable skills, and learn to read, write, and do some math. My ancestors taught in Hawaiian to help the boys learn quicker; they introduced English gradually.

Allowing Hawaiians to live with them caused some fellow missionaries to call the Lymans "radicals." They used stronger words when one of their sons, Great-Grandfather Rufus, married a member of a royal Hawaiian family. They had a lot more to say when David Belden Lyman and Sarah became citizens of the Kingdom of Hawai'i. David and Sarah and thousands of others signed a petition defying the United States' illegal takeover of the kingdom. When Kamehameha opened in 1883, it hired as its principal the Reverend William Brewster Oleson, who'd been principal at Hilo Boarding School. Oleson brought some Hilo Boarding School boys with him to help set an example for other boys. By then Hilo Boarding School was the model for educating black students at Hampton Institute in Virginia and Tuskegee Institute in Alabama. During a visit to see General Chapman Armstrong, Hampton's founder, Oleson picked up the idea of including military training in Kamehameha's curriculum. By his early twenties, Armstrong had become a Union major general in charge of African-American forces known as the Eighth and

Ninth U.S. Colored Troops. His troops pursued General Lee's Confederate Army and were present at its surrender. General Armstrong, a Hawaiian missionary descendent, hired Levi and Nettie Lyman from Hilo Boarding School to teach at Hampton. They eventually returned to Hawai'i and taught at Kamehameha Schools.

A more rigorous academic program than Oleson's was installed by Dr. Ernest Webster, a great-uncle by marriage. Webster came from Litchfield, Connecticut, to be Kamehameha Schools' president from 1913 to 1924. After helping to upgrade its educational standards, Webster went back to the fam-

Members of Kamehameha School for Boys first graduating class in 1891 included transfers from Hilo Boarding School, founded by the author's ancestors. The Reverend William Oleson, Kamehameha's first president, brought them with him from Hilo to help set an example. Included in the first row, far left, is John Waiamau; second from far right is Charles Blake. Standing second from left is Fred Beckley; fifth from left is Sam Kauhane; far right is Enoch Brown. Charles Reed Bishop paid the college tuition at Oswego Normal School (now SUNY–Oswego) north of Syracuse, New York, for Charles E. King, second from the right in the back row, and Samuel Keli'inoi, second from left in the front row. Both King and Keli'inoi returned to Honolulu and taught school. King went on to Pratt Insitute, New York City, and later became the "Dean of Hawaiian Music." *Reprinted with permission of Kamehameha Schools.*

ily's dairy and milk-delivery business in Litchfield; he was recruited by the University of Hawai'i and became its dean. Webster Hall on the Mānoa campus is named after Dr. Ernest Webster.

Frank Elbert Midkiff, successor to Dr. Webster, thought Hawaiians needed vocational skills. At one time he tried to turn Kamehameha boys into farmers. He initiated the "Antioch" program based on Antioch College, in Yellow Springs, Ohio, where students split time between studies and jobs.

It took five years instead of four to earn either a bachelor of arts or science degree at Antioch. Midkiff added a fifth year of high school to Kamehameha; students went through the ninth, tenth, low-eleventh, high-eleventh, and twelfth grades.

A graduate of Midkiff's sequence recalled, "We packed our own lunches and rode the electric trolley car to our jobs. I worked for O'ahu Railway Company earning 15 cents a day. After I graduated, O'ahu Railway Company recommended me to Matson Freighters and it became my lifetime career."

Midkiff believed the best education for Hawaiian students led to gainful employment and was proud of each one's success in the world of work. I experienced his encouraging words. Midkiff graduated from Colgate University in Hamilton, New York—near Hamilton College, where I went.

In 1931, Charles Prosser, president of Dunwoody Institute, a small technical college in Minnesota, and a $100-a-day educational consultant, prepared a controversial report on the Territory of Hawai'i's educational system. He recommended limiting high school enrollment and curbing expansion at the University of Hawai'i. He tailored his report to fit the needs of the plantations. This angered educators and parents who wanted public school children to have a choice of more than harsh plantation life, where being a *luna* (foreman) was the only chance of advancement.

Prosser warned parents against believing children would improve their social and economic status by spending more time in school. He suggested two educational systems: one for darker-skinned "peasants"—those destined for the grass ceiling—the other for fair-skinned "aristocrats."

Although his plan was defeated by the legislature, Bishop Estate trustees asked Prosser to study what Kamehameha Schools offered dark-skinned peasants. Prosser recommended modifying farm procedures at the boys' school, improving shop and class equipment, and introducing marine engineering. For girls he recommended equipment to train beauticians, registered nurses, and secretaries. The girls principal said "no," feeling these could be learned for less cost on the job or in special schools.

I was recruited while Dr. Homer F. Barnes led Kamehameha School for Boys. He believed whatever money the estate could allocate to education should be used to educate youngsters with potential to become leaders and role models. He felt this was the best way to elevate Hawaiians' status.

Barnes studied at Oxford, received a masters degree from Harvard, and a PhD from Columbia. He arrived as principal in 1930 with the vow to make the Kamehameha School for Boys one of the best schools in all of America. Barnes restructured the boys school from a military school, as it was under Midkiff's presidency, to a civilian school with ROTC—Reserve Officer Training Corps.

For fourteen years, Dr. Barnes enforced an admissions policy based on ability, sociocultural background, home environment, and the possibility for return on investment in terms of a student's future contribution to society. He required tough scrutiny of an applicant's previous school records, not only for grades but for attitudes and work habits.

His idea was to select students having the potential to benefit from the school; he held them to the highest academic standards, which explains why Nona Beamer and many other students received college scholarships and fellowships. He wanted each student to have an above-average IQ compared to mainland indices. He believed ability was deeper than skin color and was out to prove it. That's exactly what caused his problems.

While Dr. Barnes was at Kamehameha, someone composed a song describing the main private and public high schools in Honolulu: the predominately white Punahou School, where wealthy Islanders and high-ranking military officers sent their children, was known "for its pretty girls." McKinley High, with a primarily Japanese student body of 3,000 from which to draw its athletic teams, was known "for its champions." The song's last line could have been written by Dr. Barnes: "But 'Kam' is for its standards."

The 600-acre Kamehameha Schools campus was completed while Barnes was in charge. The new girls school, built on the highest ridge on Kapālama Heights, opened in 1931 with dormitory accommodations for 250 girls. The boys school had 226 single dormitory rooms and was built below the girls school. When the boys school opened in 1940, completing the campus, Kamehameha became known as one of the most beautiful schools in the United States.

Barnes believed only boarding students would gain the maximum benefits from a quality Kamehameha education. To trustees he suggested the need to set up smaller elementary country schools on the main islands as feeders to prepare students for the high school on Oʻahu.

By the early 1940s, Kamehameha Schools was second to none among local secondary schools. It was one of only two schools in the nation with both complete academic and vocational training programs—the other being Girard College in Philadelphia. As an educator of students with aboriginal blood, it had a distinctive international position. To Kamehameha students, being a scholar was as heroic as being an athlete.[1]

---

[1] The true story of Kamehameha Schools has never been told to the general public. In James A. Michener's fictional novel *Hawaii*, published by Random House, New York, N.Y., in 1959, Michener used the name "Hewlett Hall" to describe, in a few paragraphs, a school for Hawaiians that is physically perfect but intellectually limited. He explains it never occurred to its board of directors, composed of Big Five family members, that Hawaiian boys had exactly the same mental capacity as haole; consequently they forced Hewlett Hall into a trade-school mold. A character known as Dr. Hewlett Whipple (patterned after Dr. Barnes) tried to vitalize the curriculum and to find dynamic teachers, but politicians and trustees stopped him, believing Hawaiian children should not be educated above their natural capacity. In other words, they did not want Hawaiians to learn to manipulate their society. Michener attributes to Whipple the statement that trustees have condemned these people to perpetual mediocrity and that Hewlett Hall (Kamehameha Schools) is the worst thing to happen to the Hawaiians since the arrival of measles and the white man. The order should have been reversed to read, "since the white man arrived and brought measles."

# CHAPTER 11

## *Auntie Nona*

### Mid-1930s

W INONA BEAMER, known as "Auntie Nona," is regarded as one of "Hawai'i's Treasures." Preceding me by seven years, she entered Kamehameha School for Girls in 1937 at twelve years of age; she was the third generation of her family to do so.

She attended while Dr. Barnes enforced his high standards. Nona's story during and after those years is integral to the unfolding of *Lost Generations* because of her personal influence on Kamehameha Schools contemporary history.

Nona loved life as a boarding student. As with many students, it was the first time she had a bed all to herself and she shared a room with but one person. Her great-grandmother, who now taught the hula openly, told Nona to carry her culture as a bundle of love, always to hold it closely, never to let it go.

The following stories describe Hawai'i prior to World War II, when it was the playground of Hollywood's stars and others who were rich and famous.

N ona responded to a notice on the school's bulletin board asking students to volunteer to work with young children at a mission home. Her first job was to scrub eight little boys and girls lined up by a big galvanized tub filled with hot water. All had running sores and scabs of impetigo on their arms and legs.

To calm herself, Nona started chanting. The children's eyes grew wider, and two began crying. She softened the chant by a third of a tone, transforming it from a minor into a major key melody. Expressions on the children's faces softened. Soon she had the little ones in the tub, where she soothed them with her story-song while cleansing their sores with soap and water.

For the next five years, Nona continued as a volunteer at the mission, where she told stories and taught dances and songs of Hawai'i *nei*. Surely Kamehameha trustees must have heard she was using her knowledge of Hawaiian. Maybe Hawaiian was considered all right there in the slums, but not at Kamehameha.

Nona formed Hui Kumulipo, the Kamehameha School for Girls Hawaiian Club, and instructed her fellow students in chants and body movements. She taught them to use pebble-filled gourds to accentuate phrases; they beat ancient rhythms on drums and learned to play nose flutes—blowing through the nose rather than the mouth.

The *hui* was invited to perform at a trustees' tea. Nona thought guests understood what the program would be, but trustees were genuinely shocked when the young women did a stand-up chant. Hula was not to be taught at Kamehameha Schools, and trustees knew *who* was teaching it!

Later that day, Nona was packing her things in her room with the words "willful" and "stubborn" ringing in her ears. Her grandmother, Helen Desha Beamer, a school alumna and one of Hawai'i's most prolific composers, convinced officials that Nona should be allowed to return.

M issionaries considered the hula lascivious and declared it was not to be performed. They also began diminishing the Hawaiian language. They used it initially for proselytizing, writing hymns in Hawaiian and printing a Bible in Hawaiian in 1822. But Hawaiian was not allowed to be used in schools. This edict meant Hawaiians would become accustomed to speaking only English. The Hawaiian language would die through attrition.

L ouise "Dambi" Beamer, Nona's mother, opened the Beamer Hula Studio in Waikīkī in 1928. Nona taught there during school vacations, never mentioning this at Kamehameha School for Girls.

Film actress Mary Pickford, in her early forties, was Nona's first celebrity student. At Waikīkī on a honeymoon with her younger husband, Buddy Rogers, Mary wanted to learn a pretty and sexy dance quickly. Nona thought the song "To You Sweetheart Aloha" would be a good start. It was composed in 1935 by Harry Owens, who initiated the *Hawaii Calls* show broadcast over American and Canadian network radio. On the third lesson, Mary was ready for the "sexy" part, and Dambi took over.

$M$ary Pickford made her unannounced hula debut in the courtyard of the Royal Hawaiian Hotel to the music of Harry Owens' orchestra. The dark and shadowy courtyard was lit by tiki torches.

Without explanation, Mary excused herself from the guests at her table. Unnoticed, she made her way behind the orchestra and then stepped to the center of the dance floor. Once she was in place, an electrician turned on an overhead spotlight, aiming it directly at her. She was wearing a figure-hugging, floor-length white gown covered with sparkling sequins. Richly aromatic white ginger lei were around her neck, her golden hair glistening in the bright light. The music began and Mary Pickford glided into "To You Sweetheart Aloha."

Dancing flawlessly, her graceful hand motions beckoned compellingly, her hips undulating as her eyes flashed tantalizingly. Unaware of her lessons, Buddy Rogers sat transfixed as this Canadian known as "America's Sweetheart" performed Hawaiian magic near the oceanside. Even the ocean sighed while the surf receded from the sandy shore.

A few days later, Mary Pickford encouraged Uncle Alex Anderson to write the song that became known as "White Ginger Blossoms." With a twinkle in her eyes, she confided breathily, "White ginger's aroma is a powerful aphrodisiac." Mary Pickford depended on steel guitar music to unlock her own emotions.[1]

$N$ona taught the hula to Shirley Temple, Mary Astor, Dinah Shore, and to film stars' children. By teaching and dancing the hula, the Beamers came to know many Hollywood stars. A growing popularity of Hawaiian music around the world gave the Beamers celebrity status.

Nona was sitting next to George Palmer Putnam at a party in 1937 as he talked by radiophone to his wife, who was in an airplane. Her high-pitched voice crackled into the room excitedly, punctuated by the static of the radiophone they were using.

Mr. Putnam asked Nona to go around the room to collect autographs for his wife,

---

[1] Mary Pickford called on Sol Hoopii, known as "the Hollywood Hawaiian," to play his steel guitar and make her cry at the appropriate moment in silent films. Sol later toured with the religious crusades of Aimee Semple McPherson and wrote religious songs for her revivals.

giving her his fancy fountain pen to use and keep. Nona approached Bing Crosby, who was talking to her parents and suggesting they dance and be language advisors in Paramount's movie, *Waikiki Wedding*. Bing, Dorothy Lamour, Martha Rae, and Anthony Quinn would be among those in it.

A few days later Mr. Putnam's wife, Amelia Earhart, and her plane were lost mysteriously in the Pacific.

Back from Hollywood, Dambi gave Nona a memorable lesson on the importance of proper Hawaiian pronunciation, doing it through a story.

"In one scene of *Waikiki Wedding*, Anthony Quinn was supposed to yell, '*He mai!*'—'Come here!'—calling people to watch a volcano erupt. He just couldn't get it right. He kept yelling, '*He maʻi.*' All the Hawaiians laughed. Quinn inadvertently was saying, 'Come have sex!'"

Nona corrected my pronunciation as we talked. I was not articulating each "h" in Kamehameha, having fallen out of the habit while on the mainland. Fortunately, I did not alter the word's meaning.

Nona won a scholarship to Colorado Women's College and later a Guggenheim Fellowship allowing her to continue at Barnard College of Columbia University. While at Columbia, she volunteered at New York City's Stuyvesant Center Neighborhood House, interacting with African-American, Italian, Greek, and Jewish children, some having severe learning disabilities.

She'd play "radio," holding her *ʻukulele* upright as a microphone, urging children to speak into the acoustical hole to resonate their voices. She taught the children Hawaiian words to a clapping hula chanted to the cadence of "Pease Porridge Hot." They moved their bodies to the claps. Some arranged string in the complex Hawaiian "cat's cradle." Nona featured them in a neighborhood "Hawaiian Show." She remembers parents smiling, crying with joy, the crowd clapping and cheering. Hawaiian music is a great equalizer.

Eleanor Roosevelt, one of the most important women of the twentieth century, often attended Barnard's faculty teas. On Nona's turn to be the hostess, she invited a member of the first graduating class from Kamehameha School for Boys as her guest. Nona described it to me.

Charles E. King, in the music publishing phase of his life, was living and working in New York City. He was so charming. He sat beside Mrs. Roosevelt, talking with her while I served tea. They appeared to be having a lot of fun.

I looked over and saw him kneeling down by her shoes. I thought, what is going on with Uncle Charlie? He was tying her shoes. She wore gunboats—large, ugly walking shoes. She was famous for striding around New York City.

At the end of the tea, Mrs. Roosevelt said to everybody, "Are you going to invite Uncle Charles to the next tea? Oh, please do."

I thought, *Charles E. King, how can you be such a flirt? She is the president's wife.*

"Uncle Charles" indeed!

CHAPTER 12

# Charting a New Direction

## 1943

NOT EVERYONE was happy with President Barnes' ideal of a high-quality school for Hawaiians. Income to operate Kamehameha Schools came from low-yielding leases for agricultural and ranch land, and Barnes felt that limited available funds should provide quality education for youngsters meeting high standards.

A furor erupted in 1943, the year I was accepted. Senators William H. Heen and David K. Trask attacked Bishop Estate trustees. Trask accused school officials of running a high-brow school for the intellectual cream. Heen objected to entrance exams and IQ tests.

At a public hearing, Dr. Stephen Porteus, a University of Hawai'i psychologist, testified that not more than 15 percent of Island students of all races could achieve the scores Kamehameha required. "Either you are going to do 90 percent of the good for 10 percent of the Hawaiian people, or 10 percent of the good for 90 percent," he declared. Dr. Porteus favored doing 10 percent of the good for 90 percent of Hawaiians.

Dr. Pauline Frederick, Kamehameha School for Girls principal, warned: "Taking in students to maintain numbers defeats the purpose of this type of education. Admittance should be determined by the number of available serious, earnest, ambitious students, giving preference to the most intelligent. Insistence on quality would and should mean a smaller student body."

"Kamehameha was not meant to be created for the intellectually gifted," stated both Senators Heen and Trask. They didn't explain how Princess Pauahi had communicated this information to them.

Dr. Barnes' believed that the senators wanted a third-rate common school to accommodate everyone wanting in.

Political pressure caused the trustees to move away from the Barnes ideal of a small, secondary, boarding-only institution. They decided on a larger, predominately day-student school open to a more representative population of students; a school having a more diverse educational program and requiring less stringent standards.

In mid-summer 1944, the trustees invited Dr. Charles A. Prossner to return and guide them. Mr. Midkiff earned a PhD while on the mainland, returning to Hawaiʻi as "Dr. Midkiff," and became a Bishop Estate trustee.

Arriving on Christmas Eve and departing forty-five days later, Dr. Prossner recommended a curriculum emphasizing more vocational and less college preparatory work. Prossner submitted his report to the trustees on the eve of his departure. Astounded to learn it was finished, Barnes felt terribly hurt by Prossner's not consulting him once during the course of his survey. He suspected connivance.

Prossner thought Kamehameha should be recruiting 80 percent of applicants for occupational studies and 20 percent for college preparatory work. He slotted precise numbers of students for each vocational skill based on the current job market. Barnes felt it wrong for the trustees to determine these options for an unknown future.

Prossner's plan didn't make sense to Barnes since 50 to 75 percent of boys school graduates and more than 40 percent of girls school graduates went to college, and all did well. This was at a time when going on to college was not considered "a given" even to most mainland children.

Barnes and his fellow academicians opened the world of opportunity to Hawaiians, challenging their potential, raising their level of expectation, and improving their sense of personal worth. Moral training was his overall thrust. He thought this was more in keeping with making "good and industrious men and women" than Prossner's emphasis on specific skills or occupations. Barnes held to 250 as the optimum number for the boys student body; the campus was built for 250 boarding students. Learning that the trustees concurred with many of Prossner's recommendations, such as no entrance examinations and deemphasizing the boarding program, Barnes resigned.

His wife, Mary Frances Barnes, engrossed in Hawaiian history and culture, taught Hawaiian history at the boys school and took hula lessons at Beamer's Waikīkī hula studio. Just before she and her husband left Honolulu, a student reporter for the school's newspaper quoted her as saying, "I wish I could create in all of you so much respect for this beautiful dance that you would use all of your influence to keep it worthy of the respect it deserves." She stuck her tongue out at the trustees by saying, "I wish the hula was danced on every occasion as an inspiration to all who see it."

Although yielding to the Senate's educational demands, the trustees wrote to the judiciary committee chairman objecting to the Senate's fee formula. They mentioned their potentially large liabilities as trustees. Senators Trask and Heen were furious over their request.

The chairman was more magnanimous, pointing out that the bill was supposed to cover trustees for all Hawai'i's charitable trusts. He proposed what turned out to be the final fee-setting formula of the Legislature. It reduced trustees' commissions from more than $1,000 a month to about $350 a month; Bishop Estate land-leasing income was very low at the time. However, it set the stage for rich payoffs forty years later when politicians succeeded in breaking up Bishop Estate land holdings and trustees sold land at the greatly appreciated prices of the 1980s.

After Barnes left, his dedication to raising individual levels of expectation and emphasizing moral training were fostered by faculty he left behind. Charles T. Parrent, who worked with Barnes, was appointed principal-in-charge to apply the new policy changes. Parrent taught auto mechanics and physics from 1926 to 1946. He became a businessman, and in 1985 he and his wife established a $1 million fund to underwrite staff development activities and to bring celebrated artists and scholars to the campus.

## CHAPTER 13

# War Years on Campus

## Pre–World War II through 1950

Beginning in 1935, the U.S. Army secretly assigned 170 students from Kamehameha School for Boys to the Pacific equatorial region. England's expansion—not Japan's—in the Pacific was feared by the U.S. government. The army told the boys, "You will colonize and help establish claim to the Baker, Jarvis, and Howland Islands. They'll become famous air bases in a route to connect Australia and California."

Twelve students at a time were placed among the islands for six months. They were given 50-gallon drums of water and food staples. The ocean teemed with edible fish; it took only five minutes to step out on the reef and spear sufficient mullet and snapper for the day's meal.

The boys charted the weather, checked in with the army by shortwave radio, did required readings, and waited for six months to end. Should curious Englishmen stop by, the boys were to claim the islands as "their home" and radio the U.S. Army immediately. They built a church, dedicated it to Amelia Earhart, and flew an American flag over it.

When returning to school, the "colonists" were supposed to say, "We were away studying sea life for the Bishop Museum." Some boys feared, groundlessly of course, that they might be shot for talking about where they went and why.

Two were killed during air raids and a submarine shelling at Howland Island on December 18, 1941, and the Japanese shot down the American flag over their church. A U.S. destroyer rescued the survivors in late January 1942. Although noted in *Panala'au Memoirs,* a 1974 publication written by E. H. Bryan Jr., the deaths were not general knowledge until the summer of

2002 when the Bishop Museum featured an exhibit on how these boys from Kamehameha Schools served U.S. interests.

On the afternoon of December 7, 1941, the U.S. Army arrived on campus to give ammunition to Kamehameha seniors, whom they dispatched to nearby reservoirs with orders to shoot "spies" trying to poison water. This fear proved groundless.

After Pearl Harbor was attacked, the Territory of Hawai'i was immediately subjected to martial law; the army canceled Kamehameha's ROTC program, collected the 1903 Springfield rifles loaned to the school, and confiscated students' khaki uniforms.

The army took over the boys' school infirmary, a dormitory, and faculty cottages as a military hospital and stationed doctors, nurses, and enlisted men on campus to serve wounded troops. It moved into the girls school prior to offensive action in the Pacific, adding 600 patient beds.

Boys became members of the Kamehameha Military Training Corps, drilled with wooden rifles, and wore khaki pants, white shirts, and khaki ties; dress uniforms were saved for Sunday chapel and special events.

Ranch earnings allowed me the privilege of buying a secondhand blue-gray Kamehameha uniform from the school store: pants with a black stripe on the outside part of the legs; a dress coat with lapels and brass buttons on the front and sleeves; and a cadet cap with a brim. With it I wore a white shirt, a black tie, black socks, and well-shined black shoes.

Nona Beamer returned to Hawai'i shortly after World War II began. She took nurses aid training at the Honolulu Academy of Arts and was assigned to campus to administer to wounded servicemen. The Hawai'i Red Cross program and aids were headquartered at the Kamehameha Schools hospital.

She also taught and entertained on military bases, where she introduced the clapping game enjoyed by children in the Stuyvesant Center Neighborhood House. Nona said, "I taught so many children that song; it seemed strange and touching to see big men in their uniforms performing it. But they had fun, too."

Nona's "Sweetheart Grandma" came to a class; the soldiers were surprised to find her literate—more so than most of them. Helen Desha Beamer's skin color and age caused them to stereotype her initially as being less bright than she was.

The girls school relocated to the boys campus, and boarders moved into two dorms with a hill and a road separating them from lower dorms used by boys. Boys and girls shared the same classroom building but not the same classrooms; the only facilities used in common were the library and the auditorium. Because of campus sharing, enrollment was reduced by 20 percent and the seventh grade was temporarily eliminated.

$A$s I walked into my room for the first time, an upperclassman handed me typed procedures for "The Proper Way to Eat" and said, "Learn these before dinner tonight."

"A whole piece of bread," I read, was never to be buttered at one time. "Tear off a quarter of a piece, butter only that." Details on the proper way to hold eating utensils were described, as well as rules for decorum:

- You will talk, but not while chewing.
- Sit erect, bring the food to your mouth, and do not bend your head toward it.
- No elbows on the table.
- Match your eating pace with the host's.

A student officer occupied one of eight seats at each round table; he was the host. Should a student forget "The Proper Way to Eat," a quick jab from the officer's sheathed saber was an abrupt reminder.

For students raised as "old-style Hawaiians," Kamehameha was a cultural shock. For the first time, they had a bed of their own, two sheets and a blanket for sleeping, a light that didn't need kerosene and had a switch, toilets in the building that flushed and didn't have to be moved every six months, hot water showers, and no water restrictions.

They ate three meals a day from a porcelain plate instead of a tin plate and had a fresh napkin at every meal. Cutting while the fork was in the left hand and transferring it to the right hand was awkward initially for some, who learned by imitation.

We never wore a hat inside a building. Officers promptly reminded offenders: A swipe by the heel of the hand over the ears removed the hat and produced a memorable sting.

As elsewhere in Honolulu during World War II, nightlife was curtailed by total blackout from 6:00 P.M. until 6:00 A.M. No overhead bulbs were in our rooms and we weren't allowed lamps.

We did homework in designated study halls or in the library. Blue bulbs in outside passageways made it hazardous to walk up or down flights of stairs even with their painted white guidelines. Blue lights replaced white bulbs in halls and lavatories. Normal bulbs were on only in the dining hall, assembly hall, library, dormitory common room, and the senior club room. Windows in these rooms were painted black and lights had to be turned out before students could enter or exit the doors.

The bathroom was outside of the study hall; younger students learned to "hold it" rather than interrupting students by turning out the lights so they could leave the room. On some nights sirens signaled an air raid, and we'd sit in dark hallways, away from windows that might shatter. During my first drill, upperclassmen told us new students what they saw from the hilltop campus on December 7, 1941: "Pearl Harbor was crowded with ships of the fleet at anchor. A few minutes before eight o'clock, waves of planes flew directly over the girls school and swooped low over the naval base. Smoke rose from burning ships and oil storage tanks, eventually blocking the view. At about midnight, the moon rose and a beautiful rainbow arched over destruction below."

We younger boys shuddered. "Moonbow," a lunar rainbow caused by the refraction and reflection of light from the moon, is a Hawaiian omen of a victory. Whose victory was this? At that time it seemed like Japan's.

We sang while waiting out air raid drills. Anyone could start a song, and everyone added their voices. Sitting on the floor in blacked-out hallways, encompassed by four-part harmony, we sang words about Hawai'i's beauty hoping not to be bombed.

The second attack on Pearl Harbor came without warning. Hearing explosions, students believed enemy submarines were in the harbor. From the hillside campus we saw and heard it all: explosions, ships escaping, a pier on fire.

Many years later I became friends with Henry W. Schramm, a mainland-based historian. Henry, a seaman on a mine sweeper inside the harbor on May 21, 1944, was watching events through a pair of binoculars after being alerted to a base fire. He gave me his written observations and official documents of this Pearl Harbor story not previously told:

> As I watched, a gigantic explosion rocked the area. A truck, then a jeep rose above the blast, seemed to hang there forever, and then tumbled back into the inferno. Six LSTs—landing ships for tanks—loaded with ammunitions exploded.
>
> We were worried that with all the explosives at Pearl, perhaps the whole place would go up.
>
> Someone else said, "No, the big stuff was located in the ammo dump near the harbor mouth."
>
> "That's where mines and torpedoes are stored," someone else added.
>
> We saw a cargo ship, heavy smoke pouring out of her, headed for that

ammo dump. She appeared to be a run-away and drifted ever closer to the depot. It jolted to a stop.

It had run aground in the one single area where it could continue to burn and do no damage to the base's explosives, nor would it block the channel.

In just six hours, hundreds of lives had been snuffed out or changed forever, millions of dollars of war material, let alone navy ships, had been destroyed.

Seniors apprenticing at Pearl Harbor brought back a story circulating around the naval base that a Japanese welder purposely set off anti-aircraft shells in an ammunition locker with sparks from his torch. I have the U.S. Navy's investigation report declassified fifty years after the event. It states that the explosions originated from servicemen smoking on the LSTs. They were roughly handling ammunition, including 5-inch projectiles and phosphorous bombs, while smoking. A prominent sign in the area stated "No Smoking." No welding was being performed in the indicated areas of the initial explosion. There was no evidence of sabotage.

Other Islanders knew nothing more than what was relegated to a single paragraph on the front page of the morning newspaper, advising its readers of an "insignificant" fire with few casualties at the navy base. In reality, it was big enough to delay departure for the attack on the Marianas for a week, giving over 15,000 invading Americans and more than 45,000 defending Japanese an additional week of life.

We eighth graders were working in the vegetable gardens on the lower part of campus in 1944, when Eric Kalohelani began jumping up and down excitedly, calling our attention to a fighter plane streaming smoke that was coming in over the ocean. The airplane was wavering; the pilot was having difficulty bringing it down. We cheered for the pilot when the plane's wheels touched the landing strip, but it immediately burst into flames and exploded.

I tried not to look at my classmates. I was certain they were all crying as much as I.

Journalism teacher Loring Hudson had Kamehameha students join him and Dr. Kenneth Emory, ethnologist and curator at the Bishop Museum, in teaching fliers how they could survive if forced down on a jungle island or atoll. Classes were at the Bishop Museum, south of our campus. The boys demonstrated picking and using coconuts, building a shelter from the tree's branches, and using edible and medicinal plants. During trips to the ocean, we introduced servicemen to nourishing ocean plants and showed them how to pound *'ākia* leaves to release a chemical that makes fish sluggish so they'll rise to the surface to be gathered by hand.

I remember watching as the thin-bespectacled Emory looked a group of U.S. Air Force officers directly in the face and smilingly remarked: "In the coconut at this stage you get the three-in-one rations. All of you have heard of the army's ten-in-one rations, but they are no match for the meat, salad, and dessert obtainable in the coconut. In New York's finest hotels you'd have to pay $7.50 a plate for a salad made out of the heart of a palm tree. This so-called millionaire's salad is free out here on islands in the Pacific."

At the end of the war, Mr. Hudson posted an army writer's story on a school bulletin board noting that 61,608 servicemen had been schooled in these courses at the museum. The article said, "They are better prepared to 'live off the land' than are the Japanese." On it Mr. Hudson proudly wrote, "Thanks boys for your war efforts."

A n old Hawaiian man approached four of us eighth graders at the Hilo airport waiting to fly back to Honolulu after Christmas vacation. He handed each of us a package of Hawaiian food, gave me a hug, and walked off, visibly upset. The boys asked who he was and I said, "My grandfather's brother, Richard Lyman Senior.[1] He fears Kamehameha Boys will have to help defend Hawai'i."

The neighbor islands were undefended early in the war, and the entire U.S. Pacific Fleet had been reduced to the dimensions of a task force. Residents feared invasion until the Battle of Midway, a key naval engagement that took place some 1,300 miles northwest of Honolulu and changed the course of the war. If the Japanese naval fleet had won that battle, they could have penetrated into Hawaiian waters, giving Japan a base from which to shake up West Coast Americans.

O ur school dining rooms reflected Hawai'i's dependency on the United States for life's essentials such as protein products, milk, oil for cooking, and even sugar. Locally grown produce was available, but not mainland apples and oranges. We drank powdered milk mixed with water. Hawaiian sugar in its natural state was brown, like Hawaiians, but a limited amount came back from the West Coast white and was called "refined" and therefore was worth more. Even as a youth I sensed an implicit irony in the contrasting terms of "brown natural" and "white refined."

---

[1] My tender-hearted great-uncle's son, also named Richard, was the last person to receive a lifetime appointment as a Bishop Estate trustee. Called "Poppa Lyman" by students, he served for thirty years until his death at eighty-six. Oswald Stender succeeded him.

Meals were sparse; the school dietitian struggled with what was available and nutritional. Canned Spam, our only meat, was seldom served. Dinner sometimes consisted of Cream of Wheat with black olives for protein. Wartime menus made us determined to avoid demerits so we could leave campus on Saturday for chop suey. Food was always on our minds. Candy was a war casualty, and we craved it. Boarders begged day students to sneak custard pies on campus. Canned condensed milk, sweet and sticky to pour on anything, was considered a treasure.

The cheapest place for lots of food was in Chinatown, off Hotel Street, in Honolulu's wartime red-light district where the legendary Mamie Stover supposedly serviced soldiers and sailors.

At the end of a back alley, a door opened into a small room where an old Pākē (Chinaman) cooked over a gas stove. We each gave him fifty cents, he handed us chopsticks and a bowl of rice, and we sat on stools at a big round table. He poured whatever he was cooking at the time into the big bowl in the center of the table and we dipped in. Other patrons came and went; he kept refilling the big bowl and supplying fresh rice.

M any servicemen in the Kamehameha Schools hospital were in wheelchairs; they wore dark red hospital robes. Wounded men attended Saturday night movies in the auditorium with us and rode their own buses to our football games at the downtown stadium. We met servicemen hiking on trails above campus who'd say, "I hope you boys never have to go to war." They shared candy if they had any. We respected them so very much.

A soldier crippled in Saipan told me a story about a Hawaiian hero in his unit. The war hadn't been going in America's favor until Saipan. In 1944, more than 70,000 Americans were prisoners of war in Japan. Understanding that will give you appreciation for the affect this story had on boyish imaginations. I told it to everyone in school who'd listen and, years later, I obtained the censor-approved battlefield documents for verification. It is presented in World War II correspondent style.

Pvt. Willie Hokoana of Paia, Maui, was an assistant bazooka man; his sergeant said, "He's the only guy in the squad big enough to carry all the bazooka rockets." On Nafutan Ridge, Hokoana picked up a Browning Automatic Rifle (BAR), and spent days cleaning his cherished new possession. He did something different with it; other men laid down and placed the weapon on the ground to use it, but Hokoana stood up and held this clip-fed, light machine gun.

On 7 July, the enemy made their last determined effort to break the tightening American grip on Saipan. Enemy soldiers overran some American positions, and they isolated others—Hokoana's was one of the latter.

"I started shooting from a trench where three other BAR men were firing from," Hokoana recounted. "But pretty soon all three of them got hit and I figured I'd better move out." The big Hawaiian saw a tree some 10 feet ahead of the trench with a crotch about shoulder high in which he could place his BAR.

"So I ran up there and got all set," Hokoana said. "Sure enough, pretty soon the Japanese start closing in along my lane of fire. So I shot them down. Boy, I was sweating all that time."

Hokoana fired mostly in barrages of one, two, and three shots for about an hour and a half. He missed his target once: A Japanese officer dropped the saber he was carrying and scuttled for safety, then later returned to pick up his weapon. "I got him that time," Hokoana said.

Once the gun jammed and Hokoana ran to a nearby house, where he made hasty repairs, replacing the recoil spring. Several men kept Hokoana supplied with ammunition, gathering it from all around the defended area, loading it into clips and passing it on to him. Some of it came from wounded and killed automatic riflemen.

"I don't think they saw me," he said. "The enemy was in a sort of clearing and I was hidden in the leaves of that tree. They shot my way, but the bullets hit the tree or its branches."

Hokoana and his automatic rifle accounted for at least 200 of the dead enemy, according to his commanding officer.

"I figured I was done for anyhow, so I wanted to take as many of the enemy with me as I could," Hokoana said.

Uncle Willie Hokoana made it back home to Maui, living into his seventies. Family members graduated from Kamehameha, and his grand-nephew is a current student. The war was especially scary when this story of "the big Hawaiian" was shared with little Hawaiians in school uniforms. It made us feel connected to one who was brave and very cool in the heat of battle.

War was waning when Oz Stender arrived at Kamehameha in 1945. Children had stopped carrying gas masks years earlier, our ROTC program was revived, and we dressed as soldiers in army CKCs—cotton khaki clothing. We had the fun of opening the wooden boxes and removing the greasy Cosmoline from the U.S. Army's new M-1 rifles, now ours to use.

We still feared "germ warfare" because of an Asian flu that twice brought campus activities to a standstill. After the second outbreak, morning buses carrying day students stopped at the boys infirmary and the girls infirmary, where nurses examined students to make certain they weren't bringing an illness to campus. A nurse drove students home if she thought them infectious.

Col. Kent, the school's new president, wrote parents of day students to tell them that it was their duty to see that their sons wear their uniforms "even when they are not at school, for the Kamehameha uniform designates a boy who does the right things at all times." This made Kamehameha students marked persons, and word quickly got back to campus of any infraction—some no more serious than talking in a movie. Those most inclined to be tattletales may have been relatives of children not accepted into the schools. The word seemed always to reach a "Big Six" member. These hold-overs from the days of Dr. Barnes could discipline and discharge any student—no questions asked.

During my time, teacher-to-student ratio was high—one to seven—but that meant just 35 teachers to supervise 250 boarding students. Barnes' policy used students to improve the ratio. This practice was in force when I arrived: Administration officials selected six upperclassmen (thus the "Big Six") who were respected for academic and/or athletic achievements to oversee study halls, make certain each student was in his bed at night, keep roll call records, handle dorm inspections, lead grace at meals, and check out and check in students with Saturday off-campus privileges.

Should a student and his belongings disappear from campus during the night, you forgot who he was the next day. If a boy committed a serious infraction—stealing was the worst offense, but cheating on exams or smoking meant strong punishment—he would hear from "dorm rats" that "the Big Six are coming tonight."

At 9:00 P.M., lights were out and the guilty boy lay uneasily in bed. At about 12:00 A.M., a flashlight might shine in his face. A one-time Big Six member described a typical situation:

> I'd say, "Robert," or whatever his name was, "I hear you have some things that don't belong to you. Pack what is really yours and call your parents to take you home. If this is not true, come with me."
>
> If Robert were smart, he would start packing. If he didn't, I marched him into a room where the rest of the Big Six waited.
>
> When we got there, I hit him in the face.
>
> As he sat dazed on the floor, I'd say, "that's for lying."
>
> We needed overwhelming evidence to take such a drastic step.

Each dormitory had upperclassmen overseers. Faculty lived in apartments at the end of the hall behind thick doors. Students were especially quiet near the door of "Bulldog" Drummond, a crusty old chemistry teacher who, younger boys were told, could "hear everything, and his bite is worse than his bark."

We younger boarders were invited to the dormitory commons room for a retirement party held for "Bulldog." Some alumni and Mr. Bailey were there. Cake and punch were served, and we all joined in singing, "For He's a Jolly Good Fellow." Upperclassmen gave Mr. Drummond a scrapbook containing current campus scenes and pictures from alumni. Mr. Drummond had hair in some of the old photos.

He didn't look fierce as he leafed through the pages; he seemed deeply touched. It dawned on me that the warning about keeping quiet near his door was so younger squirts wouldn't disturb the old man. After reading the book, *Goodbye, Mr. Chips,* by James Hilton, I understood things much better.

E ach student started the year with 100 credits. Teachers could give demerits but only did so for being late to a class. Student military officers managed behavior by being able to issue demerits. Demerits were issued for infractions such as an improperly made bed, sideburns touching your ears, and being late for a drill. In the case of insubordination, you could expect to appear before the Big Six.

A boy couldn't leave the campus if his credits dropped below 75; if they fell below 50, he was on the edge of leaving school permanently. Boys could regain 10 credits each week by good behavior; those confined to campus worked off demerits in the Saturday labor battalion.

Pat Gandall's talkativeness made him a labor battalion steady. He could try to explain anything—even why his name hadn't been written in indelible ink on the inside collar of his T-shirt. Pat helped build the football field—digging up boulders and rolling them off a cliff. A bag lunch was their treat. Pat said, "Our dietitian saved hard-to-get food from the mainland: peanut butter for sandwiches, orange juice, and apples for us guys who stayed on campus. A kind person, she was trying to nourish us and satisfy our voracious appetites during wartime's stark shortages."

Janitorial work was part of Oz's scholarship obligation. Because he was an orphan, Lili'uokalani Trust supplied clothes, school materials, and counseling—which Oz called "nagging." He described this life stage as "assisted subsistence."

Being admitted without taking a test, he missed the chance to qualify as "academically gifted" and was placed in the vocational program to be trained as a draftsman. "I couldn't afford college anyway," he explained. On the rifle team for three years, he found hitting stationary targets easier than spearing moving fish.

Pat Gandall described Oz in this way: "No matter how badly I might treat him when he was learning to drill, he took it like water off a duck's back. He was a hard worker and a quiet person who always said 'hello' cheerfully when I passed him on the steps, even though the day before I might have been screaming at him to 'about face' properly. Oz made the effort to be liked."

Our lives were regulated for sixteen hours a day. We always were running anxiously to the next destination to avoid demerits for being late: up at 5:00 A.M. to dress in blue work clothes and make the room ready for inspection; breakfast at 5:50 A.M.; at an assigned work station by 6:50—students cleaned the classrooms and school buildings as well as shared areas within their own dormitories. By 7:30—assuming cleaning passed inspection and didn't need redoing—we had to be back in the dorm room, showered and dressed in CKCs, waiting for both personal and room inspection—uniform clean and neat, shoes shined, bed neatly made, clothes folded properly in drawers, no dust anywhere, closets clear of clutter.

At 8:00 A.M., we went to the assembly hall for morning devotions, then to class, lunch, and back to classes until 2:30 P.M. We'd change into shorts and our *hui* shirt for intramural sports—unless we went to practice on a junior or varsity team. By 5:00 P.M., we had showered and changed into khaki uniforms for retreat at 5:50. Standing at attention in our assigned company, we saluted while a bugler played and the American flag was lowered and folded. At 6:00 P.M. we stood at the dinner table, sang a prayer in Hawaiian in four-part harmony—the "Doxology" or "The Lord's Prayer"—a Big Six member chose. After dinner, some of us gathered in the assembly hall, listening as Edwin Mahi Beamer played classical music on the piano before our next scheduled activity.

Two times a week, boarders drilled at 7:30 P.M. for about half an hour. On Monday evenings boarders attended assembly, and the boys student body sang for about half an hour. Then it was on to study hall. Dormitory lights were turned off at 9:00 P.M., and we were to be in bed by the time a bugler played "Taps." During my junior and senior years, I had that duty. Being the school bugler had its benefits. Since I blew the calls for drills as well as for ceremonies, many boys in school may have felt they owed me favors. Few could afford watches, and many would yell while rushing downstairs to line up in formation: "Don't play yet, Attah . . . wait two minutes more." Of course, I'd delay blowing the final call.

There were afternoon drills, a Saturday morning formation when each student was inspected for proper appearance before leaving campus, and a monthly Sunday afternoon dress parade. All were announced by bugle calls.

In addition to daily devotional services, two school chaplains taught weekly classes, and their offices were open for student visits. Oz and I trained to become Sunday school teachers, and we both were in the Hi-Y, a Christian-oriented social club. Chaplains took us to teach at area churches—dressed in our uniforms, of course. In weekly school newspaper articles, upperclassmen reminded fellow students of how vital our religious training was:

Kamehameha helps each student prepare for his life work, including work in the Christian way. Our devotion periods help lessen the strain of our day's task. In devotion period we pause for a few minutes to give thanks and ask for guidance through the remainder of the day.[2]

With the attitude that there is a God Almighty who is always willing to listen to the pleas of mankind, the person is soon relieved of his burden. Many times it isn't possible to confide in any one person, but it is quite possible to go into meditation and disclose your thoughts to God. Therefore, one of the chief values of religion is its power to aid a person when there seems to be no other help available.[3]

Students without 75 or more demerits could board school buses on Saturdays for free time off campus; buses brought students back by 5:30 P.M. Since dormitory and room inspections were held first, this put everyone on edge, especially the younger students. If any infraction was found in a student's room or in the area a student was supposed to keep clean, such as toilets, shower room, and wash basins, the entire dormitory would be confined to campus. Everyone in the dormitory would know who let them down.

Students without demerit problems could spend one Saturday night a month off campus, if registered to stay with a designated family. You left the phone number, and a Big Six member might call.

We eighth graders, the youngest boys on campus during the war, were housed in one dormitory where a few upperclassmen supervised us. In the ninth grade, we dispersed into other dormitories to live with older students. Holdovers from high- and low-eleventh grades meant that there were some students who were six years older than I was. Being the youngest and smallest in my class made me a target until I proved my mettle.

Jimmy's beatings in California had toughened me. A few experiences on campus proved it wasn't much fun picking on me. When bruises showed on my pale skinny arms, the gym teacher asked who had hit me and I answered, "I don't know who he is."

I was small and light, making it easy for two boys to swing and toss me into vines

---

[2] Excerpt from school newspaper by Dewey Eberly.
[3] Excerpt from school newspaper by John Miller.

covering the hill between dormitories. To their surprise, I returned for another swing. Thinking I found it amusing, they stopped doing this.

When a big guy holding me over a balcony threatened to drop me, I remained inert. My not screaming or crying spoiled his fun and the incident wasn't repeated.

The meanest thing of all, "pantsing," didn't work with me; I reacted insanely as adrenalin kicked in instantly. If two or three boys tried to hold me to unbutton and pull down my pants, I'd stick my fingers sharply into the closest person's eyes with the full intent of blinding him, and I'd bang my head against whoever's head was in range.

There was a brief phase when students pressed fingers against another boy's throat to make him pass out. An older boy down the hall from my dormitory room was building his body with the Charles Atlas "Dynamic Tension" exercises—using muscle resistance to "pump" up. I had joined in, hoping to create biceps. He did the "pass-out" trick on me; other students had to help him carry me into the shower to be brought to by cold water. He was terrified I'd tell on him. I didn't, but I stayed away from him.

I learned to be useful and indifferent to pain, and I acquired skills requiring knowledge and fortitude. Being able to strike back by using my wits was a momentous discovery.

I was responsible for cleaning the showers, urinals, and toilets on the second floor of our dormitory. After a particularly difficult week of teasing, I made certain my work area wouldn't pass Saturday's inspection. Everyone was furious. I remained indifferent. The same thing happened the next week. What could anyone do? I was hopeless. From the third Saturday on, helpers put finishing touches to my work and students from our dorm were able to leave the campus for the day.

Some upperclassmen in our dorm invited me to join their shoe-shining business. We shined students' shoes, and the proceeds were saved for a chop suey feast. I did a pretty impressive spit shine, snapping the shining rag smartly—experience from shining soldiers' shoes in Kona.

The feast was scheduled for a Sunday afternoon when a day student drove the food to us. My excited chattering may have annoyed some of the older boys; two intended to "pants" me. After I struck back viciously, I beat it out of the room while they moaned about sore eyes and heads, and I ran from the dorm to hide in the bushes. I heard some of them calling for me—"Come eat" and "We're sorry"—but I stayed hidden. From that time on I avoided "the shiners." They'd violated my trust and had taken advantage of my small size.

Physical episodes associated with growing up and being tested had nothing to do with my fair complexion. No one ever called me "haole" because doing so would suggest I didn't belong at Kamehameha Schools, which was not true at all. It wasn't until my fiftieth reunion, and after Tom Hugo shared his secrets, that I found out Don Ho had been my public relations emissary.

Five of us in the Library Club were going to elect a president; since two of my close friends were voting for me, I was a shoo-in. Following my grandparents' Christian ethics, I voted for the opposing candidate. He voted for himself and won. My two friends were shocked at me, asking, "Didn't you want to be our president?"

Leadership opportunities came in other ways. The Library Club organized a memorial service for President Roosevelt's death in 1945 and chose me to do readings and summarize his career before the assembled male student body. Ham and Eggs experience had given me stage confidence. From that time on I had many chances to represent Kamehameha Schools at off-campus events where public speaking was involved.

Realizing it was an avenue to popularity, I became a camera bug. The school let me use its old-fashioned 4-by-5-inch Graflex view camera. It was heavy, had a focal plane shutter, and used sheet film. I looked into a shade to focus the full-sized groundglass viewer and composed the picture by looking down at a reflected scene, instead of directly at it. Its results were astounding: sharp images, good depth of field—old-fashioned types of photos with everything in sharp focus. By the ninth grade I was a school photographer, spending Saturdays and Sundays in the darkroom developing film and making enlargements—doing lots of cropping and dodging to produce "extra snap." Students enjoyed seeing themselves in big action pictures. I became good at it and felt useful and accepted.

With the war over, Graflex once again produced cameras for civilian use. During my junior year I found its new 2.25-by-3.25-inch Speed Graphic at Kodak Hawai'i. It used both 120 sheet and roll film. Luryier Diamond of Kodak Hawai'i had worked at Camp Maluhia in Kona, where I'd been a counselor the previous summer. He'd been kindly to me and had left the kitchen door unlocked at night because I was always hungry.

Only this one Speed Graphic was in stock; no telling where there would be another, and some professional photographers were interested in it. But "Pop" Diamond, as this man became known after he became Kamehameha's photographer, offered to sell it to me. The problem was, I didn't have enough money, and "Pop"—bless his heart—offered to buy the camera for me, and I'd pay him back when I could. I told my mother of his kindness and she was horrified over my going into debt. I found out I could cash in war bonds purchased with my rat-tail earnings before their maturity, and I was in business. Now I could make photographs by following the action, instead of waiting for it to come into the scene on a glass viewer.[4]

---

[4] In one of life's innumerable coincidences, almost twenty years later Graflex Inc. in Rochester, New York, became my national public relations client. That led to my similar twenty-two-year association with Eastman Kodak Company.

I was shy, and Kamehameha provided reassurance through many opportunities for accomplishment. Uncomfortable at being complimented, I disappeared quickly after a performance, event, or accomplishment—feeling unworthy for not doing well enough. These feelings were ingrained in my psyche long before I arrived on campus. With time, Kamehameha's opportunities and classmates' genuine kindliness reduced this embedding.

In 1944, Kamehameha School for Girls celebrated its fiftieth anniversary. Articles in the school paper and commemorative speeches described its history in carefully molding the lives of the young women upon whom Hawaiians would depend for their future.

From its beginning, Kamehameha School for Girls provided students professional training as well as instruction in homemaking. The school turned out students who went on to become teachers, nurses, stenographers, social workers, librarians, dental hygienists, recreational directors, occupational therapists—the only kinds of career positions available to Island women prior to World War II. Their job skills were important; Hawaiʻi's living cost made two incomes necessary in westernized types of homes.

I am very aware of how little I knew of girls and the girls school while growing up. Boarding students were isolated from members of the opposite sex. That and my attending a men's college made me ill equipped for what lay ahead.

Edmund Kealoha Parker, a day student, explained how to avoid my being taunted by toughs on public buses. He knew I was a prime target—a slight, white-looking boy wearing the uniform of an elite school to which a limited number of Hawaiians were admitted.

Experienced in both judo and karate, Ed was the master of appearing unruffled. "Arthur, don't look at them unless you intend to fight. Appear calm and secure. If their noise continues, move casually to the front of the bus. Stand by the driver as if you are soon going to get off."

He taught me two unconventional blows to use hard and fast if cornered. His advice on appearing detached worked well at a time when I most needed it. Bill Fernandez, another classmate, loaned me his barbells and weights for a summer so I could become stronger. Two summers later I grew over 6 inches and had biceps—not exactly like Popeye's, more like poached eggs. It didn't matter: Everyone else on campus had shrunk.

During my senior year the school nurse gave me the job of bringing three meals a day from the dining room to students confined in the infirmary. She ordered food for extra students so I would have enough to eat. When starting my senior year I was 6 feet 4 inches tall, weighed only 150 pounds, had low blood pressure, was anemic, and always felt starved. Extra food at the infirmary helped me achieve normal proportions.

On some Saturday evenings we had "supervised socialization" with the girls school for ballroom dancing lessons, movies, school plays, and sometimes a concert. Of course, no boys sat with girls and we weren't forced to dance. The ballroom dancing came during the fall that I hurt my knee, and I sat out the lessons with other male wallflowers. At other times, lower-division boys beat up on each other in a game developed to work off energy. Pat Gandall said it was his first introduction to a form of rugby—soccer played with football rules. Solidly built and low to the ground, Pat blocked taller students where it hurt the most.

On Sundays after church, we were allowed free time after the noontime meal. If it was rainy, some of us practiced a version of "sand surfing" on the lower playing field, out of sight of the main campus; if the grass wasn't wet enough, we risked turning on the lawn sprinkler—demerits if caught.

To sand surf, you wait until foam from a wave begins receding and covers the sand by a few inches. Running fast, you put your arms down as you fall and propel your body. If done quickly and smoothly, you glide over the surface as if hydroplaning. Do it wrong and you flop on your belly, stuck in place. It is easier to learn on wet grass. Geno Kaupiko—"Nature Boy"—slid three times farther than all of us, laughing with delight.

Geno stepped out of line but once, and it was in Mrs. Ann Kauaihilo's classroom; she was our favorite teacher. Speaking in Hawaiian, in what he thought was a soft voice, he described her physical charms to those of us near him. He wasn't crude, he wasn't lewd, but he *was* descriptive.

She answered in Hawaiian—we didn't know she spoke it! Mortified, Geno slid down in his seat. Looking directly down at him, Mrs. Kauaihilo said, "This is English class, Eugene, and you *were not* speaking English. I am giving you 10 demerits."

We laughed with relief, appreciating her sense of humor.

Mrs. Kauaihilo danced the hula for a red-haired, freckle-faced Coast Guardsman named Arthur Godfrey at Aunt Emma Markham's home, my designated monthly weekend residence. Aunt Em, a probation officer for the Territory of Hawai'i, told me a boy from school always phoned to make certain I was there—Big Six!

After Mrs. Kauaihilo's hula, Aunt Em asked me to sing "The Cockeyed Mayor of Kaunakakai." It's a funny song about a place where I once lived and describes a silly white man adored by all the village people on the island of Moloka'i. As a novelty, I placed the *'ukulele* behind my head and played it.

Godfrey performed "boogie woogie" on Aunt Emma Markham's piano. He wasn't a celebrity; he was just another good guy serving our country to whom an Island family extended hospitality.

When Arthur Godfrey became a famous American radio star in the 1950s, he helped boost the tourist industry by speaking fondly of Hawai'i and by repopularizing the *'ukulele* on the mainland.

In 1945, Kamehameha cadets were the honor guard for Abigail Wahi'ika'ahu'ula Kawananakoa's funeral. She was the last person of royal blood to be interred at the Royal Mausoleum.

We wore our woolen dress uniforms and followed the casket in a slow three-mile march in the hot sun from 'Iolani Palace in downtown Honolulu uphill into Nu'uanu. One boy passed out from the heat while we stood at attention at the palace. He was much bigger than me and gave me a hard time. While dressing in the dormi-

Marchers carried royal *kāhili* during Princess Kawananakoa's funeral procession from 'Iolani Palace in downtown Honolulu to the Royal Mausoleum at Mauna 'Ala in Nu'uanu. They were the same *kāhili* as those seen in this photograph from Queen Lili'uokalani's funeral ceremony in 1917. *Bishop Museum Archives photo.*

tory, he complained about the woolen trousers being "itchy." "Someone" told him to wear pajama pants under his trousers. He put paper inside his shoes, because "someone" told him this would keep his feet cool. He was set up for hyperthermia. Passing out in front of us all was shameful. He stopped picking on me.

The pomp displayed during Princess Kawananakoa's funeral seemed momentous to us because Kamehameha students weren't allowed involvement in Hawaiian cultural activities. Tall, stately feather *kāhili* (royal standards) carried by stern-faced men attested to her royal status, and profuse garlands of flower leis showed that many people loved her.

Male and female chanting was part of the service at Mauna 'Ala. This is how ancient Hawaiians originally "talked story" and passed on history. Our ancestors used their voices in many ways in chanting: Drama was added through glottal cutoffs— voice breaks caused by transitions from one vocal register to another—glides, varying vibrato, and special articulation of certain language sounds. Pitch attacks might be accompanied by a glide up—transitions receive two pitches and occur on glides. Chanters may use a yodel-like alternation of two pitches with intervals smaller than a half tone.

Chanting was a profound experience for every student present, but particularly for James Kaupena Wong, class of 1947. After graduating from Coe College in Cedar Rapids, Iowa, Kaupena studied to become the best-known performer and teacher of chant of his generation.

K amehameha School for Boys celebrated its sixtieth anniversary while I was a tenth grader. Charles E. King, a member of the first graduating class, came from New York to tell students about the early days, and he brought a new song, "Ku'u Kamehameha," which he composed for the occasion. He conducted us while we sang it.

King became a teacher after graduating from Oswego Normal School (now SUNY–Oswego); it's on the shores of Lake Ontario in the snow capital of New York State. King started composing music when he was forty and became renowned as the "Dean of Hawaiian Music." "Ke Kali Nei Au," widely known as "The Hawaiian Wedding Song," is one of his compositions. He reminded us that music was the only bit of their culture that Kamehameha students were allowed to embrace.

While he was at Kamehameha, Dr. Theodore Richards developed a new type of Hawaiian choral singing. The Kamehameha Boys School chorus repertoire was based on nonhymn songs composed by King Kalākaua, Queen Lili'uokalani, and others who were developing this new genre. Some Hawaiian composers added their own poetry to melodies that Henry Berger, the king's bandmaster, brought from Germany. If you've wondered why peppy old Hawaiian songs such as "Ninipo" have a tinge of German beer garden music, you now know why. It also explains the Prussian military sound of "Hawai'i Pono'ī," the kingdom's national anthem, with words by King Kalākaua and music by Herr Bandmaster Berger.

I had the opportunity to photograph and interview Charles King for our school newspaper. He explained to me how the Kamehameha Schools singing tradition began.

> Theodore Richards, a teacher hired from New Jersey, was inspired by discovery of the great musical talent among us boys.[5]
>
> Richards gave us Hawaiian songs to sing in four-part harmony; he was able to get into the hearts of his pupils, and that was the reason for his success.
>
> He sang the parts for us to learn. His voice was of the very high, clear tenor type Hawaiians particularly love.
>
> He had our glee club dress in white tuxedos, standing collars, white bow ties, and white patent leather shoes. He took us on concert tours around the islands, making us proud of ourselves, proud of our school, and making our Hawaiian audiences proud of our accomplishments.
>
> Dr. Richards personally paid for these glee club uniforms; we boys and our families had no money.

Richards became principal of the boys school in 1891 and encouraged singing among all students. The idea of a song contest surfaced when Uncle Ernest Webster was principal. George Allison Andrus, school musical leader, died suddenly on May 26, 1921. Webster and faculty decided on having a competition among classes to honor Andrus—and they created Hawaiian musical history. The trophy boys continue to compete for is called "The Andrus Trophy."

---

[5] We think of the world being smaller now, but consider these nineteenth-century coincidences: Richards, newly graduated from Wesleyan University in Middletown, Connecticut, came to Kamehameha School for Boys in 1889 at the recommendation of Samuel C. Armstrong, a Civil War general, whom he met at a boys camp in New Hampshire. Born and raised in Hawai'i by his missionary parents, Armstrong was familiar with Hilo Boarding School, Hilo, Hawai'i, which emphasized manual training along with academic work for Hawaiians. General Armstrong founded Hampton Institute in 1868 in Hampton, Virginia, for black students and used Hilo Boarding School as the model. Booker T. Washington, an early Hampton graduate, established Tuskegee Institute in Alabama to train the "head, hand, and heart," beliefs Armstrong brought from the Lymans. Armstrong hired Levi and Nettie Lyman from Hilo Boarding School to teach at Hampton. They returned to Hawai'i to teach at Kamehameha Schools.

In early song contests, each class sang the school song, a Hawaiian composition, and *an original song in Hawaiian composed by members of the class.* Webster and members of the music department stayed within the rules but encouraged the young men to be creative within their own cultural milieu: Even though members of the boys school weren't allowed to speak Hawaiian, Webster allowed them to use it for composition and singing.

The contest was held at night on the steps of the old school. Aunt Molly told me that on contest night, automobiles would be lined to face the boys. Car headlights were turned on to illuminate the singers.

Webster returned to Litchfield, Connecticut, after the 1924 school year to help operate the family's milk business. Because of his accomplishments at Kamehameha School for Boys, the University of Hawai'i recruited Dr. Webster from Litchfield to teach engineering and be its dean; he resided for the rest of his life next to its Mānoa campus. The University of Hawai'i's Webster Hall is named for him.

Winning a song contest gave members of the winning classes bragging rights for a year—or forever, as with the girls class of 1947, led by the legendary, vivacious Rowena Vierra. Under her direction, the class won song contests during its eighth, ninth, and tenth grades, becoming known as "the invincibles."

Girls in the senior class of 1946 never had defeated the class of 1947. They needed to do something dramatic to win. Rowena-led juniors were virtuosos. Being in the class that never won a song contest stigmatizes you forever.

Anna Eagles, the seniors' song leader, and Miss Laura E. Brown, music teacher, made song contest history. Eagles selected "Nālani," a popular contemporary song by Alvin Isaacs that had been recently recorded by Alfred Apaka. At that time, Isaacs was helping to create a new wave of sensuous modern Hawaiian music. His vocal quartet, the Royal Hawaiian Serenaders, had brought him to the attention of Bing Crosby and Hollywood.

Miss Brown created a sophisticated choral arrangement of "Nālani" with choral vocal depth to Isaac's tight major and minor harmonies. Miss Brown helped Anna teach classmates to sing like Fred Waring's "Pennsylvanians," a hugely popular mainland choral group at that time with a style that was—well, very Fred Waring-like.

The words were not what you would expect to hear on a high school stage; they were permissable because if it was only rare that students understood the forbidden Hawaiian language, judges certainly didn't. The song begins as follows:

| | |
|---|---|
| *Auhea ʻoe Nālani* | Where are you, Nālani? |
| *Auhea wale ʻoe* | Where are you? |
| *He aha no la kau hana* | What is my desire? |
| *A liko no ʻoe iʻau.* | To make you mine. |

The second verse intensifies:

| | |
|---|---|
| *Ke huli nei Nālani* | Come to me Nālani |
| *Ke 'i'ini nei ia'u 'oe* | You are the one I yearn for. |
| *Heaha no la kau hana* | What is my desire? |
| *A lilo no 'oe i'au.* | To make you mine. |

Hawaiian words to the next two verses increase with passion.

The Pennsylvanians changed tempos during a song, rose to a crescendo before suddenly dropping to a whisper, and emphasized certain sounds within words. They played on listeners' emotions. That's what Anna taught classmates to do.

Isaac's contemporary technique, Brown's tonal effects, and Anna's total control stunned the audience and judges. At times the girls sang and extended "Na-a-a-a," then briskly clipped the two-syllable "lani" to echo within the auditorium—as if reflecting a lover's impatience (comprehended only by those knowing the Hawaiian words).

Silence hung momentarily when the senior girls finished. Was this Hawaiian music? Applause began tentatively at first as an awed audience adjusted to contemporary sounds it had heard. Then the crowd roared with approval for creative and courageous senior girls who obviously had just won their first song contest. The judges' decision seemed an afterthought. The "impossible" had happened. Junior women were devastated, feeling the seniors had used trickery to beat them.

Rowena and her class won the next year's contest, melting the audience with incredibly beautiful singing of the more conventional and innocent "Lei Lokelani" ("Rose Lei"), the words and music composed by Kamehameha Schools alumnus Charles E. King in 1921. King's words are picturesque, not passionate:

| | |
|---|---|
| *Ua 'i'ike maka au* | I have beheld with my own eyes |
| *I ka nani o ia pua* | The beauty of that blossom, |
| *Puaho'ohihi na'au* | A flower to be cherished by me alone, |
| *Puia I ke 'ala* | Imbued with fragrance. |

Glorious gems of musical history sung by the girls class of 1947 are preserved for posterity on Kamehameha Schools' first-ever recording made. Col. Kent, a former broadcaster, was responsible for making the 78 record possible. "The invincibles" sang Charles King's lush "Ku'u 'I'ini" ("My Desire") and his charming "Ku'u Ipo" ("My Sweetheart"). Senior boys of 1947, led by Cleighton Beamer, are also featured on the recording.

The song contest leader, the most important person in a class, called as many rehearsals as he or she felt were needed and had the authority to browbeat anyone not trying hard enough. The only time Kamehameha students were allowed to use Hawaiian was when they sang, and class song leaders made certain the words were sung as perfectly as the music.

By the night of the song contest, you ached to do your best for this person who controlled with the flick of a finger, a glance, a raised eyebrow, or an intense look, and who reassured with a smile.

Boys and girls held separate contests on two different nights in the school auditorium while I matriculated. One song was assigned to each division; each class sang a second song of its choice. The song contest is now integrated and only the three upper classes compete. Audiences fill all 7,000 seats in Honolulu's downtown arena, and it is televised throughout the Islands and can be heard over the Internet. Classes of boys and girls sing separately and as a combined class; it is a long evening.

O ne night Don Ho heard me crawl out the window of our room onto the dormitory roof. I sat there anguishing over whether anyone would care if I ended it all by jumping to my death 10 feet below onto a basketball court. He urged me to come inside and tell him what was wrong.

I was supposed to sing an obbligato to our eighth grade class's prize song, "Beautiful Kahana," by Charles E. King—it was a countermelody soaring above the chorus. Earlier in the year, Emma Veary had sung an obbligato to her eighth-grade class's winning song; the songleader was Emanelle Vierra, Rowena's sister. Emma's performance gave our music teacher the idea that I could do the same thing; it would be novel since I was the only boy in the entire school who was still a soprano. I told Don that two ninth graders had waited on the dark stairway after study hall. They grabbed me, saying they'd "take care of me" if anyone heard me sing.

Don said, "Don't worry."

Students wore flower leis for the song contest; the sweet aroma made you dizzy as you stood nervously onstage. Bright lights from the footlights were in your eyes, and the audience was an out-of-focus mass. Every one of the 999 seats was filled. All you could see was the confident smiling face of your songleader.

Well, *usually* it appeared confident. The night of our eighth grade song contest was when Don Ho's more than forty-year career as a crowd-pleaser began. Here is how he describes it:

> I had my back to the audience and my pants kept slipping down as I raised my arms and moved them to direct. I had to keep pulling my pants up while leading the singing and heard hilarious laughter.

That gave me insight as to what makes people happy: It's when things aren't perfect.

Years later I tapped into this experience by encouraging audience involvement in my shows.

"Can you sing? Come on, be happy, come up on stage and be part of the gang." I include the lousy ones; some are so lousy that they're very entertaining.

I no longer had to worry about ninth graders' threats after the song contest—their class won. I hit all my notes, but I was no match for Emma.

Thanks to Don, we received happy cheers as well as applause. Seniors from the girls school sent Don a pair of red suspenders.

During the school talent contest, sophomore Emma Veary sang the "Italian Street Song." She astounded everyone; her coloratura soprano voice was so polished and mature.

Emma had returned to Kamehameha after spending the ninth grade at Brentwood Hall School for Girls in Bronxville, New York. She went there to study voice in New York City, encouraged by a mainland voice teacher she met in Hawai'i. The teacher abandoned her when Emma's mother refused to grant the teacher power of attorney. This would have meant full control of Emma and her future earnings.

When limousines drove up on weekends to take daughters home, fifteen-year-old Emma rode a train to New York City. The International House allowed Emma to spend Saturday nights and holidays with college friends from the Islands who resided there.

She learned performance skills on her own from attending operas, ballets, and musicals. People working in the box offices came to recognize this tall, dignified girl and gave her free passes.

Vera Brynner, sister of actor Yul Brynner, kept seeing this striking Hawaiian with the long black hair at performances and noticed how intently she studied everything that was happening. She invited Emma to become her voice student.

After winning the Kamehameha talent contest, Emma became a featured attraction at Waikīkī's best hotels. Unable to balance the Kamehameha Schools schedule with her music career, which was helping to support her family, Emma transferred to a public school. She became one of Hawai'i's most renowned and respected singers.

Two years later there was Don Ho and his group. By now, Don's pants fit and he played the steel guitar. He recruited three classmates as singers. Quiet Don was happiest just doing background music. His trio tried to sound like the Mills Brothers, then at the height of their popularity. The Mills Brothers sang close harmonies and vocally imitated musical instruments.

Students gathered outside the dormitory laundry room where they rehearsed and excitedly spread the word: "They'll win the talent contest. They're going to sing in Waikīkī hotels just like Emma Veary."

Don chose baritone Richmond Apaka as lead singer because of his name and genes. Richmond's uncle Alfred Apaka starred at the Royal Hawaiian Hotel; he was Hawai'i's greatest male vocalist and the heartthrob of middle-aged female tourists. The group kept its name a secret.

On the big night, the announcer introduced the group over the public speaking system in grand style: "And now here is the performance we've all been anticipating—'The Three Nights'. . . ."

Out came Don Ho, Wimpy Wilmington, and Richmond Apaka. The audience thought the name of the group was "The Three Knights."

The announcer paused momentarily before continuing dramatically: "'. . . and a Day!'"

Out I walked, pale, a snap in my stride, to stand at the front of the stage among two dark nights, with Don in the background by the steel guitar.

"Three Nights and a Day"—it brought the house down. Don planned it all. He had a showman's instincts—even then.

He started playing the steel guitar.[6] The three of us rhythmically snapped our fingers, waiting for Richmond to sing the single word "Gloria" into the microphone. It was the opening to our signature song. Then we'd join in harmony for a line, he'd repeat the word "Gloria," we'd add our line, and then the singing went into high gear. Richmond's one-word solo wasn't complicated; he didn't even have to be on pitch.

He stared at the spotlight and froze. Alarmed, I glanced over. Richmond was a standing dead man, eyes glazed, mouth hanging open. We kept snapping our fingers, scared to death, hoping Richmond would revive, start the song, and lead us out of trouble. It didn't happen.

Behind us, in a soft voice without a microphone, Don started singing. We snapped our fingers and bobbed our heads. We'd forgotten our parts!

Somehow this all ended. Quickly we scooted offstage, not even thinking of trying our second number, "We're Dancing under the Stars Tonight."

---

[6] Credit for invention of the steel guitar is given to Joseph Kekuku, a Kamehameha student in 1889. He experimented in the school's machine shop until he was satisfied with a slim cylinder of metal that slid on the strings, producing a distinctive portamento sound. To create "a bite" on notes, he cut finger and thumb picks out of metal and raised the strings.

Don wanted us buried under the earth that night. After that experience, whenever he saw any of us—nights or day—he'd look menacingly and snap his fingers.

Richmond had steely nerves for everything except being in the spotlight. While in the U.S. Air Force, he was one of the first pilots to recover a missile returning from space. After military retirement, he became a commercial pilot for Japan Air Lines.

Kamehameha boys contradicted stereotypes of Hawaiians with their spit-and-polish appearance, politeness, and inexhaustible spirit—especially in athletics. I destroyed that impression by humiliating Kamehameha Schools before 25,000 people.

Because our band supplied marching music for Kamehameha's cadet battalion, the Shriners invited us to perform at their 1946 Thanksgiving "Shriners Game." The two best high school football teams played each other in a stadium filled to capacity. Our school administrators didn't consider the fact that most band members were boarding students from the neighbor islands who'd be home for the holiday.

About fifteen of us showed up early at Honolulu Stadium: one trombone player, one tuba player, three snare drummers, and no bass drummer. I was the only trumpet player; the rest of the band consisted of clarinet and saxophone players. Bandleader Mr. Seivers tentatively said he would play his cornet if we wanted to go through with it. No one said anything, so I spoke up: "With your help, we'll do fine, Mr. Seivers."

The other bands' members began arriving from Honolulu's day schools. Their numbers were huge because ours was the only predominantly boarding-school band. The coeducational Punahou band stood next to us wearing shining buff and blue uniforms. I gaped. The gorgeous girls wore form-fitting blue slacks. The form of the mellophone player with the long blonde hair was particularly fitting. This was a new experience; Kamehameha girls didn't wear slacks around boys.

"Military Escort" by Henry Fillmore, our entrance march, was vigorous and stimulating when our sizable brass section performed it. Its opening was a robust fanfare with trumpets and trombones driving the melody; woodwinds kind of danced through the middle section.

We heard an announcement over the loudspeaker: "Here comes the Kamehameha School Band." Off we went, lined up in three rows of fours; two snare drummers were in back along with a clarinetist, who this time was carrying and playing the bass drum. Edwin Beamer led us forward. We resembled postmen in our secondhand blue-gray uniforms, in shabby contrast to other bands' colorful uniforms. In the open-air amphitheater, Mr. Seivers and I sounded like we were playing kazoos.

As we made our first right turn, the large bell of the tuba fell off and rolled on the ground. Rayner Kinney chased it and cradled it in his arms like a baby for the rest of the march—no oompah-pahs.[7]

Edwin Beamer marched undauntedly, playing the glockenspiel, his officer's sword swaying from his side. The vigor with which he hit that bell-like instrument—and his bravado—kept us determined.

I couldn't hear the bass drum.

The crowd's reaction began with titters, became guffaws, and, when we reached our seats in the middle of the stadium, everyone was laughing loudly. I imagined them saying: "Ha-ha-Hawaiian band."

We certainly didn't change opinions about Hawaiians that day. It was all my fault; I was the bigmouth who assured Mr. Seivers we could pull it off. My stomach had a sick, sinking feeling. I was dazed, time had slowed down, nothing seemed real, and I was unaware of any football game.

Mingling with the exiting crowd and ashamed of being in uniform, I dreaded riding on a public bus with my telltale cornet in a case. I sat in the back row. *Oh no—* Punahou's gorgeous mellophone player was getting on! I kept my head down.

Through contacts in the community, our new president Col. Harold W. Kent learned that the schools suffered from the usual negative stereotyping of Kamehameha students and Hawaiians. Too many people thought that Kamehameha taught boys to be mechanics and girls to be good mothers—period.

Some viewed Kamehameha as a caretaker institution for poor and troubled Hawaiian students. This was a public relations challenge for a great communicator, which Col. Kent believed himself to be.

Surprisingly, the Shriners invited our band to the following year's Thanksgiving game. Mr. Seivers urged us to stay in Honolulu, and we all agreed. Then our big, kindly, blond band teacher and track coach who performed jazz in a Honolulu night club handed us the music we played. He shared a secret plan he said was "fully supported by Col. Kent."

On Thanksgiving Day, 1947, our eighty Kamehameha bandsmen arrived early. All but the drummers placed their instruments in the covered grandstand area. We would sit there when we performed. We waited at the entrance gate for other school bands. Seeing us with only drums and remembering last year, members of the arriving bands thought we were there for show but didn't dare to blow—"Ha-ha Hawaiians!"

Blue-and-white Kamehameha School buses began unloading, about a hundred

---

[7] Rayner must have heard comments later from his dad, Ray Kinney, who enjoyed a fifty-seven-year musical career and the widest acclaim of any Hawaiian singer-musician of his time, particularly on the U.S. mainland.

of the schools' strongest-looking young men lined up behind our drummers, and band members were in front of the drummers. Wearing crisply starched, freshly ironed U.S. Army khaki uniforms with garrison caps, we would be the last group to enter. Were we ever keyed up!

Then came the announcement: "Here comes the Kamehameha School Band." Before anyone in the audience could titter, snare drummers and three bass drummers hit double time—180 paces a minute—and 180 of us entered at almost a run. Machine-gun bursts came from snare drums, cannons boomed from bass drums, 360 stomping feet declared our resolute vigor.

At midfield, drummers began beating "regular time" as we gave the crowd a lesson in marching precision: Our lines were razor straight, we marched straight forward, did right- and left-flank movements, two obliques, and a countermarch.

At the seating area, band members picked up their instruments and sat down behind a wall quickly formed by fellow students in the parade rest position. Waiting for us in the front row was our secret weapon: a smiling blond girl holding a piccolo.

On command, students in front of us side-stepped to the left and right like stage curtains. They stood at attention on an oblique and we held our instruments in position. In front of us, Mr. Seivers smiled merrily, raised his baton, and we burst into one of the most stirring marches ever written: John Phillip Sousa's "Washington Post March."

The piccolo rose above us in its own happy, playful melody with a few trills included as a fillip. Seated together and with acoustical help from the grandstand roof, we produced powerful cohesive music, unlike the thin wavering sounds from other bands who were strung out on the field, parading as they played.

We finished, and an excited roar poured out from the crowd. Our hearts pounded with joy. Sitting near us, Col. Kent grinned widely along with the rest of us.

In the spring, when she played the flute solo to "In a Persian Garden" with our concert band, we learned that our piccolo player was the daughter of the president of Punahou School. Col. Kent had "outreached" for us.

During my sophomore year, I began making brief Saturday visits to my grandparents' home. They politely listened to my stories of Kamehameha life. After a few weeks, Grandfather Lyman began speaking to me in Hawaiian; I pretended not to be surprised; living in Kona made me familiar with the language. He'd accepted my choice to hold firmly to my Hawaiian roots; perhaps he saw them strengthening me. Now he'd take me on adventures.

For a visit to the Bank of Hawaii, he dressed in his customary white linen suit, wore a red silk tie, but chose not to put a Panama hat on his thick white hair today.

Walking in grandly, he presented a teller the check he had written in Hawaiian using his elegant Palmer-method penmanship. Puzzled, the teller carried the check for approval to the branch manager sitting in the lobby area. He shook his head noticeably.

Standing at the teller's counter, grandfather pointed to the bank's identification on the front window and addressed the manager in his Hallelujah voice: "Is *this* the Bank of Hawaii?"

The manager stood up and assured him, patronizingly, "It is indeed the Bank of Hawaii." People in the lobby could not help but hear the exchange.

"Well then, shouldn't *the Bank of Hawaii* allow a *Hawaiian* to withdraw his own money by writing a check in *Hawaiian?*" Grandfather was still in his Hallelujah voice.

The manager, agitated, raised his voice and started a retort that sounded like it might turn out to be, "But this is not the Bank for Hawaiians."

Suddenly realizing he was headed for trouble, the red-faced young man caught himself midway, lowered his voice to a mumble, and gestured to the teller to cash the check. Grandfather walked out of the bank as proudly as he came in. That was fun.

Some might use drink to soothe the pain of falling to the grass ceiling, but Grandfather Lyman became a teetotaler after his conversion by the Salvation Army. He retaliated: In the presence of haole officials, he pretended to be a naive old Hawaiian. Then he roped them in and made them tongue tied. Wise persons deferred to his eccentricities.

M ost upperclassmen were on varsity teams so we'd have enough athletes to match up against bigger schools. Dr. Barnes initiated a varsity sports feeder system with each boy assigned to a *hui*—the Hawaiian word for club or society. They were Mōʻī (supreme), Aliʻi (royal), ʻEleu (active, quick), and Imua—the school motto ("Go forward"). Every boy chose his *hui* activities: football, basketball, baseball, track, soccer, volleyball, horseshoes, checkers, field hockey, ping-pong, mountain hiking behind the campus, tennis, and boxing.

*Hui* football was played barefoot, although pads and uniforms were worn. Young and frail boys wore shorts and played "touch" football. Twice a year every student took physical performance tests to see how he measured up to fitness classifications. Some boys had to do extra training to reach the requirements.

The *hui* system allowed boys to select sports for which they were fitted. The principal's office totaled accumulated points at the end of the year to determine overall winners. Athletes in individualized sports contributed points: a boy who was a whiz at chess was viewed respectfully by others; a ping-pong champion was a celebrity.

The Kamehameha ideal was to allow every student a chance to excel in something, be it academic or shop work—winning silver and gold pins—interscholastic sports, *hui* sports, the rifle order of arms, sharpshooting, singing, or Sunday school teaching. Everyone had recognitions listed after his name in the yearbook and stood out in a positive way.

Compensating for our being outnumbered by other schools, coaches pushed athletes aerobically by increasing running distances, demanding faster and faster wind sprints, and by loading on the calisthenics. And of course, there were the stairs.

When the schools resumed postwar "normal conditions," girls moved back to their campus. Col. Kent declared dining should become coeducational and boys climbed an additional 560 stairs three times a day. Including stairs on their own campus, this averaged 2,000 steps daily. If you raced down fast enough, two steps at a time, the soles of your shoes would clack like a machine gun—exhilarating! Vocational students had an additional walk to the shops, and athletes went farther down the hill to playing fields. Everyone was in condition.

Worn out by relentless enthusiasm, players on other teams accused Kamehameha athletes of being "nuts."

Too small at first to represent my school on a playing field, I managed football, basketball, and track teams to learn these sports. A failed attempt at football in my sophomore year ruined my knee, resulted in operations, and resulted in a seemingly permanent limp. Recovery was long and painful. While runners did laps, I hobbled around the track, eventually could walk, and finally could run.

Coaches Bill Seivers and Tom Mountain announced open tryouts for the upcoming interscholastic mile run. Kamehameha didn't have a standard-sized track and we ran five laps for a mile. A wannabe to whom no one paid attention, I lined up barefoot behind everyone else—only real runners wore track shoes.

As others tired, I worked my way through the pack. By the fourth lap I was running with the leaders. By the fifth lap I had a commanding lead, and Tom Mountain, the football coach who didn't know I was alive, was jumping and shouting. I understand that he told this story for years, and at our fiftieth anniversary reunion he greeted me as "the miler."

Our track team was decimated by the flu during the annual Cornell Relays in my senior year. Coach Seivers asked if I was willing to try to run the mile, half-mile, quarter-mile, and three laps in the distance medley relay. I answered, "Yes. Thank you."

I was lucky to be on the team after making the awful mistake of telling my mother of a stress fracture, the result of overtraining. She wanted a doctor to "break my foot" so the fracture would heal properly. This would have meant no track in my senior year. I ignored her. Her overreacting was why I didn't tell Mother about personal things. I just taped my left foot very tightly.

Coach Sievers had asked Edmund Parker to run every sprint in the Cornell Relays. Edmund flashed a grin as he finished with the leaders. Coach didn't expect any of us to equal Parker's performance, but he hoped the team could compete well with the larger schools. We won a lot of events and set an Island record in the distance medley relay. *Although numerically small, we demonstrate Hawaiians aren't slow and lazy,* I mused to myself.

This was the year the football team, starring classmates Don Ho, Eric Kalohelani, Richmond Apaka, Tom Hugo, Geno Kaupiko, and other stalwarts, won the interscholastic football title, stunning the local sports world. Who would expect this achievement from such a small school?

As football players walked off the field after each game, girls placed leis around their necks. Hawaiian men enjoy flowers and don't consider them effeminate; they are nature's symbols, and each flower has its own meaning. They are also used to send signals. Women wear a flower over their right ear to show "I'm taken" and over the left if they're not.

For the first May Day in the combined girls and boys dining hall, the top three out of four winners of the flower-arranging contest were football players. To decorate his table, football tight end Richmond Apaka made a flower decoration of a warrior's head. Running back Eric Kalohelani used flowers to depict volcano goddess Pele on a mountain. Our wideout who could catch anything, Eugene Kaupiko, used every flower on campus to concoct something eerie looking.

Julie-Bethe Perkins, a stunning beauty with the best posture in the world and a dazzling smile, was queen of the day, wearing a white satin *holokū* hugging her body at the waist, with a long train that reached the floor. Her appearance made me understand Tantalus' agonies. I'm referring to the Phrygian king, not the Oʻahu mountain slope named for him. Tantalus, for all eternity, also saw something so near but so unreachable. Julie was Tom Hugo's girl.

Kamehameha School for Girls exceptional program for life resumed once the military hospital closed and girls moved back to campus. It included a half-year of cooking, a half-year of sewing, and each senior made her own white graduation gown. They had courses in prenatal motherhood and on raising children up to ages five or six.

Pii Ellis Kinimaka, class of 1949, a clinical enterostomal therapy nurse and co-owner of an ostomy therapy practice in California, explained: "We could have delivered a child after that training. We learned the basics of health care and worked in the school infirmary, where we were expected to be available to patients at all times."

Girls worked as teachers aides with students at Kamehameha Preparatory School. Twelfth-grade girls, eight at a time, were assigned to the "Senior Practice Cottage" for eight weeks to take care of an infant loaned to the school for the academic year. Girls lived in the cottage, purchased food, cooked meals, kept accounts, and were its housekeepers. Each girl had to assume individual around-the-clock responsibility for the baby's care—feeding, changing, and bathing—for at least a week and had to make up the school time she missed. "Days just got longer," Pii said. "We learned what it was like to be a working mother."

Girls learned to be gracious hostesses. Each one had "her night," when she invited a boy to dinner at the Senior Cottage and none of the other girls were visible. She'd cook the meal, arrange the flowers, and handle the conversation. I remember telling my hostess, "This dinner demonstrates we can grow up to be elegant as well as industrious."

The industrious men and women concept, especially the Senior Cottage, caused many outsiders to believe that Kamehameha was developing a servant class. As a mainland author wrote,

The Kamehameha School [*sic*] became in reality a haole enterprise to keep the Hawaiians subjugated and docile. Boys were taught the trades that would make them good mechanics, carpenters and maintenance men; speaking Hawaiian was forbidden; and college enrollment has been insignificant in the eighty-five years of the schools' existence. Until a few years ago, Kamehameha girls were taught, in their home economics classes, to set a table with three sizes of wine glasses and four settings of silver knives and forks, "because it was evident," as a contemporary student put it, "they needed us as maids." (Franciene Du Ple Gray, *Hawaii: The Sugar-Coated Fortress,* New York: Random House, 1972; appeared originally in *The New Yorker* magazine)

Girls school students were in one of two units designated by the school colors. "White" was for those wishing to take commercial courses and enter the job market after graduation; "blue" was for those aspiring to go to college—they received a heavier dose of college-preparatory courses.

Girls wore leotards to learn modern dancing and gracefulness from a Swedish dance instructor. "This was ironic," Pii recalls. "The Beamer girls, best dancers in the Islands, were forced to do this thing instead of teaching others to do their thing.

"All lower division girls participated in the Forum Club; some continued through their senior year. A club committee selected a topic, exclusive of current events, to discuss each week and each girl had to stand up and make a statement even though it may not have been profound. They learned to be unafraid of speaking up. The school was a mixture of very shy rural girls and more sophisticated Honolulu girls." Pii believes this program is one reason many Hawaiian women became successful in public life.

We were loaned every modern and up-to-date weapon required by infantry-men, including BARs—Browning Automatic Rifles. Instructional materials provided by the army covered subjects ordinarily taught to soldiers in basic training; we learned it all.

Col. Kent wanted Kamehameha to regain its status as a military institute. A large man with a ready smile and a broadcaster's voice, he was fond of the wartime army rank and title he gained while an educational training officer in Washington. His previous experience included elementary and high school teaching and administra-tion and radio work. In his first public statement to the Kamehameha family, he pledged to improve community relations and "perpetuate the glorious Hawaiian culture."

He initiated "The Kamehameha Hour," an on-campus radio show, which gave me the opportunity to prepare and announce scripts during my junior and senior years. Col. Kent joined the board of the new tourist-related Aloha Week and arranged trips to campus for tourists. He recognized Aloha Week as a way to showcase Kamehameha—particularly its choral groups.

Although knowing little about "the glorious Hawaiian culture," he realized it deserved a more important role at Kamehameha. One of his first moves was to start a Hawaiian language class for boys with the Rev. Stephen Desha as instructor. While a minister in Kona, the Rev. Desha coined an expression for my mother: "Ruth Rath of the narrow path." In my senior year, Grandfather called him to make sure I was on the straight and narrow path; he'd heard I liked to hang out at Kūhiō Beach.

School chaplains conducted services entirely in English, but Col. Kent gave the Rev. Desha permission to have students read the scripture in Hawaiian. Never before was Hawaiian allowed to be spoken on campus by students.

Kent implemented the Territorial Senate's imposed policy for Kamehameha to admit a cross-section of Hawaiian youth, regardless of IQ scores. He worked out an exact scale of island percentages among boarders. Under Kent there was greater emphasis on vocational work and lesser emphasis on high-level academic work.

All eighth- and ninth-grade male students learned agriculture, wood carving, furniture making, and drafting; at this level, training was more for an avocation than a vocation—every boy took home a wooden lamp he made "in shop."

In the tenth grade, all boys had six weeks of orientation in automotive, machine, and electric shops. Students wishing to continue chose from programs preparing them for beginning employment in about sixty vocations. Shop students could meet the University of Hawai'i's entry requirements by doing extra academic work.

We called Oz Stender "Mr. Sunshine" because of his pleasant expression; he was never cross. During school hours, Oz wore a shop uniform—blue pants and blue shirt —marking him for a blue collar career. Everyone liked him; he was a cordial and polite honor student, earning his first silver pin for scholastic achievement during his second year in school.

"Charles G. Clark, mathematics teacher, became my father image," Oz says. "He looked after me when other boys went home for the holidays, took me places, and encouraged my academic efforts."

Clark was not lenient. One evening, after washing pots, pans, and dishes in the school kitchen, Oz came back with a sandwich from the kitchen for a night's snack; this was a violation of the rules. "Charlie Clark gave me a demerit and ate the sandwich."

Clark left Kamehameha before Oz graduated, becoming principal of two other schools, an administrative assistant to the mayor, and State superintendent of education. Oz kept in touch with Charlie Clark throughout his life and then continued his friendship with Mrs. Clark.

By his junior year, the capitalist system had made a major change in Oz's life: He had the canteen concession, the newspaper route, and wrote love letters for classmates—all for pay. The boys school canteen now sold candy and ice cream, and Oz could keep the profits. Willing to take charge of what had happened to him and to work hard, he got up at 4:00 A.M. to do his paper route before the daily school schedule began. While classmates rode school buses to Honolulu Stadium to watch football games, Oz stayed on campus doing manual work, knowing all the while he was privileged and lucky for an opportunity to make good things happen in his life.

To stimulate postwar tourism, the Hawai'i Visitors' Bureau (HVB) staged its first Aloha Week and featured Hawaiian culture. Col. Kent volunteered to supply all the warriors and singing choruses the HVB needed.

Every boy could wear a loincloth, march, and throw a spear, but only members of Hui Oiwi, the cultural society, were allowed to play ancient games. Hui Kumulipo, the girls society, could do sit-down hulas and shake gourds—stand-up hulas were forbidden. Still, Col. Kent's dedication to Aloha Week legitimized Hawaiian culture at a school for Hawaiians.

He offered a busload of juniors to help welcome the *Lurline*, Matson Line's famous cruise ship, when it made its first trip to Hawai'i after the war on April 21, 1948. Weekly "Boat Day," when tourists arrived or departed, had been a festive pre-war tradition that attracted big crowds, and we were going to help reinitiate it.

Although paler than usual from being in the infirmary with chicken pox, I didn't want to miss this outing. Zoe Iungerich, a boys infirmary nurse, loaned me a bottle of dark brown leg makeup; women had painted their legs with this liquid during the war because nylon stockings weren't available. I covered myself and wore a loincloth wrapped around my waist and groin. We native warriors started from Waikīkī in out-rigger canoes and rowed into Honolulu Harbor as the *Lurline* docked. There were 709 passengers on the ship, and a crowd estimated at 100,000 watched it arrive.

Wearing their white uniforms and hats, the Royal Hawaiian Band played, waving crowds cheered, and passengers threw paper streamers. When some of the passengers started tossing coins, Geno dived into the water. Collecting them was easy: Once a coin hit the water it zig-zagged slowly down in a predictable pattern. If you held out your hand for a zag, you'd have the coin. I joined other "natives" in the water, happily showing off for the crowd when someone pointed out that I resembled a frightened squid.

Water was dissolving my makeup and my loincloth had come loose. I was a naked, white-looking boy surrounded by an expanding ring of brown water before the whole world!

Geno swam over, retrieved the sinking fabric, helped retie my *malo,* and motioned me over to catch coins with him. No one mocked me—not even during the bus ride back to school. I was just another Kamehameha boy on the road to manhood, assisted by classmates.

Teenagers from Samoa stayed on campus for a week when I was a senior. Being Polynesians, as are Hawaiians, their language sounded Hawaiian except for conso-nants not in our language; for instance, our word "aloha" was their word "*talofa.*"[8]

The Samoan young men wore lavalavas, a skirt wrapped around their waists to just below their knees; the young women also wore lavalavas that covered their upper bodies as well.

During their last night on campus, the Samoans presented an elaborate two-

---

[8] Prior to the arrival of the missionaries, the Hawaiian language was closer to that of other Polynesians in Tahiti, Samoa, and other islands from which Hawaiians emigrated. For example, Kamehameha was known as "Tamehameha." When they created a written language, missionaries simplified it, using all vowels and only seven consonants: h, k, l, m, n, p, w. A consonant is always preceded or followed by a vowel.

hour program in the school auditorium. Kamehameha Schools had never hosted anything like it: aboriginal dancing in the school auditorium! Samoan dancing was fast and graceful, and Tahitian dancing was at presto speed—extremely fast and vigorous —my, how they shook their *okole!*

For weeks after, students imitated the Samoans, feeling they could get away with doing so; they weren't dancing the forbidden Hawaiian hula or speaking Hawaiian.

Senior girls signed pictures in yearbooks with Samoan phrases they'd picked up: "Talofa" or "Fai fai le mu"—take it easy. Even though it was close to Hawaiian, they couldn't be punished for writing in Samoan.

I practiced until I could make a loud sound by briskly bringing my arms straight down so they slapped against lateral muscles, as was done in a Samoan dance.

The only time I saw Kamehameha students do the Hawaiian hula was after the Samoans left. Day students from our class stood and danced in the bus as we rode back to campus from our senior picnic. Our faithful driver, Dusty Rhodes, wouldn't report them. Yes, Rhodes was his name and "Dusty" was what the girls called him because his reddish hair was the color of Hawaiian red dirt. Driving these girls to and from school for five years, Dusty watched them grow into beautiful young ladies. Everyone knew the legend of Nona Beamer who was expelled from school for dancing the hula, but our girls knew that wouldn't happen to them; Dusty would keep their secret.

When I graduated in 1949, 5 percent of the boys in the school were pure Hawaiian; 60 percent were seven-eighths to half Hawaiian. Charles Parrent was gone, and Leonard Calvert was principal. Kamehameha had begun its new policy of quantity over quality. New students were chosen from among those who applied for interviews, not recruited as in the past.

In his report for the coming year (1949–1950), Calvert commented on the consequences of changes in the direction advocated by Senators Heen and Trask, Dr. Porteus the psychologist, and Dr. Prossner the educational consultant. Calvert wrote: "We're moving away from a highly selective student body . . . from a small and select campus-quartered faculty . . . from boarding school to day school status. . . . To serve a cross section of Hawaiian youth, expert help is needed in testing and screening applicants, in remedial teaching in handling them after selection, and in providing professional psychological services comparable to certain public schools. I recommend we retain a psychiatrist to work on special cases of maladjustment."

The Big Six and its policy of shape up or ship out had been deep-sixed; if misfits surfaced, well, Freudian techniques could be applied.

New president Harold W. Kent, using his flair for public relations, would obscure what was happening through his enthusiastic ideas. Students kept singing, "Kam is for its standards."

Experiences at Kamehameha became links to lifetime friends. In my senior year, I did a photo story about "The beautiful Sequeiras from the island of Maui"—brother Eldridge, at the boys school, and sisters Keakealani, Kaonoulu, and Kuulei at the girls school.

Our 1949 yearbook includes more photographs of Oz Stender, a smiling junior, in the seniors' "snap shot" section—than any senior. Oz was so well liked that we made him prominent in our school memories.

Oz and Kuulei were honor students who earned Silver Pins through their eleventh year. Were their minds occupied by other than schoolwork in their senior year? The answer appears in the 1950 senior class "Wills" in the school newspaper.[9]

Oswald Stender had just one thing to say: "I bequeath all my worldly possessions, of which I don't own any except my heart—I hope I own it—to my sole survivor Kuulei Sequeira."

Kuulei Sequeira had several possessions to pass on to classmates, including her love of the gym. She concluded with these words: "and to Stender, 'How Soon?'"

In 1950, the year Oz graduated, Col. Kent realized his ambition of the boys school being officially designated a military institute. The school had its first field maneuvers. Boarders repelled a dawn attack by a force of day students who attempted to capture the schools.

This new status allowed Kamehameha boys school students to compete with seniors from mainland military institutions for additional appointments to service academies. It allowed seniors to skip basic training and enter special training directly from enlistment date. After all, we could use real weapons, and some, like Oz, were sharpshooters. Since the Korean War was going on, Kamehameha graduates going into the military had a leg up on other enlistees and a faster trip to the action.

---

[9] Principal Bailey read students' senior wills, for they sometimes provided insight on his boys. George Kanahele '48, one of fourteen children, with no hope of being able to afford college wrote: "To nobody I will nothing and to everybody I will my sense of self sufficiency. I am not going to college and hope to find a job working for the city or county." George was my roommate during my ninth-grade year and taught me how to really study. The day after the school newspaper was distributed, he was doing what Mr. Bailey demanded: filling out college application forms. George went to Brigham Young University. He served two years as a Mormon missionary and when he returned, he could not afford a dormitory room so slept in a sleeping bag in the hills above BYU and showed up early in the men's dormitory to bathe, shave, and use the bathroom. He earned a PhD from Cornell University. He is recognized as one of the leaders of the Hawaiian Renaissance that began about the time Nona started the language program at Kamehameha. George died, in his seventies, while on a lecture tour in Samoa. The week prior he had gone skydiving for the first time in his life. He may have demonstrated self-sufficiency all his life, but teachers like Allen Bailey gave him sufficient direction.

Kamehameha boys were killed in places like Heartbreak Ridge, Seoul, and Inchon. First Sergeant Everett Ho, Oz's classmate and Don Ho's younger brother, was one.

Earnest Everett was so eager to have the number-one seat in the trumpet section that I sometimes heard him practicing my solos in front of his admiring friends. He was so good it was frightening. I thought of putting alum on his trumpet mouthpiece to make his lips pucker up and slow him down. The seat was his when I graduated.

We grew from boyhood to manhood and girls to womanhood, learning lifelong values in the environment Princess Pauahi made possible. When she initiated Kamehameha Schools to help her race survive, the Hawaiian population had declined to about 40,000.

At present, there are over 200,000 persons with Hawaiian blood in Hawai'i and about that many more on the mainland. Educated Hawaiians have become an integral part of life around them, marrying haole, Chinese, Japanese, Filipino, and other Hawaiians, creating a racial melting pot having common ethnic origins.

Princess Pauahi's flowers bloom abundantly.

Some of the princess's flowers: eight children, twenty-three grandchildren, one great-grandchild—the descendants of Tom and Julie-Bethe Hugo, class of 1949. The photo was taken adjacent to the school chapel after Tom's memorial service in December 2004. Julie-Bethe is in the second row, center. *Photo by Val Loh.*

# PART FIVE

# HAWAI'I CHANGES

>─┤◆>─○─<◆├─<

### CHAPTER 14

## *Off to College*

### 1947 through Early 1950s

I RETOOK algebra during the summer of my junior year to improve my grade for college applications. The course was taught adjacent to the Bishop Museum; though over soon, it was too late for a summer job at the pineapple cannery. I went to the museum and volunteered to operate its unstaffed darkroom. There was a large backlog of developing, printing, and enlarging to do and museum officials welcomed my free help.

Dr. Kenneth Emory and Dr. Peter Buck encouraged me to study anthropology with possibilities for a career in the Pacific trust territories acquired by the United States after World War II. Dr. Emory felt financial help might be available for schooling from the University of Washington. He took me on a photographic trip to the Marquesas Islands and talked of how important it was to help islanders protect their way of life against modern society's encroachment.

After that trip, Grandfather asked about my educational ambitions, and I told him. He was furious, announcing that I would become a derelict and marry an aborigine girl. He offered to pay my way to college if I'd abandon this wild idea. I went along, but money didn't come with it. He became ill and his resources subsequently went to supporting an institutionalized daughter.

An airplane flight to college separated me by nearly 6,000 miles from friends and relatives in Hawai'i. Short of money for the next semester's college tuition in the early 1950s, I wrote to Allen A. Bailey, now boys school principal, to explain why I was dropping out, so he wouldn't think it was for academic or disciplinary reasons.

I took care of two coal furnaces; one heated Hamilton College's infirmary, the other a fraternity house. It was steady work because artificial heat is needed during much of the school year in upstate New York. I anticipated signing on two more fraternity houses, but a natural gas company extended its services to campus and coal furnaces were converted to gas. My kitchen job in a fraternity house provided only room and board.

A little over a week later, a $450 check arrived from the Kamehameha Athletic Association to help me finish my sophomore year. Hired by a bank in a nearby city when a junior, I earned enough to graduate.

Because you can't drop a lei in the ocean from an airplane, I doubted if I would return to Hawai'i. I couldn't get a job there.

A t about this time, Nona and the Pele Dancers, her twelve-person hula troupe, were touring the forty-eight states under Music Corporation of America's sponsorship. Cleighton, her brother, Kamehameha School for Boys class of 1947, and Edwin Beamer, her cousin, class of 1946, took time off from Brigham Young University and the University of California to join her.

The hula was off limits at Kamehameha, but the famous author Pearl Buck arranged for Nona and her dancers to perform it in New York City's Carnegie Hall.

While living in Hawai'i, Pearl Buck became a good friend of Dambi Beamer, Nona's mother. Now back on the mainland, Pearl Buck found homes for Eurasian children who were treated harshly within their own culture. Having white fathers—often servicemen—and Chinese mothers caused them to be considered outcasts. She operated an East-West Center in New York and brought many children from China to her home in Bucks County, Pennsylvania.

Nona told me of the troupe's adventures: "The Duke of Windsor—former king of England—sat on the floor of his apartment with us in New York City. The dutchess wasn't home. We were teaching him to play the 'ukulele and sing 'Honi Ka'u'a Wiki Wiki—Kiss Me Quickly' in that distinguished voice of his. Oh, how we all laughed!"

The Pele Dancers were guests of Nona's parents' friend, Bing Crosby, at the San Francisco Opera. They became part of the Fred Waring Show—Fred Waring's "Pennsylvanians and Hawaiians" performing on stage and on the radio.

Both Beamer men stayed in New York City to finish school—Edwin at Juilliard School of Music and Cleighton at Columbia University, where he earned an advanced degree.

W ell educated and well traveled, Nona Beamer spoke intelligently and philosophically about Hawaiian culture during dance performance intermissions and wherever else she had a chance. Back in Hawai'i, her candor in saying things like the following caused trouble again with authority figures:

> Scholars have explored the reason for Hawaiians' decline: theological, sociological, and economical. But I think underlying it all was a basic lack of any relevant way for Hawaiians to communicate with one another.
>
> Their language was suppressed, their mythical figures destroyed.
>
> People are placed at a disadvantage when their language is taken away. It can make them feel insecure: Having learned to think in that language, it is difficult to be as adept in the language they are forced to use.
>
> The hula—Hawaiians' nonverbal language—was also forbidden.
>
> We believe that outstanding Hawaiian mythical figures and their activities must be preserved. They help define us as a people. Our stories belong to us and I believe we must treasure them.

Dressed entirely in white, Winona Beamer performs the "Aloha Chant." *Beamer family archives photo.*

Nona had returned to Hawai'i and was performing at the Kona Inn when a well-known haole minister accused Nona of being a witch. "Start with the group's name—Pele Dancers—the volcano goddess," he said. His preaching frightened one female dancer and her musician husband out of Nona's troupe.

The United Press International newspaper service distributed a photo-story of the "Kona Witch." In the picture, Nona looked very demure and wore a white bow in her hair. Deciding to answer the pastor's criticism publicly, Nona invited him to appear with her on KGMB-TV's *Life of the Land* program.

On the air, the pastor quoted Bible passages to the effect that anyone even mentioning ancient Hawaiian gods was committing sin. He said that in reciting some of the old chants, Nona might cause some to waver in their faith.

Nona silenced him with these words: "I suggest you make firmer Christians then."

There were no hard feelings. His wife and daughter subsequently attended Nona's Hawaiian classes where they learned the hula. The minister returned to the mainland to serve at a church in Boston—or maybe it was in Salem, Massachusetts.

Col. Kent initiated a new cooperative part-time program during the second semester of my senior year in 1949. This allowed classmates in both general and vocational education sequences to hold a part-time job. College preparatory students were excluded. It became the opening to a lifetime career for many.

Three months after my class graduated, Col. Kent hired Nona to begin a part-time Hawaiian studies program at Kamehameha Schools that included the hula. With Aloha Week making Hawaiian culture appear more acceptable, Kent accomplished what no one previously could.

In spring 1950, senior Oz Stender began working part-time in Hawaiian Electric Company's drafting department. It became his full-time job after graduation. From his work station he saw a grass ceiling: about 250 persons were in the drafting department, and many had been doing the same kind of work for twenty-five years. He would stagnate if he didn't change his life. He needed a college education but had no money; college loans didn't exist.

In addition, he had to tell Kuulei "When."

America was fighting the Korean War; G.I. Bill educational provisions were available to veterans, so Oz joined the U.S. Marine Corps. When the war ended he enrolled at the University of Hawai'i, took a part-time job as a baggage boy for Aloha Airlines, and on Christmas Day, 1953, he and Kuulei married. With his job at the airport and Kuulei's job as a secretary for Kamehameha Schools, their future seemed promising.

By now, Honolulu's Second Revolution was under way. Repression through a caste system, low wages, and inequity made it relatively easy for labor union organizers to attract members. On strike for six months in 1949, the ILWU showed the Big Five its muscle, stopping all shipping to and from Hawai'i, bringing the economy to a stand-still.

Political dynamics were set in motion by Jack Hall, shrewd labor organizer from San Francisco who brought the so-called Communist menace infiltrating Hawai'i's labor movement. Jack Burns, a former Honolulu policeman and Democratic cru-sader, used union power and set out to challenge the Big Five's fifty-year rule.

Once the union-backed Democrats took over in 1954, they began passing land reform laws with large-scale financial benefits accruing through closely connected politicians and land developers.

In 1959 Hawai'i became America's fiftieth state, and by 1962 Democratic leader Jack Burns was governor. Statehood brought in huge federal expenditures to be managed by Hawai'i's new rulers.

Racial democracy led by Democrats affected the Islands' legal and business communities; rapid political, economic, financial, and social changes completely undermined the Big Five's prewar oligarchic plantation system. Japanese and Chinese Democrats who Hawai'i's white rulers once considered as second-class citizens retal-iated by showing loyalty to their ethnic groups, class, local community origins, and old friends, avoiding the former haole bigshots as much as possible. Succumbing to new political pressure, private clubs such as the Pacific Club opened their doors to local nonwhites.

Burns' inner circle—William Richardson, Matsuo Takabuki, Hung Wo Ching—were rewarded with Bishop Estate trusteeships, as was Myron Thompson, Burns' gubernatorial assistant.

Jumbo-jet airplanes multiplied the number of visitors and investors from Japan, for whom Hawai'i became a favorite destination. Japanese investors were eager to buy choice property; the yen had doubled in value in relationship to the dollar, Japan's stock prices were high, interest rates in Japan were about 5 to 6 percent, and Tokyo banks based loans on the value of the collateral. Anybody at all who owned property in Hawai'i was profiting by the soaring rise in values.

From the 1950s to the 1980s, Governor Jack Burns' version of Democratic gov-ernment delivered generous social programs and expanded business opportunities. Hawai'i became more and more socialistic, with "government" becoming the largest employer.

As many of the Big Five became public companies, Island family control shifted to new owners outside Hawai'i. Racial makeup of the judiciary changed as nonwhite lawyers were appointed by Governor Jack Burns. He'd helped Democrats rise to power in the early 1950s by appealing to Hawai'i's "second-class" citizens, and it was time for him to deliver paybacks.

Leading the charge for top positions were Nisei war veterans—Americans of Japanese ancestry, AJAs—who President Roosevelt allowed to join the U.S. Army in World War II. A little over twenty years after the war, Americans of Japanese ancestry comprised 29 percent of Hawai'i's population but represented 40 percent of the State Senate, 50 percent of the House, and held three of Hawai'i's four congressional seats. They'd used education money from the government available to war veterans—the G.I. Bill—and were eager to succeed in business and government; they weren't docile stoop laborers, as had been their plantation-worker parents.

Heavy clothes worn in the tropical sun protected this female Japanese sugar worker from razor-sharp cane leaves. Field workers' descendants became Hawai'i's political and economic leaders after the 1950s. *Bishop Museum Archives photo, Ray Jerome Baker, photographer.*

CHAPTER 15

# Hawaiian Culture

## 1965 to Early 1970s

I N 1965, Kamehameha Schools offered Nona a full-time post teaching the Hawaiian language, and trustees gave her the go-ahead to develop a major Hawaiian studies department.

In its precedent-setting study for the Bishop Estate, Booz Allen Hamilton Inc. made a strong case for Kamehameha taking the lead in forwarding Hawaiian culture and heritage: "The distinctively Hawaiian aspects of the state's culture should be a matter of special concentration by Kamehameha Schools. This is a distinctive role no other institution is equally able to fill."

This consulting firm urged that Kamehameha "provide effective instruction in the Hawaiian language and prepare and also refine related materials for widespread elementary use."

Booz Allen Hamilton suggested that Kamehameha Schools help the Bishop Museum, the University of Hawai'i, and the Department of Public Instruction study such major questions as the following:

- What are the important values in Hawaiian culture?
- Which of these values should be preserved in modern American society?

The school was ready for what Nona Beamer had to offer. Students wanted to learn everything she could teach. Interestingly, 145 years earlier Nona's great-grandmother had gone into rooms in lava tubes to learn the "heathen" hula missionaries forbade.

The Beamers preserved their beliefs out of sight, not unlike Christians who practiced their faith in catacombs in Rome during the first century A.D.

With Nona's help, Kamehameha Schools brought Hawaiian culture into the daylight. She also linked it with modern-day Christianity, and students reacted enthusiastically.

Nona said, "I saw them spreading what they'd learned, enriching the world around them. Best of all, they were becoming proud to be Hawaiian. Engendering such pride and confidence is what Princess Pauahi had in mind."

G ladys Brandt, Kamehameha School for Girls principal, traveled to the island of Lāna'i for the Kamehameha Schools Glee Club's inaugural performance in animated form of the Kingdom of Hawai'i's motto, "The life of the land is preserved in righteousness."

Gladys was enthralled to see this used as a Bible lesson. She and Nona's father began as classmates at Kamehameha when they were six years old. She didn't know Nona was a *kahuna pule*—preacher—and said she could understand how a Hawaiian art form could be integrated into Christianity.

T he faculty asked Nona if her students would give a short Hawaiian presentation during its annual song contest intermission.

"We sang and danced to an island medley," she related. "The power the football boys exhibited in their dances finally moved the trustees to give us permission to do many more things I hoped we could.

"For example, Ula Noweo, an ancient warrior's calisthenics hula, is done with the body supported only by the palm of one hand and the side of one foot. It requires strength and stamina.

"When students performed the Oli Chant en masse in 1967, it was the first time for Hawaiians since the days of Kamehameha the Great, who died in 1819, the year before Christian missionaries arrived."

Nona helped students tap into a seemingly limitless storehouse of Hawaiian creative expression. Through her they realized ancient Hawaiians were a naturally poetic people. She explains in the following talk story:

I t is impossible to convey that starburst of Hawaiian imagery in English alone. Even the most careful student with only the tool of English becomes bewildered that a Hawaiian could react so emotionally to sonorous words sounding so simple.

A puzzled listener may sense the exquisite quality, but miss many paths the mind can follow with depths and the moods reached through a profusion of phraseology and beautiful similes.

Depending on the westerner's frame of mind, he or she may see more than one, maybe even several images when someone asks, "Do you see the tree?"

But when persons well versed in the Hawaiian language are asked the same question—"*Ua ike lāʻau?*"—they are aware of being asked a lot more than if he or she can "see a tree" and will react to ingenious and sophisticated use of figurative language. Among images and thoughts that question can trigger are:

- Do you see the tree with your eyes?
- Do you see the tree with your mind?
- Do you have an understanding of and a spiritual insight into the tree?
- Do you comprehend how the tree grows, anchored deep in the earth?

I told Nona that, as a boy in Kona, I learned that Hawaiian is a metaphoric language, rich chiefly in words expressing sensations and images.

She explained that the old language shows strength in things relating to everyday life and natural objects, reflecting its ancient origins when Hawaiians were close observers of nature. It has terms for every variety of clouds, for all species of plants on the mountains or fish in the sea, and is particularly copious with terms relating to ocean, surf, and waves.

"Old Hawaiians had an acute power of observation, a keen sense of humor, and the ability to make striking comparisons and similes. Often the indirect method is used, creating opportunities for double meanings and hidden allusions."

I responded by interpreting proverbs heard as a child:

- "A stranger is a stranger for only one day." After the first day, the stranger must do some work?
- "The fish will not look at bad bait; you can bring home only crabs." Bad methods bring only things easy to get.
- "The sand crab is small but digs a deep hole." Size does not limit accomplishment.

Nona's sons, Keola and Kapono Beamer, demonstrated to classmates what she taught them from childhood and were adept at encouraging fellow students to share their thoughts.

Nona said, "One day I asked Keola to talk with a student from Niʻihau. She had done well in her entrance examinations to Kamehameha Schools, but her oral reports were below standard. Keola listened to me explain the problem, then went to find the young woman. He took her to sit with him under a tree on the campus and they talked.

"A little later Keola came back to say, 'She's really bright, but very shy. She is unsure of using English in class. Let her make her Hawaiian class reports in Hawaiian. After graduation, she is going to return to Niʻihau, an island where the Hawaiian language is used exclusively. She plans to be a teacher.'"

Nona said, "As a result of Keola's visit with that young woman, her oral report grades soared. Speaking confidence gradually carried over to her classes in English and she blossomed.

"My eyes fill with tears when I see today's young people opening souls to their heritage. They want so much to live and share it."

CHAPTER 16

# The Lei

## 1967–1991

I was arranging notes at the speaker's podium as members of the Hawai'i Chapter of the Public Relations Society of America socialized in the Waikīkī Hotel's dining room. Then thirty-four years old, I was thrilled to be in Hawai'i for the first time since leaving at seventeen to go east to college. I was invited to describe my company's programs, which won the society's top honors in three out of four years.

Other men in the room were wearing aloha shirts; women were in casual dresses. It was the 1960s—Islanders dressed informally for business. I had on a double-breasted white linen suit, a light-blue shirt, and a Windsor-knotted cobalt blue silk tie—Kamehameha's colors.

At Kamehameha we were taught to dress for the occasion; my garb reflected the opinion that this was an important one. I shared my grandfather's fondness for tailor-made white linen suits.

I felt a tap on my shoulder; the program chairman said softly, "Someone in the hallway is asking for you."

By the elevator stood a Hawaiian man about my age holding a rectangular box. "Arthur?" he asked, seeing me walking toward him.

Responding to my nod, he handed me the box, saying, "Open this now—it is from the Bishop Estate for your speech. *Imua!*"

He left immediately. Inside the box were *'ilima* lei. Astonishing! With the lei and the Hawaiian word, he was letting me know that the Bishop Estate wished me to be proud to "go forward" before this audience.

I learned about these rare orange leis while growing up but had seen them only on the frame of a monarch's portrait in 'Iolani Palace on his or her birthday and placed on Princess Pauahi's memorial on Founders Day, her birthday. They connote high honor and authority.

'*Ilima* blossoms remain fresh for but a day; the flower is very delicate; a thousand blossoms are needed to string a single lei about an inch or so in diameter for a person of my height. This lei had three strands—nearly three thousand flowers—picked individually early that morning. Wrapped around it were lengths of aromatic green *maile,* a vine growing on trees in dense forests.

My hands trembled with excitement as I placed the lei over my head and onto my shoulders. The circle of '*ilima* almost reaches my waist; *maile* drapes below my suit jacket.

A murmur of surprise rose from local peers seeing me reenter—they recognized an '*ilima* lei's connotations. I sensed the intensity of hushed words traveling throughout the room: "The lei came from the Bishop Estate."

This lei demonstrated that Bishop Estate trustees were proud of gradu-

Metamorphosis of the Bishop Estate from a land-rich, cash-poor entity into having a larger endowment than Harvard or Yale University, or any other educational institution, occurred after 1971. At this time new trustee Matsuo Takabuki, far left, came on the board. Second from the left is Frank E. Midkiff; continuing left to right are Richard Lyman Jr., Hung Wo Ching, and Atherton Richards. Honolulu Star-Bulletin *file photo.*

ates' achievements. I'm describing tears-in-the-eyes kind of pride—Dr. Midkiff especially acted that way, which is why I surmise he arranged for the lei.

Such pride is a reciprocal feeling; the Kamehameha *'ohana* (family) is proud of its trustees, quickly coming to their defense if ever challenged. "Honor thy Bishop Estate trustees" is our eleventh commandment.

K amehameha contemporaries were experiencing productive years. Don Ho, entertainer, and Edmund Parker, "father of karate," were world famous, but no one was as big in business as former vocational student Oswald Stender.

The James Campbell Estate hired Oz as a property manager after he graduated from the University of Hawai'i, and he kept rising. By 1989 he'd been Campbell's chief executive officer for fourteen years, senior advisor to the Campbell Estate board of trustees, director of four financial trusts and two businesses—including Hawaiian Electric, where as a draftsman he had seen his grass ceiling.

He was being groomed to be a Campbell Estate trustee to replace his close friend and adviser Herbert C. Cornuelle, due to retire in 1990. Cornuelle, former president of Hawaiian Pineapple Company, was strikingly different from local executives born of old-time families. Reflective and soft-spoken, he encouraged new methods and bright people of any race. He was from the mainland where his father was a Presbyterian minister. Cornuelle studied philosophy and political science in college and continued to read avidly in both disciplines. Oz regarded Herb as his mentor.

From Cornuelle, Oz acquired the philosophy of "closing circles." Oz explained: "Everything we accomplish depends on freely given efforts of others from the past and present." Oz treated humanity as an end in itself, never as a means only. Closing circles means helping others along the way.

The $2 billion Campbell Estate is a taxable entity with very tight restrictions. All earnings must be distributed at the end of each year, and management is challenged yearly to create new earnings, starting from zero. Campbell's sole purpose is to make rich heirs richer while positioning this limited-term trust to provide a big payoff when it terminates early in the twenty-first century.

Oz was known as an amiable manager and reliable person who made clever and rewarding deals. Using his tax acuity, he helped popularize Hawaiian property exchanges, identified by the IRS code of "1031."

His first such deal involved American Factors, a former Big Five company now listed on the New York Stock Exchange as "AmFac." In a year when forecasts showed it needed to earn more cash for a reasonable distribution to stockholders, an AmFac officer asked Oz if Campbell Estate would buy some of its Maui property—Kā'anapali Beach land and a nearby shopping center. Campbell would have to find $25 million for the transaction. Oz told me how he handled it.

Chevron leased 100 acres on Campbell Estate property it had always wanted to buy. I told my contact at Chevron they could have it for $25 million. "We'll have it appraised," he answered.

"Have it appraised, but know that $25 million is not negotiable. Let's have a swap: You buy the shopping center and trade with us for the 100 acres to avoid taxes."

Hughes Air Craft had always wanted to buy the acreage it leased from Chevron and Chevron wanted to sell but didn't because of tax implications.

I suggested a three-way swap: Hughes bought the Maui land from AmFac, traded it with Chevron, and Chevron traded with Campbell. The result was that Campbell Estate had the Maui land, Hughes owned the land it wanted, Chevron got its land, and AmFac shareholders received a good dividend.

O ffered the Kamehameha Schools Bishop Estate appointment in 1989, Oz talked with Cornuelle about how his background and experience might benefit the estate, even though he was reluctant to leave Campbell. "I realize Kamehameha Schools Bishop Estate has the potential to help more people," Oz noted.

"Do what you have to do," Herb answered, so Oz took the Kamehameha Schools Bishop Estate job. The money initially was a bit better than he was making but would be comparable once Oz became a Campbell Estate trustee. It was a sideways move.

B y this time I could afford regular trips from New York to Hawai'i to visit my mother and cousins and to share in family activities. After Uncle Richard Lyman died in 1988, I attended Founders Day ceremonies with Aunt Jane, his widow; she reserved a seat for us in the "trustees' row" at on-campus school ceremonies. Aunt Jane and I were in the trustees' section during ceremonies at the Royal Mausoleum in 1991. Oz stood with us, having replaced Uncle Richard as a trustee.

## CHAPTER 17

# Oz Becomes a Trustee

## 1990

O z  BROUGHT  thirty years of property development and management experience to the Bishop Estate boardroom. He familiarized himself with how the estate operated under Internal Revenue System guidelines for a charitable, tax-exempt entity. These were different than at Campbell, where earnings were taxable.

He explained to me that Bishop Estate land revenue had to be "passive" rental income. If it used debt to improve land, revenues were taxable. If the Bishop Estate sold masses of lots, the Internal Revenue Service would tax the sales proceeds. To avoid this, the estate leased raw land to developers who then subdivided it, built an infrastructure, and sold houses having long-term leases to be paid to the estate.

Homeowners bought the house, but the estate owned the land on which it stood. The IRS qualified lease rental income as "passive." Leases were low and homeowners could invest more money in a house than if buying the lot as well as the house.[1] The Federal Housing Authority (FHA) and other lenders required the fixed lease rent period to exceed the mortgage term. By the early 1980s, the Bishop Estate owned about 75 percent of all leased lots in Hawai'i.

The IRS allowed the Bishop Estate to create for-profit subsidiaries; one of the outcomes was the Royal Hawaiian Shopping Center, fronting Waikīkī

---

[1] The low lease payments for a fixed period of time had the unintended result of lowering the appraisal value of the lessor's leasehold interest. Hawai'i's lease-to-fee conversion law adopted decades later substantially reduced the appraised value of the estate's interest.

hotels. The estate borrowed funds to develop it through Kamehameha Development Corporation, one of the estate's taxable subsidiaries.

I learned from Oz that the Bishop Estate worked for years to be designated a tax-exempt educational institution as described in section 501 (c) (3) of the IRS Tax Code. If considered a foundation, the estate would have to pay a minimum of 6 percent tax on earnings, exceeding the cost to operate the schools.

In 1969, the year it received that favorable ruling, a "foundation tax" for the Bishop Estate would have been $24 million. Eventually this tax would exhaust the estate's resources.

A foundation is treated as an ordinary business corporation in that it pays income taxes on profits it earns. The IRS has this rule so that if a charitable trust develops its lands, it will not take improper advantage of private landowners who pay federal taxes on profits and capital gains from land development. Using its Washington, D.C., political resources, the Bishop Estate helped to pass an amendment to the Internal Revenue Code allowing educational institutions certain tax-exempt income, even if using debt to develop land from which the income is generated.

With the new IRS rulings, the estate entered an entrepreneurial mode using its infusion of cash from leaseholder land conversions. After studying estate operations, Oz prepared recommendations to share with trustees. He was accustomed to discussing matters openly with Campbell's trustees; all were chief executive officers of substantial companies. He expected similar congenial give-and-take with his new colleagues.

O z handed his memo to each of the trustees. They glanced at the first sheet and sat impassively. Looking at expressionless faces, Oz sensed a sinking uncertainty, as if it was Hell Week at a university and he, a college freshman, was assigned to present manifest knowledge to three worldly seniors and the sophomore in charge of freshman hazing.

The three seniors—Matsy Takabuki, Judge William Richardson, and Myron (Pinky) Thompson—were lame ducks in a sense; Matsy and Richardson would retire in 1994; Pinky would do so the following year.

Henry Haalilio Peters was appointed a Bishop Estate trustee in 1984 when he was thirty-three years old and is destined to remain a trustee for thirty-seven years. Henry was a tremendously able and charismatic politician. Elected to the State House of Representatives at age twenty-three, he became speaker of the House, one of the State's most important positions; he continued to hold this job during the first two years of his trusteeship. He'd graduated from Waipahu High School and Brigham

Young University, Provo, Utah, and had been in the army reserve. He was appointed to a government-funded job, the Wai'anae Model Cities Project, from which he made his political climb. At one time he seemed destined for the ministry, but physical presence and political acumen propelled him into the hurly-burly world of politics.

Over 6 feet tall, athletic, and powerfully built, Henry towered above some Asian-American legislators by as much as a foot. He had a powerful voice and an animated face. I remember his quizzical look, as if he were about to ask you a penetrating question. Many described Henry as "formidable." He was determined not to have anyone try to put anything over on him.

Matsuo Takabuki was a Nisei—a second-generation Japanese resident. Along with Myron Thompson, William Richardson, and Hung Wo Chung, he had helped make Hawai'i's second revolution possible. Rejected initially by those not wanting a person of Japanese ancestry on the board of a Hawaiian trust, Matsy became the architect and developer of the Kamehameha Schools financial future.

Pinky Thompson, a social worker for much of his life, had been an assistant to Governor John Burns.

Judge William Richardson had been well thought of as a lawyer and judge and was known for his gentle humor and impartiality. The Richardson School of Law at the University of Hawai'i is named for him.

S tanding in front of this impressive group, Oz began by recommending a five-year plan and coupling a reporting system with a strategic and financial plan so decision making and operations monitoring can be more efficient.

Trustees shook their heads, almost in unison.

He suggested an investment strategy to guide trustees in managing activities. The strategy was in Matsy Takabuki's head. Expressions he saw in the room indicated that it would stay there.

To meet the financial needs of the schools, Oz recommended developing a parallel expense and operating plan that would forecast expenses for five years.

There was more head shaking.

The trustees continued sitting stiffly. Their silence put Oz on edge. He expected to exchange views from the memorandum, not to read its formal, for-the-record style of writing. He gulped down a glass of water, waiting to see if a pause would initiate some response. When it didn't, he continued reading: "I acknowledge that neither the estate nor the schools had the luxury of taking the time to do financial planning due to negative cash flows in earlier years. With the heavy infusion of capital from leasehold conversions since 1987, we can now focus on asset management and school expansion planning."

There was still no reaction, except from Henry Peters, his hazer. Henry smiled sarcastically. It reminded Oz of comedian Rodney Dangerfield, except that Oz felt *he* was the one getting "no respect." The way Henry was looking at him made Oz uneasy, but he continued: "Observations on public relations are in the context of my close ties to Kamehameha Schools and the Hawaiian community. We can improve a negative external view of the estate by integrating with the community."

When preparing those words, he had thought, *I helped people learn to love the Campbell Estate. Campbell's mission is to create more wealth for wealthy persons; it has no built-in compensating values. Creating community support should be easier here. Kamehameha Schools Bishop Estate has the heartwarming mission of educating Hawaiian children.*

He continued reading: "It's difficult for the Hawaiian community to respond to the estate's critics and to be supportive when communications between the estate and its public are totally lacking. While higher visibility may uncover other critics of the estate or of the schools, in the overall, we will gain a greater number of loyal friends who will diffuse the critics."

Everyone gave him a fishy-eyed look when he said "critics" and "criticism."

He mentioned improving the image. Henry Peters spoke up in a cutting tone, "We accomplished that by changing the Bishop Estate name to Kamehameha Schools Bishop Estate."

"Why did you do this?" Oz asked.

"A consultant recommended placing the school's identity with our own Bishop Estate identity to soften negativity."

Such superficiality angered Oz. He slapped his memo down on the table, looked around the table, and raised his voice: "If we have a public relations problem, let's fix it, not hide it. You can't fool the public."

There was no response.

Reporters continued to refer to the two as separate entities: When describing money and power, they referred to the Bishop Estate; for articles about education, they used Kamehameha Schools. The acronym KSBE was sometimes used for brevity, but "Bishop Estate" was always cited to connote clout.

O z confided that he would have resigned after that first meeting if the estate had not recently adopted an age limit of 70 for trustees. Frank Midkiff was a trustee until he died at 96 and was replaced by Henry Peters. Richard Lyman remained a trustee until he died at 86. Three of the trustees would soon retire and perhaps replacements would be amenable to changes.

He wanted to correct structural problems: No chief executive officer served as a central manager and informational source. In-house staff reported directly to a lead trustee; other trustees were out of the loop. When a matter came to the table for decision making, it was pretty much a done deal.

At first he believed that staff reports coming to him were balanced, objective, and reviewed. Then he learned that reports were dictated by lead trustees. Those who made deals supervised the investments. If a deal went sour, they covered their tracks.

Oz wanted investment and real estate departments to have standards and prepared a written policy no one followed.

$O_z$ acquired the practice of preparing notes and memos while at Campbell and continued to do this now. Believing those running a trust should prepare records replete with information, he wrote down what he did, his thought process, and the rationale for making a decision. Whether a decision was right or wrong, he had a basis for review.

He explained: "I believe it is someone else's money; what I am doing needs to take that into account. Whoever is going to watch me should know what I know, so I put information down in writing. The Bishop Estate never documented or detailed anything. Look at the minutes; you won't know what we did in those meetings. When my wife Kuulei was a secretary to the trustees, she was required to write down everything. The new gang gave that up."

Left to his own devices, Oz learned all he could from Matsy Takabuki. Oz shared many similar investment concerns while with Campbell and knew many people Matsy worked with on the mainland.

As another of Hawai'i's major landowners, the Campbell Estate was threatened by socialistic aspects of land reform. Democrats came to power by declaring residential leasehold land should be turned into fee-simple land.

The State's Leasehold Conversion Act, aimed particularly at the Bishop Estate, forced it to sell land under homes. Public policy ignored the primary concept behind the leases—so homes would be more affordable—and also the historical context in which these leases were made, which was at a time when lease-to-fee conversion law wasn't contemplated.

The Legislature used the power of eminent domain to redistribute land ownership in Hawai'i, and the court set the price.

The Bishop Estate resisted the State's involuntary conversion of its residential leases. Losing in the federal district court, it appealed to the Ninth Circuit Court and won. The State appealed, and the United States Supreme Court overruled the Ninth Circuit Court.

"We may live to regret the day we heard about the Hawaiian land reform," stated an article in the *Wall Street Journal*. It explained that the U.S. Supreme Court decreed public use was no longer a requirement for the awesome power of condemnation under the Fifth Amendment. "The real issue is that a well-intentioned court has just opened this sphere to a host of unforeseeable harassments."

In the first case tried under Circuit Court, a jury returned a price of 18 percent of the current fee simple market value of the lot.

During a speech to a district council of civic clubs, Matsy Takabuki explained that the formula set in a legislative session meant that a lot having a value of $55,000 could be worth about $4,000 under its method of valuing the present worth of the lessor's interest. "The movement against private property is only beginning in the state legislature. In votes lessees greatly outnumbered the lessors; the survival instinct of those in politics is very strong."

Condo owners also wanted lease conversion rights; by the 1990s the estate owned land under 113 condominiums containing about 13,000 units. (I add parenthetically that this situation continued until early 2005, when Honolulu's new mayor Mufi Hanneman erased the fourteen-year-old mandatory lease-to-fee conversion law from the books. By a tight vote, the Honolulu City Council voted to repeal the law and sent the measure to the mayor for his signature. This law, known as Ordinance 38, used the city's powers to condemn the land beneath condominium buildings to help leasehold owner-occupants buy the land.)

While at Campbell, Oz recommended an early exit from the housing market to capture value while possible. He wanted the Bishop Estate to be out of the residential leasehold business by the end of the 1990s and kept repeating that to the other trustees.

In essence, the battle between the trust and lessees was over who received the big payoff for thirty years of appreciation in land values—renter or landowner? At Oz's suggestion, the Bishop Estate offered to sell its condo leases at a lower price if it could share in the profits made from subsequent resale. This met with a cold reception from lessees wanting to buy low and sell high.

Oz said that sales of fees for lots dating back to the late 1970s were about $600 million. "A more realistic pricing system would have yielded more than $2 billion. That's what the owners turned around and sold their fees for. We tracked the resales." Politicians claimed land reform was intended to lower the cost of housing for entry-level home buyers. It wound up benefiting lessees in upper-class neighborhoods.

Trustees' fees were still based on the fixed percentage of qualified income receipts established by State law back in 1943. When land sales caused the estate's receipts to increase more than tenfold, newspapers drew attention to what trustees were now being paid. In 1980, trustees earned an average of $125,000 apiece. Seven years later their commissions rose to $926,000 each. In fiscal 1990, the trustees earned just over $1 million each.

The commission schedule did not change; the increase was due to the estate's spiraling revenues from sales forced on it.

Matsy invested $570 million from the land sales under single-family units to generate revenues to meet educational needs in perpetuity. He redeployed some assets into high-yielding investments with real appreciation potential.

Because of the continuing threat of condemnation, he believed reinvestment in Hawai'i was imprudent. The estate retained Cambridge Associates for investment help outside of Hawai'i. Cambridge advises many major educational institutions on traditional investments in marketable securities and financial assets.

The Bishop Estate formed an investment relationship with some of the largest educational organizations in the country, including Duke University, the University of Texas, Harvard University, and Yale University. It worked with the McArthur Foundation, one of America's largest foundations. In one way or another, the estate became involved with many investment banking firms in New York City.

Having the highest credit rating a charitable institution could have, the Bishop Estate could issue its own commercial paper considerably below prime rate. It "arbitraged" interest rate differentials to investment entities:

- The estate offered its partners a loan at the rate a bank would charge should partners do their own financing.
- Then the estate obtained the money from a lender at its preferred rate.
- The difference, or spread, became tax-exempt income to the estate.
- It negotiated commitment fees and equity kickers for credit enhancements.

When leases on urban land in Hawai'i expired, the estate took them over; it managed shopping centers, commercial office buildings, and industrial property.

The Bishop Estate's prime jewel is 16 acres of Waikīkī land on which sit the Royal Hawaiian and Sheraton Waikīkī Hotels and the estate's own Royal Hawaiian Shopping Center. In arbitration, the land next door was valued at $1,200 a square foot, or over $52 million an acre. On this basis, the estate's Waikīkī land is valued at $832 million.

Matsuo Takabuki was an investment star known as "a home run hitter."

KSBE invested in Centre Re Insurance Company in Bermuda. In about three years, Zurich Life Insurance of Switzerland bought the interest of the financial investors, including J. P. Morgan and the KSBE. The estate exited with a substantial gain.

J. P. Morgan later introduced the estate to another major investment opportunity in catastrophic insurance in Bermuda involving Marsh & McLennan and several investment banking groups. The estate took a share in the company. In less than a year it made an initial public offering, first on NASDAQ, and later on the New York Stock Exchange. This resulted in another big payoff.

It invested in Saks Fifth Avenue with Invesco, an investment banking firm, and Saudi investor Prince Alsaud. It exited through a public offering. It was another home run.

The Simon group, headed by William Simon, former secretary of the treasury, negotiated to buy a controlling interest in the American Security Bank in Honolulu from a Hong Kong group. KSBE was the major financial investor in the deal and exited with a substantial gain.

It invested with Simon in other U.S. banks. This affiliation created the opportunity for KSBE to participate as the American component of the Xiamen International Bank in the Fujian Province of the People's Republic of China.

G oldman Sachs, Wall Street's premier private investment bank, was KSBE's principal source for placing short-term and money-market funds. Goldman Sachs asked if KSBE would be interested in acquiring a partnership for several hundred million dollars. Several partners had retired and withdrawn their partnership investment, and new money from KSBE was welcomed.

Goldman Sachs is involved in fixed income, equity, commodities, investment banking, and asset management. It offered the opportunity for immediate redeployment and diversification of KSBE's portfolio in various types of financial assets with highly competent professional management.

The nature of an investment banking firm, using debt to conduct its business, didn't allow KSBE's investment in the firm to be tax exempt. But by using one of its subsidiaries for the income, gains became taxable at a corporate level and dividends from the subsidiary to the estate, its parent, continued to be tax exempt.

Goldman Sachs' partners reinvest a portion of their gain each year in the partnership in order to maintain the percentage of their interest in the firm. This conformed to Matsy's goal of obtaining good current yield plus an annual increase in the investment capital; it assured growth of the corpus and an increasing current yield while the corpus grew. The needs of today would be met with current yield, while the growth of the principal corpus would take care of tomorrow.

Bringing Goldman Sachs and the Bishop Estate together was one of Matsuo Takabuki's crowning achievements as a trustee.

In collaboration with the McArthur Foundation, Duke University, and the University of Texas, the Bishop Estate picked an investment banker and staff willing to risk its own capital. It created a private investment banking firm that located and analyzed deals, and the nonprofit institutions considered private placement ventures firsthand.

Trustees were chary about revealing financial dealings, considering this information as classified. But Oz persuaded Matsy to give a speech in 1991 to school and estate employees at a service award ceremony.

Takabuki covered his twenty-year history with the estate, beginning in 1971 when the Bishop Estate was operating at a deficit, as it had in prior decades. He spoke with pride about the next century being "the Pacific Area," the estate's meaningful contacts in Japan and the People's Republic of China, and of the estate being a Hawaiian catalyst for Asian entities within the Pacific Basin.

Members of the press deluged the Bishop Estate offices for copies of Matsuo Takabuki's speech, believing "the secrets were out." They weren't. History was out; the secrets were still in Matsy's head. Oz felt fortunate that many were shared with him.

With the assets that Matsy helped build, Oz began to speak publicly of the princess's estate growing into a $56 billion organization: "As a result of a conservative 5 percent annual return on investment, this would yield $1.4 billion yearly for education before the year 2033."

CHAPTER 18

# Educational Vision

## 1970–1993

O z ADMIRED how Trustee Myron (Pinky) Thompson expanded Kamehameha Schools educational reach. From years of social work, Pinky realized Hawaiian students scored academically lower than other local ethnicities. To change this, he helped launch a five-year experimental program in 1970 known as KEEP—the Kamehameha Early Education Program. Students improved IQ and reading-achievement scores right from KEEP's beginning. KEEP was in its twentieth year when Oz became a trustee.

KEEP's discovery of more effective ways to assist kindergarten through third-grade children in learning has been described by educational psychologists as one of the most outstanding educational research projects in the world. Children learned to comprehend reading through a "talk story" approach instead of traditional methods of sounding out words and memorizing letters and rules.

During its tenth anniversary year, about 250 visitors from Asia, Europe, the Pacific Rim, and the United States observed activities at KEEP. The Ford Foundation sent a group of nationally known educators and researchers to examine KEEP's reading program for minority education programs.

By then it operated as the Kamehameha Educational Research Institute. "KERI," as it was known, included parent/infant and preschool programs because its studies showed that 34 percent of Hawaiian families with children under five had social or economic needs that might affect their babies.

A disproportionately large number of Hawaiian women, 27 to 35 percent, didn't receive prenatal care, particularly during their first three months of pregnancy when medical attention is of key importance. This contributed to preschoolers' learning problems.

Hawaiian girls had the highest teenage pregnancy rates in the state. KERI's studies showed that teenage mothers tend to have lower education, poorer nutritional habits, little self-esteem, more family stress, and less money. Their children are likely to have problems in pre- as well as early schooling years.

KERI's curriculum prepared children to do better in school and allowed Kamehameha Schools to reach a large number of Hawaiian children. Its single campus could barely handle 6 percent—2,600 students—from a potential beneficiary population of 34,000 children.

To demonstrate KEEP's applicability to public schools throughout the Islands, Kamehameha changed its entry-level school's name to Kamehameha Elementary School. Previously it was called "Kamehameha Preparatory School" because the students were automatically eligible for the intermediate and high school on Kapālama Heights. Admission to the prep school had been based on tests and potential students' ranking according to ability, speech, behavior, and motivation. In many ways, admission standards reflected the high academic model introduced by Dr. Barnes.

Admission to Kamehameha Elementary School was instead based on random selection by lottery, giving everyone an "equal chance"—just as everyone buying a lottery ticket has an "equal chance" to win a big-money pot. As a result, the student body was comparable to a public school in which students have wide ranges of abilities.

Oz explained, "Those who passed a screening process less rigorous than the old prep school's test were included in a pool for quotas by district. If fifty applicants applied from a district but only five were eligible from that district, forty-five families would be disappointed and the brightest kids might be excluded."

The intermediate and high schools on Kapālama Heights still used a selective admission process. Movement from Kamehameha's elementary to its intermediate school was not automatic. More sixth graders were in the elementary school than the seventh grade could accommodate, and the admissions department admitted those who tested highest. This meant that 33 percent of the sixth-grade students admitted by lottery made it into Kamehameha Schools' seventh grade and 67 percent were kicked out.

Oz learned about this and urged trustees to change procedures. They said, "Too late," but he brought up the subject relentlessly. The elementary school went to selective admissions instead of a lottery in 1991—a partial answer.

After holding meetings and workshops with teachers, staff, and administrators over a two-year period, Dr. Chun, president of Kamehameha Schools, developed a "bottom-up" educational plan. It contained student outcome measures, with resources identified to meet the outcomes. He submitted it to the trustees in 1990; they wanted to keep it on hold for the new trustees to consider. He updated and resubmitted it in 1993; this new plan also sat on their shelf.

O z thought often about quitting. Out of frustration, he decided to walk away from the Bishop Estate job in 1992. He'd missed the chance to be a Campbell Estate trustee when Herb Cornuelle retired, but another Campbell trustee would retire in 1993. Campbell Estate beneficiaries and employees who knew Oz was unhappy urged him to come back. He told this to mentor Herb Cornuelle, who replied, "You became a Bishop Estate trustee because you felt you wanted to make changes. You're frustrated because you can't make headway. But three new trustees are soon to be appointed. If judges pick the right people, you can create change."

In 1994 Matsy Takabuki and Judge Richardson would go; their replacements would be selected in December 1993. Pinky Thompson would reach 70 a year later. Oz thought doing something so the right people would be picked to replace them was a grand idea.

Alumni in the legal and trust fields helped Oz prepare selection standards and a job description to assist supreme court justices in making their selection. He wanted Hawai'i's most qualified people to become nominees. If the new trustees were dedicated to some of the changes he advocated and kept momentum going, KSBE would be a far different entity after the 1990s were over.

By the time Oz and his group finished their work, another person had filled the position open for him at Campbell Estate.

Oz's group gave the justices their recommendations and received a letter back stating, in a sense, "We know what we are doing." Oz erred in interpreting the judges as meaning that they knew what to do for the good of the schools. What they meant was, "We know how to ingratiate ourselves with the Democratic Party."

O z was extremely optimistic shortly before the two new trustees were appointed. He told me he might seek to become chairman of the board, but only if the trustees agreed to have a strategic plan for the estate and only if they supported his efforts to communicate openly with the public.

The Bishop Estate had created two classes of Hawaiians: those who went to Kamehameha Schools and those who didn't. The Islands have at least 200,000 Native Hawaiians who didn't go to Kamehameha Schools, and many resent being left out. Oz felt it was vital to bring the two groups together.

He wanted Kamehameha to run public schools in predominately Hawaiian communities. Discussing this with Department of Education officials, he suggested that DOE pay the cost of educating non-Hawaiian children in the same manner as the U.S. military does for its dependent children attending public schools in Hawai'i: The State might reimburse Kamehameha Schools an amount per student to teach non-Hawaiian children.

He believed the will's insistence on Protestant employees and the subject of unions were hurdles that could be cleared.

Oz set the stage for a "New Kamehameha Schools and Bishop Estate" through an active speaking schedule. He predicted what Kamehameha Schools could become by the year 2028, on its 150th anniversary. His spiritual link to the princess is reflected in these two sentences: "As trustees, we must speak for students not yet born and for the Hawaiian people. We are charged with the responsibility of ensuring that Kamehameha Schools help every Hawaiian on earth achieve his or her potential through education."

He foresaw Kamehameha Schools becoming a worldwide influence in the field of educating children. In thirty-five years, its trustees might include prestigious international business and educational leaders.

Oz was specific and all-encompassing about changes that he envisioned:

- Sixteen trustees from around the world paid only a fee for attendance at each meeting.
- School operations involving early education, focused on prenatal, postnatal, traveling preschools, and parent/guardian counseling.
- Special education programs on the Kapālama campus with upgraded programs for students with IQ levels of 120 and above and scores in the upper quartile of national tests of achievement.
- Psychological counseling and positive image/self-esteem building for special needs and at-risk children with social, learning, and dysfunctional problems.
- Satellite schools operating in partnership with Hawai'i's Department of Education and school campuses located on each island.
- A preschool program expanded into every community having a minimum of fifty persons of Hawaiian ancestry. Hawaiian language immersion and vocational educational centers on each island.

- Financial aid funds—vouchers—provided to Hawaiian students attending trade schools, special needs schools, other preparatory schools, plus post–high school financial grants.
- Grants for activities to help communities address social needs.

He looked forward to sharing these ideas with new trustees selected by criteria he and alumni helped develop. Feeling he'd soon be rewarded for his patience, Oz confided, "I know the princess will be pleased."

# PART SIX

# ABANDONED CHILDREN

>—⊷>─○─⊰⊷—<

CHAPTER 19

## Dickie and Lokelani Appointed

1994–1995

O z WAS driving from work to his home in Kailua when he heard the bizarre news on his car radio: The State Supreme Court had appointed Dickie Wong and Lokelani Lindsey as trustees. Aghast, Oz almost swerved off the road. Governor Waihee enjoyed telling jokes, and these appointments seemed bad ones.[1]

R ichard Wong had a twenty-six-year career in State politics and owned a real estate company. He'd served in the State Senate for eighteen years, thirteen as president; and was in the State House of Representatives for eight years. He was the quiet and effective former business agent and assistant division director of the United Public Workers' union.

After attending Maryknoll, a small Catholic school across the street from the Punahou campus, Dickie received a degree in social work from the University of Hawai'i. Shortly before his appointment to the Bishop Estate, some of my cousins began noticing Dickie at Central Union Church, the well-known Congregational Church attended by many missionary descendants. He was now married to Marni Stone, an attractive blond who resembled Punahou girls of his era.

---

[1] While at an official event of the Daughters of Hawai'i at 'Iolani Palace, Governor Waihee greeted my mother quite loudly with this statement: "Hualani, you are hanging in Hilo." That stopped all conversation. Then he explained—relieving my mother that he was not announcing a forthcoming event where she would be featured. The governor had just returned from visiting the Lyman Family Museum, now a state museum. According to him, Ruth Hualani Lyman Rath, now in her eighties, was "the identical image of her great-grandmother, missionary ancestor Sarah Joiner Lyman, whose portrait 'is hanging' in the Hilo museum."

Known as a keen negotiator, a person who could quietly get things accomplished, Dickie's calm demeanor was a contrast to the more volatile Henry Peters.

$M$arion Lokelani Lindsey, the first woman appointed to the Bishop Estate board, was known as a strong-willed former gym teacher, bartender, dishwasher, and tour bus driver. She dropped out of school at the age of sixteen to marry a mainland serviceman, had a child, finished high school, and earned a bachelor's degree in physical education from Brigham Young University–Hawai'i. At the age of thirty-seven, she obtained a master's degree in Pacific Island studies from the University of Hawai'i. After having two children, she divorced and married Stephen Lindsey, a cowboy with five children. Stephen Lindsey was Governor Waihee's relative and good friend.

Lokelani Lindsey worked for twenty years as a school administrator. She was Maui district superintendent for ten years and an unsuccessful Democratic candidate for mayor of Maui.

She had a mercurial personality—it charmed some and alienated others. Some people loved her, others hated her guts.

Oz always referred to her as "Mrs. Lindsey," having real difficulty in using her Hawaiian name of Lokelani, which means "a rose from heaven." Most persons called her "Lokelani," in Hawai'i's informal style.

$I$ met Lokelani Lindsey at the Royal Mausoleum Founders Day ceremonies shortly after she was elected. Tall, solid, with a shock of hair, she gave me a politician's greeting: big smile, firm handshake, and an energetic "glad to meet you." She exuded friendliness; I thought it was great for the justices to have finally appointed a woman trustee.

Hawai'i is a matriarchal society: Women are bosses in most households, and they raise children, control money, and run the household. High living costs make an income-producing wife a fact of life in civilized Hawai'i.

Looking and acting like an authority figure, Lokelani moved quickly, becoming lead trustee on education and then supervising communications as well.

$O$z served on the board of other independent schools, and he invited Mrs. Lindsey to join him in workshops sponsored by the Hawai'i Association of Independent Schools. Giving her a copy of the "National Association of Independent Schools Principles of Good Practice for Independent School Trustees," he suggested that she attend an NAIS conference on governance.

"It is unnecessary. I have thirty years of educational experience," was her answer.

Mrs. Lindsey would repeat that phrase to Oz whenever he offered a suggestion about Kamehameha Schools. "She was like a broken record," he said. "She kept reminding me I didn't have her 'thirty years of educational experience.'"

It was was not long before Mrs. Lindsey would make major changes. Oz detected it from her frequent criticisms of Dr. Chun, Kamehameha Schools president, whom she described as "unqualified," and from her extreme negativity about the community outreach programs.

Dr. Chun was beloved by students and alumni and respected by teachers for his management accumen.[2] He used to run up and down the school stairs until Lokelani moved into an office on campus, directly opposite his. His pep faded after that.

She wanted Rockne Freitas to operate the schools under her direction. Rockne, from Kamehameha's class of 1963, earned all-pro honors with the Detroit Lions, played football with the Lions for eleven years, and then earned a PhD in education at the University of Hawai'i.

L arceny can start through careless thoughtlessness. An employee who takes business property such as pens and note pads home for personal use may pad an expense account. Once that becomes habitual, progression to other forms of self-enrichment may slip in because it's so easy to do. Mrs. Lindsey's exploitation of Kamehameha Schools Bishop Estate began with "pooper scoopers."

She'd been invited to represent the island of Maui as a *pā'ū* rider in the Aloha Week parade. She would wear a long gown and rose lei, and her horse would be festooned with blossoms.

She told school officials she wanted students walking behind her to shovel up horse droppings and carry them in a bucket. Years of educational experience should have made her aware of how humiliating the public nature of this task would be to teenagers. No one volunteered.

She insisted the school provide this service, so members of a music appreciation club became "pooper scoopers." Instead of paying the club herself, she ordered the estate to write a check for $100.

Lokelani needed a building permit to remodel a beach house she'd bought from the Bishop Estate. The shoreline changes she wanted required a new variance through a planning consultant costing $12,000. She told a KSBE land development manager

---

[2] Mrs. Lindsey scorned his background: a PhD in Environmental Engineering and an MS and BS in civil engineering, all from the University of Kansas. He had been an associate professor of public health at the University of Hawai'i and was director of the Department of Public Works for the City and County of Honolulu before being picked as president of the schools. He'd been an all-around academic and athletic star at Kamehameha Schools, class of '61.

to process the permit. Believing it inappropriate, he spoke with Tony Sereno, general manager of KSBE's Asset Management Group. "Do it," Sereno told him. "This new trustee is vindictive and might take it out on our group."

KSBE land managers worked 180 hours on the matter and appeared at a public hearing where the project was approved. Lokelani didn't offer to pay them. Two years later, a newspaper published a story about her use of staff at her beach house. It was the first the trustees had heard of this.

"Tell the newspaper the estate corrected a surveying discrepancy," Lokelani ordered Elisa Yadao, estate communications director.

"In that case, we'd better go find someplace else where there might be a survey mistake and fix it," Tony Sereno advised. Elisa understood that Sereno's suggestion was so KSBE could claim it had helped other homeowners.

Elisa told a reporter what Lokelani directed her to say: "It is not a violation of policy for trustees to use staff for personal work. KSBE corrected a survey of Mrs. Lindsey's property and KSBE would do the same for anyone."

Oz asked Mrs. Lindsey to reimburse the estate. "General Counsel Aipa said repayment was not necessary," she told him.

Oz asked Aipa about it, and he denied Mrs. Lindsey's statement.

She recanted: "Tony Sereno told me I didn't need to reimburse the estate."

Tony Sereno was not available for comment. He had died.

D uring her first year as a trustee, Lokelani took the first of sixteen free trips to Las Vegas, Nevada, a city she grew to love. She also went to the Rose Bowl, the Super Bowl, and the Olympics at the expense of KSBE vendors such as Xerox and Educational Management Group (EMG). She started by flying in commercial airplanes and two years later was demanding private jets.

She'd become involved with EMG while with the Maui school system. Lokelani introduced them to Kamehameha Schools for what she described as "a breakthrough in distance learning." EMG proposed 500 teacher/student workstations, software, network systems, and related items costing between $30 to $50 million dollars. It offered to install seven demonstration stations free of charge.

"This system won't interface with the schools computers and is difficult to configure and maintain," the schools information technician warned.

Lokelani told Dr. Chun the schools specialist was not to interfere with her idea. With her urging, the trustees agreed to fund EMG's proposal, authorizing $1.2 million for hardware used in the "free demonstration" program. Custom curricula didn't work; teachers couldn't link with interactive systems because of the four-hour time difference between the data center in Arizona and Hawai'i. Five years later, the estate was still paying EMG's $285,000 yearly fee for inactive computers.

Lokelani fell for a $400,000 gold bullion scheme involving a Philippine Islands seller and potential Arab buyers. Money laundering through gold transactions is popular in some parts of the world; a gold dealer supplies gold in exchange for checks and cash received; a cash transaction in one country is completed by a gold transaction in another.

Her friend Benjamin Bush invested approximately $800,000 in the same venture. The person who sold them on this scheme died, and Lokelani and Bush lost their investments.

To help her fellow investor, Lokelani brought KDP Technologies, LLC, to the trustees' attention. KDP wanted to develop an Internet database called "Star Book" for models, actors, and entertainers to showcase their talents to casting agencies, promoters, and producers. KDP agreed to pay Ben Bush a $90,000 annual salary. Lokelani didn't tell the trustees of her connection.

Oz objected to the investment because KSBE had no experience in this area, there was no patent, it was an unknown nonexclusive service of a dubious nature, and he questioned the principal's creditworthiness.

KSBE not only invested over Oz's objections, it made Lokelani president, vice president, director, and manager of KDP Technologies, LLC. She controlled it all.

She gave Randy Stone, trustee Dickie Wong's brother-in-law, a consulting contract with an incentive clause that could pay him up to $500,000. Lokelani didn't tell the trustees that the Federal Bureau of Investigation asked her questions about Ben Bush's alleged illegal transactions early during the venture.

She wouldn't provide financial reports. She didn't advise the board when KDP developed a program called "Love Mate," an Internet dating service, linked to online pornography.

The company closed when cash from KSBE slowed once Bush's criminal prosecutions became public. By then, KSBE had put $1.3 million into KDP, including payments to Randy Stone.

After participating in a "Hawai'i Diet" program, Lokelani decided to bring it to the campus for some of her community and campus friends.[3]

---

[3] Breakfast: poi, fish (2 oz.), sweet potato, taro, banana, tea. Lunch: poi, *laulau, poke* (raw fish 2 oz.), sweet potato, taro, *limu* (seaweed). Dinner: poi, *laulau,* taro, fish (2 oz.), *limu,* banana, water. Eat only during early morning and before sunset. Pork and chicken are allowed on special occasions only, red meat is not included or is very limited. This is the ancient Hawaiian diet. It was similar to mealtime at Oz's grandfather's home.

The diet consisted of healthy old-time Hawaiian food such as fish, fruit, and vegetables. When Rockne Freitas asked her how to pay for it, she said, "Use school staff development funds." The president's budget for that was $140,000, which included money for fifty-seven mainland staff development activities, tuition registration, summer study grants, workshops, and conferences.

At a cost of $3,500 each, thirty-six persons including Lokelani ate their way through two sessions. Lokelani signed checks totaling $128,800 for the diet doctor's foundation. President Chun didn't know his budget paid for Lokelani's weight-loss program until it was finished.

Lokelani took over the estate's communications functions, and this included employee and alumni interactions.

While with Campbell Estate, Oz had invited employees below the management level to have lunch with him. He wanted to know more people instead of just those with whom he worked. He was continuing this practice at the Bishop Estate; each month the Personnel Department selected between fifteen and twenty file clerks, accountants, and other employees, half from the school, half from the estate side. There was no agenda or speech from Oz, just exchanges of goodwill.

Before Mrs. Lindsey's arrival, Oz took staff on monthly bus tours around the island of O'ahu to see Bishop Estate properties and developments. The tour included a picnic lunch alongside the ocean. She thought these staff tours were inappropriate, and Oz gave them up, but he continued the staff luncheons. He also organized yearly bus tours for alumni.

Mrs. Lindsey wanted to be involved with the alumni tour; Oz had assigned a bus to her. Alumni gravitated to Oz and Neil Hannahs' bus. Neil, class of 1969, was the community relations director. Lokelani resented riding with "leftovers," as she referred to stragglers who boarded her bus.

"I told Neil we'd have uniforms for the alumni next year with logos on shirts and baseball hats, and we'd wear shorts," Oz said. "Mrs. Lindsey frowned when she saw us in our alumni uniforms."

Oz's secretary asked her, "How was the bus trip?"

"It was fine except your stupid boss and Neil Hannahs wore those stupid uniforms."

Oz explained, "I was beginning to understand her character and personality by her petty behavior." He reduced his observations to doggerel:

> *The problem is that Mrs. Lindsey doesn't know.*
> *And she doesn't know that she doesn't know.*

*She thinks she knows everything,*
*But she doesn't really know,*
*And she doesn't know that she doesn't know,*
*And that's why she does all of those stupid things.*

Neil Hannahs sent a memo to all trustees asking how they wanted their name displayed for a sign on the car they'd ride in during the Kamehameha Day Parade. "Oz, Kuulei, and Ulilani Stender, class of 1950 and class of 2007," responded Oz. Ulilani is the Stenders' granddaughter.

With that sign on his car, Oz drove into the parade marshaling area to line up with other trustees whose cars had signs stating their name and title. Outraged at Oz's sign, Mrs. Lindsey scolded Neil publicly. "She could have come to talk to me about it," Oz said. "But she picked on Neil and people heard her humiliate him."

"I asked everybody what they wanted, but Oz was the only one who responded," Neil explained to her.

On Monday, Mrs. Lindsey called Luana, Neil's secretary, into her office. "Why didn't you ask me what I wanted to put on my car?"

"I did," Luana replied. "I wrote you a memo."

"I never saw it."

"Your secretary did and I followed up when I didn't hear from you. Your secretary said you wanted 'Trustee Lindsey' on your car, so that is what we did."

"I said no such thing," retorted Mrs. Lindsey.

Luana left her office, grabbed Mrs. Lindsey's secretary by the hand, pulled her into the room and said, "Did I ask you what Mrs. Lindsey wanted put on her car? Did you answer 'She said put "Trustee Lindsey" on it?'"

"I said no such thing," interrupted Mrs. Lindsey.

Luana broke down in tears.

For the next year's Kamehameha Day Parade, Oz's car sign read: "Tūtū, Tūtū Kāne, and Moʻopuna"—"Grandmother, Grandfather, and Grandchild."

"That really ticked her off," Oz told me. "She resented me and Dr. Michael Chun because we were popular with the faculty. It irritated her that people didn't respond to her but did to Michael. That's why she tried to get rid of him."

"Henry took over as lead trustee for investments when Matsy retired and kept me out of anything financial," Oz said. "I became his enemy because I had more experience and knowledge and wouldn't let things slide."

Oz cultivated relationships with people on Wall Street and in Washington while at the Campbell Estate. He arranged introductions for Henry Peters, who was bothered by Oz's personal links.

"Henry liked power and control," Oz said. "He was chairman of the board of every subsidiary we owned—this was wrong. He wouldn't put outsiders on the board of our for-profit organizations. It was either him or staff from our Royal Hawaiian subsidiary under his control.

"Still in political office after being appointed a trustee, Henry remained director of industrial relations for Dura Contractors Inc., a company receiving millions of dollars in business from the State of Hawai'i and the Bishop Estate.

"Henry took credit for Matsy's work, claiming that since his appointment in 1984, he was responsible for the trust's vast investments. He called me cautious and conservative. I would refer to experiences with Campbell, because they were parallel comparisons."

"'We don't give a s--- what Campbell does,'" he'd answer, determined to do things his way.

"Other trustees felt I was trying to show them up," Oz said, "so they put me down and ate me up.

"Henry made sure I wouldn't be able to pin him down. Sometimes he tried to be condescending and came to talk to me—but it was rare. Women employees sparkled when he came in to my office. They wanted things to be nice and friendly at Kawaiaha'o Plaza. His visits were just after or before he did something."

The trustees received only information the lead trustee wanted them to know. Oz had to do his own investigations because what he got was incomplete. "Mrs. Lindsey manipulated school information. Henry Peters manipulated investment information."

"What about Dickie Wong?" I asked.

"He seemed oblivious to daily doings. Dickie behaved as an archetypal political figurehead," Oz explained. "He managed the big picture, leaving details to others. For that to work, you have to trust your organization. Dickie did; this was the path that led to his becoming a trustee.

"Lokelani controlled all details for every responsibility she could grab. Dickie trusted her. She showed her dark side against those who denied or defied her.

"Henry wanted to make big financial gains for the estate, to assure its growth and future. In the process he sought retribution and paybacks for once downtrodden Hawaiians. He was relentless and had the resources, authority, and aggressive personality to carry it off. He was ready to be a home run hitter like Matsy Takabuki.

"His flaw," Oz observed, "was blatant prejudice and even anger against descendants of races who took advantage of Hawaiians. This dark side surfaced and caused bad business judgment."

Oz provided the following examples.

The Bishop Estate sold lease rights for the Kaiser Estate in Hawai'i Kai to a Japanese real estate investor who paid Bishop Estate $1 million a year. The investor wanted to own the land in fee simple and offered $24 million. It was appraised at $22 million.

"Take it," Oz said.

"I want $30 million," Henry answered.

"Why?"

"He is Japanese and can pay."

"Stick it in your ear," responded the Japanese investor, who left town.

"We got the property back," Oz said. "With luck, we may be able to get $10 to $15 million. Meanwhile, it is costing the estate $1 million a year to maintain."

Residents of a Kāhala Beach condominium asked Oz, "Can't we buy the fee?"

"Trustees have a policy of not selling beach land," Oz explained.

A staff member he asked to appraise the property came up with $75 million as the cost of the fee. The estate was receiving $80,800 a year in rent.

"We had a major asset sitting there. I asked the condo manager to invite me to talk with the owners. I asked if they would be willing to pay $500,000 an apartment for the fee—that would give the estate about $77 million. They were eager to do it."

Oz had a property staff member submit a report recommending the sale.

"No way will I sell this," Henry said.

"Why not?"

"Nothing but f---ing rich haole live in that building."

"That was his rationale; he wouldn't vote for it."

If the trustees made what he thought was a bad decision, Oz filed the information into his computer system. Here is what he recorded:

I reexamined the Kāhala Beach property a couple of years later. The Japanese investment bubble went away and the value dropped down to $60 million, but it was still an opportunity.

When it came time to renegotiate the lease, we had to reappraise the site and it was down to a $50 million range. According to the lease, we could receive only 4 percent return on the property value, so the estate takes another hit—bringing our income down to $50,000 to $60,000 a year, hardly enough.

In the meanwhile, the Honolulu City Council passed an ordinance allowing lessees in condos to have the city condemn the properties for conversion. These people took that step.

They purchased the land for less than half of what we could have received earlier.

An American development group went belly-up after starting to build a Four Seasons hotel and roughing out a golf course on Big Island land owned by the Bishop Estate. Its Japanese partners would continue supplying money but needed a new developer-manager.

"This project is no different from the Sheraton, the Lauluani, the Mauna Kea, and they are all half empty," said a partner in the Phoenix firm taking over the project. He drew the attention of the Japanese representatives, Henry, and Oz to a project next door. "The Kona Village is a low-key, single-story project. It is very successful and has repeat customers. That is what we should be doing. I recommend blowing up our building and starting over." This would wipe out the $25 to $35 million investment at that point.

"Who the f--- are you, coming in here and telling us what you are going to do?" yelled Henry. "It is our land. We tell you what to do!"

When the meeting dissolved in confusion, Oz called the planning consultant in Arizona, who had done lots of business with the Bishop Estate. "I don't share Henry's sentiments. You know how Henry is: He shows his power by insulting others. That is why you should have come yourself."

"Investment managers gave trustees quarterly reports. Henry would say they don't know what they are doing," Oz explained. "You don't insult people in a group in front of other people. That is rude. It was his way.

"It worked. People brought in reports containing information, not issues needing to be discussed. They laundered information, producing only what Henry wanted to hear. No one dared tell the emperor he was wearing no clothes."

Oz had an idea that would remove Trustee Henry Peters immediately. With the estate's financial resources under his jurisdiction, along with his political power, Henry would be a dominant force within the estate and the Islands over the next two decades. Oz wrote to Chief Justice Ronald T. Y. Moon:

> It is a common practice of major corporations to "recycle" its chief executive officer within a ten to fifteen year period.
>
> Inasmuch as the estate's trustees assume the role of chief executive officers, I suggest justices appoint trustees for a period of ten years. This would provide options to recycle trustees should their energies or performance decline over the years of service.

Reversibly, if the trustee continues to be a valuable contributor to the management of the estate's affairs, that term could be renewed or extended. This is my own suggestion made for the benefit of managing the trust.

Judge Moon didn't reply.

As a storyteller, I recount others' actions without judging or criticizing these individuals as lacking spirit and values. God lets his voice be heard through others' work to help each of us understand darkness—ego, greed, anger, sadness. We can contrast that to light—selflessness, giving, peacefulness, and love—and come to our own conclusions.

Oz served Princess Pauahi's beneficiaries in a very bright light. Other trustees also gave for the sake of others within their own narrow focus. Each absolutely controlled his or her feudal fiefdom by keeping others uninformed and off of their turf. It was Lindsey's school, Peter's investments, and Dickie's political leadership. Oz, in charge of nothing, became the estate's watchdog and stepped everywhere.

Trustees made decisions at a whim; one would say, "This is what we are going to do," and others would acquiesce. Oz's suggestions, supported by memos, were ignored.

Everyone makes mistakes, but it was the volume of bad mistakes that worried Oz. "They must have blown $300 to $400 million dollars in investments because of bad decisions," he told me. "Henry complained over spending money for due diligence on a complex deal. I told him that if we spent 1 percent of a proposed investment on due diligence, it would be worth it. Isn't it worth spending $500,000 on due diligence if you are considering a $5 million deal, rather than making a $5 million mistake? This helps you to find out if you shouldn't make an investment; if you do choose to invest, it'll identify things to watch for and straighten out."

Frustrated over the political appointment system, Oz said, "Supreme Court justices appointing those trustees didn't understand they weren't qualified and shouldn't be in charge of the endowment. By using its wealth wisely, the Bishop Estate could rank with the top 400 companies in America."

While at Campbell, Oz talked with the owner of Maui Land and Pine about the possibility of Campbell buying a shopping center on its land. One of Maui Pine's large stockholders didn't believe in selling real estate. After death, his Maui Pine stock went to a foundation headquartered on the mainland.

By this time, Oz was a Bishop Estate trustee. He contacted the foundation, and it was amenable to selling its Maui Pine stock for $60 million. Oz didn't think Bishop

Estate should buy Maui Pine unless it controlled the company. He found a retirement investment account managed by the Bank of Hawaii, and the bank was willing to sell the Maui Pine stock in the account for $20 million.

Now the Bishop Estate could own half of the company, 25,000 acres of Maui real estate, a shopping center, a resort, and a pineapple company for $80 million.

How could the estate pay for it? The money could be raised by selling some golf courses. Oz talked with the Club Corporation of America, which was willing to pay $25 million a course—KSBE had three, so that made $75 million. For an outlay of $5 million, the Bishop Estate could own 52 percent of Maui Land and Pine. Oz explained what happened next:

> It was a no-brainer as far as I was concerned. But the trustees wouldn't do it, because I presented the plan.
>
> Okay, if the estate won't do it, I'll do it myself.
>
> I talked with three New York investment firms, including Goldman Sachs. However, the sister of the majority stock holder didn't like the idea of my bringing in high-powered Wall Street firms to finance the deal. She thought of it as a takeover with the possibility of down-sizing and employee layoffs. I backed off.
>
> Mrs. Lindsey wrote me a note about using insider information for my own gain.
>
> Gerry Jervis instructed the law department to come after me.

A reporter from a local television station called Oz saying they were told he had breached his fiduciary duties to the estate. They showed him a package of documents that had been turned over to them.

"They originated from the Bishop Estate. I didn't believe the estate should be paying private investigators to investigate a trustee without the trustee's knowledge. I decided to bring everything into the open and called a press conference."

The story was given a ten-second play by the television station that had brought it to Oz's attention. Newspapers didn't cover the story. Mrs. Lindsey accused Oz of controlling the local media.

I attended alumni meetings in Washington, D.C., when Oz was scheduled to speak. Yearly he'd join us to place flower leis on Kamehameha's statue in the Hall of Statuary at the nation's capitol and sing Founders Day songs. I asked school representatives, "Where's Oz?" when he began missing East Coast alumni meetings.

"He had a schedule conflict."

That didn't sound like him. Nothing interfered with Oz's attending alumni meetings.

He'd been pushed out of the inner circle, and meeting notices didn't reach him. With three votes out of five, Henry, Dickie, and Lokelani ran the estate as they wished.

Oz and I talked periodically by phone. He hoped that a strong new trustee would help him to initiate open discussion within the boardroom. The following story describes a turning point in his life.

O n the morning of December 12, 1994, Oz was sitting in his office reading in the newspaper that Hawai'i's Supreme Court had appointed lawyer Gerard Aulama Jervis as a Bishop Estate trustee. Most of Oz's information came from outside sources by then. That's how he found out about five impressive candidates recommended by a panel of community leaders. Gerard Jervis was not among them.

This news was shocking. Chief Justice Moon had promised panel members the justices would choose a trustee from their list of candidates. It took Oz four years to advance the selection process to this point. In making this decision, justices also disregarded Princess Bernice Pauahi Bishop's will, which states that Bishop Estate trustees are to be Protestants. Jervis was a Roman Catholic.

Feeling a sharp pain, Oz stood to stretch. Was his ulcer acting up? He took deep breaths, sat back down in his office chair, and symbolically tossed the newspaper into the wastebasket. Oz had nothing against Jervis, but his appointment was so blatant.

S upreme Court justices, supreme arrogance, he thought to himself.

It was 6:00 A.M.; he'd give Gerry Jervis a congenial call later. Oz habitually was at work hours before anyone else, allowing uninterrupted thinking time. This appointment was another example of Princess Pauahi's dream being diverted into a political resource.

Justices used the panel as subterfuge, assuming it would recommend Governor John Waihee for the opening. In that way justices could avoid criticism for hand-picking the governor, who had personally appointed each of them to the Supreme Court.

Oz heard they were angered that panel members didn't include the governor on their list of candidates. He was tipped off that the panel would exclude him because too many former politicians now were trustees. So the justices appointed the governor's good friend and confidante instead, knowing that Trustee Gerard Jervis would help take care of John Waihee when he left office the following year.

A patter song from Gilbert and Sullivan's *HMS Pinafore* popped into Oz's mind as he visualized each justice's face: "I always voted at my party's call and never thought of thinking for myself at all."

The panel thoroughly screened each of its candidates; how about the justices?

Was Jervis really qualified? Did his experience apply to the Bishop Estate's mission? Would he be a worthy exemplar for a school with deep religious roots?

Princess Pauahi's will stipulates that Hawai'i's highest court shall select trustees to manage her estate. This has become its fatal flaw. She believed this court would choose Hawai'i's best business leaders. She didn't anticipate statehood, political intrigue, or corruption in high places.

The Bishop Estate was not as healthy as it outwardly appeared. Supreme Court justices initiated the decline by appointing politicians without qualifications and character to manage assets and sustain an educational vision.

Oz had suggested that the estate hire the best chief executive officer that money could buy and for trustees to become advisors who are paid minimally, as once they were.

Oz was very different from the other trustees. He was a businessman, formerly chief executive officer of Hawai'i's second-largest estate, and was registered as a Republican in a state the Democratic Party had dominated for about forty years. Each trustee's annual commissions averaged $1 million, and their lifestyles reflected this.

But not Oz, who gave away most of his income to scholarships and charity. Married for forty-five years, Oz and Kuulei lived on the same amount he earned long before he became a trustee. Theirs was a modest home in which they raised their son and daughter. He drove a six-year-old car.

In the boardroom he was analytical, only to be told he was critical. Trustees were indifferent to his financial and educational ideas. Three out of five trustees constituted a majority, and he was always outvoted.

Humiliated with trustees' decisions and angered by their boardroom behavior, Oz had fallen into the habit—only when with friends—of referring to the other trustees as "jerks" and rolling his right index finger around his right ear whenever Mrs. Lindsey's name was mentioned.

A highly respected Island businessperson and close friend told Oz that he was the right person in the right place at the right time—and by lucky accident.

When he was appointed in 1990, the justices were at an impasse among candidates, to whom each was politically beholden. Oz realized that they chose him because his experience made him a safe compromise.

He was a graduate of Kamehameha Schools; only one other graduate was a trustee many years ago. He hadn't applied for the job because as a Republican and a graduate of the school, he didn't think he had a chance. He was phoned and asked to come over right away. Arriving ten minutes later, he was told he had been chosen to be a Bishop Estate trustee. There was not even an interview.

He was seven years from mandatory retirement at the age of seventy. The estate and the futures of children it was established to educate would be in the hands of the other trustees for the next twenty years. That could prove disastrous.

For his own lifetime security, all he had to do was let the years roll by. He wasn't required to do any work—other trustees didn't want him to. He'd receive commissions and then at least $250,000 yearly in a pension. It'd be easy and rewarding to do nothing.

The pain in his stomach was gone. Oz sensed a solution. If he *was* the right person in the right place at the right time, then he needed to see to it that all trustees were removed to fix the Bishop Estate's problems, even if he left with them. Judges had to be shamed out of rewarding members of their political party. The Bishop Estate needed a fresh start.

This meant challenging government, the courts, every businessperson, and every lawyer in Hawai'i with ties to the Bishop Estate—it included almost everyone with power and would be dangerous. How could one person challenge a state?

Leaning back in his chair, Oz closed his eyes to reflect on his favorite prayer. Slowly saying the words, "Lord, give me the strength," he visualized a phalanx of young men facing him, standing at attention on the field in front of the Kamehameha Schools auditorium—just as he used to do prior to Sunday worship service in the late 1940s.

They wore military uniforms from many eras; some were in khaki, some in blue-gray, and some in gray high-collared West Point–style uniforms. On the left side of the field, on stairways and balconies of classroom buildings, stood a mass of young women in white dresses, their heads turned in his direction.

Oz opened his eyes. He had the answer: He would be a warrior for the princess. He must do this so that Hawaiian children would have the opportunities intended for them.

Princess Pauahi would inspire others to move forward and ally with him. He was positive she would.

## CHAPTER 20

# Fear and Intimidation

## 1995–1996

L OKELANI EXPECTED people to come running at the snap of her fingers, but she demonstrated her total control through delays and insults. She called staff members "incompetent" and spoke of the director of communications, the general counsel, and the school president as "insubordinate." She made teachers feel inadequate and scared.

Oz beseeched her not to scream and insult staff and direct gutter language at them. Other trustees let her do as she wished, and her behavior worsened.

School president Dr. Chun couldn't protect faculty and staff from Lokelani's top-down management because he reported to her, not to the board of trustees. He used to fill vacant positions; now he needed her approval. He tried to avoid confrontation and harassment.

Lokelani formed a communications committee and instructed Elisa Yadao, director of communications, not to distribute the minutes to trustees.

Through focus group sessions, mainland consulting firm Sheppard Associates sought to learn why KSBE employees were unhappy with compensation. The consultants learned that employees' concerns went far beyond their pay: They felt unappreciated, undervalued, anxious, and disenfranchised. They were upset at being evaluated by how they conformed to Hawaiian values, when the trustees themselves did not practice such values.[1]

---

[1] In his book, *Ku Kanaka* ("Stand Tall"), George Kanahele reported on traditional Hawaiian values. Here is the summary: love and humanity, giving of yourself to others, humility, generosity, hospitality, spirituality, obedience, cooperativeness, cleanliness, graciousness and manners, industry and diligence, patience, playfulness, competitiveness, keeping prom-

The Sheppard Report was supposed to be presented to trustees in November 1996, but Lokelani told Elisa she would do so when "they could focus on it." She kept the report from the trustees. Seeing one on an employee's desk, Oz phoned the consultant for a copy.

Peter Harris, another consulting firm, included alumni in its focus group sessions and promised confidentiality. Mrs. Lindsey hid this report as well. She asked Elisa for the names of alumni who spoke in the focus groups. Fearing they'd be subject to retribution, Elisa "somehow" could not find them.

Lokelani acquired hiring power at Kawaiahaʻo Plaza. Once a supervisor selected an employee, the personnel department took the recommendation to Lokelani for approval. It waited on her desk indefinitely—nothing happened until she said so.

President Chun requested approval from Lokelani to hire principals for elementary schools on neighbor islands slated to open in August, and then made a second request. Not until seven weeks prior to the opening of school did he receive her approval to hire the principals, staff, and to purchase equipment and supplies.

She delayed mailing teachers' yearly contracts until the day before school started, leaving them uncertain as to whether they would be invited back after the summer. Teachers have mortgages, car payments, and children to support. Can you imagine the anxieties they experienced? Was she trying to make them more grateful when the contracts arrived?

"Teachers aren't working hard enough and don't take advantage of available resources," she declared. "Some aren't really teaching, some are incompetent, and some are spoiled."

Lokelani downgraded the faculty before alumni, making comparisons between KSBE teachers and those in the State Department of Education. She compared class loads and gave examples for the need to tighten up at KSBE. She frightened them into needing her goodwill.

She gave Principal Ramos one of her "research reports." Claiming to have reviewed the records of elementary students who applied to the seventh grade, Lokelani stated that some schoolteachers were more effective than others. She discussed her "research" at a meeting of seventh- and eighth-grade teachers, telling them she could track the students' successes by which teachers they had had.

---

ises, forgiveness, intelligence, self-reliance, excellence, courage, helpfulness, balance, harmony, unity, dignity, leadership, achievement, and honesty.

She wanted teachers' appraisal forms to include information on students' standardized test performance. She delayed teachers' contracts until learning that no other private school evaluates teachers that way.

Once creating fear and distrust, Lokelani demonstrated vigilance and her ultimate authority. In fall 1995, Nina Aldrich, eleventh- and twelfth-grade vice principal, was called to the secondary school principal's office. Lokelani sat there with a drug gun used to detect marijuana or cocaine. Two sales representatives had scanned about a hundred cars as Lokelani watched with keen interest.

Walking with her to the student parking lot, Principal Ramos told Ms. Aldrich, "Have these three vehicles and the drivers' bags and lockers searched."

Security guards took the drivers out of their classrooms and ordered them to move their cars behind the school dorms. Guards examined the cars, even taking the seats apart.

No drugs were found in the first two students' cars, bags, or lockers. A marijuana pipe and some marijuana seedlings were found in the third student's car.

Principal Ramos expelled the student immediately under the schools "zero tolerance" policy. Looking on approvingly, Lokelani ordered a drug gun for the school.

The Hawaiian language program Nona Beamer began in 1965 now included 902 students and 10 teachers. It developed its own course materials and received administration approval in 1992 to update and expand the high school Hawaiian language curriculum to be authentic and teenage friendly. The program included words developed by a lexicon committee of Hawaiian language professors who coined or created new Hawaiian words for use in modern society.

Sarah Keahi, a longtime Hawaiian language teacher, received a call from Lokelani during the middle of her class. By Lokelani's tone of voice, Sarah knew she was upset. "May I phone you back after class?" Sarah asked.

"I am concerned about your initials on a request for approval of a T-shirt design for the girls basketball team," Lokelani told Sarah when she called back.

"It uses the current Hawaiian word for basketball—'pōhīna'i,'" Sarah explained.

"I have a committee who reviewed the T-shirt and it disagrees with your interpretation," replied Lokelani. "I also have a new policy regarding the Hawaiian language."

"Would you be willing to discuss this with the language teachers?" Sarah asked. Lokelani did, explaining that her own Hawaiian language committee included her secretary and several persons not connected with the school. She didn't explain her definition of "traditional" Hawaiian language. Mrs. Lindsey doesn't speak Hawaiian, by the way. To cover this lack, she got her own experts.

Teachers asked if she would include one of the school's language teachers on her committee. "You are too busy. My committee meets during class times and at evenings."

"We'll make time for such an important task," Sarah answered.

They didn't hear from Lokelani.

Principal Ramos told teachers, "She wants only language used in the mid-nineteenth century, when Princess Pauahi was alive. Use just words in the Pukui-Elbert dictionary."

"But it includes twentieth-century words," Sarah replied.

Lokelani wouldn't amend her directive; she didn't render her definition of "traditional" Hawaiian language in writing.

Teachers stopped working on their four-year curriculum project and no longer used videos, comprehension tapes, or any other materials containing modern Hawaiian words. Because University of Hawai'i professors include the modern lexicon, Lokelani's edict put Kamehameha graduates behind other university Hawaiian language students.

Sarah thought that Lokelani's setting herself up as language authority was illogical and unprecedented. She had taught under nine trustees, three school presidents, and seven school principals; never was she told to teach only "traditional language"— whatever that meant. Enrollment in the Hawaiian program dropped from 900 to about 600 students.

Mrs. Lindsey chose Dr. Paul Ahr, president of Corporate Psychology in St. Louis, Missouri, to help her create a new kind of Kamehameha Schools. Oz asked Mrs. Lindsey for copies of Dr. Ahr's previous studies, but received none. Dr. Ahr's web site referenced experience in conflict resolution, not in educational planning.

Mrs. Lindsey and her consultant named the program "Go Forward," the English translation of "Imua," the school's slogan. She didn't allow faculty and staff to help develop it. Unlike Dr. Chun's educational plans, still sitting on the shelf, Go Forward was a top-down decision-making process from Lokelani to which all trustees except Oz gave their tacit approval. Go Forward changed the mission, goals, and direction of Kamehameha Schools.

No documents set forth Go Forward's objectives, no integrated planning document analyzed its development, implementation, and costs. Despite this, Go Forward set out to implement major changes in human resources, facilities, education programs, curriculum, admissions, and the organizational structure of Kamehameha Schools. Oz told me the estate paid Dr. Ahr $1.2 million for his consultation.

$D$r. Ahr was a senior advisor to the mainland-based Ernst & Young accounting firm. He hired this firm to examine the schools extension programs, and it recommended closing them all. Ernst & Young charged $2 million for its report—the same as the cost of outreach programs for a year.

Based on statistics only, Ernst & Young took apart programs developed over twenty-five years, claiming they were failures.

Oz tried reasoning with trustees, but it was becoming clear that the entire Go Forward scheme was designed so that Mrs. Lindsey could say, "I did this." She was remaking Kamehameha Schools in her own image.

After KEEP was cut, Oz received information in envelopes without return addresses from those who had been involved with the programs. "I was shocked," he told me. "The national accounting firm manipulated information."

$T$rying to save outreach programs, Oz developed the following thoughts for trustees to consider after sharing them with his focus groups:

> Special needs programs cost about $2 million, less than 2.5 percent of the schools average operating cost over the last three years.
>
> They benefit more than 4,700 students. The cost is $150 a student for summer school and up to $4,000 each for alternative education. These employ 170 persons, some of whom came up through the programs. Besides helping participants, the public relations benefit to KSBE is immeasurable.
>
> The Internal Revenue Service is auditing how we use earnings for education. How do we explain cutting these programs in light of our surplus of over $250 million accumulated during the past ten years and a $13 million surplus for the year just ended [1995–1996]?

"I sat in the boardroom and expressed my views," Oz explained. "Trustees did what they wanted anyway. At first I tried to fit in with them, believing we would have differences of opinion. But their decisions made no sense. I served on other boards; I knew how they ran and how board members behaved.

"This place was an absolute joke. I wrote memos to chronicle what was happening. They told me I should stop. I asked, 'Why?'"

"'Because you may regret what you say in those memos.'"

"I wrote memos because trustees didn't fully understand what I said in the boardroom. I wrote memos before meetings and afterwards so there were no mistakes as to what I meant or tried to express. I don't know if trustees ever read what I wrote."

Dickie Wong stifled Oz's voice at meetings by not including his memos on the agenda and calling him "out of order" when Oz spoke up. Dickie pushed things forward or blocked them. Four votes against his kept Oz powerless.

"It must be frustrating trying to communicate with people who ignore you," I commented.

"That's why I carry this prayer around with me." He pulled a typed card from his pocket and read to me what is known as "The Serenity Prayer":

> *God grant me the serenity to accept the things I cannot change,*
> *Courage to change the things that I can,*
> *And wisdom to know the difference.*[2]

"Sometimes when things were so bad, I had self-doubts: Should I be doing this? Am I overreacting? Am I letting my personal feelings be in the way of a sound judgment? When that happened, I read the prayer again and reflected. I needed to think about things I couldn't change, as well as those I could.

"I would meet with members of my focus groups. We'd have a cup of coffee and talk to see if I was off base. They'd tell me when I was overreaching or overconcerned."

Lokelani's consultant discouraged trustees from supporting government-funded programs. Oz, the only Republican in the boardroom, disagreed: "The government can't carry the entire load. Programs will be jeopardized by financial constraints on the Department of Education."

Being a board member for a school serving at-risk and socially troubled students, Oz knew that public-assisted programs fall way short in addressing children's needs. "Privately sponsored programs serve dysfunctional young adults but are very expensive. Not many Hawaiian families can afford them. Without them, many children will be relegated to juvenile court and go on to Oʻahu Correctional facility or be permanently enrolled on state welfare rolls."

Oz wanted to help children who otherwise would lose an opportunity for a better life, and he used memos to explain to trustees how this could be accomplished:

---

[2] "The Serenity Prayer," as it is now known, is attributed to Reinhold Neibuhr, theologian and recovering alcoholic who wrote it in the 1940s. The Neibuhr version has five verses, the second of which is "Living one day at a time; / Enjoying one moment at a time; / Accepting hardship as the pathway to peace."

174 · Lost Generations

"Don't ignore those whose childhood environment won't prepare them to be 'good and industrious men and women.' Expand our programs to serve children who otherwise never will receive a decent education. Help handicapped Hawaiian children whose families can't afford to meet their special needs. If we don't aid youngsters handicapped by dyslexia—spatial, visual, and auditory disorders affecting reading and other learning—they'll be disabled forever."

Oz told me that Go Forward's limited educational approach disturbed him greatly. "Many Hawaiian children come from dysfunctional situations, including substance abuse and learning deficiencies due to families' economic conditions. The community had programs to help these children. The Bishop Estate had money sitting in a money market fund. But trustees wouldn't deal with kids having problems!"

He was determined to keep outreach programs going and explained to trustees why:

How an individual functions in adolescence and adulthood hinges on the individual's childhood experiences before the age of three. Brain development is much more susceptible to environmental influences than was ever suspected. Early years are critical for laying health and learning foundations. Education and family care are interdependent for young children. These two cannot and should not be separated.

Parental education has the most positive influence on a child's development. Families need to participate in the early learning process. Kamehameha has been nationally recognized for its leadership in this area. Why back out now?

Unsuccessful in convincing trustees, Oz placed parts of KEEP elsewhere. He organized an alternative to Kamehameha's Traveling Pre-School at the Liliʻuokalani Children's Center in Punaluʻu. He helped establish "Healthy Start," similar to Kamehameha's previous parent-infant care program, at the Hauʻula Shopping Center. He worked with the Castle Foundation for permanent funding and sought to build a facility with another foundation's help. These alternatives reached only a lucky few.

CHAPTER 21

# Determining Hawaiian Children's Future

## Mid-1990s

LOKELANI BECAME a literature connoisseur while Oz worried about the futures of unborn children. Robert Van Dyke had asked Oz if KSBE would purchase his Hawaiian book collection. Oz asked Ms. Sigrid Southworth, in charge of the schools Hawaiian Collection, to review a sample; she had thirty-five years of professional library experience.

"We have 55 percent of these titles," she reported. "Only one book in the remaining 45 percent is educationally appropriate."

Oz declined Van Dyke's offer.

Trying to sell it to Lokelani a year later, Van Dyke wrote and said, "Trustee Stender examined the collection." Not asking Oz for his opinion, she purchased the books and old-time photographs for about $423,000.

She told an estate lawyer to draft a bill of sale. The young woman was concerned by the lack of an inventory or appraisal report, but Lokelani told her, "I'll supply information to use in a report."

When the report was prepared and ready to present, Lokelani didn't list it on the board of director's agenda, knowing Oz would make a point to attend the meeting and object to the purchase.

Oz was on the mainland trying to recover money in one of the estate's troubled investments when Lokelani brought the report to a trustees' meeting. To gain Henry's vote, she agreed to pay his longtime friend, attorney Albert Jeremiah, over $7,000 a month for as long as it took him to catalog the photographs.

In ways like this, the estate's career politicians used alliances and blunt habits from the halls of State government to run the charitable trust, bartering and horse-trading for votes just as once they lobbied for votes in the Legislature. "Taking care of friends" is fundamental in politics.

The estate paid Van Dyke $100,000 in earnest money, with the balance in escrow until an inventory was made of the collection. "If you need anything more, just let me know," Lokelani told Van Dyke when releasing another $152,500 before the books were inventoried.

The books were stacked floor to ceiling in three rooms of a downtown office building. Dusty and dirty, most had active mold, and some had cockroach and termite damage. Over the next seven and a half months, at a cost of almost $175,000, the Hawaiian Collection librarian, an attorney, and others cleaned, inventoried, and packed the books into boxes for delivery to campus.

Among the 23,000 books, Ms. Southworth found just one item for which she had been actively searching to include in the Hawaiian Collection. She found numerous inappropriate items, including books on green manure, swine kidney worms, and condom use in Japan. They had little educational value.

S chool communications such as programs, fliers, and graphics used to be approved by department heads and the dean of student activities. Once Lokelani moved on campus, all such items went to her.

She reviewed communications to parents, standardized forms, school programs, invitations to large events, and examined external communications in draft and final form.

The communications director needed Lokelani's approval before returning calls to news media. Such actions sent her message: "I can't trust your professionalism."

Her efforts to be so careful became absurd. She claimed she had to review graphic material because a lesbian alumni group used the Kamehameha logo on its T-shirts.

She liked to apply her "innate color sense," but her opinions changed with her mood. Seeing gym clothes made up from material she previously authorized, she objected that "It does not flatter dark skin."

A cross-country coach asked Mrs. Lindsey to approve a well-known artist's drawing of running Hawaiian warriors to be printed on a T-shirt. He waited and waited. Finally she responded with a note: "Find another picture, the depiction of the Hawaiians is not flattering." She may have meant the best, but it was too late for runners to have their own T-shirt when other athletes wore theirs on "Athletes' Recognition Day."[1]

Rene Martin divided a class of her fall students into small groups for a project that included forming a company, selecting a product to sell, developing a marketing plan, and executing it. She'd base students' grades on the profit they earned.

Five students in one group chose to sell T-shirts and canvas bags with either a turtle or a plumeria flower design; there was no wording or use of the school logo. Students collected $2,500 in deposits.

Needing Lokelani to approve their designs, they forwarded them to her in the middle of November. Students became anxious when she did not promptly okay them; their sales were targeted for the Christmas season.

Ms. Martin left daily phone messages with Lokelani's secretary but received no reply; by the second week of December designs still weren't approved. Her students canceled the project and refunded deposits. They were concerned about their grade because their company would make no profit. Given their presales, each of the five students expected to earn $300 for their own Christmas spending.

On December 18, the day before Christmas break, Lokelani faxed Ms. Martin a note with these encouraging words: "Tell the kids to go for it."

It was too late. Their opportunity was gone.

Lokelani managed by walking around, making unscheduled and unannounced visits to classrooms. Seemingly omnipresent, she kept teachers on their toes. She startled a ninth- and tenth-grade Hawaiian culture teacher by shaking her finger at him as she walked into his room in the middle of class. Lokelani directed him to the hallway for a talk.

"Students' parents call and tell me you say trustees sit around all day and collect money."

---

[1] As a former gym teacher, Lokelani should have realized that being unrecognized as an athlete is extra tough because long-distance running is not perceived as a "real" sport by high school youngsters, who place a heavy emphasis on being in the mainstream. Developing running potential means self-discipline, dedication, and sacrifices while accumulating the miles necessary for maximum fitness. The reality is discomfort, whether training or racing. No other sport, except possibly crew racing or canoeing, is based on a steady, prolonged increase in physical discomfort as a normal condition. One of the things long-distance running does so well is to define one's character, but everyone enjoys recognition; it's the reason so many adults proudly wear T-shirts commemorating "runs" and "rows."

"You may have misunderstood. I merely asked students if they understood trustees' responsibilities," he answered carefully.

Giving him her famous glare, she said, "Everyone has to be a team player," and stomped off. Students had watched their teacher be humbled.

Seeing student art hanging in an art teacher's room, she said: "It's stupid. Looks like laundry." After she left the room, the elementary students asked if they could draw caricatures of Lokelani for an assignment. Their lack of respect was very apparent.

She set a date by which kindergarten students must identify KSBE trustees by their pictures and say something flattering about each. Older readers may reflect that this sounds like propagandist Joseph Goebbels' youthful brainwashing during Hitler's rule.

Oz continued criticizing Mrs. Lindsey's Go Forward plan. "A strategic plan should be aggressive and visionary, with input from the entire education group staff. Even the best-laid plans won't succeed without participation from those charged with its implementation," he wrote.

There were no cost information or financial models for either the capital funding requirements or the operation cost components. The plan was unimaginative, traditional, and costly.

Now having billions of dollars, the schools enrolled the same percentage of Hawaiian children as it did in the early 1960s when its assets were a few hundred million dollars. The estate could provide educational services to virtually all Hawaiians, but Kamehameha Schools rejected nine out of ten students because of the limited space on the Kapālama Heights' campus.

Oz said the Go Forward plan lacked vision because it did not address the need to serve the wider community of Hawaiian children. It claimed to be directed at the brightest of Hawaiian children but ignored the educational needs of 90 percent of the Hawaiian student population.

Dr. Barnes took that approach in the 1930s through 1944, when Bishop Estate income was only enough to educate a few hundred students of what was then a smaller Hawaiian population. This was no longer the situation. Kamehameha was the richest school in the world and could broaden its mission for the larger Hawaiian population.

Wanting money spent on education, not edifices, Oz suggested ways to serve more students. Silenced by Dickie Wong in meetings, he used memos to present ideas. Oz wanted to educate more Hawaiians; Lokelani sought to make Kamehameha Schools in her grand image.

Dickie had built his reputation on his skills as a political leader, coalition builder, and group manager. He could prevent Oz from speaking at cross-purposes with Lokelani's schemes.

Oz kept forwarding memos. Did trustees read and understand them? They probably did not.

Because the highest quality education is provided by Hawai'i's private schools, Oz suggested that the estate provide a "voucher" system for bright students at other private schools to compensate for lack of room at Kamehameha.

He was a director at 'Iolani, one of Hawai'i's finest schools. At 'Iolani it cost $13,000 a year to educate a student. At Kamehameha it cost $17,000 to educate a day student and $37,000 for a boarder. 'Iolani charged $8,700 for tuition and subsidized each student at about $4,000 each.

For the cost of one day student at Kamehameha, two students could be given vouchers to attend 'Iolani, and 'Iolani would subsidize each at $4,000. In other words, for a net cost of $4,700 each, Kamehameha could educate two students at 'Iolani.[2]

He said this voucher system could be similarly applied at Punahou and other top-notch private schools.

Oz's issue was that Kamehameha rejected bright students because of space limitations; those unable to afford other private schools attended public schools with lesser standards. He suggested financial aid based on need, no different than the need-based college tuition Kamehameha provides to all post–high school Hawaiian students—not just those from Kamehameha.

To enhance educational readiness, he urged revisiting the zero to three-year-old group Kamehameha had abandoned. While it was unlikely trustees would reopen those programs, others were being established elsewhere.

Those programs used public funds and could not be directed solely to Hawaiians, who had the greatest need. He wanted KSBE to provide vouchers to help Hawaiian families enter the programs, feeling this would improve the estate's ability to reach more Hawaiians in a cost-effective way. Through voucher systems, KSBE could place programs in areas with high needs.

---

[2] Tuition for 'Iolani was $12,200 as this book was readied for publication in 2005–2006. 'Iolani's cost per student has risen to over $18,000; therefore, its subsidy per student is in the $6,000 range. Kamehameha reports that its cost per student is about 87 percent more than what it charges for tuition fees and is called a "tuition subsidy." Kamehameha's charge for students in grades 7–12 is $2,686; boarders in the same grades are charged $4,998; financial aid is available. The ratios Oz described in 1999 still apply. Kamehameha Schools can subsidize two students at 'Iolani and other fine schools for about the cost of educating one on its Kapālama Heights campus.

He suggested partnerships with the Department of Education. Statewide, twenty-five DOE elementary schools were serving enrollments with 50 percent or more Hawaiians. These totaled 6,525 Hawaiian children in place at zero capital cost to KSBE. Why build schools in these same areas?

T rustees wouldn't change Go Forward and gave President Chun four months to prepare an educational strategic plan consistent with it. He felt that input from teachers should be included; they were away for the summer break. Falling seriously ill, Dr. Chun was unable to meet the deadline but presented the plan a few months later. Trustees rejected it, as they had his previous reports. "Get a consultant to assist you," they told him.

Dr. Chun collaborated with two highly regarded and experienced educators. Trustees rejected this plan as well.

"Because of her thirty years of educational experience," Dickie asked Lokelani to prepare a strategic plan. She selected just administrators, no teachers, to help.

The content of her educational plan was similar to both reports Dr. Chun prepared. The format was flashier. Dickie, Henry, and Gerry accepted Mrs. Lindsey's plan.

Oz didn't quit offering information. As Mrs. Lindsey and Dr. Ahr continued with their schemes to enlarge the main campus, Oz used a trustee retreat as the opportunity to discuss ideal school size.

He referenced a study in which authors used a database of almost 10,000 students from 800 public, private, and Catholic schools. Researchers sought to find out how school size affected student learning and whether this was similar for different income levels and ethnicity. The criterion was how much learning took place during the four-year period between grades nine through twelve. Using the same tests, researchers used the difference between scores on math and reading tests given to the same students in the eighth and twelfth grades.

"The researchers found out that learning is best in high schools with 600–900 students, whether the schools are more or less affluent or whether more or fewer minority students are enrolled," Oz explained. "Above and below a size of 600–900, learning falls off, especially so in really small and really large high schools (less than 300 or more than 2,100).

"The difference in learning between more and less affluent students is smallest in small high schools and gets bigger as school size increases. Compared to rich kids, poor kids do better in small high schools than in large high schools."

He told trustees and Dr. Ahr why: "Small schools tend to have a good school climate; students and staffs know each other, and the learning environment is personable. However, these don't usually have the money for expanded curricula as do larger schools.

"Larger schools, while having the resources to obtain elaborate curricular and instructional choices, tend to become bureaucratic and impersonal."

Oz concluded, "We're lucky to have the resources for a series of smaller schools with optimal learning potential for between 600 and 900 students."

He warned against the Go Forward plan's approach: "Our student count for grades 9–12 is now over 1,700. Increasing the size of the Kapālama campus may make it harder to create an effective learning environment."

This was new information for Dr. Ahr, whose credentials didn't identify him as an educator. Despite this lack of experience, he and Mrs. Lindsey were determining Hawaiian children's future. Mrs. Lindsey was also attempting to influence Hawaiian culture by undoing Auntie Nona's efforts.

# PART SEVEN

# THIRD REVOLUTION

## CHAPTER 22

## Help the Children

### 1997

O z was agonizing: The princess's estate was meant to provide education to perpetuity, but unstable investments could bring it to a sudden end.

The Estate of King Lunalilo should have been larger than the Bishop Estate by now, but its land was sold and bad investments reduced the estate to $8 million. This provided only enough income to run a small home for old folks.

The Bishop Estate was wasting away, quietly and unnoticed. Investment returns were negligible. Inflation was eroding assets. A purging was imperative; trustees could not be dethroned without one, but Oz couldn't pull this off alone.

A revolution could be ignited if the court master uncovered and reported on the estate's true financial conditions. Momentum would grow if the Circuit Court judge became angry at trustees' malfeasance. Justice for the princess's beneficiaries might result if the current attorney general took on the estate and its lawyers.

But no one—court master, Circuit Court judge, or attorney general —had ever dared to challenge the Bishop Estate trustees. Might a public groundswell change this?

So many people fear Kamehameha Schools Bishop Estate: It owns the land on which they live, is a dominant employer and buyer of goods and services, and has links to powerful politicians. In addition, Hawaiians have a natural disinclination to challenge authority.

Outvoted trustee with no boardroom power, Oz decided to carry his battles outside of the boardroom. He would undertake guerrilla warfare by assuming the tactical offensive, selecting the forms, times, and places. The outcome would be determined by the extent to which he could raise public indignation. By assisting potential warriors who were destined to appear, he could harass entrenched trustees and their sycophants.

Minds of the masses blow with the trade winds. To obtain and sustain allegiance, his efforts had to be reinforced by a spectrum of information to erode the strength of the trustees and their cohorts. To organize a loose amalgam, he would become a "disguised champion."[1] This is a term from ancient Hawaiian tales where the hero does not come forward as a conqueror but uses spiritual powers to ensure victory to those who are fighting his causes. Disguise and surprise would be Oz's greatest advantages.

Others could play the part of vicious gnats stinging a large, clumsy beast, until it retreated in fury and aggravation.

He recognized the potential power structure residing in several branches: teachers, alumni, parents, community leaders, the attorney general's office, the court master. These branches could indoctrinate others to support the validity of his type of guerrilla war. Sheer numbers might be able to influence politically motivated persons such as justices of the Supreme Court, who sat on the fence, waiting to see the best way to jump. They were like the people of Laodicea, who, caught between two big powers in Biblical times, straddled the fence.

His objectives had to coincide with the aspirations of Hawai'i's people if he was to gain their sympathy, cooperation, and assistance against the entrenched political patronage system.

"Help the children" would be his rallying cry. No one loves children more than Hawaiians; their efforts would further the princess's dream.

---

[1] Kuali'i, king of O'ahu and Kaua'i, connected with the highest families of Moloka'i, is considered the epitome of the "disguised champion." He would remove his royal raiments and create a diversion among enemy troops by infiltrating and slaying huge numbers. Even in his nineties, according to legend, he defeated younger men with his own hands. Kuali'i lived to be 175 years old, according to a Lyman Museum publication, and died in 1730. Shortly before his death he called his trustiest *kahu* (priest) to his side, giving him the duty of hiding his bones after death so no one could get at them or desecrate them. When Kuali'i was dead and the body had been dissected and the flesh burned, according to custom, the *kahu* wrapped the bones in a bundle and started off, as everybody thought, to hide them in a cave or sink them in the ocean. Instead, he went to a lonely spot and pounded up the bones of the dead king into fine powder. Secreting this about his person, the *kahu* returned to court and ordered a grand feast in commemoration of the deceased. Chiefs from far and near attended. The night before the feast, the *kahu*, unobserved, mixed the powdered bones of Kuali'i in the poi prepared for the feast. At the close of the meal the following day, the *kahu* was asked by the chiefs present if he had faithfully carried out the wishes of the late king regarding his bones. With pride at his successful device, the *kahu* pointed to the stomachs of the assembled and replied that he had hidden his master's bones in a hundred living tombs. My Hawaiian bloodlines come from Kuali'i.

CHAPTER 23

# Colbert, the Court Master

## 1996 and Retrospective

Aᴄᴛᴇʀ ᴠɪsɪᴛɪɴɢ Colbert Matsumoto at a Zen Buddhist dojo, Governor Ben Cayetano said, "It was like being on the set of *Kung Fu*"—Colbert's head was even shaven.[1] "Colbert is spiritual and one of the most honest and decent persons I've ever met, and is strongly committed to the needs of the less fortunate"

Colbert's background was similar to many of Hawai'i's third-generation Japanese who became successful professionals. His grandmother, Kimiyo Kaya, came to Hawai'i as a picture bride for his grandfather, a contract worker in the island of Lāna'i's pineapple fields. Picture brides were expected to have strong backs, and she joined her husband in the fields.

When old enough to do stoop labor, their daughter Matsuko was there as well, wearing a straw hat, bandanna, and protective denim, laboring ten hours daily in the hot sun. In the late 1970s, when equal rights for women became a leading issue in our nation, Colbert's mother became a supervisor and later a field superintendent. Until then it was inconceivable that any woman could rise to a supervisory position on a plantation.

Yukio, Colbert's father, served in Europe with the 442nd Infantry Regiment during World War II. Shortly after he returned home from war, Yukio's father suddenly died. Yukio had to abandon plans to use G.I. Bill educational benefits and supported his widowed mother by working as a carpenter for the pineapple plantation on Lāna'i, later becoming an office clerk. Yukio became

---

[1] Almost every episode of the *Kung Fu* television series, starring Richard Carradine, included scenes of students learning mental discipline and karate skills in a temple.

a leader in the International Longshoremen and Workers Union (ILWU) and was involved in the plantation's major labor struggles.

While a youth, Colbert labored in the pineapple fields. His family instilled in him the Japanese sensitivity to not do anything that would bring dishonor or shame upon his family or community. "My father also taught me courage," Colbert said. "He encouraged me not to just accept things the way there were, but to consider different alternatives and perspectives. He supported my youthful experiences in challenging institutional authority, ingraining fearlessness within me."

Colbert spent his freshman year at the University of Hawai'i and completed his undergraduate education at the University of San Francisco, where he worked as a dorm counselor to pay for his room and board. He attended the University of California's Bolt Hall School of Law, in Berkeley, California, and returned to Hawai'i to practice law.

Colbert became a member and later president of the Honolulu Chapter of the Japanese American Citizens League. This chapter helped Hawai'i's World War II evacuees and returnees obtain redress and reparations for dislocation and internment during World War II.

His friendship with Benjamin Cayetano began when Colbert volunteered as a campaign worker on Cayetano's first State Senate campaign in

After exchanging pictures and having a broker arrange the marriage, brides from Japan joined their new husbands in Hawai'i for a lifetime of back-breaking work in the pineapple or sugarcane fields. *Kodak Hawai'i photo.*

1978. He spent many hours with Cayetano campaigning on pineapple and sugar plantations.

I n January 1996, the State Probate Court appointed Colbert as court master to examine the Bishop Estate's records for fiscal years 1994, 1995, and 1996. Princess Pauahi's will specified that the court have her estate reviewed annually.[2] Masters' reports have been as serious as the person appointed and just as flexible. Some were glowing, some were critical.

The job of court master was considered a rewarding though inconsequential assignment. It was inconsequential because trustees—recent ones, anyway—paid little attention to what masters wrote. The report is a public document accessible to the media and general public. Because the legalese in which they are usually written creates sleep-inducing yawns, court masters' reports receive scant attention.

The master is accountable to the probate court. However, there is no practical way to determine if a master has done a complete job of reviewing the trustees' account.

Colbert explained to me the initial frustrations this assignment brought him:

Approaching mid-1997, I was still fumbling my way along, struggling from lack of information, trying to scope out issues for concentration.

Trustees didn't disclose enough for me to figure out what kind of a job they were doing.

They certainly didn't view the annual review process as an opportunity to report their good work and promote public confidence in their stewardship. Their staff monitored me closely, limited my access to their books and records, and imposed copying restrictions.

I felt as though I was reviewing the CIA's finances rather than those of an educational organization. Previous masters weren't subjected to such restrictions. Why did trustees want to cover up the past three years' performance?

---

[2] "I also direct that my said trustees shall annually make a full and complete report of all receipts and expenditures and of the condition of said schools to the Chief Justice of the Supreme Court, or other highest judicial officer in this country; and shall also file before him annually an inventory of the property in their hands and how invested, and to publish the same in some newspaper published in Honolulu." Bernice Pauahi Bishop, "Wills and Deed of Trust: Bernice P. Bishop Estate."

CHAPTER 24

# Randie, the Music Maestro

## 1997

R ANDIE FONG, widely respected teacher of Hawaiian culture, attended Kamehameha Schools from kindergarten through high school. Unfortunately for him, he had to consult periodically with Lokelani Lindsey, who allowed little academic freedom.

Each year, Randie Fong hired instructors to teach voice parts to approximately 1,800 students for the song contest. Lokelani heard of this and they were "unhired."

Embarrassed over loss of face in the musical community, Randie had to tell the teachers he couldn't promise they would be paid for work up to that point. Lokelani later said all instructors could come back except for one individual. Randie had to promise not to tell anyone she caused the interruption. Her late approval meant Randie lost many veterans no longer available. Then she criticized him over youthful instructors.

Lokelani exercised detailed control over the annual song contest. She had final approval over announcers, program, student introductions, and the *hō'ike*—intermission entertainment while the judges tabulated the results. All this was formerly handled by the president's office.

She had to approve who was invited to the reception, the kind of leis people would be given to wear, and contest seating arrangements.

After the contest, she called in school executives to review a tape with her of the entire two-hour television broadcast as she criticized it. She did the same thing for commencement and baccalaureate ceremonies. Instead of being respected as a person deeply concerned that school events were well orchestrated, her management style caused others to regard her as a "control freak."

In 1997 the student body raised her ire to a nearly hysterical level. They spontaneously booed Trustee Lindsey when she was introduced during the song contest rehearsal.

By contrast, they cheered resoundingly when Dr. Chun was introduced during the actual contest.

Lokelani was furious and tried to launch an investigation to throw out the students who instigated the booing.

Booing Lokelani was not model behavior, and teachers lectured students on the importance of showing respect for others.

While Trustee Lindsey had her way, school president Dr. Michael Chun behaved with dignity and outward calmness, setting an example for students. *Photo courtesy of Dr. Michael Chun.*

When told of the incident, Dickie Wong declared: "I don't give a f---
about the song contest. I'll cancel it in a minute if the kids continue to show
such lack of appreciation for us." Thinking like a politician, Dickie was prepared to punish severely if opposed. His threat quieted things down, but it
didn't create appreciation.

R andie worked for two years on a campus Hawaiian Cultural Center approved by
trustees. His committee reviewed plans with over 300 community representatives; he
sent reports and information regularly to Lokelani. At the end of two years, he gave
her a comprehensive status report and videotape.

She told him he was working against the wishes of the trustees because he had
not planned a little house and unnecessarily involved lots of people. This was the first
time he heard she wanted a shack on the site. She killed the project—just like that.

Randie later told her he was leaving the school because of the way his life was
being affected, and, inexplicably, Lokelani stood up and started yelling irrationally:

"Who the f--- does Doctor Chun think he is? Ever since I've been here as a
trustee, no one has appreciated what I have done for the schools. And who the f---
does he think he is?"

*What is happening here? Why bring up Dr. Chun's name?* Randie wondered.

CHAPTER 25

# The Student and the Trustee Bully

### April 1999, Retrospective to April 1997

A PRIL, THE MONTH of Ching Ming, is party time at Chinese grave sites across Hawaiʻi. Families flock to the Mānoa Chinese Cemetery when the heavenly gates are open for spirits of the dead to visit.

Some groups remain at the grave all day, munching on whole roast pig and other treats. Food for the ancestors is arranged at the grave in sets of three or five; it must be in odd numbers: five cups of tea, five bowls of rice, and equal amounts of tasty treats. If the honored ancestor enjoyed a beer or two in life, that too is offered and poured out next to the grave.

Families bring food and liquor for their own enjoyment as they put life into perspective—renewing family ties, talking story about the old folks, and sharing a feast.

In addition to burning incense and lighting firecrackers, the families bring bags of *tum ngun* to burn: gold- and silver-flecked spiritual paper money folded into small, flat boats. The gifts appease the spirits, who can assure good fortune for their earthbound kin. Uncle Fred Wong burned spiritual money for his recently deceased wife Auntie Marion's "use in the afterlife."[1] Heart problems and cancer ended her struggles.

I was with the Wongs two years earlier when Marion and Fred included Mother and me in a party at their home. They called her "Auntie Ruth" and always included her in family events; they honored her for being the oldest person they knew. Appreciation for elders is one of the many things I like about the Chinese. As always, Fred Wong's cooking was superb, and he pre-

---

[1] Uncle Fred Wong told this story, relating some of it from an article writer Carol Chang filed with the Library of Congress.

pared extras for my mother to take home—enough to live on for almost a week.

Fred was Episcopal as was Marion, and the *tum ngun* ceremony was in the name of good spirits. Whether they embrace Buddhist or Christian teachings or none at all, Chinese come to the cemetery to share a family occasion; all of Hawai'i considers Ching Ming a month of great fun.

Chang Apana, the famous Honolulu detective who inspired the Charlie Chan series of adventures, is here in the Chinese Cemetery. He used to grant spiritual exemptions for gambling on the day Ching Ming begins.

I came to Honolulu in 1999 during Ching Ming. Being in town gave me the chance to meet Kamani Kualaau, a 1997 graduate of Kamehameha Schools. Oz and Kuulei Stender hosted a dinner for us at Sam Choy's restaurant.

Kamani had come back to Honolulu to encourage area prep school students to apply to Princeton University. He was student body president during the 1996–1997 year, when Mrs. Lindsey had the Kamehameha campus roiling.

O z described Kamani to me as "one of those kids who stands out." Very interested in the schools drug education program, Oz attended its functions, believing it was important for kids to see that a trustee cared. Kamani was on a panel; Oz, impressed with his demeanor, talked with him.

Kamani sometimes visited Oz in his trustee's office. For Oz, talking with Kamani was a way of closing circles—helping another as he himself had been helped by Charles Clark, Herb Cornuelle, and members of his focus group.

In 1997, while Chinese were partying and Oz was preparing for war, Kamani became an innocent symbol of the ends to which Lokelani would go to justify her meanness.

K amani described it to me:

> I suggested to other senior class officers that we express our concerns in a letter to trustees and print it as an advertisement in the newspapers. Naively, we thought if we did such a public thing, trustees would take care of the problem. We'd publish it after graduation to be safe.
>
> I spoke with the dean of student activities about it. He said we couldn't use class treasury funds for that purpose, so I collected names of alumni to approach for publication costs.

On the evening of April 30, Oz returned the call I'd made earlier in the day.

I told Oz, "Dr. Chun's job status is being discussed on campus. We want to pay for a full-page newspaper ad containing a letter to the trustees expressing students' love and admiration for Dr. Chun."

"That would be expensive," Uncle Oz told me. "Why not mail the letter to the Supreme Court justices instead?"

Kamani recalled Oz saying, "It looks like they're ready to get rid of him," meaning Dr. Chun. He said the telephone conversation lasted no more than five minutes.

After the phone call, Kamani looked for the senior class president to enlist his help in writing the letter they'd both sign. An English teacher proofread it.

"I carried the letter with me the next morning, May 1, 1997, and asked teachers if they'd allow me to read it out loud in class. I wanted to gauge students' feelings. Our letter noted that Kamehameha Schools was in a state of turmoil, several of its best teachers will be resigning or retiring, and many more are dissatisfied with the current board of trustees' new leadership and management styles. We said this situation adversely affects students."

After reading it to two classes, Kamani was ordered to the principal's office at 1:00 P.M. When Kamani appeared, Principal Ramos told him Mrs. Lindsey wanted to see him at 1:30 in her trustee office at Kawaiahaʻo Plaza. His parents were not contacted; the principal simply drove him there for a meeting lasting two and a half hours.

It began with Lokelani telling Kamani, "I do not call people into my office unless I have three things on them."

She read from a note pad: "A mother of an intermediate student told me that the student body president was doing a petition on campus and that intermediate students were being pressured. That is the first thing.

"You initiated a letter-writing campaign against the trustees and for Dr. Chun. That is the second thing.

"The third thing is that Trustee Stender called you and said the trustees are going to fire Dr. Michael Chun and that you, Kamani, needed to do something about it. Oz would pay to put your letter in the newspapers."

Kamani denied the first two things, and responding to the third said, "Trustee Stender did call me. But he didn't ask what you said."

The two interrogators tried to convince Kamani he was being used by Oz. He explained repeatedly he was not.

"Is President Chun going to be fired?" Kamani asked.

"There's never been discussion in the boardroom to fire him," Lokelani answered. Then she turned on him: "Do you know you're accused of being behind the applause for Dr. Chun at the song contest?"

At that point Kamani began crying.

With fervor, he said to me: "I couldn't believe people would disrespect Dr. Chun so much as to believe people weren't cheering because they love him!"

Lokelani pointed her finger at Kamani: "How would you feel if I wrote a letter to Princeton and told them you were a rabble-rouser?"

Accepted by Princeton for fall 1997, Kamani needed a Kamehameha Schools scholarship to help cover costs. Mrs. Lindsey could squash that.

"You have done something that can bring you to court. If you publish your letter, you could destroy the entire Kamehameha institution."

"I was frightened," Kamani said. "It was a scare tactic to stop me and it worked."

"If anyone finds out about this meeting, it will be because you told them," Lokelani said as she dismissed Kamani.

While driving him back to campus, Principal Ramos asked, "What are you going to do now?"

"Nothing." Kamani felt that if he did, he would be back at Mrs. Lindsey's office with her finger stabbing at him.

Oz was in a board meeting when Kamani had called earlier in the day. During the meeting he'd handed each trustee a memo and started speaking before Dickie had the chance to declare him out of order.

His memo was a "manifesto" in which he stated his intentions. In it he described morale problems and the loss of good people because of Mrs. Lindsey's micromanagement.

> It is an affront to all Kamehameha alumni and current students for Mrs. Lindsey saying in public that the school needs to be "cleaned up."
>
> Prior to Mrs. Lindsey's changes, Kamehameha reached more than 30,000 Hawaiians at a net cost of $61.95 million. It provided education to Hawaiians from prenatal and postnatal education to post and higher adult education.
>
> By contrast, in the past year with Mrs. Lindsey as lead trustee for education, the school touched about 3,200 Hawaiians—one tenth as many—at a net operating cost of $87.60 million.
>
> For her to state that the entire administrative staff at Kamehameha is not competent or qualified to do their job is an affront to good people recognized in the education community as among the best.
>
> I am concerned about huge sums of money being spent by trustees on contract services without consulting the affected staff. On the other hand, we "nickel-and-dime" staff requests to no end.

In board meetings, Mrs. Lindsey often told Oz that what he had to say was inappropriate because he was not "an educator." This day he replied to her nagging criticism: "There is very little difference between managing a business and managing a school. People are your most important asset and how you treat them individually or as a group is with care and respect for being the professionals they are."

He declared war against boardroom secrecy: "From this point forward, I will express my concerns openly, especially on anything relating to education.

"I love Kamehameha for what it has done for me and what Kamehameha represents to all Hawaiians everywhere. While it pains me to have to go through this most trying time for Kamehameha—I must."

No one reacted to his impassioned remarks.

*What will it take to wake them up?* Oz wondered.

CHAPTER 26

# Nona Writes a Letter

## 1997

"MAYDAY" is the international radiotelephone distress signal. "May Day is Lei Day" in Hawai'i when, as a song goes, you toss aside a load of care and wear a flower wreath. Sarah Keahi used both associations on May 1, 1997, when she phoned KGMB-TV, leaving a message for Winona Beamer to call after she finished her "Lei Day" interview.

"Auntie Nona, you must help Kamehameha," Sarah began when Nona returned her call. She tossed her load of care to the 74-year-old. Sara was anguished by drastic changes in the Hawaiian language department.[1]

Nona lived on the island of Hawai'i, about a half-hour's flying time from O'ahu. Listening to Sara made her feel that her family's belief system was being attacked. It was as if Lokelani had slapped her in the face. Nona Beamer believed that the past was good, but we must build on it. She began using the word "Hawaiiana" in 1949 to describe the process she developed as a part-time teacher at Kamehameha Schools; it combined both the old and the new.

Lokelani's edict put Kamehameha Schools students at a disadvantage at the University of Hawai'i. Kaliko Beamer Trapp, descendent of the famed

---

[1] If Lokelani read the "Acknowledgments" to the *Hawaiian-English Dictionary* of 1957 that she endorsed, she would have read these words by its authors Mary Kawena Pukui and Samuel E. Elbert: "[Hawaiian] is one of the oldest living languages of the earth . . . and may well be classed among the best . . . the thought to displace it or doom it to oblivion by substituting the English language, ought not for a moment to be indulged." I knew Aunt Mary when I worked at the Bishop Museum; she worked at the front door, had a flower in her hair every day over her right ear, and usually wore a *kukui* lei. I went to school with her daughter Pele who became an outstanding chanter, often appearing with Kaupena Wong, who also studied chanting with her mother.

singing Trapp family on whom the musical *The Sound of Music* was based, had been adopted by Auntie Nona into the Beamer clan as a *hānai* son—a foster child. He dropped the "von"—the Austrian term of nobility—from his surname and added Beamer. A Hawaiian language scholar, editor, writer, and composer, Kaliko was helping to develop the Hawaiian language curriculum at the University of Hawai'i–Hilo; he was a neologist who created new Hawaiian words for modern English words.

The young Trapp had picked up the Beamer way to keep a culture alive: adding freshness through creativity. The talented Beamer family is famous as innovators in modern Hawaiian music and hula as well as preservers of tradition. They keep it interesting so mainlanders as well as Islanders will want more. Her Aunt Aggie Auld, who danced in Hollywood movies, taught Spike Jones a novelty version of the "Hawaiian War Chant" and instructed Sonja Henie in hula-on-ice routines. No one composed more hapa haole (half white) songs than "Uncle Alex," Alex Anderson, a family friend. Hapa haole music has English words and a melody conveying the lilt and gaiety of Hawai'i—it makes Island music widely popular; many songs sung by Don Ho are of this genre.

Auntie Nona loves to talk story and include you within her experiences. She told me, "The first time Uncle Alex saw Aggie dance, he heard someone say, 'Aren't her hands lovely?' Remembering this phrase, he composed 'Lovely Hula Hands' while on a friend's yacht; he 'saw' the line in the song: 'Gliding like the gulls over the ocean.' He wrote the words to "Blue Lei" based on flowers from a jacaranda tree, a sea of blue, that was in the Beamer yard; my brother Milton wrote the music."

"Recordings by my sons Keola and Kapono Beamer helped popularize Hawaiian 'slack key' guitar with its unusual tunings and baroque playing style."[2]

After hearing from Sarah, Auntie Nona decided to stay on O'ahu for a few days with my cousin Kea until she could find out what was happening on campus. Calling

---

[2] This music, like falsetto singing and steel guitar music, is specifically Hawaiian and combines musical elements of traditional chant (original talk stories) with those of foreign sources. The six strings are loosened, or slackened, to the pitches of a major triad, although the outline of the triad is avoided in the bass strings. In the key of G, the common tuning woud be D G D G B D (taro patch tuning). Many tunings exist and they are kept secret within the 'ohana—extended family. A slack key guitar is plucked rather than strummed, the melody accompanied by a plucked bass. Keola Beamer began popularizing it widely in 1973.

scores of people—teachers, alumni, parents—Nona learned that Sarah was just one of many angry persons.

She was told, "Mrs. Lindsey acts as if Kamehameha Schools are personal property over which she has complete control. She even handed out the graduation diplomas, an honor formerly handled by the schools president and principals. Everyone is afraid of her. Faculty was considering forming a union to protect their jobs."

Knowing she had a constituency, Auntie Nona prepared a letter on May 3, 1997, directed to justices of the State Supreme Court. Kea faxed a copy to me in New York and I phoned back to say, "Don't change a word." It came straight from Auntie Nona's heart.

She read her letter to Oz over the phone. When Oz told her that the strong tone of her letter might cause her to be sued, Auntie Nona replied, "I'm too old to care and I don't have any money." She signed it with her name and stated that it was written on behalf of countless students, faculty, staff, parents, graduates, friends, and associates of the Kamehameha Schools.

R oy Benham, former alumni association president, was among those from whom Nona gathered information about what was happening at the schools. "Hold off on sending your letter until alumni can discuss it this week," he requested. Cousin Kea gave Nona's letter to Paulette Moore, class of 1952, to take to a May 4 meeting at an alumnus's home.

"I read it to the group," Paulette Moore told me. "Both Oz and Roy were there; we discussed Lokelani's hanky-panky and how politicians were dragging down the school. Those present wanted to add their signatures to Nona's letter. I was afraid to do so because my daughter worked in the KSBE investment department. My name on the letter might jeopardize her job."

Kea sent a fax copy of the letter to Greg Barrett, a reporter she knew at the *Honolulu Advertiser.* He called her back excitedly, saying his editor wanted to run the letter as a newspaper feature article, and he might write an editorial. She recalls his words: "This is big. It will shake everyone up. Nona Beamer's reputation is top rate in the Hawaiian community and in Hawai'i in general. She is recognized as a 'Living Treasure' and has done a great deal for the culture and for Kamehameha Schools."

Here is Nona's letter:

An appeal to the Supreme Court of the State of Hawai'i:
Kamehameha Schools trustee Lokelani Lindsey has shamed the Hawaiian people!

Her high-handed tactics on campus with students, staff and faculty have completely demoralized the entire Kamehameha 'ohana!

The deep concerns have spread through the community, neighbor islands, and farther.

Mrs. Lindsey's micromanagement methodology is an utterly diabolical plan of a self-serving egoist!

We call for impeachment and Supreme Court redress!

There had been no previous public criticism. Oz had taken his anguish no farther than to close friends within his focus groups. There'd been no reason for the newspaper to take on the powerful secretive estate, with its influence permeating virtually every aspect of Hawaiian business.

Hawaiians always rallied to defend the Bishop Estate in the past. But what a person of Nona Beamer's stature wrote and was published in a reputable newspaper could not be ignored.

In its May 8, 1997, article the *Advertiser* stated, "Nona was stirred to action when plans to update the Hawaiian language curriculum were canceled recently by trustees." In what proved to become an understatement, the newspaper quoted Governor Cayetano as saying, "The Hawaiian community has brought the problem to light."

In an editorial, the *Honolulu Advertiser* responded to Auntie Nona's letter with the following prophetic excerpts:[3]

> A painful "family" dispute within Bishop Estate/Kamehameha Schools has become public, but not public enough. Lindsey's opponents say she is a disruptive micromanager who has usurped the authority of popular school president Michael Chun. . . .

> The schools and the estate operate on a tax-exempt basis, so every taxpayer has at least a related interest. . . . Kamehameha Schools is a unique institution, one that brings international attention to the Islands and the Hawaiian people.

Adjacent to the editorial was a cartoon of the famous statue of King Kamehameha I labeled "Kamehameha Schools." The artist drew the king seated, instead of

---

[3] In addition to clippings supplied by my "aunties" in Hawai'i, e-mail with copies of radio and TV broadcasts and comments on Internet items began arriving daily from friends in Hawai'i, often with a note attached. The note attached to this "file" stated, "The *kūkae* has hit the *kāhili*"—saying, in essence, "fecal matter has hit the fan." The royal symbol of a *kāhili* has a somewhat fanlike appearance.

standing; he looks depressed and holds a limp spear. Two spectators are looking at him; one questions the other about the possible cause of the king's impotence—"Low morale?"

During her twenty-three years at Kamehameha, Winona Beamer taught Hawaiian children not to be afraid to express themselves. Now she would demonstrate her own fearlessness.

After the newspaper published Auntie Nona's letter, Lokelani's attorney issued a subpoena to Nona. Lokelani used this procedure routinely to intimidate anyone crossing her path. Nona called Kea, who contacted one of our relatives who is an attorney. This lawyer explained to Lokelani's attorney that Nona had been hired to teach the hula on a cruise ship and couldn't be in court when they wanted her: "How about having a conference call?"

The three-way conversation included Lokelani's lawyer, Nona's lawyer, and Nona. Lokelani's attorney wanted Nona to say she got her information about Lokelani from Oz.

"I am not going to say that. It is not true."

"He must have told you those things about Lokelani Lindsey."

"No such thing. I have been hearing this information for over a year."

"When did Oswald Stender tell you about Lokelani Lindsey?"

"He has never said anything."

Nona said later that it was obvious they wanted to use her to get at Oz. "That was contemptible. Oz is a good, honest man who cares about Hawai'i's children."

The conference call ended it for the moment. Auntie Nona took the cruise ship job. She would show Lokelani Lindsey's lawyers how to dance later.

## CHAPTER 27

# The Integrity of the Trust

### 1997

O N MAY 5, Colbert was having dinner with a Kamehameha Schools graduate who told him, "Dr. Chun is going to be fired."

"What? What are you talking about?" Colbert responded.

"Yes, the trustees are going to fire Mike Chun. On top of that, Randie Fong is resigning and going to work for Punahou."

Colbert knew who Randie Fong was. "Why would he resign? Randie's been there almost all his life?"

"Lokelani Lindsey is causing a lot of controversy on campus. Auntie Nona is planning to write a letter to be published in the newspaper that will blast the trustees."

Colbert knew this man was well connected with other alumni. During the next day, he thought to himself, *What my friend said must be reliable. If someone like Nona Beamer is willing to criticize trustees publicly, things must be pretty bad.*

Colbert realized his report would now be in the public spotlight turned on by Auntie Nona. He told me his reaction after reading a newspaper editorial discussing Auntie Nona's letter.

"I decided to go to the schools' archives to read Princess Pauahi and Charles Bishop's writings. I reviewed background material from their era to understand the historical context of what they wrote. The whole point of the court master's work is to determine if the integrity of the trust's original intent is being maintained.

"The school archivist showed me other information critical in shaping my thinking."

Colbert studied Booz Allen Hamilton's 1960 report aimed at meeting the challenges statehood and Hawai'i's imminent growth and expansion presented the Native Hawaiian population. The consultants had recommended expanding the Hawaiian cultural efforts started by Nona Beamer in 1949. They suggested adding an extension program and giving college-bound students scholarships. Colbert said, "Booz Allen demonstrated the kind of analysis and thinking that needs to be in a proper strategic plan. The estate had done nothing like it for forty years."

Colbert went through Trustee Midkiff's collection of documents; they shed light on past controversies and issues considered by trustees. He found the Barnes' ideal of the 1930s and 1940s for a small, elite school—instead of the all-purpose school Midkiff favored—particularly illuminating in view of the current goals.

"I was impressed by how cautious and conservative past trustees were about making changes. They consulted regularly with the court to make certain they were well within the will's parameters. In contrast, over the last ten years trustees never went to the court for instruction. The concept of accountability had eroded significantly."

He reviewed court masters' reports. In the late 1980s, when the estate began to amass income, some masters suggested the need for long-range planning.

The Bishop Estate had evolved from being a real property landlord, passively collecting lease rents from tenants on its Hawaiian land holdings, into a complex business organization with wide-ranging, sophisticated domestic and international financial investments. Management practices had not kept up with the new dynamics.

Colbert worked in the quiet archives of the Midkiff Learning Center, as I did over the years. He touched and read material in its original form. During breaks he walked on campus and observed beneficiaries in their learning atmosphere. "These experiences motivated me to achieve the princess's wishes for full disclosure," he confided.

I understood: Colbert had become a warrior for the princess. He would become the most formidable and aggressive person ever to evaluate the Bishop Estate—and possibly the most enlightened.

CHAPTER 28

# The Alumni Meet—and March

## 1997

AFTER NONA'S letter was published, thirty alumni held a three-hour meeting at the Pacific Club. Oz arranged it and was there.

These alumni decided to name their new organization "Nā Pua Ke Aliʻi Pauahi"—"The Flowers of Pauahi." This was because they represented beneficiaries of the princess's will and weren't acting as an official alumni association. Nā Pua's list of concerns centered on three points:

1. Return management of the schools to the principals and president;
2. Reinstate talk story sessions with alumni, parents, and students;
3. Allow faculty, staff, and students to express thoughts and concerns without fear of retribution.

Dutchy Kapu Saffrey suggested presenting the list to the trustees at their offices in Kawaiahaʻo Plaza.

Months earlier, trustees had scheduled talk story meetings with alumni for May 13 and 15. When they heard alumni were eager to uproot rumors of Dr. Chun being in danger, they realized attendance at the meetings might be large.

Alumni weren't adversarial; they were saying among themselves, "Trustees can make mistakes as do the rest of us. Our differences can be resolved." Some of them referred to it as the chance for *hoʻoponopono,* a talk story session leading to healing.

After checking with Lokelani, who opposed it, Dickie Wong canceled the talk story sessions, claiming "trustee scheduling difficulties."

Oz shook his head while recalling this: "It was the critical moment for trustees to hear members of the Kamehameha family voice concerns. Trustees blew it. I felt they would."

According to Roy Benham, "If the four trustees had come away from our talk stories and said to Mrs. Lindsey, 'Hey Lokelani, back off,' she would have had to. Otherwise she has their support and all trustees must take blame for her actions."

The problem was that Mrs. Lindsey, Dickie Wong, and Henry Peters had no respect for alumni. Oz told me what they said about us in the boardroom:

When he wanted alumni to demonstrate at the State Legislature prior to a bill being voted on, Dickie remarked, "Eh, those Hawaiians, all you need do is give 'em beer, stew and rice and they'll come out."

Mrs. Lindsey asked trustees to help her write a letter to alumni.

"Have the PR department prepare it," I said.

Mrs. Lindsey answered, "We have to be very careful about how we word this thing because it is going to a lot of people who can't even read at an eighth grade level."

"Mrs. Lindsey, this goes to Kamehameha alumni," I reminded her.

"Well—they can't read."

Roy asked Oz how the alumni group should make their demonstration at the trustees' headquarters. Oz suggested visiting chief justices as well and offered these ideas: "Each of you phones a Kamehameha friend and asks that friend to call another friend to build the size of the protest. Do not carry signs, do not shout, and do not in any other way diminish the name of our princess. Walk with dignity and wear a lei. Remember, we are doing this to help the children."

Members of the group echoed his words: "To help the children. . . ."

He suggested holding the march early enough in the day for coverage in the evening papers and on television stations' early evening news broadcasts.

Dr. Chun warned students not to skip school to march; this would be considered an unexcused absence. According to school guidelines, unexcused absences resulted in one grade drop for each class missed.

Faculty didn't join in because a clause in their yearly contracts prohibited actions or statements critical of Kamehameha Schools or the Bishop Estate. They were not even allowed to have an association.

Risking their jobs, an ad hoc group calling themselves "Nā Kumu O Kamehameha"—"Teachers of Kamehameha"—met three times off campus the week before the march. They prepared a document listing concerns, proclaiming loyalty to the school and its students, and asking trustees to meet with them. Their communiqué closed with these words: "If there is no action, we will nail this to a church door"—indicating that their statement would be made public anonymously.

Roy Benham agreed to present Nā Kumu's material to the trustees along with Nā Pua's.

While the alumni's planning was underway, Auntie Nona's letter was creating a groundswell. Greg Barrett, the reporter to whom Kea sent a fax of Nona's letter, did a follow-up on his earlier story:

> The frustration of teachers, parents, and alumni over what they say is micro-management of Kamehameha Schools by the trustees was given voice this week when alumna Nona Beamer complained in a letter to the Supreme Court, which appoints the trustees.
>
> Problems that stem from excessive regulations, declining teacher morale and the shrinking authority of school president Michael Chun have been building for months, and some say years, according to people who called our paper yesterday.
>
> Two years ago Stender had to talk a frustrated Dr. Chun out of resigning and taking the chancellor's position at Chun's alma mater, the University of Kansas. Teachers have been complaining, even crying sometimes, in the office of performing arts director Randy Fong, one teacher told us.

The story concluded with an alumnus's optimistic words: "We all love and value Kamehameha and its students. We just have to discuss things and work toward a resolution in a traditional Hawaiian fashion."

By calling it a "march," the media had almost everyone using that word for the event that brought public attention to Kamehameha Schools problems. "It was really a walk," said Roy Benham, who helped organize it.

"Mrs. Lindsey's behavior provoked the Kamehameha family to do a very un-Hawaiian thing," U.S. District Court Senior Judge Samuel P. King told Steve Kroft of the CBS *60 Minutes* TV show. "They staged a protest march. If the trustees had just sat down and conferred with them, none of this would have happened and they could have gone on their merry way ripping off the trust without beneficiaries worrying about it."

Newspapers quoted persons using the word *"ho'oponopono"* to describe the kind of discussions alumni sought. As Roy Benham confided, "Trustees wouldn't understand anything that formal. We just wanted to talk."

Puristically, Roy, class of 1942 and former president of the Kamehameha Alumni Association, was right on both counts. Alumni did not "march" in parade formation.

They walked for 3 miles; one alumna, the late "Rockie" Pokuhara, rolled in a wheel-chair. Except for Oz, trustees were emotionally incapable of talking story in *ho'opono-pono* style.

*H*o'oponopono is a peacemaking process generally—but not exclusively—considered for family or extended family disputes.

The word means "to make things right." Its ingredients include a belief in God or a higher power than one's self, a mutual desire to solve the problem under such spiritual support, and agreement to accept the resolution reached through *ho'opono-pono*. It includes prayer, absolute truth, confession, repentance, release, and healing.

All involved agree to commit themselves to it for resolution. All acquiesce to the process: Everything said or done is in absolute confidence and not to be discussed again; all speak the truth openly and extend respect to each participant.

Should the problem prevent a feeling of mutual understanding, participants must restore "aloha"—the Hawaiian word encapsulating respect and kindness toward others.

The leader is selected by his or her character, integrity, and impartiality, not by popularity. Participants speak only to the leader, who directs everyone in prayer, discussion, and sometimes silence. The leader asks all questions. No one speaks to another until the leader's final prayer. A figurative cord linking members of the group in mutual unpleasantness must be untied by all.

The usual conclusions are hugs and sometimes tears of relief.

*T*he day before the march, Roy Benham and Tomi Chong, an alumna, arranged to meet Dickie Wong on campus. To their surprise, Mrs. Lindsey was present.

"This is your last chance to talk with the alumni," Roy explained.

Roy and Tomi were carrying out an ancient Hawaiian tradition in which chiefs of opposing forces met the day before battle to discuss possible resolution or terms of the battle. The two trustees neither reacted nor mentioned they had selected a fact finder that very same day.

Gerry Jervis had suggested hiring a fact finder to determine if there truly was a morale and micromanagement problem. His legal training led him to believe that if the fact finder determined Mrs. Lindsey innocent of what Nona Beamer had written, then Nona and her letter could be discredited.

Trustees signed a petition on May 14 asking the Probate Court to appoint retired Judge Patrick Yim as fact finder for the trustees. The judge seemed a safe choice: He was a loyal Democrat, and one of his maternal aunts was married to Henry Peters' father.

Paulette Moore describes the now-legendary walk to Kawaiahaʻo Plaza:

About 200 of us gather at the Royal Mausoleum at mid-morning on May 15. We wear lei with all colors of the rainbow, bearing fragrances of ginger, jasmine, gardenia, plumeria, carnation, and maile. We carry lei to place on the princess's tomb. We pray there and sing "He Inoa ka Wahine," Pauahi's name song.

Dutchy Kapu Saffrey and Roy Benham lead us downtown. The obligation to save the estate is more important than helping my daughter preserve her job, so my husband Bobby and I go near the front.

Dutchy chants a sentence in Hawaiian in her strong, resonant voice. We repeat its last few words in traditional Kamehameha Schools four-part harmony. The eighteenth-century chant describes King Kamehameha the Great's lineage. Dutchy continues the chant as we walk.

I chant the scripture in Hawaiian at St. Andrew's Episcopal Cathedral, but without a chorus responding in rich chords like today's. It is thrilling and strengthens our resolve. We walk proudly, shoulders back, looking straight ahead—as when students.

Spectators stand on sidewalks and on condominium balconies.

Without intending to, we become jaywalkers—the traffic light changes as we are in the middle of crossing the street. Motorists wait patiently, some nod approvingly so we can continue and stay together. Most smile, some wave; no one honks or says mean things.

Once we are downtown, alumni join us from business offices. Police arrive to halt automobile traffic.

---

We walk to Washington Place, the queen's former home; at that time it was the governor's mansion. Governor Ben Cayetano and Mrs. Vicky Liu Cayetano are back from their honeymoon—they were married ten days ago. They invite Roy, Tomi, Dutchy, and Fred Cachola to come in. Roy tells us Attorney General Margery Bronster was with them; they were cordial and impressed by our turnout.

At ʻIolani Palace, we present flowers at the base of Queen Liliʻuokalani's statue and sing "Makalapua," the hauntingly sweet song she composed about a queen fond of flowers. Since we don't have permission to enter the palace as a group, we stand beneath the room where our Queen Liliʻuokalani was kept prisoner when Americans overthrew her kingdom. We sing "The Queen's Prayer" in Hawaiian, using four-part women's harmony, as we did before dinner sometimes at Kamehameha School for Girls.

Approximately 700 alumni march from ʻIolani Palace to Bishop Estate headquarters at Kawaiahaʻo Place as a show of concern about trustees' school management. Honolulu Star-Bulletin *photo by Craig T. Kojima.*

The Queen wrote it in the room just above us; she was asking God to pardon those who rose up against her: "Behold not with malevolence the sins of man, but forgive and cleanse." Everyone in the congregation sings it as part of the Eucharist during the Hawaiian Mass Sundays at St. Andrew's Cathedral.

We cross the street to the statue of King Kamehameha. Our ranks have swelled to over 700 alumni, and we vigorously sing "Imua Kamehameha," our school fight song.

><

We are expected at the Supreme Court. Roy and Tomi and four others are invited inside to present our list of concerns to Chief Justice Ronald Moon. Roy said that Justice Moon explained, "After the trustees are appointed we can do nothing; management is in their hands."

We become silent when nearing Kawaiaha'o Church. This was the princess's church and we show reverence. Even our footsteps are slower, almost muffled as we pass.

We walk around the block surrounding the trustees' headquarters before

Pausing from their march, alumni and supporters emotionally sing "Imua Kamehameha," the school's fight song, in front of the statue of King Kamehameha. Kea, the woman second from the right, the author's cousin, marched to represent Nona Beamer, who was on the Island of Hawai'i at the time. The letter Nona Beamer wrote to judges and a newspaper while at Kea's residence earlier in the month led to this show of alumni outrage. Honolulu Star-Bulletin *photo by Craig T. Kojima.*

entering the courtyard. Mrs. Lindsey has staff members photographing marchers to identify participants. We know she will strike back if she can link students or employees with marchers.

I hear Roy call out teasingly, "Save me some pictures to send to my grand-children."

Paulette says she was frightened as she approached a photographer, but the man taking the pictures knew her and put his camera down as she and Bobby passed by. She concludes her story with these words: "My daughter darts behind a pillar and waves. Friends say, 'There are your mother and your father.'

"My daughter answers, 'No one can stop my mother, including my father.'"

C ousin Kea saw trustees looking out of their second-floor windows; Oz waved cheerily, Gerry Jervis looked sick, Lokelani Lindsey scowled, and Henry wasn't seen.

Roy spoke up, expressing Nā Pua's concerns and handing the Nā Pua and Nā Kumu statements to Dickie Wong, who came to the outside plaza area. Giving a big toothy smile, Dickie promised the assembly that all trustees would meet with them next week. "Please, bring no more than twelve Nā Pua representatives."

After delays, the meeting was finally scheduled, but only Dickie, Gerry Jervis, and a Bishop Estate attorney appeared. Feeling insulted, Nā Pua representatives, including former trustee Pinky Thompson, walked out before Dickie called the meeting to order.

The march became the symbolic end of the opportunity for *ho'oponopono*. Jan Dill, class of 1961 and vice president of Nā Pua, explained: "We were naive. Nobody thought the trustees would stonewall everything."

F aculty waited vainly to meet with trustees. Their situation under Mrs. Lindsey was similar to a dysfunctional family trapped in an abusive relationship: Every time an abuse occurs, family members are threatened and told not to say anything to anyone.

There was even denial by the abuser. As in a domestic abuse case, Mrs. Lindsey controlled through fear and intimidation, claiming what she did was "for the good of the school."

Instead of releasing their two-page statement anonymously, four teachers representing over 200 members of Nā Kumu Kamehameha personally stepped forward. They bravely put their names on the statement so local newspapers would be willing to publish it.

By ignoring the faculty, trustees inadvertently shifted campus discussions into a public forum. Faculty was included among the protesters.

Oz realized trustees would keep the dispute over Lindsey's role clouded in secrecy and confusion by declining to talk. This left critics with the dominant voice; trustees buried themselves in a silent, defensive bunker—Kawaiaha'o Plaza was their fortress. Faculty explored different models for organizing formally; a union was one model. They asked one of my cousins by marriage for help; a mathematics teacher, he headed the faculty union at Mid-Pacific Institute, another private school, and helped to "unionize" them.

T rustees petitioned the Probate Court for "privileged advice and counsel" by their hand-picked fact finder, meaning no one else could receive the fact finder's information. Secrecy would cover up problems Nā Kumu was trying to address.

Nā Pua planned to object to Circuit Judge Patrick Yim's selection as the fact finder. Oz relayed the advice that trustees wouldn't proceed with anyone but Yim: "Don't fight that battle."

N ā Pua developed a web site, initiated "chat" groups, held meetings, issued news releases, and retained Kea's friend Beadie Dawson as its lawyer. She served free of charge.

Beadie, a former deputy assistant state attorney general, described Nā Pua as "guardian ad litem of unborn Hawaiian and part-Hawaiian children." Because trustees' attorneys claimed that the physical school itself is the sole beneficiary of the princess's will, Nā Pua initiated a legal action to recognize *people*—not buildings— as beneficiaries.

Nā Pua's directors included Kamehameha's student body president, senior class president, a representative of the association of parents and teachers, and a representative of the board of presidents of the Kamehameha Schools Alumni Association. This association included alumni in the Islands and on the mainland.

Nā Pua opened its membership to others beyond the Kamehameha *'ohana* (family). Beadie, a Punahou graduate, was an example.

Toni Lee, Nā Pua's president, did not march on May 15. She needed to be on the mainland where her daughter, Brook Lee, Miss USA, was in the Miss Universe contest the next day. George Hamilton, the pageant's host, asked each finalist questions to address to the audience. Among those the well-tanned movie star posed to Brook was, "How does it feel to be Hawaiian?" She'd learned to be proud of her heritage at Kamehameha Schools. The 1989 graduate's answer helped Brook win the Miss Universe contest

Toni returned home immediately after the contest to help Nā Pua grow to almost 3,000 members. In a news release, she echoed the faculty's complaint: "Instead of sitting down with concerned groups to discuss resolution, the trustees asked the court to allow their fact finder to prepare a secret report exclusively for their review."

Jan Dill pointed out that Kamehameha *'ohana* identified the problems, not the State government, not outside observers. "We sought repeatedly to discuss issues privately with trustees. How did they react? They went outside the family to the Probate Court. They wanted the court to appoint a cordial fact finder who would deliver a report covering everything up. Instead of relying on all the powerful values that have allowed the Hawaiian culture to touch the world with love, defined by the word 'aloha,' the trustees wanted protection and cover."

Oz and allies turned on the intensity. Distinguished members of the community prepared a major essay for publication having fervor similar to Thomas Paine's. His writing inspired American's action against the mighty British in the Revolutionary War.

I n early June 1997, Nā Pua's attorney Beadie Dawson argued before a circuit judge that Kamehameha Schools alumni, students, and their parents are the Bishop Estate's beneficiaries. She told the judge that Attorney General Margery Bronster supported this claim. Beadie also suggested that the judge remove herself from the matter because her husband's law firm had done work for the Bishop Estate.

The judge recused herself and the court ruled in favor of Dawson's request for temporary continuance of Nā Pua's beneficiary status. It granted Nā Pua's request that Judge Yim's fact finding report be made public. Both decisions strengthened Nā Pua's resolve.

A newspaper ran Kamani Kualaau's story about being interrogated for two and a half hours by Trustee Lindsey. He was welcomed by Princeton University and out of Lokelani's reach.

In another newspaper article, Oz wrote:

The trustees' Gestapo-like atmosphere seems paranoid at best; clandestine at worst. They accuse me of going behind the scenes to direct criticism at them.

All I'm trying to do is keep the focus and get on with the process. I'm steering things in a way that will help everyone.

My office phone is bugged. When discussing sensitive issues surrounding the Kamehameha issue controversy, I turn up the volume on my office radio to drown out my words.

It isn't KSBE anymore, it's the KGB.

Oz was shadowed by a private investigator whose activities were supervised by fellow trustee Gerry Jervis.

Oz described the estate's newly decorated offices as resembling a nightclub, having $4 million touches such as *koa* wood paneling, black marble floors, and an indirect lighting system.

Yet in budget meetings, Mrs. Lindsey combs each teacher's request, line by line. She questioned an order for 250 pens costing 10 cents each, a total of $25.

She spends a huge amount on new hires and contract services without discussing them. On the other hand, she nickels and dimes staff requests to no end.

O z told me that Gerry Jervis threw the newspaper containing the article at him. When he stood up to leave the boardroom, Gerry flamed up and yelled, "Go on! Get the f--- out of here. You're not part of the team."

Oz retaliated in writing to this treatment by the trustees:

"Gerry's abusive language is typical of trustees' behavior. It is this way of dealing with people that has brought us to this point. How much more pain from this sort of treatment can our people endure before we see a revolution of change?"

Gerry Jervis, lead trustee for the legal department, used a private investigator to keep track of Oz. Honolulu Advertiser *photo by Bruce Asato.*

He wrote the word *"revolution"*—not *"evolution."*

The trustees didn't get it—or they didn't care. They were used to pressuring persons they didn't think could strike back.

L okelani barred teachers from meeting in the school cafeteria. They met at a public intermediate school to discuss their concerns. That's where my cousin, president of the teacher's union at Mid-Pacific Institute, helped "unionize" Kamehameha teachers.

On August 9, Lokelani had teaching contracts for the new school year mailed with a notice that the offer would expire if the signed contract was not back by August 11—the same day most teachers received the contracts. This should have been done by March; teachers have families, mortgages, and other obligations making their job uncertainty tortuous.

Her lieutenants in the alumni office outwardly criticized alumni. One refused to let Toni Lee, Nā Pua's president, continue serving as an usher at school events. When an alumnus came to the office for tickets to a reunion event, another asked, "Were you in the march?" Without waiting for a response, she went on, "You old folks do nothing but make trouble."

After listening to one of Lokelani's lieutenants, alumni association members voted not to support "the radicals" in Nā Pua until the fact-finding process was completed. "That lousy decision gave trustees a sense of security," Roy Benham told me. "Presidents of alumni chapters from Hawai'i and the mainland were misguided; they were led to believe they were showing loyalty to their school by not allying with us Nā Pua militants."

T rustees couldn't control Nā Pua. Growing public awareness baffled them, even though Oz had stated he would "go public."

Beadie Dawson spoke to the Honolulu Rotary about Nā Pua's activities and the Bishop Estate. Rotary voted to give Nā Pua a $10,000 grant as the club's favorite nonprofit. Rotary now included persons of my grandfather's "sort."

On August 9, "Broken Trust" appeared in the *Honolulu Star-Bulletin*—pages and pages of it. The title alone was as attention grabbing as were Thomas Paine's opening words to an essay: "These are the times that try men's souls."

CHAPTER 29

# "Broken Trust" Appears

## 1997

"IF THE MARCH had not occurred, the chance that the governor would have appointed the attorney general to look into the estate is minuscule," says Randy W. Roth, law professor at the University of Hawai'i and longtime critic of the trustees. Randy teaches wills, trusts, and taxes at the University of Hawai'i law school named after Judge William Richardson, retired Bishop Estate trustee. He told me of his own efforts.

"I had been following the Bishop Estate from a professor of trust law's point of view. I was fascinated not only by the mission and history of this particular trust and the size of the estate, but also by the fact there were obvious breaches of trust seemingly done with impunity. Accountability had broken down."

When the alumni marched in May, he decided to write something that would address breaches of fiduciary duties. Randy had a Sunday morning radio interview show, *The Price of Paradise*. Almost every week his upcoming guest would write an op-ed piece for the *Honolulu Advertiser*—an article published opposite the editorial page. "This helped build an audience, forced guests to think ahead about the topic, and enabled me to prepare good questions," he explained.

Randy described what he had in mind to the *Advertiser*'s editorial page editor: "It will be controversial and could result in a lawsuit. I promise to check my sources carefully and to seek additional legal opinion."

The editor indicated that his paper would be willing to work on it. Randy met often with the editor, who confided to his staff members that the upcoming essay would be "the biggest story to hit Hawai'i since statehood."

Randy interviewed about three dozen people formerly holding high positions in Hawai'i: members of the judicial selection commission, trustees, justices of the Supreme Court, and masters who had prepared reports. He assured them he wouldn't use anything they said without permission.

Judge Sam King was among those he interviewed. King, senior federal district court judge, had been a State Circuit Court judge. After about two months, Roth asked the judge to take a look at the draft. "You are painting a target on yourself, Randy. You should understand the personal implications of your doing something like this." King gently explained that the essay coming from a haole, a non-Hawaiian, might not be effective.

"Would you consider coauthoring it, Judge King?"

"Yes," King replied.

Randy recruited three more part-Hawaiian authors who were also highly respected and influential community members: Monsignor Charles Kekumano was chairman of the Queen Lili'uokalani Trust, a retired Catholic priest, and former chairman of the police commission. Walter Heen, a retired judge of the State Intermediate Court of Appeals, was a former state legislator and city councilman then active with the Native Hawaiian Advisory Council. Gladys Brandt, former principal of Kamehameha School for Girls, was chairwoman of the University of Hawai'i Board of Regents. Randy explains the process as follows:

> The coauthors took me and my draft through the wringer and back again. They vastly improved it, making it more sensitive to the reader's perspective generally, but writing it specifically for the Hawaiian community.
>
> We turned a key word or phrase to reflect their wisdom and judgment. The writing became more effective than what somebody like me, with just raw training, would be able to do.
>
> I became the recorder and wrote what the group wanted to say. The authors felt the letter to the editor Nona wrote was vital in preparing the Hawaiian community for the notion that one could criticize trustees without being disloyal to the trust itself.
>
> The authors were inspired by Oz and the great courage shown by the marchers. They were deeply impressed by Nā Kumu, the faculty group who handled themselves admirably and were teaching wonderful lessons to students.

They discussed what they hoped to accomplish through their essay. Randy explained: "If the attorney general was encouraged to do the job previous attorney generals should have been doing over the years, if the Probate

Court was embarrassed into doing the job they should have been doing over the years, then the Bishop Estate could be greatly strengthened."

Randy talked with Oz at least six times before "Broken Trust" was published. "Without Oz we would not have been able to write something as powerful. He was concerned about his duty to hold certain things in confidence. But he realized he had a duty to take action against serious breaches being committed. Oz was ready to explode from frustration over the trustees' behavior when the process of writing 'Broken Trust' started. His frustration had turned to outrage by the time it was completed." Many of the concerns addressed in "Broken Trust" were in Oz's memos to trustees.

Writing "Broken Trust" was easy compared to getting it published in the *Advertiser*. A new editor for this Gannett newspaper gave Professor Roth and his collaborators the runaround, despite being told by his staff that it was a "blockbuster."

After three weeks of unsuccessful attempts, Professor Roth took it to the *Honolulu Star-Bulletin*. They ran it as four full pages the next day, Saturday, August 9, 1997. The protest was no longer "a Hawaiian thing," it was now a State of Hawai'i event.

To illustrate their quest for absolute power, Trustee Henry Peters actually admitted during the CBS *60 Minutes* show, "The only thing we couldn't control was the press. We should have bought the *Honolulu Star-Bulletin* when we had a chance."

The authors opened their essay declaring that the "web of relationships between the judiciary and our beloved Kamehameha Schools Bishop Estate has pushed two great institutions to an absolute critical point. Immediate action must be taken."

To help readers understand the underlying causes, the coauthors included stories such as this one (the complete 6,400-word essay was filed on the *Honolulu Star-Bulletin's* web page under "Broken Trust"):

# Yukio and the Boys

We are greatly disturbed that the trustees would hire Yukio Takemoto as their director of budget and review after he left the state as director of budget and finance under Gov. Waihee. This was in the wake of serious questions involving the investments of the $5 billion state Employees' Retirement System and a $150,000 airport consulting contract that was increased to $52 million without competitive bidding or outside review.

Here's how Oswald Stender has described the circumstances and consequences of Takemoto's hiring.

"When Dickie indicated that he wanted to hire Yukio Takemoto for another person's unfilled job, I told him I didn't think it was a good fit. That was true, but I also was thinking of the fact that Yukio had left the state under a cloud.

"Besides, we already had some really good people on staff and I like to hire from within when possible.

"When I raised these additional objections, Dickie got upset saying:

"'Hey, I've already hired him so none of that matters.'"

"It didn't take Yukio long to hire a bunch of 'his people.' Can you believe it, now he's got it up to 13 people and an operating budget of $1.6 million.

"Already, I've spotted a few non-bid contracts involving Dura for over a million dollars each. (Trustee Henry Peters was a Dura officer and director.) Usually something like that would go out for a bid.

"It's the same kind of stuff they did when Yukio was director of the state budget."

The "Broken Trust" essay recommended the following steps to heal the trust:

1. The Bishop Estate should draft and widely distribute a strategic plan for both protection of the endowment and operation of the schools.
2. The state attorney general, and the Supreme Court justices, if they elect to participate, should authorize a blue-ribbon panel of community leaders to develop criteria and procedures to select trustees.
3. The state attorney general should begin a comprehensive review of trustee conduct and trust performance. If trustees do not cooperate, a lawsuit should be filed. The term of appointment for trustees should be limited to a fixed number of years with no expectation of reappointment.
4. The Hawai'i State Legislature should repeal the current scheme for determining trustee compensation and replace it with a statute providing for reasonable compensation as is prevalent in other states.
5. The Legislature should appoint and fund a watchdog to monitor the performance of charitable trusts in Hawai'i.

On Monday, three days after "Broken Trust" was published, Governor Cayetano asked Attorney General Margery Bronster to investigate the trustees.

Colbert Matsumoto, the court master, was in the Kamehameha Schools archives studying the writings of Princess Pauahi and Charles Reed Bishop.

Nā Pua was initiating court action to make Judge Yim's fact-finding report public.

Warriors were coming forward. The behemoth would be stung relentlessly.

CHAPTER 30

# Reactions

Summer 1997

Publicity-shy KSBE was the biggest story in town. The day after "Broken Trust" appeared, the *Honolulu Advertiser* ran a banner headline and front-page article stating the Bishop Estate was in danger of losing its tax-free status. It quoted U.S. Senator Daniel Inouye: "Charges of mismanagement could cost the school its charitable standing with the IRS."

In the same article, Oz explained the implications: "If the charitable status is revoked, Kamehameha Schools program funding will be slashed in half."

Oz had learned the estate could afford its disbanded outreach programs while keeping other Kamehameha Schools programs intact. Quoting from Oz's earlier memos, the reporter included his new information: "The board's Go Forward plan dismantled programs touching 30,000 Hawaiians at a cost of $61.9 million. Last year, with Go Forward in place and campuses added on Hawai'i and Maui, Kamehameha Schools educated a total of 3,200 children for $87.6 million. Trustees approved extensive program cuts without reviewing a financial plan."

Oz explained to the reporter that there were 1,100 applicants for 80 kindergarten openings. "The estate has money to serve more children." The newspaper estimated Bishop Estate's wealth at that time at up to $10 billion, placing it in the company of Ivy League endowments: Harvard (then $8.8 billion ), Yale (then $4.8 billion), and Princeton (then $4.4 billion).

Oz said KSBE had enough money to be on the cutting edge of education, but it was operating as a huge public school. He wanted the board reorganized. He was quoted as if he were the amanuensis (ghostwriter) for the princess:

"In today's economic, social, and educational environment Pauahi Bishop would say this business is so huge, five people cannot manage it. She would want to form a mega-corporation and have 14 or 18 people on the board who we can hire. Get the best brains in town. Then the board is rented for a few hours a month at a cost of two or three thousand dollars."

That same day, during a press conference on another matter, Governor Cayetano responded to an inquiry about the Bishop Estate situation:

> I've asked the attorney general to examine charges reported against the Bishop Estate [referring to "Broken Trust"].
>
> For those distinguished Hawaiian leaders to come forward with their concerns must bring great pressure on them and presents the likelihood that there is substance to the issues they raise.
>
> The attorney general will do a preliminary assessment to determine whether there are grounds for a probe. She has the authority to pursue the matter in the probate court.

Gov. Cayetano was distancing himself from his predecessor, John Waihee. All trustees—except Oz—were close friends of the former governor.

Chief Justice Ronald T. Moon, now sensitive to Governor Cayetano's perspective, had suddenly become open to the public for ideas on how to hold the schools managing board accountable to the trust. "We are willing to listen to anything. The justices can greatly tighten the Bishop Estate appointments." His was a remarkable change in attitude.

A week later, on August 17, 1997, reacting to criticism that it had been "scooped" by a smaller paper, the *Honolulu Advertiser* responded with a rebuttal to "Broken Trust." It included articles from KSBE chairman Dickie Wong, Supreme Court judges, and *Advertiser* editor Jim Gatti.

Dickie Wong lauded trustees' good work in the writing style known as "puffery": "Judge Yim, because of his integrity and skill, was doing fact finding and trustees would invite a nationally recognized education outfit of some kind to review whatever he says should be reviewed."

Strangely, Dickie ended his article by quoting advice from two elderly Hawaiian women. One said, "We must look to our culture to find the solution that will help us heal" *(ho'oponopono).*

The other urged, "Resolve the perceived problems by listening to each other without prejudgments and communicate with mutual respect."

Both suggested the kind of talk story Dickie had carefully avoided.

Supreme Court judges wrote, "'Broken Trust' was a lengthy but factually inaccurate, distorted, irresponsible opinion piece.

"The authors expressly and implicitly impugned the integrity, honesty, ethics, intelligence, qualification, competence, and professionalism not only of the members of the supreme court as individuals, but also of the court as an institution."

Their article went on and on in similarly pompous, abstract language.

*Honolulu Advertiser* editor Jim Gatti stated that it was his decision not to publish "Broken Trust" because "It required more editing and reporting time to ensure fairness to all involved." Could this be true even after months of preparation and meetings?

Big and round, with porky facial features and bushy hair, Lokelani had the kind of look loved by newspaper editorial cartoonists. They drew her as a witch; as a Gestapo-type dominatrix in jodhpurs—riding breeches cut *very full* across the hips—and boots, holding a whip; as a Wagnerian Valkyrie with a horned helmet, looking down contemptuously from her castle; as the fat lady singing at the end of an opera's final act, with dead bodies scattered on the stage; and sometimes just sitting on and squashing schoolchildren. Lokelani was a very versatile subject.

Within their Kawaiahaʻo Plaza fortress, trustees could snicker at Hawaiians by claiming subsets wouldn't work together. "They're like ʻaʻama crabs," they smirked. The trustees couldn't conceive that Oz would inspire unity.

Mature ʻaʻama crabs are about the size of a nine-year-old child's hand. For an interesting experiment, put five of them in a pail. Take five of *any other* type of crab—we'll refer to them as "B" crabs. Put them in another pail, just like the one holding the ʻaʻama crabs. Type "B" crabs do the following: One crab stands next to the side at the bottom of the bucket. The second crab climbs onto the first crab. Then a third crab braces itself next to the first crab to create a strong foundation for the other crabs. The fourth crab climbs onto the second crab. The fifth crab climbs onto the fourth crab and reaches to the top of the pail. Having all their weight on one side of the bucket allows the crabs to tip it over and crawl out. They have the instinct to escape through teamwork.

ʻAʻama crabs exemplify selfish attitudes: "Never let anyone rise above you . . . every crab for itself." If one ʻaʻama crab climbs on another, the others pull it down; happens every time.

Gerry Jervis discovered that people on the Kamehameha campus weren't 'a'ama crabs: They were pleasant and cooperative, though very frightened and somewhat desperate.

He seemed to mellow from being on campus and visiting with teachers and alumni. Gerry encouraged employees to talk to Judge Yim without fearing retribution. He talked on that subject on campus, at Kawaiaha'o Plaza, throughout O'ahu, and on the neighbor islands. He even wrote an apology to Oz for throwing that newspaper at him a month earlier.

Oz wrote back, "I agree you lost your temper. None of this focuses on the issue at hand: mismanaging processes and people. This problem could have been avoided if the trustees gave our teachers, students, parents, and alumni an audience, and if we took time to listen to their concerns. The course I have chosen has taken a heavy emotional toll on my family and me. However, my mission is to preserve the legacy for eternity, to give it dignity and economic substance with the ability to provide greater hope for all Hawaiians."

After reading that last paragraph, Gerry began siding with Oz. He was beginning to realize this man was not all memos and no muscle. Others, too, were criticizing trustees.

## CHAPTER 31

# Margery, the Attorney General

## 1997

GOVERNOR BEN CAYETANO appointed Margery Bronster as state attorney general because he wanted someone bright, competent, and independent. All things being equal, it was time for a woman to hold that office. He was convinced Margery would tell him whether what he wanted to do was right or wrong.

State budget director Eric Anzai, one of the governor's closest friends, said: "Margery won't be intimidated. She stands behind principle to an extreme and will not suffer fools."

Oz arranged a lunch meeting for me with Margery Bronster. He asked her to talk to me because I knew the school from way back. I arrived early, sat at the outdoor table he'd reserved alongside Waikīkī Beach, and appreciated both a cooling mai tai and the sight of female sunbathers turning golden brown in front of me.

I stood up when I heard an enthusiastic voice just behind me saying, "Thank you for your help." Margery had arrived. She was a young woman, slim and small, with a pageboy haircut. The maitre d'hotel, a smiling young Hawaiian who I later found out graduated from Kamehameha Schools, brought her to the table. Margery's nice "girl-next-door" appearance and personality captivated me immediately.

Oz is a wise facilitator; he allows people time to get to know each other before he arrives—and after he leaves. He joined us shortly and had a cup of coffee. After seeing how happily Margery and I were chattering, he excused himself "because of a sudden emergency." I learned later that he went shopping with Kuulei.

Margery was born in Queens, New York, to parents of the Jewish faith. Her dad moved the family and his precision metal parts factory to Tenafly, New Jersey, where Margery went to high school and became interested in China.

"The best way to learn about a country is through its language; I entered Brown University, class of 1979, because it was the only school then offering a Chinese curriculum. China hadn't opened yet to the Western world. College classes were Monday through Saturday at 8:00 A.M.—possibly to scare away nonserious students."

Margery majored in Chinese language, literature, and history, and had a language immersion sequence in Taiwan. After Columbia University Law School, she joined a New York City law firm representing Chinese government entities. She worked with Chinese-speaking clients, specializing in commercial litigation and international and business securities law.

Margery met Mark Fukunaga, a New York City lawyer from Honolulu. Margery and Mark married and moved to Hawai'i, where he became chairman and CEO of Servco Pacific, Inc., his family's business. With traditional Japanese resourcefulness, Mark's father started Servco in the garage of the family home, building it into one of Hawai'i's leading automotive, marine, and real estate development enterprises. In less than two years, Margery Bronster, as she remained known in business, became a partner in a Honolulu law firm.

She became known as one of the smartest attorneys in the state. When she left her law firm to become attorney general, a former partner remarked, "She's forceful when necessary and will not relent. No one can put anything over on her."

She described how she met Oz to me:

I read in a magazine that Kamehameha Schools educational endowment was then right up there with Harvard's. This surprised me.

I saw Oz for the first time when we were both on the same airplane and recognized him from the picture appearing with the magazine's article. He looked wise, friendly, and patient—the way I imagined the trustee of an important philanthropy should be.

He phoned not long afterwards to ask if I would be willing to talk with him privately in a friend's office.

A former attorney general told Oz I was considering investigating the activities of the Bishop Estate and its trustees. As I was not from Hawai'i, he wanted to give me some background.

Margery said Oz described the Bishop Estate and its political links.

He asked about my career plans in a very kindly way.

"Are you planning on practicing with the Supreme Court?" was one of his questions.

He explained the intrigue involved in being selected.

"Think very carefully before you take on the Bishop Estate," he advised. "It won't help your career no matter what you choose to do here."

I remember his phrase: "Once you let the genie out of the bottle, there's no telling what will happen."

He wasn't attempting to intimidate me. He wanted me to understand the Hawaiian political situation.

My actions would create headlines if I investigated the estate, he warned. "Would you be willing to proceed to prosecution?"

"Absolutely," I replied.

Hearing that, he let out a big a sigh of relief. With great intensity, he told me about "the lost generations of children."

Although not delving into the estate's financial affairs, he confided, "The estate accumulates income in violation of the princess's will. She wants money spent on education." I noticed his using present tense when referring to the princess.

He made another statement I shall not forget: "Once the chance to educate a generation of children is missed, we can't go back. Their opportunity is gone. They become a lost generation. The time when children are most open and eager to learn is so short and elusive; if properly encouraged and in the right environment, children have the chance to reach their potential."

"*A lost generation*"—I understood his perspective. Emily, our daughter, is at Punahou where the education she is receiving is helping her become smart so fast it's almost spooky. Mark and I are lucky we can afford a school that stimulates her to strive for such high achievement.

Oz suggested I consult with Edward Halbach, former dean of the University of California at Berkeley School of Law. Dr. Halbach is one of the country's foremost experts on trust law. Oz wanted me to seek his advice on legal requirements pertaining to the Bishop Estate.

He mentioned, as an aside, "The princess needs your help." He subtly used the present tense again.

We'd finished lunch. I thanked Margery, said I'd keep in touch, and went for a swim in Waikīkī's pleasant 75-degree water.

CHAPTER 32

# Bobby Harmon Loses His Job

### 1997, Retrospective to 1996

O z STENDER hadn't been the only insider questioning trustees' decisions. Bobby Harmon served for eight years as the estate's "risk manager"—in charge of its insurance programs—and as president of P&C Insurance Co., a for-profit subsidiary he helped organize. By 1994 he had reached the pinnacle of his career, and life was good. Bobby prided himself on his high principles and professionalism.

Federal Insurance Company, Inc., a member of the Chubb Group, conducts business through insurance brokers as well as through licensed general agents of the company. In Hawai'i, one of Federal's licensed general agents is Marsh & McLennan, Inc. "M&M," as it is known, is the world's largest insurance brokerage firm. It was very chummy with the investment arm of the Bishop Estate.

It was a coinvestor with the Bishop Estate in Underwriters Capital Ltd., a short-lived Bermuda company with losses of several million dollars in its first year of operation. As was his practice, Henry Peters became a director for Underwriters Capital. The Bishop Estate also invested heavily in a former M&M subsidiary acquired by Terra Nova, another insurance company.

W hile president of P&C, Bobby received an insurance management proposal from M&M for services on a time-and-expense basis, at an estimated annual cost of around $70,000. There was no mention in the proposal that M&M would charge an additional $200,000 annual fee for brokerage, risk management, or other services.

I interviewed Bobby years before he was coerced into signing a document of silence about his dealings with the Bishop Estate. In deference to his subsequent agreement, I reference facts distributed by mail and posted on the Internet before his agreement.

Bobby refused to pay the $200,000 service fee for work he felt was not under contract and unjustified. He pointed out that premiums to M&M for insurance could be obtained through other insurance brokers at substantially lower cost.

It became apparent to him that Nathan Aipa, his direct supervisor, and Henry Peters wanted tight control over all insurance matters, including parceling out related legal work to attorneys they selected.

O n October 11, 1996, Bobby was called into a meeting by Henry Peters, acting in his role as Bishop Estate trustee and chairman of the board of P&C. With him was Nathan Aipa, Bishop Estate general counsel and assistant secretary and assistant treasurer of P&C. "You can be replaced as president of P&C if you fail to follow Nathan's directives," Henry said. Bobby didn't "sell his soul" and continued working for the good of the trust.

He told representatives of Coopers & Lybrand, the estate's auditors, of his concerns over apparent sweetheart deals with M&M. He said he would not sign P&C's annual financial statements because of the apparent conspiracy among certain trustees, managers, directors, and officers at Bishop Estate, P&C, and M&M to defraud the Bishop Estate, P&C, and the IRS.

Bobby learned that Nathan Aipa approved P&C's annual financial statements. Coopers & Lybrand said nothing about M&M or the Bishop Estate not reporting certain potential claims. Bobby also told Price Waterhouse, the estate's accountants, of these improper activities. Neither firm did anything.

A month after Bobby was warned, Peters fired him from P&C and Aipa fired him from the Bishop Estate.

Almost a year passed. Then, in August 1997, three months after Auntie Nona demonstrated that it was possible to criticize Bishop Estate trustees, Bobby fearlessly stepped forward.

H e spoke to an Associated Press reporter, a local TV reporter, and a *Honolulu Advertiser* reporter about how the Bishop Estate was exposed to hundreds of millions of dollars in damage claims and millions of dollars in legal fees because trustees tried to keep their insurance company and the public from knowing about embarrassing lawsuits on the mainland.

He told them Bishop Estate employees "controlled" and "managed" claims directly with outside lawyers and disregarded insurance company guidelines regarding use and payment of these firms.

He talked with reporters about a $2.3-billion lawsuit in 1993 against the trustees and others who had participated in other ventures with the Bishop Estate. Henry Peters and his cohorts viewed Bobby Harmon as a loose cannon on the deck of their jolly ship. At times, Bobby visualized a skull and crossbones as this vessel's flag.

N ames of those involved in ventures included Dave Thomas, owner of Wendy's restaurants and coinvestor with the Bishop Estate on several other projects; William E. Simon, former U.S. Treasury secretary and coinvestor with the estate on projects including HonFed Savings & Loan, Sino Finance, Xiamen Bank (China), and SoCal Holdings; Wayne Rogers, an actor, who brought suit against KSBE for its Kona Enterprises deal; and Frederick "Ted" Field, who was also the estate's partner in the corporate takeover of European conglomerate DRG, Inc. Field also brought suit against the estate in another coinvestment deal.

T he story of the estate's $85 million investment in McKenzie Methane Inc., a Houston-based energy company, had been covered by local newspapers two years earlier. Several trustees and estate executives added $3 million of personal investment to this venture. It went into bankruptcy. Local newspapers stated that the troubled deal could cost the estate as much as $65 million in lost capital and at least twice that much in lost earnings and tax benefits. One of the anticipated benefits of the deal would come from the tax-exempt estate's selling federal energy tax credits from the transaction to others.

This was no longer "news," but a $2.3-billion legal suit was. The estate was entitled to legal defense reimbursement under an insurance legal liability policy. Bobby learned of this lawsuit several months after it was filed, only as a result of his inquiring about unreported claims as he prepared to renew the insurance policy. When he reported this claim to the insurance carrier, Aipa immediately took control and directed that all correspondence to or from the carrier should come to his attention.

"Nathan Aipa repeatedly refused to furnish information to the insurance company regarding the claim, despite frequent and urgent requests," Bobby said to me before signing an agreement to say no more.

Eventually, the insurance company closed its files on the case due to Aipa's failure to respond to requests for information. The actual cost to the estate is unknown, but Bobby estimates that the loss of legal defense reimbursements alone could easily have been in excess of a million dollars, I was told.

A ipa and others did such a good job of concealing this information that Bobby was unaware of coinvestments by trustees and others until reading about them in the newspaper. None of the court masters since 1989, nor the State Probate Court, nor the state attorney general's office, which also are required to review Bishop Estate operations annually, knew about the personal investments estate trustees and employees made in the estate's McKenzie Methane investment.

"The investment portfolio appears complete and well-maintained," wrote one master. "More than adequate information is presented to provide the master with an appropriate understanding of the investments," declared another.

Bobby said the estate spent $500,000 defending against an $86.7 million lawsuit brought by movie producer Frederick Field, stemming from another partnership with the Bishop Estate. This was not reported to the insurance company for reimbursement.

Actor Wayne Rogers, an investment partner, filed a lawsuit against a partnership not reported and thus not covered by insurance.

As principal executive of the legal group, Nathan Aipa had ultimate approval of all legal bills including P&C's. Bobby reported that he would frequently pay these legal fees and costs from his general counsel account, without approval from the insurance companies. He told me, "Often the amounts billed by the law firms exceeded allowable fees and costs provided in the insurance company guidelines. When, if ever, the Bishop Estate submitted the legal bills to the insurance company, many of the charges were disallowed. This practice led to the loss of millions of dollars never recovered from the insurance companies."

Estate attorneys claimed Bobby leaked sensitive information. Experienced as an attorney, Governor Cayetano commented: "You cannot hide information. The confidentiality provision should stand only if it is in fact protecting the trust and its beneficiaries—and not protecting the trustees."

K amehameha Schools Bishop Estate's lawyers sought and got a contempt of court charge against Harmon for releasing confidential information. They went after the reporters with subpoenas for notes from meetings the reporters had with Harmon. The television station answered, "We will provide only what we broadcast and not notes or outtakes."

"I never gave reporters more than a synopsis of information I had written out," Bobby stated.

The court ruled that the press was not a party to any kind of alleged improper activity in obtaining the information. But estate lawyers shot Bobby down. He ended up bankrupt and unemployable in Hawai'i. Bobby symbolized what can happen to persons who challenged the trustees.

CHAPTER 33

# Judge Yim Releases His Report

## November 1997

THE FACT-FINDING report Lokelani thought would vindicate her was due on August 29, 1997. Although he had collected information and comments from over a thousand people, Judge Yim felt it was too soon to make a final judgment.

He met once with the trustees as a group and also with each individually. Finally, on November 10, he sat before all trustees to present his preliminary report. His findings were directed at Lokelani Lindsey:

> She lacks the basic understanding of her role and responsibilities of a trustee. . . .
>
> Her volatile personality and rash utterances create an oppressive and hostile environment on campus. . . .
>
> Her intemperate, inappropriate and ill-advised comments lower morale of teachers and staff. . . .
>
> She should step down. Trustee Lokelani Lindsey must immediately relinquish or be removed from any position of control regarding the direct oversight, management and/or administration of KSBE education. . . .
>
> She should apologize to some of the people she offended. . . .
>
> Trustees must return governance of the school back to President Chun.

Lokelani was shocked. Judge Yim had focused on *her* and *not* on President Chun!

Henry spoke up angrily. But Yim continued. He urged trustees to engage in mediation and attempt to reach some kind of internal resolution to the controversy. "I want ultimately to file a report with the court that simply has two words: 'All *pau.*'"

"I want to tell my story," Lokelani retorted angrily.

She had two bankers boxes of documents delivered to Judge Yim, along with a note stating: "These include complaints and allegations against President Chun, the basis for my lack of confidence in his ability to manage and lead the education group." She hadn't told trustees she had been collecting this information—or creating it.

The judge wrote back: "Appointment of the fact finder was to address trustees' lack of knowledge and inability to determine the genesis of the controversy—not to conduct a performance appraisal of President Chun."

Lokelani's storage boxes remained unopened.

Lokelani prepared to protect her position. Around November 23, she retained Doug Carlson, a public relations specialist, to help her deal with the news media. "Mrs. Lindsey is eager to respond to questions and set the record straight when the report is leaked," Carlson wrote in his notes.

He stated that his public relations objectives were "to ensure Oz's credibility is damaged and to ensure Mrs. Lindsey's standing is elevated."

He arranged for her to be interviewed by Greg Barrett, the *Honolulu Advertiser* reporter who wrote the story about Auntie Nona's letter and later interviewed Oz, who described "Gestapo" conditions within the estate's headquarters.

"The purpose of the interview is to provide Mrs. Lindsey an opportunity to tell her story for the first time," noted the PR man, who was being paid $15,000 a month for his services.

On November 27, the *Advertiser* printed her story on its front page with a banner headline: "Lindsey Breaks Silence on Estate." Barrett described her plush, immaculate office as regal, a virtual museum of framed memories and memorials.

"Her husband Stephen is pictured with former heavyweight boxing champion Joe Frazier, a photo taken at the 1996 Olympics when Mrs. Lindsey said she was doing Bishop Estate business, while a guest of Xerox Corporation."

He referenced a large hanging on her office wall showing a shark, "her family god," and wrote of her difficult early days: "Stephen and I had nine children at home to take care of, we had a farm with 1,000 chickens and cattle and water buffalo. In addition I had to go to work and go to college during the day. I worked as a waitress, bartender, and tour bus driver and was a hula dancer at the Polynesian Cultural Center."

She told of advancing rapidly from being a physical education teacher and track coach during the 1960s into administration. She ran for mayor on Maui and spent $150,000 in a failed effort in the Democratic primary.

The reporter checked other sources. A former Hawai'i State Teachers Association field-worker described Mrs. Lindsey as "a very difficult woman to work with, extremely hostile." She told Barrett, "I investigated teachers' complaints at Kaimukī High where Mrs. Lindsey was a principal. Her posture, her body language, her whole modus operandi was intimidation."

"Critics say she plays loose with facts," Barrett wrote and included a line from an earlier story he had done with Oz: "She lies and lies."

The reporter described an incident between her and Oz: "Once, in front of the entire board, Mrs. Lindsey accused Oz of seeking her removal by writing to the Supreme Court justices. Stender denied it. But she insisted and told the trustees she had the very letter Stender had penned. When Oz asked to see it, Mrs. Lindsey declined saying it was 'confidential.' 'Why would it be confidential to me if I wrote it?' Oz asked."

Barrett's article suggested subtle inconsistencies. She said to another *Advertiser* writer that she never sought the trustee position and wasn't aware she was being considered. The following day she backtracked, telling the *Advertiser* "the reporter had misunderstood." The truth was that she had flown home from a mainland vacation to be interviewed by the justices.

Deviousness surfaced about her religious affiliation. She claimed she was baptized at Kawaiaha'o Church, a congregational church, where she was a member. When Barrett tried to follow up, the church secretary declined to answer. "Mrs. Lindsey does not want me to reveal this information." Through family history records, the reporter found that she had converted to the Mormon faith in 1959 while attending Brigham Young University in Hawai'i.

"Broken Trust II" appeared in the afternoon paper on the same day the morning paper, the *Advertiser,* published Mrs. Lindsey's story. Professor Roth planned the essay and helped coordinate it, as he had done with the first "Broken Trust" essay, but he was not identified as a contributor. The five authors, all educators, included Auntie Nona, one other Kamehameha School for Girls graduate, a former KSG principal, a former state government executive, and the former headmaster of Punahou School— the only person not of Hawaiian ancestry.[1]

---

[1] The authors were Isabella Abbott, Kamehameha School for Girls class of 1937, professor of botany at the University of Hawai'i; Winona Beamer, Kamehameha School for Girls class of 1941, teacher, Hawaiiana consultant; Gladys Brandt, former principal of Kamehameha School for Girls and director of its secondary division; Robert McPhee, former headmaster and president emeritus of Punahou School; Winona Rubin, former assistant to the president of Kamehameha Schools and former State director of human services.

The article's headline read: "School's gross mismanagement must stop now."
The subhead was: "Tyranny, distrust, poor decisions reign at Kamehameha." "Broken
Trust II" described Mrs. Lindsey's reign on campus:

> Lindsey's choice to run the school is Rockne Freitas, who is not taken seriously
> as an educator by the bulk of the faculty. A telling anecdote is Freitas' reaction
> to a proposal that students be required to demonstrate skills such as the ability
> to think critically and communicate effectively: "If a kid gets into college, what
> we care if he can write effectively?"
>
> At first educators in attendance thought he was joking. But to their hor-
> ror, they soon realized that he was dead serious. To the faculty, Freitas appears
> to be nothing more or less than Lindsey's surrogate.

The "Broken Trust II" essay concluded by stating, "We believe the best interests of the schools require that Lokelani Lindsey be removed immediately along with
Dickie Wong, Henry Peters, and Gerard Jervis, fellow trustees who allow her to ter-
rorize the school."

L okelani and her PR man gave the morning paper an immediate written response.
Beaten again by a Broken Trust essay in a competitive newspaper, the *Advertiser*
placed excerpts from Lokelani's reply on its front page, headlined "Lindsey Con-
demns Critical Essay." I wonder if the headline writer considered that "critical" can
mean "essential information" as well as "fault finding?"

The article quoted Lokelani: "I am committed to telling the truth and will do
so relentlessly in the days to come." That same day, Lokelani gave separate interviews
to four network-affiliated Honolulu television stations. She discussed a wide variety
of issues relating to school management, saying nothing of its educational program—
not yet.

CHAPTER 34

# The Court Master Releases His Report

November 1997

COLBERT MATSUMOTO reported the estate's business for fiscal year 1994 in the 109th Court Master's Report, dated November 17, 1997.

Although the estate took about a year to provide asset and investment information, it didn't disclose enough for him to figure out what kind of a job trustees were doing. Minutes of meetings contained little information, avoided financial matters, and didn't mention Oz's dissenting votes. By sheer determination, he'd found what trustees wanted hidden and now made it public.

The media spotlight that Nona Beamer had turned on six months earlier beamed brightly indeed. Court Master Colbert Matsumoto scathed, scolded, and startled trustees. When Nā Pua and the *Honolulu Star-Bulletin* posted Colbert's reports on the Internet, it was the first time a master's report had become so readily and widely accessible to the public.

In 1994, the Bishop Estate lost more than $264 million from its for-profit subsidiaries, Colbert reported. It had about $1.9 billion in at-risk investments. The potential loss figures did not include liability from the pending litigation and pending billion-dollar suits Bobby Harmon tried to make public.

From a list of twenty-one ailing investments, Colbert cited the following as 1994's top losers: a $49.4-million loss from the remains of a failed methane project; a $47.2-million loss in a Durham, North Carolina, office complex; a $34.5-million loss in a southern California savings and loan; and a $29-million loss in a California real estate venture.

These were based only on investments for which Colbert could find information after reviewing records of the estate's accounting firm. They certainly were not available from trustees. What lurked beyond his reach in the for-profit subsidiaries?

The balance sheet showed that the net equity of the estate grew by $222 million, or 16.8 percent more than the prior fiscal year. Of that, $204 million came from real property sales carried on the balance sheet at low historical values. Over $79.7 million came from its stake in Goldman Sachs & Company. The estate avoided running in the red by selling some of its diminishing Hawaiian land.

The estate and subsidiaries prepared separate financial statements; this deviation from generally accepted accounting principles resulted in an incomplete and potentially misleading view of the estate's financial status.

Colbert noted that there were "excessive amounts of cash regularly kept in demand deposits and a single money market account." The estate's guidelines establish a target cash allocation of 3 percent of the total assets of the estate—$16 million maximum. Despite this, on June 30, 1993, the estate held $56.4 million in cash, and on June 30, 1994, it held $155 million in cash.

There was no approximation of the current fair market value of the estate's assets. Neither was there a year-to-year comparison of changes in value or the rate of income produced from investments.

Colbert noted that expenses connected with managing the investment portfolio should be deducted from investment income *before* determining the income yield—of course, this would lower trustees' commissions.

The estate ignored its own asset allocation guidelines, which called for 3.8 percent to be in marketable fixed commodities (bonds) and 6.7 percent in stocks. As of 1994, only 1 percent of the total portfolio of the estate was in such investments.

In fiscal 1994, at the beginning of one of the strongest bull markets in history, the estate put more in oil and gas investments that soured than it did in stocks and bonds that soared.

Colbert criticized its aggressive investing as "entrepreneurial in nature, volatile, and therefore not stable sources of income." He questioned whether the portfolio's proportion of high-risk, high-reward ventures might be too great.

I saw two sides of Colbert's personality in the report. The first was his politeness and balanced thinking. The second, perhaps from his father's early directives, was disdain for arrogance and unfairness. You sense this in Colbert's statement, "I felt as if I were investigating the CIA's finances rather than a charitable educational institution."

"High-risk investments don't provide stable income, are volatile, and principal can be lost readily," he noted. He pointed out that trustees invested repeatedly with the same people. William Simon, former secretary of the U.S. Treasury, was an example.

Remember the childhood game "Simon says?" The estate played a version. The estate loaned SoCal Holdings, a failed savings and loan, $30 million in 1992, then forgave its loan and $2.6 million in unpaid interest in place of more equity. When "Simon said . . ." the estate kicked in another $42.5 million.

Colbert disclosed that potential loss exposure was substantially greater than liabilities reflected on the balance sheet. "The estate has guaranteed loans by subsidiaries and other third parties, and for $100,000 a year insured Robert Rubin's $100 million personal investment portfolio." Rubin was secretary of the U.S. Treasury and a former Goldman Sachs top executive.

The estate owned 367,509 acres of land in the Hawaiian Islands. Some 25 percent of its Hawai'i holdings were commercially zoned lands that supplied 88 percent of its real estate rental income. Residential property supplied another 9 percent of its income from leaseholders; the remaining 3 percent of income came from agricultural land. No income resulted from conservation land.

Trustees determined the commissions payable to themselves on a maximum of 2.5 percent of cash principal, capital receipts, and final disbursement of capital. Colbert noted a lack of provisions to adjust commissions when its revenues were adjusted, such as those disallowed by an IRS audit.

He questioned the practice of taking commissions on interest payments on subsidiary loans and commissions on a return of capital, since these are not infusions of new cash—only a return of original equity investment.

Trustees paid themselves commissions based on the original capital investment in the partnership rather than limiting them to the income or gain generated from that investment.

The lead trustee system made it easier for a trustee to act without the knowledge of the full board. He explained: "This may result in horse trading between trustees who want special consideration for matters outside their subject matter but within the area of another lead trustee."

Colbert pointed out that Oz was the only trustee with previous estate experience and was the lone trustee without a designated area of governance.

He criticized how trustees ran their meetings: "While minutes were prepared for each meeting, they lacked any significant detail or specificity. There was nothing in the minutes to indicate the nature of any discussion or debate among trustees.

"Trustees failed to live up to other masters' recommendations to develop a strategic plan. Their fortress mentality cloaks the estate in secrecy."

Several times he mentioned the lack of any reasonably reliable or approximate indication of the fair market value of the estate's assets.

It seemed to him that the board was not fulfilling the estate's purpose. It decreased spending on school and financial aid while it increased spending on administration and professional services. Although assets grew, the school did not.

Investment losses Colbert reported were sharp blows to Henry Peters' vanity. He ordered the estate's Communications Department immediately to launch a newspaper and radio advertising campaign titled, "The True Bottom Line on KSBE's Financial Performance."

Print ads and broadcast commercials touted "compounded average investment returns of 17.3 percent between 1980 and 1994." Trustees contended that "This record compares favorably against various investment benchmarks and returns reported by other institutions."

Court master Colbert Matsumoto, left, reflects on the statements a Bishop Estate attorney makes to a TV news reporter. Honolulu Star-Bulletin *photo by Craig T. Kojima.*

This is the kind of "spin" politicians apply to facts. When asked why the court master's calculations were so different from what the estate advertised, Henry Peters answered, "We use different time frames and formulas to calculate rates of return."

Estate lawyers replied to the Court Master's Report with ninety pages of explanations, denials, and blistering sarcasm. They called the master's report "the product of a flawed analysis." They charged that it was "factually incorrect and grossly misleading" and questioned the competence of Colbert and the accountant he hired to review the estate's finances. This is called "destroy the messenger"—another political tactic.

It was now up to Circuit Judge Colleen Hirai to decide whether the trustees handled finances properly in 1993–1994 (fiscal year 1994). If she approved, her ruling would insulate trustees from personal liability for any actions during that period. Should she withhold approval, trustees might have to repay the estate for harming it.

Back in the boardroom, it was not business as usual once the Court Master's Report was publicized. Trustees found it very difficult to communicate with each other.

Oz told a reporter he hoped the Circuit Court turned some of the master's recommendations into court orders. He wanted the estate's management structure changed to one chief executive officer.

Beadie Dawson, Nā Pua's attorney, told the same reporter, "Other trustees will never go for it. They use the fiction of being five CEOs to rationalize their nearly $1 million compensation each."

Attorney General Bronster supported Colbert's recommendations. She called the estate's account of its operations "materially deficient" and challenged it to provide detailed information requested by the court master. If they didn't, she threatened contempt of court, denial of their pay, or removal.

"Her experience as a commercial litigator will help her in confronting the Bishop Estate," stated Budget Director Earl Anzai. "Commercial litigation is all-out war."

# CHAPTER 35

# Lokelani Begins Damage Control

## Late Fall 1997

DENNIS WALSH worked with Lokelani while she was a school superintendent and helped prepare her application to be a trustee. She rewarded him with the job of special projects officer for trustees. The day after Judge Yim suggested Mrs. Lindsey step down, Walsh and Lokelani started preparing her "Education Report."

Six days later they had written five single-spaced pages of allegations against President Chun. They included everything about him she deemed unacceptable: financial management, educational leadership, personnel management, facilities management practices, tasks assigned by trustees, and his services as a community representative.

After completing this diatribe, Lokelani developed charges against students' academic performance.

Walsh was neither an educator nor an academician and had no education evaluation and testing background. He wrote what Lokelani dictated.

She contended that the class of 1997 included more than thirty graduates *"who can't read"*—italicized for emphasis in her report. She further claimed that "The longer students stay at Kamehameha Schools the more poorly they perform as measured by standardized scores. Elementary teachers don't use a curriculum that links students to their next grade."

She directed trustees to investigate eight irregularities of unauthorized expenditures of funds involving Dr. and Mrs. Chun.

On the cover she put these words: "Essential information contained in this report must remain confidential." She later told Walsh, "Change the last word 'confidential' to 'internal within the board.' The word 'confidential' isn't strong enough."

Her memo to trustees, dated November 25, accompanied the report: "We are facing serious problems in the quality of the education we are providing to our students. . . . To release this report would be harmful and damaging to staff and students."

Taking Mrs. Lindsey's memo to heart, Oz gave his copy of the report to an estate attorney to hold until he could study it.

Lokelani later sent President Chun the report with the added warnings: "Confidential attorney-client privilege, handle with extreme care." She allowed two days—until December 4—for him to respond.

O n December 4, Judge Yim presented his final report to the trustees. Public relations man Doug Carlson noted Lokelani's reaction: "I've seen the fact finder's report and I'm scared to death. The fact finder completely missed the point. Kill the messenger. I am devastated. I am the target for everything that's perceived to be wrong at Kamehameha Schools."

Judge Yim had told Lokelani to step down as lead trustee overseeing education and to leave the campus. He urged everyone "to support and provide the president of Kamehameha Schools with all necessary means to accomplish the mission of the Kamehameha Schools."

He called for what Oz long advocated: "A thorough audit of the educational functions and programs of Kamehameha Schools so trustees and Kamehameha ʻohana (alumni and parents) can create an educational/operational strategic plan that guides Kamehameha Schools and Hawaiʻi's children into the next millennium."

The Go Forward plan was far below these standards, said the judge. Oz had earlier described Go Forward as "the kiss of death for the Hawaiian community."

Judge Yim concluded with these thoughts: "At times I was greatly saddened by the suffering, angst and pain brought on by the controversy. I hope and pray that my efforts will be the catalyst for positive change for the sake of Hawaiʻi's children and for the future of *nā kanaka maoli* [indigenous Hawaiians]."

Unexpectedly, especially to Cousin Henry, Judge Yim metamorphosed from a messenger for the trustees into a powerful and respected warrior for the princess. He had become intellectually allied with Oz.

Lokelani needed to work fast to bring public opinion to her side before December 19, when the judge's report would be filed. She realized the attorney general would use it harshly against her.

The next day, December 5, she took her education report entitled "An Imperative for Educational Change" to an interview with an *Advertiser* reporter. She gave the reporter its first twelve pages. She didn't tell trustees about this.

"By releasing the report Mrs. Lindsey thought she could balance the scales of justice a bit by letting the public know her concerns," Carlson explained.

The next morning, December 6, the *Honolulu Advertiser* published a front-page article headlined, "Trustees say school failing to teach, money misspent." The subhead read, "Kamehameha President Faces Board Investigation." It detailed Loke-lani's purported concerns of poor student performance, weak faculty curriculum, and unauthorized spending of school money by President Chun. It highlighted her assertion of failure: "The longer students stay at Kamehameha, the lower they score on standardized tests. . . . More than 30 members of the class of 1997 can barely read at grade 12 levels [she had modified this statement]."

Placed in a negative context, that assertion about reading levels was misleading. "Reading level 12" is a classification for scholarly journals, not for twelfth-grade high school material. Most newspapers publish material written at about grade-level five.

Lokelani claimed that a report she compiled showed that 52 percent of the class of 1997 did not score well enough on the Scholastic Aptitude Test to meet the University of Hawai'i's admissions standards of 510 verbal and 510 math. "The problem is the curriculum and direction the school is receiving."

Faculty immediately rose to Dr. Chun's defense, despite contractual agreements that could get them fired for speaking to reporters.

These critics recognized what Lokelani was attempting. One faculty member said, "She's been looking for a publicly acceptable way to fire Dr. Chun for a long time. We're weary and wary of her. We strongly urge the public to question the integrity of her statements."

Six college students declared, "Dr. Chun instituted the curriculum that put us where we are today at Princeton, Notre Dame, Stanford, Dartmouth, the University of Southern California, and George Washington University."

The *Advertiser* wrote of Lokelani's accusing Dr. Chun and his wife, a prominent Island executive, of improper spending. Lokelani had given Judge Yim and trustees copies of her report claiming they squandered $220,000. "That's totally inconsistent with the man I know," said a school program and evaluation specialist. "Does that jibe with the image of a man who writes a personal check each year to make up the difference between Kamehameha's United Way goal and employee contributions?"

Money she accused the Chuns of squandering was used to make the on-campus president's home suitable as a hospitality center for alumni, students, parents, staff, and others. They are official hosts to students from all grades, to local organizations, and to visitors from local and mainland universities. Mrs. Chun bought furniture at discounted prices from the Kāhala Hilton and at auctions for the schools renovated dormitories.

I seriously doubt that editor Jim Gatti allowed "editing and reporting time to ensure fairness to all," the reason he gave for holding off on the first "Broken Trust" essay.

That afternoon, Roy Benham dispatched Nā Pua representatives to both campus gates with signs expressing pride in students. Tall Roy held a big sign over his head reading, "You're OK." He said, "We responded quickly because we wanted students to see us standing up for them before they went home."

I offer this aside: The Bible tells us to love our neighbor as ourselves. While it is hard not to blame Lokelani Lindsey for the turmoil she imposed on children, those who believe all things happen because God allows them might view Mrs. Lindsey's actions with human Christlike forgiveness. We might pray now, as we do for others, that when she comes back around she finds peace. But at that time, she was behaving as a pagan, a whirling dervish consumed with justifying her actions by destroying others.

Carlson issued a press release to other media with this lead sentence: "Trustee Lokelani Lindsey today released data that she said reveals serious problems about Kamehameha Schools ability to adequately educate its students, including the longer they stay the lower they score on standardized tests."

Oz was appalled and horrified. She released her report after making it clear to trustees it would harm the school, students, and faculty.

Gerry demanded of Lokelani, "Did you intend to give Dr. Chun a fair forum or was the entire exercise a calculated set-up?"

The class valedictorian said she had hoped if there were problems they would be addressed in the school and not made available around the world by the Internet and wire services. She was worried that Yale University, her "dream school," would not accept her because her education was not good enough. (It did.)

A student in New England stated that education at Kamehameha Schools had prepared him well for Massachusetts Institute of Technology, especially in mathematics.

Campus students joked with gallows-type humor: "We're all a bunch of stupid Hawaiians."

"*Stupid.*" Hearing that word is particularly painful to those of us who are older.

"Stupid Hawaiians." Racial stereotypes and slurs lie so near the surface of the skin, don't they? They penetrate so quickly, and deeply, don't they? Mrs. Lindsey resurrected feelings of inadequacy that almost wiped out our race.

Ninth-grade students in a basic geometry course plaintively said to their math teacher, "We're not very good, are we, Mr. Follmer?" He commented that self-esteem is particularly important to students in the lower-ability classes. They were deeply hurt.

Oz told me Mrs. Lindsey released her education report two weeks before public release of Yim's report to deflect criticism from her: "She defended her own interests at the expense of students she was responsible for protecting."

M argery Bronster asked Judge Hirai to unseal and make public Judge Yim's half-inch thick fact-finder's report. It singled out Lokelani for "overall damage her volatile personality inflicted." He peppered his report with damning descriptions and revealed disturbing revelations about trustees tampering with Kamehameha's highly competitive student admissions program.

"We have suspected that our admissions recommendations have been shunted," stated a faculty member. "We have interviewed sensational kids over the years who've not gotten in even though we gave them highest recommendations."

In a thirty-six-page rebuttal, Lokelani responded to all thirty-four of Yim's findings. These were treated in a "point and counterpoint" format by the *Honolulu Advertiser*—Yim vs. Lindsey. This is one example:

*Yim's point:* "The court's order does not require the fact-finder to conduct a performance appraisal of Dr. Chun's work as president of the Kamehameha Schools, and the fact-finder believes it would be inappropriate to do so."

*Lindsey's counterpoint:* "The fact-finder unilaterally decreased the scope of his inquiry, leading to skewed conclusions. It would appear obvious that actions considered in a vacuum without weighing of any justification can often be construed negatively. Furthermore, this decrease in the breadth of the fact-finder's mission undoubtedly frustrated the expectations of those who may have commented negatively on the short-comings of the administration."

Huh? Is that written at a twelfth-grade reading level? Who'd bother reading it?

Oz told Gerry, "We need to have Mrs. Lindsey removed."

"No way," he answered.

"I am going to have her removed and if you don't join me, I am coming after you when I get her removed. If you support her and she did wrong, you are equally guilty."

Oz explained, "After talking with attorneys, Gerry decided to join me to save his skin. He said right off he wouldn't pay any costs. His lawyers even billed me for photocopies I needed."

Two hours after the Probate Court unsealed the fact-finding report, Oz and Gerry held a press conference to state that they had requested Lindsey's resignation as a trustee. Gerry read from the letter they delivered to her:

> Last week it became shockingly apparent you are willing to put your own personal defense ahead of interests, feelings, and pride of our students.
>
> Release of your so-called education report falsely and unfairly casts a deep shadow on the quality of the education of this institution without including its many positive improvements and educational achievements.
>
> You knew that damage would be done to the students, teachers, and administrators if this so-called report were to be released. Nevertheless, you willfully engaged in a reckless and irresponsible action that casts serious doubt on your judgment and fitness to continue serving.
>
> We urge you to do the right thing. If not, we will petition the Probate Court for your removal.

She ignored them.

On December 20, four out of five of the Hawai'i Supreme Court justices removed themselves from the century-old process of appointing trustees to the Bishop Estate. This was only seven months after Auntie Nona wrote her letter, igniting the conflagration now scorching so many.

On December 29, 1997, Oz and Gerry signed a petition with the court for Mrs. Lindsey's removal as a trustee.

Lokelani resigned from her responsibilities as lead trustee for education by the end of December but continued as a Bishop Estate trustee. She later claimed that in August she'd told Dickie she gave up the lead trustee position. She made this statement so she could state she wasn't forced out by the fact finder.

A newspaper quoted one of her lawyers: "Oz describes her as the Wicked Witch of the West, who circles above the campus on a broomstick." Hawaiians love synonyms and repeated that one a lot.

The wizardry of Oz proved more challenging than she expected, but Lokelani was still covering the campus, reconnoitering and churning her malevolence into malignity. After all was said and done, she was still Trustee Lokelani Lindsey, a powerful million-dollar-a-year executive. She, Henry, and Dickie were in control. Her campus spies, snitches, and lieutenants remained in place.

It wasn't time yet for Hawaiian munchkins to sing joyfully.

CHAPTER 36

# Why Can't the Trustees Behave?

November 1997–July 1998

"WHY CAN'T they behave?" asked *U.S. News and World Report* in an article describing the estate's wealth and trustees' compensation. Bishop Estate trustees' behaviors made national publications' headlines for about six years, drawing attention to Kamehameha Schools.

Lokelani Lindsey's tactics could backfire, suggested an editorial in the *Honolulu Star-Bulletin:* "Her attack on Kamehameha Schools and the performance of President Michael Chun is a transparent attempt to shift attention from criticisms of her behavior in Judge Patrick Yim's report."

The writer quoted Oz as saying, "She is attempting to blame and discredit others, instead of remedying damage her own wrongdoing caused."

Lindsey fired back, accusing Stender of orchestrating the campaign against her. She referenced her education report as proof of mediocrity at the world's richest school.

Adding balance to this drama, the *Honolulu Advertiser* published a two-part feature on the Kamehameha Schools secondary education program. It explained what was ignored in prior comparisons between Kamehameha and the Islands' other preparatory schools:

> About one-fifth of Hawai'i's population includes persons of Hawaiian ancestry, a requisite for admission to Kamehameha. By contrast, other schools draw from top performers of all races—Caucasian, Chinese, Filipino, Hawaiian, and Japanese.
>
> Kamehameha has a smaller pool of potential students resulting in a broader range of academic ability. Throughout the islands, Hawaiian students

continue to be in trouble academically, scoring lowest on math and reading among all racial groups.

The Princess established the schools to increase Hawaiians' pride. When Kamehameha wins a football game, Hawaiian men walk with their heads held high. When Mrs. Lindsey criticized Kamehameha test scores, she was talking about Hawaiians' test scores.

Local and national education experts noted that Kamehameha students' performance on key test scores improve steadily and impressively. This is especially meaningful because more of its 2,500 students walk in the door in seventh grade with fewer advantages than students in other private schools.

All Kamehameha students take the Standard Admissions Test, even those who say they are not college bound. In 1997, Kamehameha's average scores were 557 on math (vs. 511 U.S. nationally) and 515 on reading (vs. 505 U.S. nationally). Hawai'i's other private schools, by contrast, averaged scores of 583 on math and 544 on reading.

"Normally the higher the percentage that take the test, the lower the scores," stated an admissions director of the western region of the College Board.

The *Advertiser* reported that Kamehameha applies the Comprehensive Testing Program for measuring progress from one grade to the next. It quoted experts: "Kamehameha students improve as much as those nationally, except in seventh and eighth grade reading—which is their entry level to the school. Most recent reports show the school exceeding targets in math, but falling short in reading, vocabulary, and writing in the higher grades. The reason is that as students improve, targets become higher and harder to achieve."

Low verbal scores didn't bother a University of Hawai'i director of curriculum research, who said the state has a large immigrant population and many Islanders use forms of pidgin English. Helping students overcome pidgin is a mighty challenge for educators because it's such fun to use.

M rs. Lindsey was setting up Dr. Chun to be fired, but his performance statistics didn't help her. Since Chun's arrival in 1990, the number of students going to college increased to 98 percent. Four-year college enrollment went to 78 percent—half going to the University of Hawai'i and half to the mainland.

Dartmouth's dean of admissions said he was glad to have the two or three Kamehameha graduates he typically accepted each year. "They do well, are involved on campus, and are kids who make an impact."

The University of Washington enrolled twelve members from Kamehameha's class of 1997. An administrator reported, "Making the University of Washington cut off is not easy; out-of-state students must have an A– average to get in."

The University of Wisconsin tracked the success of Kamehameha graduates attending there over the previous thirteen years. All had grade averages of B– or better, and some went on to earn a graduate degree.

Mrs. Lindsey remained as bellicose as ever. She told the *Honolulu Advertiser,* "These figures of academic achievement are not a significant rise, given the amount of money we spend. They ought to be way better."

"We're just not producing the kinds of kids we want to produce," was Dickie Wong's sparse comment.

Through Doug Carlson, her PR representative, one of Mrs. Lindsey's mainland consultants spoke anonymously to the writer preparing the series. He agreed that Kamehameha draws from a smaller pool of students but said that should not cause lower test scores. "They try to use that limitation to explain lack of achievement. I don't buy that. They still have a heck of a lot of children to choose from and any limitation should be overcome by their unlimited resources. The children spend enough time at school so the school's influence should be able to overcome any disadvantages they may have experienced at home."

"We are going to take you from where you are and take you as far as we can," Principal Ramos, class of 1958, was fond of promising incoming students.

The newspaper described how the schools' proud atmosphere and Hawaiian focus caused a girl to enroll at Kamehameha after being accepted at 'Iolani and Punahou—absolutely top-notch academic schools. Her mother, extremely upset with her choosing Kamehameha, volunteered to be a room mother for six years to watch over her daughter. Six years later she told the newspaper, "It's been a great experience for a mother who once was ashamed to be Hawaiian. At Kamehameha, children live in the real world. There were people of all kinds for my daughter to learn about."

The lead to one of Mrs. Lindsey's news releases read: "The only way to stop Trustee Stender and contain the damage he already has done is to go public with his record of obstruction."

In a speech to the Honolulu Rotary Club, Mrs. Lindsey rejected the demands for broader enrollment that Oz advocated: "It is not the responsibility of Kamehameha Schools to educate all children of Hawaiian ancestry. It is the job of the State of Hawai'i to educate all children between ages 6 to 18—including Hawaiians."

She wept while whining that she had been "unfairly singled out."

A messenger hand delivered an envelope from four Kamehameha Schools faculty representatives to the attorney general's office. Marked "Confidential," it contained the following memo addressed to Margery Bronster and supporting exhibits. Teachers recognized that Bronster, who values education, could be a powerful ally.

The increased severity of our situation prompts us to communicate directly with you. Our students are achieving at high levels. To claim anything less, as does Trustee Lindsey, is inaccurate and does not honor our students' achievements and the support they receive from faculty and from their families.

In 1997, on standardized achievement verbal tests, Kamehameha students scored above or comparable to national private school norms at each of the tested grades along the K–12 continuum. They achieved at significantly higher levels than national norms for affluent suburban public schools.

In math, from grades K–12, Kamehameha students scored significantly higher than national private school norms and strongly out-performed national averages for more affluent suburban schools.

There has been a steady trend of improvement in College Board scores. When compared to national college-bound students (the top 40 percent of the nation's students), Kamehameha seniors, since 1990, have scored at or above the national average for verbal aptitude and since 1985 have scored substantially above average in math.

These facts call Trustee Lindsey's motives into question. Selected examples help establish her pattern of purposeful misinformation.

Here is a copy of her requirements that kindergarten children be able to identify each of the trustees by Christmas. She claimed what is attached as an exhibit never existed.

She criticizes the education group for not having an adequate curriculum and implies none existed prior to her appointment to the board. Neither is true.

Good school curricula reflect current educational research, the needs of the specific student body, and the projected needs of the society. They exist as living, evolving documents. Over the years we've gone through a number of curriculum reviews; each resulted in updating.

The *Honolulu Advertiser* reported Mrs. Lindsey's claims that there was no educational plan prior to her arrival. This is inaccurate. Kamehameha Schools has consistently planned for its future. Dr. Chun worked with us from fall of 1990 through spring 1992 to produce a secondary school strategy, the plan implemented during the 1992–93 school year, and was undermined by the trustees.

At the elementary school level, administrators and teachers developed a ten-year plan to accommodate the transition from a lottery to a select student body, as directed by trustees. The existence of both these plans stands in contradiction to Trustee Lindsey's claim that none existed prior to her initiatives.

Trustee Lindsey's recently released statements are misleading and appear to be primarily focused on personally vindicating herself while vilifying key personnel. Her statements are replete with half-truths—false impressions created by omission of facts, faulty analysis, and statistical manipulation.

She and her trustee supporters are willing to sacrifice anything—Kamehameha's standing as a quality school, self-esteem of thousands of students, confidence of the parents, long-standing pride of alumni, and the reputation of hundreds of teachers—to salvage their public image.

While they know they are achieving at high levels, students are outraged and bewildered to see themselves and Kamehameha Schools degraded in the manner Mrs. Lindsey did with her "Education Report."

With the help of Henry and Dickie, her gang of three, Mrs. Lindsey found the perfect way to attack her nemesis, Dr. Chun. She could destroy him once and for all and make a fool of Oz in the process. Fact-finder Judge Yim recommended that trustees hire an educational consultant. It was time for the gang to find one it could manage and perhaps manipulate.

Oz dutifully tried to help the trustees prepare for Judge Yim's recommended educational audit. He spoke of it as being critical "to the future of the children we are entrusted to educate." Oz relates what happened in the following talk story.

I spoke with acquaintances at the National Association of Independent Schools for names and references on organizations that do this kind of work. I asked the president of 'Iolani, and Michael Chun asked the president of Punahou for suggestions.

By the first of the year we had a list that included UCLA, Stanford, and Booz Allen. The schools educational office helped us draft a request for a proposal.

At a trustee's meeting on February 24, Henry announces: "We're going to use the Peterson group."

"Who are they?" I ask. "They're not on our list."

Henry says, "Somebody told me they are the best, so we're going to hire them."

"Wait a minute, wait a minute. I want to know who they are. I want to send out requests for proposals so we can evaluate them."

"No need," Henry answers. "These guys are good."

"Where did their name come from?"

I learned later the Peterson Group had a working relationship with William McCorriston, who led the lawyers who would challenge the attorney general's investigation. The topic of appointing a consultant was not on the meeting agenda, otherwise Gerry would have been present at the board meeting to add his indignation to mine, even though we'd be outvoted.

By a three-to-one vote, the gang of three selected the Peterson Group without due diligence review. We had no idea as to their qualifications, experience, intended scope of work, fees and costs, and references.

No businessperson in his or her right mind would select a consultant in this way, especially considering the magnitude and importance of the project. Peterson was given a "no-bid" contract.

Peterson didn't submit a proposal for the work it would undertake until after it was selected. Résumés of its team members showed three having extensive finance and business-related experience, but no education training and experience. Peterson's people had no understanding of the Hawaiian foundation of Kamehameha Schools.

Only two of the persons they brought in had background in educational matters; one had dealt with bilingual education and minority students in Hispanic and Asian communities. The other's experiences involved special education students.

Peterson confirmed their experience in "assisting management audits, investigations, forensic discovery, trials, and appeals." They quoted a fee in the $400,000 range plus expenses for three or four months work.

Nā Kumu did some investigating and found that Peterson presented itself on its own web site as "providing services which allow clients to manage the economic aspects of commercial problems, disputes, claims, or litigation." It stated capability to assemble "specialized teams bringing accounting, economic, financial, engineering, computer, lending, and investment expertise." A list of its nineteen client categories did not include education institutions. Nowhere on its web site were educational services or experience mentioned.

Oz told me, "I am convinced they were given orders as to what they had to come up with, and they prepared a scathing report on the schools."

Since 1964, the Kamehameha Secondary School (grades 9 to 12) has been accredited by the Western Association of Schools and Colleges (WASC). Accreditation is particularly important to college-bound students because it shows that the student's high school meets certain standards of excellence. Historically, WASC accredited Kamehameha Schools for six-year periods.

Its current process began in 1997 with a yearlong school self-study under the theme "Focus on Learning." Teachers and staff were asked to develop this through committees and focus groups. They were to talk with students, send out questionnaires, and develop action plans that addressed concerns and problems at the school. The completed self-study was given to members of the WASC committee to review prior to its March 9 to 12 campus accreditation visit.

The WASC committee read its completed report to the Kamehameha faculty. It praised the schools programs. Under a section on "School Purpose, Governance, Leadership, and Staff," Thomas Read, a member of the visiting committee, stated that Kamehameha Schools had an "outstanding curriculum, very rich and comprehensive, high quality and professional, with a dedicated and committed staff."

The report sharply criticized the trustees' governance of the school: "A perverse application of top-down decision-making has openly undervalued, if not scorned, the professional expertise, talent, and commitment of the non-administrative staff. It has produced an oppressive, intimidating, and fearful professional climate at the school."

The accreditation report cited several trustee decisions as "unethical acts of interference" that have "negatively affected the school."

The WASC visiting committee felt that while there was a lack of clarity in the role of the board, the principal damage had been caused by "micromanagement." As part of its protocol, WASC does not evaluate individuals, and the report was written to avoid identification of individuals.

On March 14, Principal Tony Ramos sent an e-mail to a Kamehameha Schools consultant regarding the WASC report. He stated that the visiting committee "got a standing ovation from the faculty upon the completion of reading their report. The trustees will not be pleased by their recommendations."

Principal Ramos told a reporter that the visiting committee said Kamehameha Secondary School is a world-class school, but they saw signs that governance would soon be affecting the teaching process. They hit the trustees hard on governance and communication between the board and the school.

Against Oz's protests, trustees ordered the 250 distribution copies of the 1998 report to be stamped "Confidential Internal Document." No prior WASC accreditation report had ever been marked confidential. Oz told me that other private schools distribute their WASC reports proudly and widely.

On March 19, Mrs. Lindsey read an article in the *Honolulu Advertiser* headlined "Team Rakes Bishop Trustees." It included the WASC's findings.

"She went ballistic," Oz said. "Her scheme was undone. She wrote a memo to

General Counsel Aipa asking for an immediate investigation to find out who released the WASC Accreditation Report to news media."

Oz and Gerry told other trustees an investigation was inappropriate because the release of the report caused no harm to the school; it praised the school, criticizing only the trustees.

Mrs. Lindsey said it was improper and unprofessional to release the report to news media before WASC had submitted its "final report." This was despite the fact that a visiting committee report is considered final once it is read to the school faculty. When the visiting committee left the school campus on March 12, its report was considered "final."

An accreditation report is considered "owned" by the school and there are no restrictions on its use. But Mrs. Lindsey's thirty years of accumulated educational experience was devoid of private school acumen. She wanted the WASC report hidden because it described harmful effects of her campus monarchy and praised the basic goodness of the school.

The Peterson report, now being prepared, was meant to be the final barrage to oust Dr. Chun. She wanted Rocky Freitas to take his place. From her perspective, things continued to worsen.

WASC wrote to school administrators that it was shortening its accreditation term from six to three years because of trustees' heavy-handed, top-down management. This news arrived at a time when the teachers were voting to form a union, feeling left out of school decision making.

Lokelani demanded to know who released the report. The board asked President Chun to conduct an internal inquiry. It didn't discuss retaining McCorriston's law firm to conduct an investigation, but Mrs. Lindsey sent a handwritten note back to Nathan Aipa, in-house counsel: "I want McCorriston to investigate."

She felt WASC's flattering report was released for someone else's agenda. She didn't directly accuse Oz, choosing to proceed circuitously with all the panoply and ceremony of an inquisition. She called it "a formal investigation."

On the school campus on June 1 for a meeting, Gerry Jervis heard staff members were in a conference room being questioned by lawyers from the McCorriston firm; a court reporter was recording the proceedings. Staff did not have their own lawyers and were asked to submit to a polygraph test. Gerry dashed into the room and saw an employee being questioned in tears and scared to death. He bellowed for questioning to be stopped.

Lokelani justified her actions in a memo to trustees: "In internal investigations, the employee does not have an attorney. It's an internal matter and usually means an employee did something wrong."

The gang of three voted to continue with the investigation.

Oz and Gerry objected because KSBE risked legal exposure by employees not being represented by counsel. They told trustees they would seek a temporary restraining order if the McCorriston law firm continued to interrogate KSBE staff members. Dickie, Henry, and Lokelani weren't intimidated. This forced Gerry and Oz to go to Probate Court.

The gang of three compromised by agreeing to use in-house staff. Lokelani demanded the investigation continue—as it did for eleven months. She never found out who allowed the schools accomplishments to shine.

Can you guess who might have stood up for the princess and sat Mrs. Lindsey down hard?

Oz and Gerry spoke to reporters about "this vindictive, ugly witch hunt, symptomatic of Kamehameha's basic dysfunctional governance."

One of Lokelani's attorneys had lots to say to the press about Oz and Gerry: "Their objecting to investigating 'the leak' speaks volumes to their guilty conscience by breaching responsibility to fellow trustees and the estate."

This same attorney prepared the way for the second coming of another education report, this one by the Peterson Group. He stated to newspapers: "The Peterson report will corroborate everything Mrs. Lindsey said in her education report. Dr. Chun will be very depressed by what he hears. The report could lead to the ouster of Dr. Chun. The Peterson report is going to vindicate Mrs. Lindsey: The school is a factory of failure."

He elucidated: "If the school is a factory of failure, who does it go to? The president of the school. That's where the buck stops."

"The school is a factory of failure." This description of Kamehameha Schools appeared on the front page of the *Honolulu Advertiser.* It became attributed to Mrs. Lindsey even though it was first said in public by her attorney. It erupted in articles all over the United States: "The world's richest school is a factory of failure."

This shocked everyone associated with Kamehameha Schools. "Factory of failure" was the type of attention-getting "sound bite" broadcasters could and did use repeatedly.

Being a lawyer, Gerry recognized the tactics; he said: "Discussing the Peterson report in advance of release and in public validates our strong concern that the report will be biased in her favor. His brazen comments clearly display ignorance and insensitivity."

The "confidential" Peterson report, completed on July 14, was about to surface. Meant for trustees' eyes only—as reputedly was Mrs. Lindsey's Education Report—she had a copy delivered to a newspaper almost immediately after it was collated and bound.

Oz wrote a memo of his assessment for the files. Dated July 14, 1998, it stated: "This is tailor-made to justify Mrs. Lindsey's Education Report."

He said to me, "It was a hatchet job, a vendetta against Mike. The Peterson people came into the school and told Mike to his face he was doing a good job; behind his back they tried to hack him into pieces."

"It confirmed our worst fears when Peterson was selected," Oz explained. "The report, countering the findings of WASC, was a whitewash for Mrs. Lindsey and a disgraceful waste of money."

With two reports, media had more confusion than clarification: WASC described the school as "world-class," whereas the Peterson report pointed to it as a "factory of failure."

"Criticism of Dr. Chun is hard to fathom," stated an editorial in the *Honolulu Star-Bulletin*. "The Peterson analysis confirms an earlier assessment that Mrs. Lindsey has been micromanaging the school. That makes blame affixed to Chun difficult to comprehend."

The editorial writer continued: "An accrediting team from WASC issued a scathing report in March; it found that the trustees' dysfunctional management and decision making harmed Kamehameha, weakened leadership, destroyed faculty morale, and damaged the climate of learning.

"Unlike the accreditation team, Peterson seems to accept some trustees' assertion that micromanagement was necessary because the school president was unable to fulfill job demands."

The *Honolulu Advertiser* said much the same thing: "Peterson slams Chun for his lack of leadership and stops just short of calling for his removal. Earlier reports by the accreditation team and the fact finder praised the schools program and called Dr. Chun a victim of a dysfunctional and overbearing board."

Beadie Dawson, Nā Pua's attorney, commented sharply: "The shallowness of Peterson's investigation and the narrowness of their focus on just one year lead me to wonder if there was some other motive for preparing the report."

The Peterson report became one more bit of ammunition in the war among the trustees. It made Kamehameha Schools appear anything but world class. It placed much of the blame on Dr. Chun, but it also could be interpreted as an indictment of the trustees.

Peterson judged student performance mainly by test scores from preschool to high school. It cited declining results as they advanced through grades 1 through 6 as well as weak college entrance exam scores. McCorriston, the trustees' lead attorney, said he gave more weight to the Peterson report because it was "an independent study."

I read the Peterson report on Nā Pua's web page. Scanned in, it bears terse, angry notes in handwriting resembling Oz's.

Peterson reiterated much of Mrs. Lindsey's education plan. Where facts were positive, Peterson offset them with negatives.

For example, Peterson reported that on the SAT tests, 47 percent of students scored above 510 on verbal and math, and 48 percent of seniors had a grade point average of above 3.0 (equivalent of a "B"). However, it pointed out, the school had "only one National Merit semi-finalist in its 1997 senior class that year."

The report included statistical charts with narrative and non sequiturs seemingly out of the blue. Here is one such example of a Peterson pejorative: "The schools ratio of almost 49 percent instructional staff compares favorably to the U.S. national average of 45 percent, but falls short of Japan's national average of 76 percent."

Why did Japan enter the Hawaiian education scene? In Hawai'i, students attend school for 180 days a year. The typical middle-school student in Japan spends the equivalent of 300 schooldays in class.

From my lay perspective, the consultants tried to offset anything good with a quick "gotcha" slap, no matter how irrelevant.

Oz commented, "They were given orders as to what they had to come up with, and they delivered a scathing report on the schools. Their bill ballooned to $500,000.

"The firm's vice president and project manager had the nerve to phone asking me for more work. I told him, 'You dinged Michael, you dinged the students, you dinged the faculty, and now you are dinging me by thinking I'm so stupid as to give you more work?'

"Some consultants will do anything for money, even coming up with a report to destroy an adversary."

O z continued meeting with members of his focus groups. One of them described Oz's position as similar to that of President Abraham Lincoln's during the Civil War: "Lincoln wasn't trying to destroy the South," he explained; "he was trying to save the Union, making America whole again as the United States of America." Oz wasn't attempting to "get at" the other trustees; he was trying to preserve the estate.

The following words are from a focus group confidant I've known much of my adult life. We worked together in a public relations agency on the mainland, and he came to Honolulu when a Big Five company hired him. William "Doc" Stryker elegantly elucidated Oz's position as a warrior for the princess.

> I believe you must continue to represent what trusteeship is supposed to mean and that you must remain visible in that role. This does not mean that you should be at the vanguard of protest or actively urging the overthrow of your fellow trustees, but you must perform your function in a manner that objectifies the concept and dignity of trusteeship.
>
> Those whose arrogance created the problem are absolutely depending on the tendency of Hawaiians to heal wounds rather than to solve the problems that caused the wounds. Sentiment can be a beautiful thing, but the cynical and

arrogant pragmatists with whom you are dealing regard it as a weakness to be exploited.

If judges can act against the public interest in their capacity as individuals, how are we to consider that they are beyond reproach on the bench? That is why your efforts to remove them from the selection of trustees are so important.

I believe Hawaiians of whatever blood quantum and the general public want a cleansing and a rebirth. It should be accomplished without personal malice, self-serving rhetoric, or an eye to the political main chance. Realism, honesty, and perseverance are required. You are the person, and Kamehameha Schools Bishop Estate is the institution.

O z had to sacrifice himself. He recognized this in December 1994 when Jervis was appointed as a trustee. He was prepared to be the first to go to set an example. If he had been concerned about what could happen to him in battle, he would not have become a warrior. Oz realized his vulnerability, but he was fearless, thanks to Tūtū Kāne, the Kamehameha School for Boys, the United States Marine Corps, and Kuulei's consistent faith and love.

The faculty regarded Oz as a champion who defied the majority and eventually attracted the support of Gerard Jervis. But they had been through too much for too long. Two years earlier, 171 faculty and staff were unceremoniously terminated. Among them were people with thirty-five years of service and outstanding evaluations.

In union they found strength and a voice; they progressed from humiliation to anger. Through the attorney general, they could strike back. They urged Margery Bronster to get rid of all the trustees, even though her sights were aimed at four and excluded Oz.

Nā Pua wanted all trustees out and "the morally bankrupt estate placed in receivership." Over 800 students signed a petition seeking the ouster of all trustees; 3,000 parents, alumni, and staff members signed as well.

It was impractical for Mrs. Lindsey to demand that McCorriston and his army of lawyers interrogate all petition signers. There wasn't much time left, and after lawyers scorched the earth, the school might be broke as well as well as broken.

CHAPTER 37

# Letting the Genie Out of the Bottle

## 1997–1998

A TTORNEY GENERAL Bronster completed her report on Kameha-meha Schools Bishop Estate to Governor Cayetano about August 29, 1997. She said beneficiaries' rights could be at great risk and wanted to continue the investigation.

By then she'd talked with "Broken Trust" authors, past court masters, and members of Nā Pua and would investigate any improprieties after the court master and judge's fact-finding reports were done. She was determined to remedy perceived problems and to take action against individual trustees.

The process Margery Bronster would use has always existed to ensure compliance with trust obligations. She was the first official daring enough to apply it.

She told me, "Governor Cayetano has a very strong sense of what is right and what is moral. He gave me the responsibility and didn't become involved."[1]

Over Oz and Gerry's protests, Dickie, Henry, and Lokelani hired six law firms to defend the estate against the attorney general's investigation. Two

---

[1] In the tradition of other immigrant groups, Filipinos glorified every achievement of their countrymen as they advanced from the fields into the mainstream of island life. The person making them proudest was Benjamin J. Cayetano, who, after winning six elections to public office, was twice consecutively elected governor of the State of Hawai'i (1994 and 1998). He graduated from UCLA and Loyola Law School, both in California, and was raised to success by his single-parent dad, a busboy in the Outrigger Club dining room.

were in Honolulu and two in Washington, D.C.; the last two, in Atlanta, Georgia, and Seattle, Washington, would handle research.

William McCorriston, former U.S. attorney practicing law in Honolulu, was leader and spokesman for the estate's team of attorneys. Oz was present as he described the team's plan for obstruction and delay. Lawyers would make every inquiry so difficult that the attorney general's office would either become confused or give up. They wanted to discredit Margery Bronster.

Oz thought this unjust, and said so: "I've met her and believe she wants to determine if there's truth to allegations made by the general public. She wants to protect the trust. Judge Yim's investigation is no different from the attorney general's. We are giving Judge Yim full support and encouragement to find the truth. The tactics you describe will frustrate her investigation and be costly. Let's work out a quick resolution with her. We don't need so many attorneys. Are we trying to protect the legacy or trustees?"

Ignoring Oz, McCorriston drew up battle lines. Oz and Margery were on one side, his army of Honolulu's highest-priced attorneys and minions were on the other.

Margery explained:

> Oz could give me little without a subpoena, which I was not ready to do. If trustees sued him for divulging information, a subpoena would protect him.
>
> Normally an attorney general can simply open an investigation and start doing interviews with people. The office starts issuing subpoenas to get documents, and information usually comes within an anticipated time frame.
>
> Instead, we got motions that were incredible: objections, lawsuits, and everything else to try and stop us from receiving information.
>
> It took us thirteen months to get the response to one subpoena. And then it had to go to the Supreme Court.
>
> Trustees had a legal right to appeal to the court to withhold documents. But their appeals process slowed investigators, consuming hundreds of hours as the estate's legal team fought through subpoenas and went back to seek clarification from judges.
>
> This became a war in the courts. Trustees' lawyers said they would cooperate, but actions belied their words.

I asked her, "How did you handle it?"

"One step at a time, as I did with Chinese. Learning that language was a daunting proposition; I did it by taking it slowly and not being scared off by the task."

The estate's lawyers tried to limit the attorney general's authority and avoided disclosing information. They objected to requests for documents on numerous grounds, including relevancy, attorney-client privilege, work product, and even right to privacy and qualified immunity.

They filed motions to quash a subpoena and for protective orders. They didn't produce documents. When orders were granted to comply with three of the attorney general's first subpoenas at issue, they drafted an appeal as well as a motion to stay enforcement. When these failed, the lawyers sent an appeal to the Supreme Court.

The lawyers developed a "destroy the opposition" strategy to silence or discredit whoever was perceived as the opposition, whether it was an employee, a reporter, the attorney general, a judge, or a court master. They researched "journalists' privilege" in order to legally support efforts to obtain sources from a reporter. They researched whether the attorney general had a conflict of interest in order to have her disqualified.

In what had to be the ultimate show of arrogance, they drafted complaints against the Internal Revenue Service for the refusal to communicate and complaints against the attorney general and the master for interference about their right to communicate.

They researched the possibility of restricting the attorney general from issuing further subpoenas and went to the State Supreme Court with that motion.

They filed an injunction prohibiting the attorney general from contacting Kamehameha Schools Bishop Estate employees. They investigated the prospects of civil liability and criminal charges against Margery Bronster.

Henry Peters discussed the possibility of Racketeer Influenced and Corrupt Organizations (RICO) Act violations against Margery Bronster. Lawyers researched the issue. RICO allows organized crime victims to sue for punitive damages.

Lawyers worked on a motion to disqualify Colbert Matsumoto as court master on the basis that he had publicly supported Governor Cayetano, who was responsible for the trustees being investigated. His support consisted of signing his name along with a list of others who endorsed the governor.

The trustees' lawyers even considered action against federal judge Sam King for ethical violations in coauthoring "Broken Trust."

Oz had warned Margery Bronster, "Once you let the genie out of the bottle, there is no telling what will happen."

A reporter wrote, "The attorney general's seven-month investigation is stalled because the interests of KSBE, the courts, government, and business are interwoven and impossible to separate."

Dutchie Kapu Saffrey, who helped lead the Nā Pua march, stated, "Our school and the estate are the goose that lays golden eggs; the political machine cannot afford to let go."

$M$argery confided the following points:

If I was not committed to doing this, we would have stopped. Without information, how can you do an investigation?

Allegations were very serious; a tremendous asset was being wasted. But witnesses were so petrified it was difficult to get them on record.

A lot of things were open secrets. Everyone in the community could tell you this, that, or the other. Hearsay is not evidence, and we needed to develop a case.

The State of Hawai'i could not match the Bishop Estate's spending. Governor Cayetano told Margery expensive delays were hurting the State's legal budget, but he didn't dissuade her from continuing.

By well into 1998, no documents had been produced, despite discussions that the Bishop Estate would turn over all documents it did not consider confidential.

Oz and Gerry filed a request in Probate Court for the appointment of an independent administrator to decide what information to hand over. Margery joined in support of the Stender-Jervis petition. Oz went to court to stop trustees from deciding which documents to hand over. "We need a special administrator to do this; otherwise, the fox is guarding the hen house."

Margery argued that trustees slowed her investigation by maneuvering not to comply with subpoenas. She asked the court to enforce specific subpoenas and even sought sanctions.

Judge Colleen Hirai denied the petition. "We are not seeking a ruling on specific subpoenas, but merely asking her to prevent the trustees from acting in a conflict of interest," Margery explained to me. "We didn't want the people we were investigating to decide what documents we received."

Delaying tactics by the estate's lawyers and the obstacles presented by judges in Probate, Circuit, and the Supreme Court left no room for her to move. Margery said, "Justices were sending a message to the lower courts, turning a temporary delay into a longer one. Add up the pieces and it smelled of politics."

One of Mrs. Lindsey's five attorneys argued, "Stender and Jervis are a minority on the board and they are using the court to force the majority members to do their bidding."

Margery earlier suggested that Supreme Court justices step back from matters involving her investigation because of conflicts on two fronts: One, under terms of the will, justices appoint the trustees; two, the appointment process itself would be part of her examination and justices could be in the position of ruling on subpoenas aimed at themselves.

The Supreme Court could force the estate to hand over subpoenaed documents crucial to the attorney general's investigation. She asked justices to hasten their decision to recuse themselves and to avoid further delays. Instead, the justices said they would seek an advisory opinion from the Commission on Judicial Conduct. This could take months.

Beadie Dawson worried about foot-dragging by the Hawai'i Supreme Court, the only court to which the attorney general could appeal. After five weeks, it had not ruled on the recuse proposal. She commented: "This is scary for Hawai'i. Is this a demonstration of the power trustees have? Or is there some Dr. No behind the scenes pulling strings?"

Margery said the delay would slow her investigation. "The real injury is to the students," she stated, remembering Oz's comments about becoming "a lost generation." She noted that justices previously recused themselves at least three times from cases involving the estate and had never before sought advice from the commission. She thought the decision would be easy, since four of them announced they had removed themselves from the trustee selection process.

Since their appointment powers were given to them as individuals, the justices were acting as individuals. Each justice could excuse himself individually in response to the attorney general's petition. But no, they helped the trustees they appointed.

Circuit Court judge Kevin Chang ruled he would not punish trustees for withholding subpoenaed documents from the attorney general. Margery had hoped that a fine of $600 an item or a reprimand would be a warning that their withholding documents would result in the loss of protections in keeping business matters out of the public record.

The attorney general's office found information by subpoena to other sources: Milton Holt's charge card records came from the Bank of Hawaii; the Van Dyke purchase records arrived from a third party involved in the sale.

The Commission on Judicial Conduct told justices of the Supreme Court to step away from the State's investigation of the trustees. They replaced themselves with Circuit Court judges.

By now the 1998 school year was beginning. Almost a year had passed; the attorney general's office still had not received any documents from the Bishop Estate.

Margery said, "Oz, in direct response to a subpoena, gave me my only help. He provided some of his memos and suggested things to pursue. The others hoped I'd give up."

# Interlude

So much was occurring on- and offstage at this point that it is time to pause and reflect on the drama.

- Margery Bronster, attorney general, was attempting to develop information to determine whether or not trustees had committed breeches in their responsibility to the estate. The estate's lawyers didn't want her to have anything and believed they could rely on a politically friendly judicial system to keep documents out of her reach.

- Meanwhile, Colbert Matsumoto, the court master, was uncovering secrets the trustees wanted hidden. Margery was counting on his report to galvanize public opinion and provide leverage to build her case.

- Trustee Lokelani was creating havoc with her "Education Report," known familiarly as "They can't read," to justify her actions in micromanaging Kamehameha Schools and ousting Dr. Chun. A fact-finding report by a judge had made her frantic. She was trying to discredit his work. Everyone was wrong except her.

- Oz was communicating quietly, creating support for Mrs. Lindsey's ouster. He wanted the system cleaned up so the trust could start fresh.

- Henry Peters was covering his tracks; the Master's Report and an IRS investigation could be his undoing, but he had a slick idea how to get out of it all.

- Dickie Wong was into some personal trouble through business deals with his brother-in-law.
- Gerry Jervis was not behaving.

The outcome centered on the efforts of two warriors for the princess. One of them, the court master, was a deft martial arts enthusiast who knew how to hit where it hurt most. The other, the attorney general, would finish the battle; she believed that if she could learn Chinese, she could overcome any challenge.

This was guerrilla warfare, where the unexpected can happen. While Lokelani flailed, public ire grew.

Auntie Nona was willing to speak up; I would talk with her soon. But for now, two quiet ceremonies reflect the perspectives of those who worked with children at the school and those whose lives were formed by it.

In August, on the eve of the new academic year, about fifty faculty and staff members spent two hours in a quiet ceremony in the parklike setting at a gravestone.

All five trustees were invited, but only Oz came. Leis were spread beneath Bernice Pauahi Bishop's nameplate on the polished marble of the monument honoring the last of King Kamehameha's descendants.

There were no political speeches nor protests against trustees, only ʻukulele, candles, and gentle singing. It was a time of quiet reflection and prayer, asking for light to lift the gloom over the school and the children everyone there loved—the children known as "Pauahi's flowers."

After a concert by the Royal Hawaiian Band, members of Nā Pua held a church service at Kawaiahaʻo Church. Jan Dill, class of 1961, Nā Pua's vice president, made a rallying cry:

> Public controversy since this past May prompted me to know the persona of Bernice Pauahi Bishop as revealed through her contemporaries' writings. She was exceptional, by any standard of measure.
>
> As I read more, I realized she was a woman of deep and abiding faith in God. He used his servant Bernice to bless and provide for her people in a time of great trauma and turmoil.
>
> A phrase from her will describing her vision for its beneficiaries helped me understand its application to my own life: "Kamehameha Schools should produce good and industrious men and women."

Studying that phrase and relating its English language to the Hawaiian—as she must have done—helped me comprehend her gift to me.

"*Lokomaikaʻi*" is the Hawaiian word most reflective of the English word "good." It connotes responsibility, active pursuit and maintenance of right and wholesome relationships—of bringing what is good and proper into all facets of what we think and do.

The fundamental right relationship is a relationship with God as Pauahi lived it. This is expressed in Psalm 24; we memorized it to recite during Founders Day ceremonies.

Remember this excerpt? "He that hath clean hands and a pure heart . . . shall receive the blessings of the Lord."

This psalm also reminds us that "the Lord is strong and mighty in battle."

In addition to being "good," beneficiaries of Pauahi's legacy are to be "industrious."

Capturing this meaning are the words *"hoʻohana me ke manaʻolana,"* encompassing a concept of contributing to a future characterized by hope and well-being.

The Hawaiian version of "industriousness" calls on us to improve our communities. The princess invested in good and industrious men and women to bring healing and hope to her people.

I recently discussed Kamehameha Schools issues with a fellow graduate. Like most of us, he tries to live a life in the calm, in the sheltered harbors, avoiding controversies, content to be where he is in control and can clearly see the horizons of life.

As a result of what was happening with the schools, he could hear God calling him to come out of the harbor and to surf the big waves outside the breakwater: "Come on, be more daring, jazz up your life!"

God was calling him to engage in the important issues we face and to stand without apology for what is right and for what brings hope and healing to our community. It is time to apply the goodness and industriousness she imparted within us:

Leave the safe harbor; be brave and nobly stand together hand in hand.

Charles Reed Bishop, the remarkable husband of Bernice Pauahi Bishop, ended his speech at the first Founders Day ceremony on December 19, 1888, with this thought: "Honor the memory and the name of Kamehameha Schools founder by your good conduct in mature life as well."

Jan concluded with Mr. Bishop's final words: "So long as we are in the right, we may reasonably trust in God for his help. So let us always try to be in the right."

*Interlude* · 265

For years I'd studied the developing drama at Kamehameha Schools Bishop Estate, sensing that a stage director, someone inside, was managing this. Timing was exquisite. As a seasoned public relations counselor and dramatist, I recognized mastery at work.

I said to Oz, "Spiritual effects from time spent on Kapālama Heights are evident among alumni I visit: It is seen in their kindness, dedication, earnestness, and sincerity. Something profound is happening: Hawaiians are looking beyond self-interests, they're acting unified. The princess is directing this through someone," I suggested.

Oz sat and thought for awhile. Then he said: "Arthur, I will tell you what no one knows. I've been working behind the scenes to help make possible what is occurring. My fingerprints are everywhere."

When he told me, everything came into place.

CHAPTER 38

# The Court Master's Consolidated Report

## August 1998

WHILE MRS. Lindsey and Oz attacked and counterattacked and estate lawyers engaged in a document tug-of-war with Margery, Colbert Matsumoto carried out Probate Court judge Colleen Hirai's orders.

She told him to consolidate the 109th, 110th, and 111th annual accounts so she could judge trustees' performance by the combined report. She also directed Colbert to hire an international accounting firm to conduct a full financial and management audit of the Bishop Estate.

"The trustees wanted a 'bigger name' than the local firm I used for the interim report," Colbert explained to me. From "big five" accounting firms, he chose Arthur Anderson LLP to consolidate the financial data of fiscal years 1994, 1995, and 1996 in generally accepted accounting practices.

For the first time since the Bishop Estate became rich, the court would receive a comprehensive overview of the complex business entity into which the princess's estate had been transformed. It would be more in keeping with formats used by Harvard University, Yale University, and other educational institutions with large endowments.

The court master finished nine months later. Whereas his interim report was a figurative shot across the bow of the vessel known as the Bishop Estate, the consolidated report was a direct hit. Previously Colbert scolded; his criticisms now struck with force in the following seven vital areas.

1.  Failure to meet the educational mission: The estate accumulated more income than it spent on education and served only 6 percent of Hawaiian children.

Trustees reclassified accumulated income rather than appropriating these funds for education under terms of the will. They decreased spending on school and financial services and increased spending on administration and professional services. Assets and bureaucracy grew; the school did not.

2. Miserable financial returns: Based on the trust's own numbers, its average total return on investment for the three fiscal years 1994 through 1996 was –1.0 percent. This amounts to a *minus* 1 percent loss.

Over the five-year period from 1992 to 1996, the total return on investments was 2.4 percent.

Both the three- and five-year rates were far worse than interest or returns investors could earn on a bank passbook savings account.

He said the trust keeps too much cash in a single money market account and should make that money work harder to earn more interest. In fiscal 1994, at the beginning of one of the strongest bull markets in history, the estate had more invested in oil and gas investments that soured than it did in stocks and bonds that soared.

Goldman Sachs provided the Bishop Estate with more income than all other investment sources for each of the three fiscal years. Colbert noted that the income for Goldman Sachs was misrepresented each year. Holding a 9.5 percent interest in the investment banking firm, the Bishop Estate was required to account for the investment on the cost-basis method. Instead, it applied a hybrid cost and equity method that over- or understated yearly amounts by as much as $33 million.

It suffered almost $400 million in losses and loss reserves on its long-term investments from 1991 through 1996.

Colbert explained to me, "Trustees defended their financial performance by crediting themselves with obtaining positive returns each year. They missed the point or didn't want to deal with it. A more meaningful discussion and analysis of the investment performance would focus on its rate of return on investments. However, trustees were silent in that regard."

3. Exaggerated success: The advertising campaign "The True Bottom Line on KSBE's Financial Performance" failed to note that most of the income claimed by the trustees was attributable

to land sales and changes in accounting principles. Its residential land was lessening (in 1994 the estate received $199 million, in 1995 $83 million, and in 1996 $51 million).

4.   Greed: Trustees used a labyrinthine maze to hide losses and assets and shield financial information. These obscured negative performance. They did this to protect their own commissions by transferring losing investments to for-profit subsidiaries whose losses were not included when calculating trustees' compensation.

He was uncomfortable with the aggressive nature of many investments, describing them as "entrepreneurial in nature, volatile and therefore not stable sources of income." He questioned whether the proportion of the portfolio in high-risk ventures was too great. High risk meant greater potential commissions to trustees.

To substantiate their high commissions, trustees had authorized two compensation studies within months of each other costing $169,296.

Colbert noted that trustees' personal interests conflicted with the trust when they hired firms to lobby against the Federal Intermediate Sanctions law. One component of the law is that an organization can lose its tax-exempt status if any principal executives receive excessive benefits in the form of high compensation, interest-free loans, or other instances of self-dealing. He wanted trustees to explain why they shouldn't reimburse the estate over $1 million out of their own pockets for those lobbying expenses.

5.   Ignoring advice, no planning: Studies in the school archives helped Colbert discover how trustees deviated from past recommendations. For example, the 99th Master's Report helped to establish internal audit functions. In 1995, trustees removed the internal audit and stopped pending audits, concealing and protecting their improper transactions and conduct from discovery.

Much investing was done with little due diligence by the estate and with heavy reliance on advice from coinvestors— that is, former Treasury executive William Simon and former McArthur Foundation executive Lawrence Landry.

Colbert pointed out that in 1983 Cambridge Associates, Inc., consultants to universities with large endowments, recommended that the Bishop Estate use "financial equilibrium" for its investment and spending programs to give, at a minimum, the same level of service to future generations while preserving the corpus of the estate's endowment. In an update, it suggested spending based upon 5 percent of the value of the endowment yearly on education, as did Yale and Harvard Universities.

Trustees moved in a contrary direction. Without portfolio planning, they became more opportunistic, investing in high-risk and illiquid non-Hawai'i real estate ventures, private equity investments, and oil and gas ventures. While some investments performed well, many became controversial and resulted in heavy losses.

In 1992 the Bishop Estate adopted its first investment policy without involving Cambridge. It lacked objectives for return requirements and risk tolerance for each asset class in the portfolio and had no benchmarks for acceptable time horizons, liquidity requirements, and other special circumstances.

In 1996 Cambridge was back to review the asset allocation in light of trustees' concerns over liquidity of cash flows with the start of the Go Forward program. Its consultants commented on the Bishop Estate's reliance on sizable capital gains from principally illiquid investments as a primary cash generator for discretionary capital expenditures.

Cambridge recommended improving cash flows from the core Hawai'i real estate assets, increasing liquidity reserves to 5 percent of the fund, building a core global stock portfolio to 5 percent of the assets, investing in liquid assets that offered risk-adjusted returns, and deemphasizing additional illiquid noncore real estate and financial asset investments. Trustees acted on none of these recommendations.

6. Go Forward is a step backward: Colbert identified Go Forward for what it was: a program prepared by a person inexperienced in educational planning. Dr. Ahr, Go Forward's mastermind, was a clinical psychologist and former director of the Missouri Department of Mental Health.

Colbert had asked the estate repeatedly for Dr. Ahr's background studies but received only a disparate assortment of surveys and reports. "There was no coherent planning document, no analysis underlying the development of the initiative."

Colbert stated, "An institution such as the trust estate should have the best of talent available to it to help it plan its most fundamental mission." He could not understand why Go Forward was announced so hurriedly.

He told me that Ernst & Young's financial study for the program was not developed until a year after Go Forward was announced. "What should have been welcomed as the most significant and ambitious educational venture for the trust in decades turned into an episode clouded by mistrust, misunderstanding, and antagonism."

7. No strategic plan: The master felt that this alone compelled court intervention.

Trustees failed to take into account available financial resources. Colbert said, "Wherever there might be a semblance of direction—such as suggested by Cambridge—there is a weak commitment to abide by it.

"There is no centralization of financial reporting responsibilities, leading to inconsistent, erroneous, and untimely reporting. Trustees are too involved in running the business; they are not providing planning, supervision, and evaluation."

O z had given Arthur Anderson representatives his memos. There was great congruity in what Oz had urged and what Arthur Anderson recommended.

The consulting firm pointed out that the last time KSBE had performed a strategic plan for the organization was in 1965. Since then, any planning had been sporadic and piecemeal.

No considerations were made for changes to the educational spending levels as the estate was faced with the reinvestment of over $1 billion in cash, and later planning ignored spending the return off the investment portfolio.

Trustees did not include any new revenues in educational planning when, in fact, surplus revenues existed.

Arthur Anderson echoed Oz's appeals that the educational mission guide every decision and that individual efforts—educational and investment—be coordinated. At the trustees' request, the Anderson report was sealed by the court.

"I found Oz very approachable and thorough," Colbert told me. "He has the personality you would expect of a trustee. I am not surprised that he is so warmly thought of by the students at the school, who call him 'Uncle Oz.' From all that I learned, the person that comes closest to his stature as a trustee is 'Papa' Lyman.[1]

"Give Oz credit as the catalyst for everything that happened," Colbert said to me. "When he brought me his memos and background material, I was surprised at the extent to which he had engaged in a personal battle with the trustees. He clearly documented every situation. I realize his had been a lonely voice for a period of time. He was extremely brave in a very uncomfortable position."

Oz suggested that Colbert comment on the estate's failure to follow generally accepted accounting principles. He urged him to investigate surplus funds being accumulated instead of going into education. Oz pointed to a lack of planning, paying lobbyists to maintain trustees' high commissions, and potential dangers from an Internal Revenue Service audit.

All of Colbert's information was now available for the attorney general to use and was on the Internet for anyone to read.

Governor Cayetano told the public that potential witnesses shouldn't fear reprisals. He stated that even if former Bishop Estate employees had confidentiality clauses written into their employment contracts, such clauses are subservient to the law. They couldn't be sued for breach of contract if they responded to the attorney general's subpoenas.

The fact that he would not be bombarded again was a relief to Bobby Harmon, first to carry live ammunition against the estate.

Trustees demanded that Arthur Anderson not disclose anything related to the estate's investment in Goldman Sachs. However, immediately after the Master's Consolidated Report was issued, KSBE spokespersons informed the press of a $3-billion value for the estate's interest in Goldman Sachs.

Colbert commented, "Trustees disclose financial information only when it serves their own purposes."

---

[1] "Papa" Lyman was famed for the way he announced the winning classes at the schools annual song contests. He prolonged the suspense with talk stories as students squirmed anxiously in their seats. Just as he finished one, he'd "happen" to think of another that was "absolutely appropriate" to one of the songs sung in the contest. Oh, the exquisite agony! He loved to tease kids the way a papa will.

CHAPTER 39

# Lawyers Crank Out a Response

## 1998

LAWYERS FOR the band of four responded to the Court Master's Report with sixty pages of corrections and explanations attributed to Henry Peters, Dickie Wong, Lokelani Lindsey, and Gerry Jervis. Oz filed his own response that agreed with the master.

Lawyers filled their pages with history, explanation, references to other legal cases, and material on trust law presented in a dissertation format as a tutorial. For instance, a response to the master's comments on its investments read as follows: "The risk factor most frequently overlooked is the inflation risk in any investment or portfolio. The danger to a dynastic trust today is less likely to be that the fiduciary will invest too aggressively than that the trustee will not invest aggressively enough to offset the effects of inflation. A failure to invest in such a manner as to offset the effects of inflation results in a radical diminution in corpus as inflation takes its yearly toll."

In their imperious style, Bishop Estate lawyers noted that operating losses in one year may be offset in another year by operating income as an investment's fortunes improve: "Years under review are a snapshot of the process whereby the estate has evolved from being almost entirely invested in Hawai'i real estate to holding hundreds of millions or billions of dollars in equity investments. Investment ratios are goals and cannot be treated as absolutes."

Trustees authorized millions spent on such banality.

Colbert had commented briefly on the trustee's investment in land formerly comprising the Hāmākua Sugar Company plantation on the Big Island. This transaction of $21 million was not included in the minutes of trustee meetings, nor was it listed in the schedule of real estate transactions for fiscal year 1995. Based on later questions, Colbert found that the investment did not meet the standards of prudent investment. Its 30,500 acres had been offered at a bankruptcy auction. A report by an estate staff member estimated the value at $500 an acre, or roughly $15 million, and recommended it be a cash acquisition rather than debt-financed. This was due to the low return for leasing the land for agriculture or forestry, the estate's intended use.

The only advantage to the purchase, stated the staffer, was that at the end of twenty years the investment would pay for itself and the estate would own more acreage in that area. Without minutes or material, Colbert had to accept the claim from one of the trustees' attorneys that further analysis showed a profitable return could be obtained on a price as high as $25 million. The trustees authorized a bid of $21 million.

There were no minutes on this decision, only a file memo by Henry Peters. To finance it, the estate spent over $1 million yearly on interest.

Colbert commented: "The purpose of the estate is to establish and maintain Kamehameha Schools, not to amass large amounts of Hawai'i land with inadequate regard to the investment consequences of such a use of the estate's assets. Over 330,000 acres of agriculture and conservation lands made up more than 98 percent of the estate's land holdings in Hawai'i."

The estate's lawyers' rebuttal was that Hāmākua Coast provides some of the most productive growing conditions for timber/fiber production anywhere in the world. Financing the purchase of this land would "position the estate to benefit from a predicted worldwide shortage of pulp and timber."

After making challenges and explanations, KSBE's attorneys said trustees would agree to accept the court master's nineteen recommendations. They could not resist including this rather oblique comment: "While the trustees do not find the substance of most of the recommendations unacceptable, the master is in error when he urges the court to 'order' the trustees to undertake discretionary activity."

This was followed by more written history in which the lawyers pointed out that the master is the agent of the court; it served no purpose for him to express his feelings.

Colbert ignored this put-down. Trustees agreed to his recommendations, and the attorney general now had what she needed.

CHAPTER 40

# The Attorney General's Preliminary Report

## Fall 1998

B Y SEPTEMBER 1998, a year had passed and the attorney general's office was still without Bishop Estate documents. Trustees' willingness to accept the court master's recommendations wasn't enough for Margery.

She issued a preliminary report stating that the intent of Bernice Pauahi Bishop is not being implemented and a trustee may have breached the fiduciary duty owed the beneficiaries. Her allegations included deceit, influence peddling, and misuse of perhaps millions in trust assets: "There are simple, very fundamental messages here: When an organization that is supposed to be open by the terms of the princess's will becomes so secretive, it must be doing something wrong."

She sought the immediate interim removal of all five trustees and the appointment of a receiver. She said she would petition for permanent removal of any trustees found guilty of breaches of fiduciary duty.

Based on the Court Master's Report, the attorney general alleged that the trustees had financially mismanaged the charitable trust, failing their responsibilities. Margery outlined what she expected trustees to do:

- Return their commissions to the estate for what she described as various breaches of responsibility over the past three years (1997, 1996, and 1995);
- Return $900,000 of estate money they spent lobbying against federal laws that include limits on trustee compensation;
- Reimburse the estate for legal fees spent to defend them personally during her investigation.

She also mentioned the possibility of criminal charges against some trustees. The State had evidence to back up the charges from interviewing 200 witnesses and reviewing more than 100,000 pages of documents.

These words finally caught the attention of estate lawyers, and the long-awaited documents arrived a month later. She had expected sixteen boxes of documents with 17,000 pages or more covering transactions dating from January 1, 1993. The trustees' lawyers delivered four boxes.

During a hearing before Judge Chang to determine whether the trustees should be held in contempt of court, estate outside counsel McCorriston commented, "What's the evidence that we didn't give them everything? Bronster has a shoot first, ask questions later investigative style."

Margery heard that a secretary for Lokelani was shredding documents and deleting computer files so they could not be resurrected by the network server. She asked Judge Chang to order all employees to return, repair, restore, and undelete any files, records, and documents destroyed since the beginning of the attorney general's investigation. This would protect employees from being fired who came forward with information about the removal or destruction of documents.

Threatened by contempt of court, McCorriston himself delivered the missing documents.

Into the attorney general's office went staff from the *Honolulu Advertiser,* rolling a small photocopy machine to copy details of Bishop Estate finances for 1995 and 1996. This accounting consisted of 841 pages of computer printouts listing dates, names of companies or individuals, and how much the Bishop Estate paid. Now the newspaper could report on who received the Bishop Estate's billions.

CHAPTER 41

# Fattening Local Bank Accounts

## Fall 1998

FROM LISTINGS of Bishop Estate expenses, newspaper staff created a database by entering names of island business firms they recognized. Phoning these companies to find out what kind of work they did, the researchers ended up with information on 540 Hawai'i businesses that were paid over $38 million by the estate. Many had ties to former governor Waihee and his friends Henry Peters and Dickie Wong.

These financial records were for the nonprofit side of the Bishop Estate's operations. Records of more than a dozen for-profit subsidiaries and ventures representing its global financial activity weren't given to the attorney general.

Despite its digging, the *Advertiser* staff could reveal only that the Bishop Estate was a huge part of the local economy. The estate spent $6.3 million on computer-related expenses, $2.99 million on consulting services, and $1.3 million on advertising and public relations services. It reinvested more than $900 million, of which $14.9 million went to Goldman Sachs and $12.8 million to Smith Barney, another investment firm.

That year's legal fees of $7.1 million were distributed by Gerry Jervis, who supervised an in-house staff of eight lawyers and an in-house general counsel. He commented, "We're an island community. It is no surprise I know attorneys we hire."

The newspaper wanted stories it could tie to trustees. It reported that the estate spent $8.6 million doing business with a company headed by Henry Peter's nephew and also did business with Henry's former employer.

I looked into the Watermark Towers environmental remediation project. Lokelani's stepson was a key employee for the firm receiving the contract. It had never done this type of work; the firm told its insurance agent it was in the composting business. When first attempts on working with the hazardous chemical PCB were unsuccessful, a change order was issued doubling the original bid. All contracts were handled by KSBE legal staff.

"Of course people hire friends; nothing wrong with picking people you know to do business," Judge Sam King said to an *Advertiser* reporter. "But what is the business they are doing? Are they doing real work or just being given money?" He commented that the estate had lost its financial innocence from fifteen years earlier when it had to sell land to meet its payroll.

My own sources found well-known national names with Bishop Estate business dealings. High-profile individuals often are attracted to entities with deep pockets; the $10 billion claimed by the estate was luring. We referenced archives, reviewed wire service articles, and searched the Internet. When clues—or dots—emerged, it was a matter of finding how the dots connected to the estate.

Over the years, the Bishop Estate made substantial investments in unorthodox or risky ventures under the persuasion of charismatic financial experts who flaunted their connections, dazzled potential investors with credentials, and used other people's money when placing investment bets.

Houston oil and gas man Lester Smith was one such person. The estate invested $3.75 million in Smith Offshore Exploration, a Smith company that did gas exploration in the Gulf of Mexico. Later it deposited $10 million in INEXO, another Smith company that did not do well. Bishop Estate partners included Harvard Management Group, the investment arm of Harvard University, Yale University, and Duke University.

Smith approached the Bishop Estate about the McKenzie gas deal, and it committed $20 million. He wanted a piece of the project but didn't have the money to buy it. As a tax-exempt organization, the estate could not make such a loan, but McKenzie lawyers showed them a way around it. The Bishop Estate guaranteed three loans to Smith and his company from the Bank of Hawaii, the estate's principal banker. The loan bought him an interest and gave him money to pay development costs.

Oz, not a trustee when this occurred, later accused McKenzie of diverting investors' money to projects in Poland, Egypt, and elsewhere. When Smith defaulted, the estate paid the tab for the $23.7 million loan and recovered Smith's interest, which Oz says was about $3–5 million. It never went after Smith for repayment.

Former U.S. Treasury secretary William Simon convinced trustees to invest with him. His technique was to pump money into a savings and loan about to go under and then sell it for a profit. He told the *New York Times* of his plans to develop a financial empire reaching throughout the Far East. He anticipated using Bishop Estate money to accomplish this.

Simon was the estate's business partner in a banking deal with HonFed, later sold to Bank of America. The State Insurance Commission took legal action against Bank of America, Goldman Sachs, and other brokerage companies in connection with the failure of Investors Equity Life Insurance, which sold annuities through HonFed. Simon and the Bishop Estate were tied in with Investors Equity Life through its HonFed investment.

Investors Equity ran up a $90 million deficit because one of the two sole shareholders made highly speculative leveraged investments known as "derivatives." It conducted sham real estate deals and used the insurance firm's assets to pay large fees to one of Investors shareholders and the companies with which Simon was connected.

Simon joined the Bishop Estate in investing in the McKenzie Methane gas drilling project. This led to Auto Fuel, another Texas-based company. It signed an agreement with the Bishop Estate on the same day it signed a revolving credit and loan agreement with the Bank of Hawaii and the Bank of New York. A year later, Auto Fuel signed a stock pledge and security agreement with Bishop Estate. Auto Fuel went into bankruptcy, and a wholly owned Texas subsidiary of the Bishop Estate filed a claim to recover $29.6 million, of which $24.76 million was secured by collateral.

Robert Rubin, worth an estimated $100 million, resigned from Goldman Sachs to join the Clinton administration. To avoid a conflict of interest, he sold his Goldman Sachs partnership to the firm. To avoid depleting cash reserves, Goldman Sachs gave Rubin a note promising to pay principal and interest over a number of years.

This caused a potential conflict for Rubin. His huge investment in Goldman Sachs might be affected by his government actions; an example was making a decision on whether or not to bail out Mexico, where Goldman Sachs had huge investments.

Rubin phoned friends at the Bishop Estate, who agreed—for $100,000 a year—to insure his stake in Goldman Sachs and guarantee a rate of return. A Treasury official commented that the estate was ideal for this transaction, rather than a major financial firm, because it was not likely to be affected by his government work.

L awrence L. Landry worked with the Bishop Estate while he was chief financial officer at the Chicago-based MacArthur Foundation. The estate invested in his Boston-based investment fund and a Florida apartment complex.

Landry came into the news after paying over $1 million in finder's fees to persons recommended by a former Connecticut state treasurer convicted on federal racketeering and money-laundering charges and for funneling bribes and kickbacks through his and others' political campaigns. Said to have authorized hundreds of millions of dollars in public pension fund investments, he involved lobbyists, lawyers, and politicians from both parties who collected finder's fees for lining up deals for him. Well-connected people in Connecticut received a percentage of nearly every state pension investment. That's one way to make political kickbacks.

I n the 1990s through 1998, the Bishop Estate had $235 million in capital losses and wrote off more than $100 million in bad investments. This was more than three times its $100 million annual educational budget.

A write-off means the estate considered the complete investment a loss. A capital loss represents that portion of an investment that is impaired. It wrote off $50 million from its investment in Cadillac Fairview Corp., a Toronto-based office and retail property development.

The capital loss in McKenzie Methane Inc., a Houston-based natural gas producer, was estimated to be between $65 and $100 million. Mark McConoghy of Price Waterhouse worked with the estate, investing his own money in Bishop Estate's methane deal. He was an associate of former Senator Robert Dole and trustee of Elizabeth Hanford Dole's blind trust, and he served on the National Commission on Restructuring the IRS. He was considered as a potential trustee candidate the year Jervis was appointed.

The Bishop Estate's purchase of Hanford's, Inc., a North Carolina ornament maker founded by the family of Elizabeth Hanford Dole, ended up as a multimillion-dollar loss. The estate lost $27.7 million in Accessory Place and $20.2 million in Best Products.

Trustees loved how McConoghy of Price Waterhouse helped to make them richer. In 1986 he concluded that the estate's Royal Hawaiian Shopping Center could be transferred from a taxable subsidiary to its tax-free parent. This gave board members additional tax-free revenue.

The Bishop Estate recorded a $30 million loss in 1992 from its investment in Pembridge Associates, a company that acquired a large England-based paper products and packaging materials conglomerate named DRG in a $900-million leveraged buyout. One of its partners was Frederick Field, an heir to the Marshall Field department store fortune and an investor in McKenzie Methane. Clay Hamner, a North Carolina investor, was involved in this and two other money-losing ventures with the estate.

Field struck back at the estate for "usury" arising out of its loan to him of over $29 million at an interest rate of 20 percent per annum.

The estate was in financial and ethical trouble with the Robert Trent Jones Golf Club in northern Virginia. The club's members included former president George Bush, U.S. Supreme Court justice Sandra Day O'Connor, ex–AT&T Corp. chairman Robert Allen, and Washington power broker Vernon Jordan. It was designed by legendary golf course builder Robert Trent Jones. The partnership included the estate and Durham, North Carolina, developer Clay Hamner. The estate guaranteed Jones' loan of $40 million from a North Carolina bank.

The club's financial problems in 1994 prompted partners to sell the leasehold interest in the club and its two-story, 40,000-square-foot clubhouse to members. The estate retained the fee interest, following its Hawai'i custom. That deal was largely engineered by Henry Peters, who also served as a trustee of the golf club.

That relationship prompted two club members—Benjamin Stone and Robert Basham, president of the Outback Steakhouse restaurant chain—to sue Henry and other partners, saying the fee price was too high and that Henry had a conflict since he served as a trustee of both institutions. The suit was settled after the estate gave club members a favorable forty-year lease and an option to buy the fee interest.

During the 1990s, most charitable trusts spent at least 5 percent yearly of their value directly on charitable activities. The Bishop Estate spent 1 percent, reflecting the trustees' personal attitudes toward charity.

Oz volunteered to collect donations from trustees for the United Way. He gave $12,000 and thought others would donate at least $10,000 each. He kept after them to submit their pledge cards, so their payments could be made through the estate's payroll deduction plan. Mrs. Lindsey said she had given $250 to the Maui United Way and saw no need to donate any more. Henry Peters gave $2,000. Dickie and Gerry didn't respond.

Well-known names were identified with some of the Bishop Estate's successes. Richard Rainwater, a Texas billionaire deal maker who helped Governor George W. Bush acquire his pre-presidential wealth, joined with the Bishop Estate in two rewarding deals.

In 1993 the estate invested $30 million in Mid-Ocean Reinsurance Co. with partners J. P. Morgan & Co., Marsh & McLennan Co., and Rainwater. Its 5.36 percent in the Bermuda-based reinsurance company that went public in late 1993 was worth about $106 million.

Rainwater helped bring the estate into Columbia/HCA. Columbia was responsible for the largest health care fraud investigation in history, involving Medicare and other federal programs. It was structured with Goldman Sachs' assistance, and the Bishop Estate became a major investor along with Richard Rainwater.

The Bishop Estate began the twenty-first century with a heady success from its investment in the Palm Beach, Florida–based Westport Advisers Limited. This is the general partner in Westport Senior Living Investment Fund, a retirement community buyer and developer. It owned 69.2 percent of Westport Advisers and put up $25 million in the Westport Senior Living Fund itself. The estate invested $37 million into WCI Communities Inc., in 1995, becoming its biggest stockholder.

Six years later its shares were valued at $160 million, the result of an initial public offering. WCI owns One Watermark Place of the Palm Beaches in West Palm Beach and was constructing a fifteen-story building overlooking the Intra-Coastal Waterway. It stated intentions to bankroll a wave of new developments including its thousand-home Evergreen development and the Old Palm Golf Club, both in Palm Beach Gardens.

The $230 million deal, perhaps south Florida's largest in recent history, encompasses nearly 15,000 acres, spanning Palm Beach, Martin, and St. Lucie counties. WCI has since sold all but 2,500 acres, generating $132 million. The company is now headed by chief executive officer Alfred Hoffman, former national cochairman of finance for George W. Bush's presidential campaign.

Verner, Liipfert, Bernhard, McPherson and Hand, a Washington, D.C., law firm, lobbied in Washington on aviation, highway, and mass transit funding issues for the State of Hawai'i during Governor Waihee's term of office. The firm includes two former Senate majority leaders—Bob Dole and George Mitchell—and former Treasury secretary Lloyd Bentsen.

When Waihee's term expired, Verner et al. set up a Honolulu office and hired him. The lawyers recommended relocating Kamehameha Schools Bishop Estate to the Cheyenne River Sioux Reservation in South Dakota, where the 12,000-member tribe sits on land about the size of Connecticut. It has 60 percent unemployment and welcomed an entity such as the Bishop Estate. The reservation has had a government-to-government relationship with the United States since 1880.

Trustees wanted to make KSBE a for-profit entity so they could pay themselves whatever they chose. They had the Verner law firm lobby Congress to lower the so-called exit tax levied on organizations relinquishing their tax-exempt status.

As an aside, the James Campbell Estate—where Oz could have been a trustee —is a private for-profit trust set up to benefit the heirs of Scottish seaman Campbell. It has over $2 billion in assets. Each trustee was entitled to receive $1,850,000 in commissions for the year ending, but as in past years, the trustees waived off a huge chunk of the amount, each giving up $1 million in 1996. The commissions set up by estate law, described earlier in this book, entitled them to receive 7 percent of the first $5,000 of income earned by the trust and 5 percent of income above $5,000.

Because of dropping values in the late 1990s, the Bishop Estate began divesting itself of many under-performing assets. It sold 608 acres of industrial land near Atlanta to a mainland investor for about $13 million. The parcel is part of the 1,200-acre Gwinnett Progress Center project launched by the estate and its partners in the late 1980s. The trust wanted to sell its assets in its Treyburn LLC subsidiary. Treyburn is the developer of master-planned residential communities in North Carolina's Research Triangle area. The estate had invested $59.5 million in various Treyburn projects, but property values dropped to about $14 million.

The Bishop Estate was worth at least $10 billion early in 1990, according to its own reports. But in 1996, after the court ordered the trustees to value all estate assets, its total was only $5.7 billion. Then it dropped to $5.5 billion, despite a $3 billion windfall from its investment in Goldman Sachs. Where did over $5 billion go? It couldn't all be due to bad investments.

Professor Randy Roth expressed his thoughts: "Untold millions were illegally siphoned off to coconspirators in quid pro quo deals. How do you embezzle this much from a tax-exempt charitable trust?"

Randy also pointed out that trustees used 1965's assessed values as a starting point in calculating gains from involuntary land sales. "Had they used assessed values at the beginning of the period in question, the result would have been substantial losses, not gains. If you sell a piece of property for $300,000 that at current market prices is valued at $1 million, you do not have a profit."

The estate claimed its land in Hawai'i was worth $1.6 billion, using 1965 values. The City and County of Honolulu assessed its land on O'ahu alone at almost $5 billion, using current prices.

When seeking connections to the missing $5 billion or more, dots metamorphose into zeros.

CHAPTER 42

# Lokelani Goes to Trial

## 1998

LOKELANI LINDSEY'S trial began on November 11, 1998, eleven months after Oz and Gerry petitioned for her removal. They were seeking to prove that she mismanaged Kamehameha Schools, abused her power, was a key factor in problems festering on campus for almost two years, and misused trust assets.

Her attorneys wanted six months more time to prepare. Circuit Court judge Weil said no: "Students and faculty were hurt enough by the controversy and it needed to be ended."

Judge Bambi Weil came to Hawai'i from Tacoma, Washington, in the 1970s as a local television station's political reporter. Eight years later she studied law at the University of Hawai'i's William Richardson School of Law, where she excelled, becoming editor of the *Law Review*, a criminal justice tutor, a legal research assistant at the law school, and law clerk in a local firm. Hard work didn't daunt her.

Judge William Richardson, remembering Weil's incisive reporting on complex legislative issues, hired her as his clerk after she earned her law degree. "She would arrive for work on Friday and not leave until Monday," Judge Richardson said. "No one was expected to work that long."

Becoming a district court judge promptly after completing the required five years of practice, Weil became a circuit judge six years later.

This trial before Judge Weil was separate from actions initiated earlier by Attorney General Margery Bronster. She sought interim removal of all trustees except Oz and then permanent removal of any trustee found guilty of wrongdoing.

Gerry Jervis seethed about this. Margery excluded Oz from temporary removal because his memos showed he had argued with trustees about their not spending money meant for educating children. By then, Gerry had allied himself with Oz. He told Margery many incidents occurred before he became a trustee in December 1994; he tried to paint himself as a "victim."

Then he told reporters Margery offered him a deal: If he made a public statement or court filing for the removal of the other three, she would not ask for his removal. This infuriated Margery; she had said no such thing.

By trial time, Lokelani had reimbursed the estate for work on her house and paid vendors for some of her trips. Five lawyers and a personal spokesman were working for her. Her two courtroom lawyers simulated a "good cop–bad cop" routine that police interrogators sometimes use. The "good cop" was courtly and smiling. The "bad cop" was more aggressive; he's the one who had coined the term "factory of failure" to describe Kamehameha Schools. He had accused Oz of using "Wicked Witch of the West" as Mrs. Lindsey's synonym.

I spoke to Auntie Nona after the "bad cop" lawyer had her on the stand. He'd intimidated and diminished her; she was terrified about making another appearance. She described being subjected to that lawyer: "I didn't have my composure, my heartbeat was erratic, and my blood pressure was going up to my ears. It was one of the worst experiences of my life. I think he wanted to destroy my credibility so he could throw me off balance and make me look foolish."

Kea said to me, "Lokelani's lawyer tried to make Nona appear as a *kua'āina*— a country hick. He reduced her into acting as a little old lady who was just trying her best."

Nona and I talked for a long while on the telephone. I encouraged her to apply her innate charm and to proceed slowly. "Pretend he is a dense hula student to whom you are describing the fundamentals of a dance."

I also said, "If he snaps at you, think of how you would handle an annoying brat. Look at him steadily with an unflinching gaze, study his character. Don't give him 'stink eye' [an island term for staring someone down]. Speak carefully and distinctly."

By the next day her *kua'āina* behavior was gone, and Auntie Nona felt like an authoritative teacher again. Judge Weil dropped the *h* when speaking the name "Kamehameha." From the witness stand, Nona spoke up and politely explained to the judge, "In Hawaiian, all *h*s should be articulated."

Judge Weil smiled warmly and said, "I stand corrected."

Auntie Nona was back.

Lokelani's sarcastic lawyer tried to discredit Nona, claiming her knowledge of Lokelani's alleged misdeeds came from secondhand or thirdhand accounts or rumors.

He tried to force Nona into admitting she had no basis for writing her letter and starting the furor. He said angrily to Auntie Nona, "You have no knowledge of morale on the campus."

She bridled. Her grandson attended the school. Longtime friends taught there. "When people you love tell you something, you believe it to be true," she firmly declared.

Responding to his allusions that her accusations were not truthful, Nona leveled him, saying, "If I lied, I'd be *make* [pronounced mah-kay] die dead." She was saying "dead, die, dead," which is about as dead as dead can be.

This pidgin English expression made spectators erupt with laughter. Looking confused, Lokelani's lawyer quickly ended his questioning. He was no match for the metamorphosed "Living Treasure."

A newspaper reporter referred to Nona as a "respected *kupuna*"—a grandparent—and gave her age as eighty-five, ten years older than she actually was. She asked my cousin, "Why did they make me so old, Kea?"

"Because of your big mouth. You put everybody in their place, as if you were too old to care."

Auntie Nona Beamer explains to the court why she "started the whole thing" by suggesting Lokelani Lindsey should be removed as a trustee. Honolulu Advertiser *photo by Richard Ambo.*

In the courtroom, Lokelani lost her capability to intimidate others. A high school math teacher told the court, "Lokelani was the spark that ignited the union. She was a threat. Her selective use of data bothered me; math scores have been steadily improving every year since I began teaching in 1988.

An art teacher stated, "After Mrs. Lindsey released her education report, students asked me: 'Does this mean I am stupid?' Some were teased about going to 'that stupid school.'"

The stories told by many witnesses for the plaintiffs appear earlier in this book, as they happened. In the courtroom Lokelani faced a parade of forty of them; some shouted, some cried, others dispassionately recounted misdeeds and errors.

The courtroom galleries were packed with members of Nā Pua, who monitored the trial daily for four months.

The Secondary School's head of curriculum and instruction gave hours of testimony on how Lokelani misused information by relying on flawed studies to support the conclusions in her education report. "Lokelani had access to studies and analyses of test data that proved her conclusions were wrong. She would not use available test information that disputed her claim that 'the longer students stay at Kamehameha Schools the worse they perform on standardized tests.'"

Others, such as Robert Witt, executive director of the Hawai'i Association of Independent Schools, said "She didn't have adequate working knowledge of commonly agreed upon and highly researched principles of practice followed by more than 1,000 private schools."

James Popham, retired professor from UCLA's School of Education, stated: "She is so out of her depth that she doesn't know what she doesn't know."

A student from MIT and one from Yale said, "She used her studies about student performance to prove her point that Dr. Chun was doing a bad job. She didn't care about students' personal reactions."

Her report on the thirty seniors who could barely read was described as the result of a classroom prank. Students didn't take the unexpected superfluous test seriously because its outcome wouldn't affect their grades or college acceptance. They were retested and their scores were remarkably better. This information was given to Lokelani, but she chose not use it.

Lokelani silently mouthed objections to some testimony. She stared witnesses down, with her eyes darkly edged and magnified behind large-framed glasses: stink eye.

Sarah Keahi, whose phone call to Auntie Nona started the revolt, told the judge, "She said we must teach the language as it was spoken during the lifetime of Bernice Pauahi Bishop. Teaching language from the nineteenth century ignores how language and culture grow."

Oz stated, "Get her in a social setting and she is the nicest person you have ever met. Put her in a control situation and she freaks out."

Defenders described Lokelani as a caring educator, a champion of technology, a hands-on manager who likes to get things done. Dickie Wong, her chief supporter, said, "She was concerned about the children." Dickie acknowledged receiving Stender's memos about morale problems before the May march and admitted ignoring his warning. "I didn't know there was a morale problem until 700 supporters arrived at estate headquarters." He said photographs and identification of marchers was done "for historical purposes."

As the trial continued, former journalist Judge Weil took copious notes.

On the stand, Dickie appeared unfamiliar with basic school issues and operations. He didn't give direct answers to many questions, going instead into tangents on subject areas beyond the questions posed. At times his testimony appeared to contradict testimony he'd given just minutes earlier. At one point, Dickie testified that Lindsey stepped down as lead trustee over education in August 1997. He later said she did not step down until December 1997, following the Yim report.

The former president of the Senate appeared nervous, had trouble remembering dates or events, and didn't recognize many estate documents directed to his attention at some point in the past. Oz described Dickie's behavior at the trial: "He's not interested, he's just there." Dickie's testimony made this clearly apparent.

Dickie conceded that he did not agree with Lokelani's directive about kindergartners being able to identify and laudify trustees: "[It] shouldn't have been put in the curriculum."

He defended her against Yim's fact finding: "I don't think it was a balanced report. I support her. What has happened to her has never happened to anyone in the State of Hawai'i."

He said to a reporter, "I told the court I thought she did a good job. I didn't believe holding onto the teachers' contracts until just before school began would adversely affect morale."

An eighty-five-year-old woman, Mrs. Lindsey's Hawaiian expert, said Lokelani favored "quality and not quantity." She explained: "Quality is when you use an original Hawaiian word. Quantity is when English words are added to the language and the Hawaiian is removed."

According to her, "A modern word such as 'television' should not be translated into Hawaiian with a newly invented word. Instead, the function of television should be described in existing Hawaiian words. Thus a television becomes 'a box that throws out moving pictures.' A radio is 'a box that throws out voices.'"

Members of Nā Pua comprised much of the audience; they maintained a polite silence out of deference to her age. Nona Beamer was not in the courtroom to hear about boxes that throw things.

Lokelani defended herself by putting blame on others. She told the court her unraveling came at the hands of Oz, who leaked confidential documents to the press, to the attorney general's office, and to a vocal minority of Hawaiians. "There was an enemy within. I've been tried in a kangaroo court since Oz and Gerry sued for my ouster in 1997. Oz has waged a three-year campaign to discredit me. The Yim fact-finding report repeated allegations, rumors, and innuendo Stender planted."

Lawyers asked Beadie Dawson about Nā Pua's role in the fact finding. "Nā Pua had facilitators, trained by private investigators and prosecutors, to help potential witnesses understand the Probate Court's order guaranteeing confidentiality. People came to Nā Pua with relevant stories but were afraid to talk to Judge Yim fearing they'd lose jobs or scholarships." Beadie explained, "We helped them overcome that fear and 75 percent became comfortable enough to talk with Judge Yim."

Doug Carlson, Lokelani's spokesperson, described Nā Pua's screening as "sinister." He claimed the fact-finder's report was a compilation of Nā Pua–inspired innuendoes and rumors provided by the people it screened. "They are using the controversy to get control of the trust," he asserted.

Lawyers for Lokelani said they might ask the attorney general to investigate whether the *Honolulu Star-Bulletin* and *Honolulu Advertiser* were working in concert against her. A *Star-Bulletin* reporter was present when she spoke to the Rotary Club and wrote that she wept and lashed out at critics during the speech. This information was run on the Associated Press wire service. The *Advertiser* used the AP story. Doug Carlson claimed she "teared up" and did not "lash out."

Lokelani testified that problems were not caused by her actions but by a conspiracy of two other trustees and several unidentifiable people. "They put the blame for all things at my door."

Her lawyers defended Lokelani as the misunderstood champion of better education and claimed she was a victim of malicious rumors and unfounded horror stories fueled by Oz. "Rumors were fed to inspire a faculty uprising to oust Mrs. Lindsey and save Dr. Chun," she herself stated.

She claimed that Dr. and Mrs. Chun were part of the conspiracy, along with Beadie Dawson of Nā Pua and Douglas Ing, one of Oz's attorneys. "Roy Benham kicked off the whole campaign against me."

The defense team tried to discredit testimony by teachers, administrators, and former students by suggesting that "they had no firsthand knowledge of Lokelani's directives or actions." The lawyers claimed "Stender created an environment that made it difficult for Lokelani to do her job."

In the end, her lawyers asked for sympathy. The "good cop" asked the judge to dismiss the case because the plaintiff failed to prove that Lokelani Lindsey was a serious threat to the trust.

Her courtroom attorneys portrayed Lokelani as well intentioned but faced with severe leadership and curriculum problems. "When she tried to reform the school, the school staff turned on her."

Lokelani promised, "If I return I will be gentler in implementing changes and will be more communicative with the Kamehameha Schools community and the media."

G erry Jervis felt edgy about his own job during the long trial. Would he be able to return if temporarily removed? After a tedious day of listening to testimony, his impulsive nature got the best of him.

Libidos unrestrained, Gerry and his companion left their dinner table in a Waikīkī hotel to have sex in the men's room. A man entering for conventional purposes heard their enthusiastic joy of sex behind a toilet stall door. He dashed out to call hotel security.

The security officer interrupted the pair, escorted them to his office, filed a report, took a photograph, and said, "Never come back. Our staff will identify you from these photos."

If it weren't for deep remorse over what followed, the public wouldn't have learned about this reckless Waikīkī adventure.

At about 4:00 P.M. the next day, her husband found Rene Kitaoka, 39, sitting in her Buick, its motor was running inside the closed garage. He called the fire department, but carbon monoxide fumes had done their lethal work. Next to Rene was a cellular phone and a newspaper opened to a story about KSBE. She left no note. In her purse was a credit card receipt from her final dinner at the Hawai'i Prince Hotel—signed by Gerry Jervis.

For eight days, the police called it an "unattended death." This baffled people. Why did it happen? She and her husband had no children, they seemed close, and their lovely home in a cul-de-sac commanded a spectacular view of Kāne'ohe Bay and the Ko'olau Mountains. She was attractive, bright, had a good sense of humor, and people liked to be around her. Her husband was an electrical contractor, she was a lawyer, and they shared the superficial glamour of modern life.

Avoiding shame runs deep within Japanese culture. An acquaintance later said, "I don't blame her for what she did, knowing this might come out publicly."

*Poor Butterfly. . . .*

Rene grew up on Maui, went to law school at Georgetown University, and was working in one of KSBE's primary law firms when Gerry met her. Gerry was chairman of the board of Kamehameha Investment Corporation, the development subsidiary of the estate, and he hired her as its general counsel.

Gerry disappeared from public sight the day Rene died, not appearing at Lokelani's trial until a week later. He was stopped by a reporter in the courthouse hallway who wanted to ask about Rene's suicide. Gerry charged out abruptly. Back at home, Rene's fifty-year-old paramour sought to follow her, taking massive doses of sleeping pills.

He was discovered and rushed to a medical center. Gerry's wife, a former State legislator, came to the hospital to be with him.

The reason for Rene's death was now public, and a banner headline and subhead in the next morning's newspaper read: "Trustee overdoses after friend's death / Her apparent suicide follows sex incident."

Three stories plastered the front page: the men's room episode, Rene's suicide, and Gerry's attempted suicide. Newspapers across the country ran this story of sex and suicide at the scandalous Bishop Estate. The stories had all the tawdry elements of a TV daytime soap opera. A newspaper's front-page headline in England described trustees as creating corruption and destruction. Jan Dill, Nā Pua's vice president, said he was especially saddened that a large picture of Princess Pauahi was published with the story by a London newspaper.

Dr. Chun appeared on the school's closed-circuit TV and asked students to pray. He didn't have to tell them for whom. He talked about "forgiveness, the need to have sympathy, to feel for people as a family, and to remember *we* are a family."

Reporters called Nona at her home on the Big Island for a statement, and she responded: "The princess's will asks trustees to provide instruction in morals. What's happening is not just embarrassing, it is heart wrenching. For the sake of the children the whole trustee saga must come to a conclusion."

Four days after Gerry's overdose, about a hundred estate employees attended a prayer service at Kawaiahaʻo, the princess's church; it was led by the school chaplain. This was a Hawaiian way of coping with tragedy.

Gerry wrote a public apology for his mistakes, the pain caused his wife and family, and said he was sorry for disappointing students, faculty, staff, and alumni.

Hawaiians are very forgiving. A newspaper quoted alumnus Roy Benham: "Our aloha and prayers go out to Gerry as he embarks on his difficult road to recovery."

Margery Bronster was not as charitable. She wanted an emergency hearing to remove Jervis as a trustee for being incapacitated from his overdose. "This would be a temporary removal until he could demonstrate to the court his fitness to serve."

Her associates echoed the theme of Margery's ongoing crusade for the children. Hugh Jones, deputy attorney general, told reporters, "Every day that goes by is another day the beneficiaries and the children of Kamehameha Schools are harmed."

A court expert said, "Jervis' behavior is a serious factor because the trust's purpose is to educate children."

Temporary removal could oust Gerry. There was no precedent to forcing a trustee to resign. This once was investigated by another estate having a trustee afflicted with Alzheimer's disease; the issue didn't go to court because fellow trustees persuaded the Alzheimer's victim to resign.

Rene's name surfaced during the attorney general's review of travel expense statements. Since 1996, she and Jervis often traveled together on estate business. Gerry worked out a way for the estate to subsidize their personal relationship, which is why his credit card receipt for dinner and drinks was in her purse. She would have submitted it to Kamehameha Investment Corporation (KIC) for reimbursement. Gerry signed off on Rene's travel and entertainment reimbursements. Between charges on her KIC card and those on Gerry's, they were able to cover their trail of frequent lavish dinner charges.

As reporters will, once on to a story, they used the attempted suicide as the platform to publish other information about Gerry Jervis. They described his close relationship with John Waihee, their days together in the University of Hawai'i's law school, and Gerry's early law career when he was known for his impulsiveness and temper.

Jervis headed Lieutenant Governor Waihee's legal division. Dickie Wong, Senate president, appointed Jervis to the prestigious Judicial Selection Commission. Gerry supplied names of Supreme Court justice nominees to the governor, who appointed the five Supreme Court justices. The justices returned the favor by picking Jervis as a Kamehameha Schools Bishop Estate trustee.

Early in his trusteeship, Gerry considered doing some work for the McCorriston law firm, but other interests began occupying his time.

CHAPTER 43

# Personal Profiteering

Fall 1998–1999

THE BISHOP ESTATE leased oceanside land in pricey Hawai'i Kai, a Honolulu suburb, for a new condominium complex. It took back a $21.9 million note from the developer, secured by the land.

Completed in 1993, the 229 luxury condominium units did not sell as projected, so the developer sold out to One Keauhou Partners (OKP), a partnership between National Housing Corporation and Pacific Northwest Ltd. Fifty percent of Pacific Northwest was owned by Jeffrey Stone, Dickie Wong's brother-in-law.

The Bishop Estate restructured the note; Henry was the lead trustee, and it passed with Dickie's and Lokelani's vote. They lowered the principal amount, waved an annual 5 percent increase in principal, extended the balloon note due date, reduced the amount of collateral required for security, and set the interest rate at 2.75 percent.

Now worth far less to the trust than the original note, the new deal conferred millions of dollars of additional profit to OKP. Jeffrey would realize this through the interest rate spread between the 2.75 percent OKP paid to the trust and the high rate it collected from the mortgages it provided condo unit buyers.

Stone rewarded Henry and Dickie through complex financial schemes. For $570,000, Henry sold a condo unit serving as his Honolulu residence to an entity controlled by a business associate of Jeffrey Stone. This price was considerably above fair market value. Peters used the money to buy a penthouse apartment in the same building. Henry's primary residence was on the windward side of the island.

Eight days after buying Peter's apartment, Stone's intermediary made a $5,000 profit by selling it to OKP for $575,000. Stone concealed the transaction by not recording the deed until three months later.

OKP sold Henry's apartment to an unrelated third party for $395,000. This was $180,000 less than it paid Henry and was how it laundered Henry's bonus.

This technique had worked a year earlier when Pacific Northwest Ltd. rewarded Dickie. It purchased an apartment from him for $613,000. This, too, was far above the fair market. Pacific Northwest promptly sold Dickie and Marni Wong's apartment to a third party for $425,000. This was $188,800 less than it paid the Wongs.

The Wongs bought a unit for $1,108,000. Dickie paid with the $613,000 from the sale of his apartment, $130,000 in cash, and a note to Pacific Northwest for $395,000.

Inflated prices paid to Peters and Wong were quid pro quo for the Stone brothers' benefits.

While KDP Trust was headed by Lokelani, Henry arranged for it to loan KDP Tech $105,000, and $50,000 of the proceeds went to Randy Stone as a loan he didn't repay. The estate continued to advance money to KDP until Ben Bush, its treasurer, was indicted for federal mail fraud and money laundering—crimes for which he was convicted and sentenced.

In September 1998, when the attorney general petitioned the Probate Court to permanently remove several trustees, Margery's office focused on Henry's alleged repeated acts of self-dealing and mismanagement.

Three weeks before the election, one of Dickie's lawyers told the press that there was evidence investigators working for the attorney general might use video cameras to raid Dickie's home to enhance Cayetano's standing in a surprisingly tight race. He claimed:

> It is part of a plan to gather evidence for criminal indictments against Wong and Peters to rally voters behind Cayetano in the November 3 election. Margery Bronster plans to remove one or more of the trustees at a hearing scheduled before Judge Hirai on October 30.
>
> They'll use this raid to get indictments. It's not hard to get indictments: You can indict a ham sandwich in Honolulu.
>
> They'll do this before the end of the month and include Judge Hirai's decision on interim removal so they can win the election.

Henry Peters and Dickie Wong were masters in political strategy. In this instance, Dickie used a "pre-spin" to make a nonevent beneficial to them.

What started in 1997 with a letter by Auntie Nona as a protest over Lindsey's overbearing style had gained momentum to reach this sad state of affairs: Henry Peters and Dickie Wong were under felony theft indictment on charges of profiting in a kickback scheme; Gerry was under a psychiatrist's care; Lokelani Lindsey was waiting for Judge Weil's decision; and Oz had offered to resign as trustee on the condition that the others step down.

I t would have been convenient for the band of four trustees if Ben Cayetano lost his reelection for governor; they'd be rid of Margery Bronster. Nothing like her had been in the attorney general's office; once she was out, the mold would probably be broken. Oz suggested to Margery that the estate pay Mrs. Lindsey and other trustees to leave, but she was determined to pursue justice.

During his campaign, Governor Cayetano said Margery Bronster would not accept a possible nomination to the Ninth U.S. Circuit Court of Appeals because of the important work she was doing, including her work on Kamehameha Schools Bishop Estate.

The Ninth Circuit is the largest federal appellate court. Its twenty-eight judges cover California, Hawaiʻi, and seven other western states, an area that includes about one-fifth of the nation's population and is roughly the size of Western Europe.

"She has pledged her support to continue the investigation," Cayetano reported proudly. Hawaiʻi is one of the few states where voters do not elect an attorney general.

It would seem reasonable that his party would give the reelected governor latitude to choose his own help and make his own judgment on their performance. The Senate has the authority to reject gubernatorial appointments, but out of courtesy would do so only for substantial breaches of public duty. Its function is not to second-guess the executive.

Trustees' friends lobbied against Margery, collecting commitments from some senators whose hands were in the estate's pockets. Margery's confirmation hearing on April 16, 1999, was the first sign her reappointment might face trouble. The judiciary committee listened to several hours of testimony against her, much of it criticizing her handling of the Bishop Estate investigation and her pending lawsuits.

Days before her reappointment was slated for a vote, Margery obtained criminal grand jury indictments against Henry, Dickie and Marni Wong, and Jeffrey Stone.

Dickie's was for theft in the first degree, for making misleading statements to a grand jury, and for criminal conspiracy. Marni was indicted on criminal charges for hindering prosecution by making misleading statements. The Wongs' trial, scheduled for August, had a potential penalty of up to ten years in prison and $500,000 in fines.

Jeffrey Stone was indicted on charges of commercial bribery and criminal conspiracy. Henry was indicted on charges of theft for money he received from Stone.

After the hearing, followed by a week of lobbying, Margery's nomination to a second four-year term as the State's highest legal official was up for a vote. She describes the event:

> I sat with my staff in the packed gallery during the roll call vote on my confirmation, keeping track of votes on a sheet of paper. After three-quarters of the senators announced their votes, I stopped counting.
>
> Other deputy attorneys were counting votes, too. They kind of looked up at me.
>
> I shook my head and said, "We didn't make it."

She was rejected by the State Senate, with fourteen voting against her and eleven voting in favor of her.

The State Senate also rejected the confirmation of the governor's good friend, budget director Earl Anzai. He lost by fifteen "no" to ten "yes" votes. Anzai brought a blunt style to the state budget crisis Cayetano inherited. Instead of sugarcoating the truth about a projected $250 million shortfall hobbling the State, he fixed it. Within three months of his failed reconfirmation, the State would have a surplus of $180 million.

Margery explained her defeat in this way: "I believe it had to do with the fact that I took on some very powerful opponents, people who previously were in the Legislature and knew how to manipulate it a whole lot better than I ever could."

One senator rationalized his vote by saying: "On the morning of her nomination she told the press she will proceed with an indictment against one of our colleagues. That is not only a threat against him, it's a threat against us as a senate and for that reason I'm strongly opposed to her nomination."

The public was outraged. Scores of letters to newspaper editors carried the warning that senators must now face voters: "Senate hit new low in political incredibility. . . . We're mad as hell and won't take it anymore. . . . List will be published of old-boy senators. . . . Welcome to the real world of influence peddling. . . . Vote spells the end of Democrats' power. . . ."

An American of Japanese Ancestry (AJA) reflected angrily:

> The Democratic political takeover in the mid-1950s was led by AJAs to abolish years of oppression and discrimination rendered by the Big Five regime. It has been replaced by the "old boy" Democratic Party. Despite economic malaise, poor public education system, union influence, constant battle against progress, the party that was so successful two to three decades ago in providing opportu-

Supporters applaud their emotionally drained champion Margery Bronster after State senators rejected her appointment 14 to 11. Honolulu Advertiser *photo by Richard Ambo.*

nities for all is the very party eliminating opportunities today. For this state to revive opportunities for all, the AJAs and others must be removed including tenured politicians such as. . . . [The writer included a list of politicals with Japanese surnames.]

I studied notebooks filled with supportive phone messages called in to Margery's office the day after she was turned down. One with true local-boy frankness came from Andy Jamila: "For a woman, you've got balls. All of us in Waimānalo stand behind you." I called Andy, who is a vigorous community activist. He explained his comment: "She was completely fearless and stood up to all of those bigshots without flinching."

Many sent cards and letters describing their affection. One said this of Margery, the thirty-nine-year-old mother from a New Jersey Jewish family: "We'll miss Bronster, a Hawaiian at heart."

My cousin Kea was one of many wearing a T-shirt reading "Remember Bronster," on which was stenciled names of senators who voted against her confirmation. Seven senators were voted out. But anger proved transitory; still in place in the Senate (2005) are some of those who voted against her: Carol Fukunaga, Brian Kanno, Colleen Hanabusa, and David Ige. Kameo Tanaka remains in the State House.

Hawaiian culture is replete with symbols and metaphors pertaining to nature. A group of women carrying five young *kukui* trees wrapped in a newspaper came to tell Margery the following story before she vacated her office.

Through your brave efforts against all odds, you forged forward to the light. You served alumni, parents, students, taxpayers, and more importantly, the unborn children. You shone your light brightly, giving us faith in the justice system.

With these special tokens of our Hawaiian people we say, *"Mahalo a nui loa."*

*Kukui* served as the light . . . medicine . . . the sap was used as glue for canoes. These five *kukui* trees symbolize the five lights you have turned on. You healed our hearts by restoring our faith and trust in mankind . . . especially for our children. You have fastened each of our canoes so we look forward to our new journey in the millennium with great promise for our children of today and for those to come.

Five unshelled *kukui* represent the unborn children you cradle.

May these five *kukui* trees be cherished by being planted in a place you deem appropriate for the children of Hawai'i. They come to you from the land once owned by our beloved benefactor Bernice Pauahi Bishop.

Each planted tree will represent one of the five trustees whom Pauahi entrusts with the care of her beneficiaries.

This *kukui* lei we give to you to wear conveys meanings:

White nuts symbolize the source of light of our creator . . . you are the light.

Brown nuts symbolize the Hawaiian people.

Black and white nuts symbolize everything in the dark that you have brought into the light.

We purposely wrapped five *kukui* trees in this morning's *Advertiser*. When imprisoned, Queen Lili'uokalani was unable to receive news of her kingdom. News was delivered to her by flowers wrapped in the daily newspaper. It was her sole source of information.

In the same manner we present to you this historic newspaper containing praise for your courageous stand for her people.

Thanks to you, we are no longer prisoners.

The sea was rough between the governor and the Legislature, particularly the channels between the Senate and the governor. One thoughtful person wrote, "In this economic downturn the Legislature and governor should work together to find some solutions to problems. When you have this kind of rift going on, it doesn't speak well for Hawai'i's future."

Shortly after the Senate dismissed Margery, news broke that lawyers representing Hawai'i in the tobacco industry lawsuit were awarded $90.2 million in compensation. This would be in addition to the $1.38 billion Hawai'i will recover through the tobacco settlement over twenty-five years.

An arbitration panel praised former State attorney general Margery Bronster for leadership of the national "small state" caucus that brought thirteen states together to negotiate.

She had been visited by tobacco industry lawyers who tried to dissuade her from entering the national lawsuit, telling her she would be attacked politically and could not legally hire contingent-fee lawyers to help her. The companies paying the settlement sued her in federal court alleging she was violating federal laws. Only she and her senior deputy attorney worked on the case; other states had scores of lawyers helping.

Margery missed the chance to complete her crusade on behalf of Hawaiian children. Wily politicians in Bishop Estate headquarters and their army of lawyers knew how to use Hawai'i's Democratic machine to remove this dauntless warrior from the battlefield.

I've prepared the following as a political obituary—at least for now. It could be headed, "Margery Bronster, former State of Hawai'i Attorney General: Sic Transit Gloria":

- Her four-year term was dominated by her handling of litigation against tobacco, oil companies, and the Bishop Estate—as it was originally known.
- She was the most aggressive attorney general to serve in Hawai'i.
- She was an outsider in Hawai'i politics, a Wall Street lawyer who enforced tougher laws against domestic violence and registration of sex offenders.
- She had an important job that she was doing well.
- That took _____ (word of your choice).
- She was not afraid to move ahead in ways that were important.
- She did it for the children.

## CHAPTER 44

# Oz and His Attorneys

## April 1999

O z's attorneys graduated from Kamehameha Schools: Crystal Rose, class of 1975, and Douglas Ing, class of 1962. The plaintiff's case against Lokelani Lindsey would end with Doug's closing statement. He was speaking for us as well as Oz, conveying our passion for Princess Bernice Pauahi's gift of education and helping the judge understand our anguish for how it was besmirched. We had waited patiently. Now, five months after the trial started, all beneficiaries were included in what he said:

> Each year during the end of the first semester at Kamehameha Schools, her spiritual children recite verses and sing songs to Princess Pauahi and say words meant to guide them throughout life.
>
> The men of Kamehameha recite the Founders Day Pledge standing before the granite stone marking the crypt of the Kamehameha Dynasty.

As he reached this point, an astonishing thing happened: As he said the pledge, lips of men and women from ages eighteen to eighty moved silently with his. Only Doug's voice was heard; we mouthed the words:

> *To give more time and strength,*
> *To gain all she wished us to gain,*
> *To strive to honor her name wherever we may be;*
> *And we do this to have such conditions*
> *As shall tend to keep and develop for our race,*
> *All those noble traits of character she possessed.*

Tears flowed as Doug paused. A sense of awe lingered in the silent courtroom; it was akin to witnessing a rainbow rise over a valley after a storm. He allowed a moment to pass, then continued:

Many witnesses came forward to tell you about intimidation, manipulation, hurt, and hostility. These included students, teachers, administrators, and alumni. These are people who risked their jobs or other retaliation from the majority trustees.

Why did they come forward?

Many friends and supporters came to this court day after day, month after month, to observe these proceedings.

Why did they come?

Why are they here?

What is the bond we share?

No great mystery, it is the essence of this case: We all have stood at Pauahi's resting place and paid respects for her generosity. We know and understand the meaning of "good and industrious men and women."

We are deeply offended by what Mrs. Lindsey has done. Hostility engulfing the school cannot be swept away. It chokes and stifles us. It ignites in our conversations. We cannot stand by and watch this happen.

And so we come before you as Nā Pua O Pauahi. Her children have risen to defend her legacy by removing from it arrogance and hostility.

The casual indifference Mrs. Lindsey showed when she released her education report leaves us dumbfounded. She is entirely unapologetic about how she mocked Kamehameha Schools to which she swore loyalty.

December 6, 1997, will be remembered as a cruel and heartless day for us. This was a day when a sitting trustee, embarrassed and devastated by a critical fact-finding report, chose to shield herself by publicly slandering the school and its students. It was an outrageous act of disloyalty and imprudence. It cannot be swept aside by false claims of "deteriorating academic programs."

Mrs. Lindsey is oblivious to her fiduciary relationship with this institution and she has the insolence to blame this spectacle on Michael Chun. She acted with a disdain for everything other than her own self-preservation and welfare. She is unrelenting in her refusal to admit she was wrong.

Kamehameha will not emerge from such poverty of character until she has been permanently removed.

Heart pounding, tears in his eyes, and with a huge lump in his throat, Doug Ing looked beseechingly at Judge Weil.

"You need to end this charade of 'trustee educator.' When you do so by the stroke of your pen, you will begin to restore for this great legacy 'all those noble traits of character Pauahi possessed.'"

Judge Weil would reflect and prepare her decision.

CHAPTER 45

# Influence Peddling

## 1994–1999

H ENRY PETERS, Dickie Wong, Mrs. Lindsey, and Gerry Jervis may have been well intentioned when joining the Bishop Estate. They never had been part of a business and educational environment of comparable size. Suddenly responsibility and power was thrust upon them. Apparently they didn't know how to handle it. Oz, on the other hand, had been trained by the Campbell Estate to fill such a position and served on other private school boards. Oz explained his perspective to me in this way:

The arrogance of the political process by which trustees were selected resulted in some arrogant individuals becoming trustees.

By "arrogance," I mean disdain for the opinion of others. One aspect of arrogance is the inability of a person to recognize the limitations of his or her abilities. This can be the fatal flaw personal conduct brings to public view, the ultimate cause of the fall of the mighty in story and fable.

They felt all-knowing instead of listening to others and trying to adjust. They were untouchable and did things their way.

I remember where I came from. Other trustees had humble backgrounds and were not that well educated. For some reason, they resented where they'd been. Once they became a trustee they set out to prove they were different.

I was like you, Arthur, in many ways. There was a time I didn't know what it was like to have a home. I was orphaned at age two and spent a part of my youth living with various family members who were able to take care of an extra person. I didn't have my very own place in this world, but I didn't know any other life. I didn't know that I was what today you'd call very much "at risk."

From the time my mother died when I was two until today, good people have come into my life, and I am thankful.

A rural lifestyle taught me the values of sharing, of caring, of survival, of being ever thankful for those who sacrificed to care for me. I never experienced what it was like to be wealthy until I used my newspaper route earnings to buy myself a $25 pair of shoes in 1949 dollars. It was the equivalent of $150 today.

Oz recollected his personal experiences of telling teachers of disadvantaged children about how important they are in influencing young people's lives: "Sometimes you look at your students, many of whom are at risk, and all you see are coarse, disrespectful, self-centered problems. Sometimes you forget what their lives may be like away from school. Sometimes you forget what a difference your job can make by providing these young people with tools to build a better future for themselves and generations to come."

For years, the Bishop Estate operated as "a million-dollar candy store for the state's political establishment," according to University of Hawai'i professor Randy Roth.

Its government relations division directed tens of thousands of dollars to the campaigns of Island legislators and entertained scores of State and County officials. Nam Snow, Bishop Estate's head of government relations, "warned" our alumni task force that any such activities would jeopardize the estate's tax-exempt status. She failed to tell us that getting around IRS rules was her profession. That fact remained under cover until her office files were opened after her death. What was in her files detailed the services performed by the Bishop Estate's legislative teams:

- Drafting bills for legislators;
- Writing floor speeches;
- Planning and coordinating demonstrations, rallies, and legislative receptions;
- Providing crews for sign holdings, door-to-door canvassing, and coffee hours;
- Paying for supplies and refreshments for political activities and legislative strategy sessions;
- Networking with private civic clubs and trade organizations;
- Writing and submitting letters to the editors in Honolulu's daily newspapers;
- Maintaining a database on politicians; it included legislators' real property ownership records and their voting records on key bills;
- Investigating lessees who criticized the estate's lease-to-fee conversion prices;

- Creating front organizations to conduct grassroots lobbying on legislation without registering the activities with State regulators;
- Operating campaign finance schemes and distributing and collecting fund-raising tickets for trust employees to buy.

Human billboards are Hawai'i's popular way of "politicking." Candidates' supporters hold signs, flashing big grins and waving at people gridlocked in cars at the beginning and end of business days in downtown Honolulu and throughout the Islands. The Bishop Estate supplied sign holders for candidates and causes it favored. Did it pay for these services with beer, stew, and rice—the way Dickie Wong suggested appealing to alumni?

It helped to feed government officials. Over a five-year period, the Bishop Estate's Government Relations Department hosted more than 700 meetings with State and City officials at local restaurants. The House speaker was treated to over sixty-five meals by estate personnel and earned a $132,000 commission on a "do-nothing" land deal the estate set up for him. He is still in office as this book goes to press. In two instances, the department directed architecture and engineering firms to pay bogus bills that would cover campaign debts owed by State senators.

The estate attempted to influence, pass, stall, or defeat legislation. Trustees claimed they "did not lobby but provided information at lawmakers' request" or monitored legislation that potentially affected their interests.

After purchasing the former Hāmākua Sugar Co. lands, the estate inherited the cost of keeping up the Hāmākua Ditch. It lobbied State lawmakers for a lease arrangement allowing the State to take over the ditch's operations and repairs but barring it from taking the property through condemnation.

The estate relied on front groups to lobby on its behalf. One group attended court hearings, wrote to legislators, sent letters to the editors of two daily newspapers, and took part in sign waving for local political candidates at the request of the estate.

During the early 1990s, the estate created an organization to lobby against controversial mandatory lease-to-fee conversion measures. It produced and aired print, radio, and television ads criticizing the City's mandatory leasehold bill, scheduled numerous news conferences attacking the bill, and held editorial board meetings with Honolulu's two daily newspapers advocating their view.

Although the City Council passed the bill, the estate's Government Relations Department claimed it blunted the damage.

"You needed connections to win government contracts in Democratic Hawai'i," locals say. "It's not what you know, but who you know."

The going rate for kickbacks in the year 2002 was 1 to 1.5 percent for public works projects. Contractors sliced off up to $150,000 for each million they charged, slid it to the source for the bribe, and inflated their charges. This easy way to richness explains the high cost and slow pace of construction in Hawai'i. It put government in the hole, but so what? Public debt in Hawai'i averaged $600 for a family of four in the 1950s when the Democrats came into power; by the 1990s, it was up to $20,000.

Rewarding others for favors was common in Hawai'i. All trustees except Oz accepted free country club memberships. Oz loves golf as much as any of the other trustees, but he felt such a "gift to the landlord" was unethical.

Tragically, Milton Holt didn't follow the warning in his school song: "Be strong and deny ye, oh sons of Hawai'i, *allurements* that your race will overwhelm."

Opium was so popular back in the 1880s that King Kalākaua wanted to legalize it to gain taxes from something people use anyway. The Reverend Oleson was a strong advocate against drugs and alcohol, and that was why he warned against such allurements when writing the Kamehameha alma mater.

Milton Holt, class of 1970 at Kamehameha Schools, was bright, personable, and seemingly destined for great things. He had been the starting quarterback on the Harvard University football team, making him a hero in sports-happy Hawai'i. He was first elected to the Legislature as a State representative at the age of twenty-six. In the words of fellow Ivy Leaguer Margery Bronster, who investigated him, "Holt had no holds barred—the world lay before him."

Peers regarded him as a brilliant lawmaker and power broker. Margery felt he was on the fast track to becoming governor. Holt was head of the judiciary committee that appoints judges, putting him in a favored position for appointment as a Bishop Estate trustee.

Milton had run the Bishop Estate's Government Relations Department. In the 1994 session he helped draft the bill introduced through the Senate president giving landowners the right to buy back any lands taken by eminent domain. Holt's role was not disclosed. The estate expected Holt to use his position in the Legislature to provide the trust with political intelligence; his boss referred to it as "G-2 intelligence," the type of information a spy acquires at the battle lines.

There were indications that Milton's clever mind conflicted with his duties as a State lawmaker. At one point, a committee chairman said he would hear a measure being held up only if he received a request to do so from the general public. The committee granted the bill a hearing after a Bishop Estate staffer provided testimony using the guise of being part of a family holding company.

Allurements overtook Milton and he fell apart. Attempting to name the wife of a friend to the Supreme Court, Governor Waihee counted on Milton to shepherd things through. Milton took off on a spree instead, getting arrested for drunk and disorderly conduct in New Orleans.

Holt's private life became public knowledge. There are no secrets if you get into trouble in Honolulu; your public record is readily accessed at a terminal in the Criminal Court Building. After twenty-two years in State government, he lost his Senate seat in 1996 and went to work as a special projects officer for the Bishop Estate.

When he lost reelection, an audit uncovered that the Bishop Estate's Government Relations Department directed some of its architecture and engineering firms to pay bogus bills covering his and another Senator's campaign debts. During his campaign, he wrote four checks to a graphics supplier who returned cash to Milton for his personal use.

Milton became the Bishop Estate's master of ceremonies, entertaining State politicians at local strip joints, restaurants, and Las Vegas casinos between 1993 and 1997, according to documents subpoenaed by Margery Bronster. She discovered that he owed $21,000 on Bishop Estate credit cards. Henry gave Milton a tax-free retroactive bonus to pay the credit card bills.

When his socializing in clubs such as Misty and Saigon Passion became public knowledge, no effort was made to investigate politicians that Milton made happy. The word on "the street" was that "accepting double handfuls of the strip club goodies hostesses offered was not intended as a bribe."

Milton's problems mushroomed. He was arrested for spousal abuse. He agreed to stay drug free as a condition of bail when pleading "not guilty" to stealing money through kickbacks. But this was not to be. He tested positive two days after telling a pretrial services officer he had never used illegal drugs. He used drugs the day he showed up for a court appearance, testing positive for crystal methamphetamine use.

Likable Milton's bright mind was overwhelmed, and he joined politicians who in rapid succession went to jail.

One State senator was jailed for improprieties in his legal practice. A burglary charge was based on his taking a $7,000 payoff from a farmer after threatening to evict the farmer from leased land. Instead of returning an advanced fee after failing to expunge an arrest record, he laundered it, giving it to a businessman who parceled it back to him in small amounts. Both occurred after he was given probation for campaign spending violations.

The speaker of the House was jailed on fifteen felony counts, including fraud and theft of campaign funds. In a letter written to a newspaper editor, a reader complained that this was unfair: "What he had done was nothing more than common practice and half the legislature was doing the same." Another member of the State House of Representatives found in violation of similar acts was not prosecuted. Maybe the writer was right that this was "common practice." Witness the following actions:

- A member of the State Senate was convicted and jailed for mail fraud.
- A State Democratic leader and former State senator served time for theft and tax evasion.
- A Honolulu city councilman was jailed for theft, bribery, extortion, wire fraud, and witness tampering.
- Another Honolulu city councilman was jailed for theft and the misuse of both staff and campaign funds.
- A city councilman and former chairman had his law license suspended and was fined for leaving the scene of an auto accident he had caused and covered up.
- A State House member was under indictment for crimes involving tax laws and control over foreign bank accounts.
- A member of the mayor's cabinet was arrested on suspicion of theft and racketeering.

Being a Democratic politician in Hawai'i used to mean sinecure and safety before Governor Cayetano's appointees made changes. Unhappy politicians complained: "This guy isn't a real Democrat."

CHAPTER 46

# Trustees the Nail, IRS the Hammer

## Spring 1999

CHARITABLE DONATIONS dried up across America after the nation's press reported about the United Way's president supporting his lavish lifestyle through million-dollar fraud and embezzlement. He'd held the position for over twenty years. By far the largest organization raising money in American workplaces, the United Way channels funds to thousands of small local charities that otherwise would struggle to find donors. It also creates its own programs to address community needs.

When the angry public cut back on giving, philanthropies of all types suffered. In response, politicians proposed a new law aimed at directors and officers of nonprofit organizations. The IRS's only punishment was to revoke an organization's tax exemption, and it rarely used this harsh penalty. An intermediate sanctions law would be a new weapon in the IRS's arsenal.

Astute politician Dickie Wong realized this new law could drastically affect Bishop Estate trustees' way of life; it would eliminate excessive compensation, sweetheart deals, and other private enrichment. The gang of three hired Verner Liipfert Bernard McPhearson to lobby Congress and keep "intermediate sanctions" from becoming a law.

Former governor John Waihee, now a lobbyist with Verner et al., discussed the proposed legislation with top White House officials such as President Clinton's deputy of staff Erskine Bowes and Treasury Department deputy Lawrence Summers, whose boss was former Goldman Sachs manager Robert Rubin. Waihee's partner, former Senate majority leader George Mitchell, talked with President Clinton's chief of staff, Leon Panetta.

For added protection, trustees sought to eliminate an "exit tax" giving the IRS power to charge hefty fines to charities converting to a for-profit corporation. Without the tax, if the estate converted to a for-profit status, trustees could pay themselves what they wished free from the overview of the IRS or other federal agencies. Bishop Estate lobbyists made calls, held meetings, and wrote letters to Senators Robert Dole, William Roth, David Pryor, and House Ways and Means chairman Bill Archer, among others. The lobbying was successful and the exit tax was eliminated.

The U.S. philanthropic community banded together, urging congressional representatives to pass the intermediate sanctions law. Leaders felt public confidence might be restored in their organizations by their backing legislation severely punishing persons who robbed from the poor.[1]

The Bishop Estate could not kill the legislation on its own, and Section 4958, containing intermediate sanctions, became part of the Internal Revenue Code. It was signed into law by President Bill Clinton on July 30, 1996. Final regulations, effective as of January 23, 2002, became retroactive to September 14, 1995.

Some Washington insiders felt the estate's heavy lobbying provoked IRS resolve to revoke the Bishop Estate's tax-exempt status. Some individual trustees' transactions might be used to "test" the new law.

H aving recused themselves in early 1999 from dealing with the IRS three-year review of the estate's finances, Oz and Gerry asked Judge Chang to remove trustees from the audit—and he did. Trustees fought it to control outcomes of the audit and limit personal damage.

Colbert Matsumoto petitioned the judge to order the resignation or temporary removal of all five trustees and to appoint an independent panel to work with the IRS. He suggested Constance Hee Lau, treasurer of Hawaiian Electric Industries, Inc.; Robert Kalani Uichi Kihune, retired U.S. Navy admiral, who was a 1955 graduate of Kamehameha Schools; David Paul Coon, former headmaster of 'Iolani School; Francis Ahloy Keala, former Honolulu chief of police; and Ronald Dale Libkuman, an attorney. The panel met with IRS representatives on April 19 in Los Angeles and made its report in sealed court documents.

Panel members told Judge Chang the IRS was applying pressure on the Bishop Estate. The IRS wanted removal or resignation of the five trustees because it was concerned trustees would hide assets beyond the reach of the agency, perhaps in the guise of legitimate investment activities. IRS officials told the five-person panel they

---

[1] It takes a long time to regain public confidence after a scandal. Nationally, as of 2003, United Way contributions were lower, after adjusting for inflation, than they were a decade ago, even as charitable giving in general has doubled overall.

were checking on individual actions of trustees, their personal expenses, and their moving money and investments among for-profits and nonprofit arms of the trust to obtain maximum tax advantages.

The IRS offered interim trustees an accelerated negotiation process to allow the estate to bypass nine usual administrative levels. They demanded that the estate establish a policy for reasonable trustee compensation and hire an internal auditor to police its finances. The IRS wanted to see drastic reforms, believing it could not be rehabilitated under current management.

In documents filed with Hawai'i's Probate Court, Internal Revenue Service officials confirmed what they told the panel: They were considering revoking the Bishop Estate's tax-exempt status if all five trustees didn't step down. Colbert told Judge Chang that losing this would cost the estate tens of millions of dollars each year. He recommended that the court remove trustees temporarily.

Oz offered to resign temporarily if other trustees would do so, pending the outcome of the IRS audit. He declared, "The Bishop Estate must retain its tax-exempt status so that Kamehameha Schools may educate as many children as possible during present and future generations."

McCorriston blamed former attorney general Margery Bronster for convincing the IRS that trustees were diverting assets. He subpoenaed her to testify before Judge Chang that she orchestrated the IRS's ultimatum. She asked that the subpoena be quashed. Chang ruled in her favor, saying her testimony was not relevant to the issues before the court.

This was the situation on May 1, 1999, exactly two years after Sarah Keahi, Hawaiian language teacher, gave Nona Beamer a "May Day" signal of distress and laid a load of care on her:

1. The Internal Revenue Service threatened revocation of Kamehameha Schools' tax-exempt status if trustees were not removed. A judge's decision was expected that week.

2. Henry Peters had been indicted by a grand jury for theft. Peters' move to dismiss the case was rejected and a circuit judge set a trial date.

3. Richard "Dickie" Wong had been indicted for theft, conspiracy, and perjury, along with his wife and brother-in-law.

4. A motion for the temporary removal of Peters, Wong, Lindsey, and Jervis was filed by the attorney general's office. Margery Bronster said board members withheld $350 million that should have been spent on Kamehameha Schools. However, confirmation of her reappointment was denied two days previously.

5.     Permanent removal of three trustees was sought from Probate Court by the attorney general, who alleged that Henry, Dickie, and Lokelani engaged in a widespread pattern of self-dealing and mismanagement.

6.     A judge would decide the outcome of the Lindsey case that week. The trial had lasted more than five months and had involved more than fifty witnesses.

Judge Bambi Weil ordered the immediate and permanent removal of Lokelani Lindsey on May 6, reading from a tightly written two-page statement. Her full report would follow.

After hearing five hours of arguments on why trustees should not resign or be temporarily removed, Judge Kevin Chang accepted the resignation of trustee Oswald Stender and ordered the removal of trustees Henry Peters, Richard Wong, Lokelani Lindsey, and Gerard Jervis.

Lokelani Lindsey is stunned when the judge dismisses her as a trustee. Honolulu Advertiser *photo by Cory Lum.*

An evidentiary hearing on whether the resignation and removals should be permanent was scheduled for ninety days after a petition for permanent removal was filed by the new State attorney general, as Margery Bronster was now out of office. If such a petition was not filed in ninety days, then the "incumbent trustees" could petition for a review of Judge Chang's order.

Judge Chang named the special panel of five persons as the interim trustees who would deal with the Internal Revenue Service. Colbert Matsumoto had suggested the names of eight persons, including those on the panel.

M ore disquieting news reached Henry. The IRS let it be known that Bishop Estate trustees' dealings would be used as a national test case on the new federal intermediate sanctions when signed into law. In addition to correction—that is, returning the fair value of the property, as in the case of the Hawai'i Kai transactions—25 percent, 200 percent, and 10 percent fines could all be imposed on the same person. The IRS was also looking into penalties on any payment or perk it deemed excessive—including free country club dues.

Reporters seek information from Oz Stender after hearing Trustee Lindsey is ousted. Honolulu Advertiser *photo by Deborah Booker.*

CHAPTER 47

# At Last They Go!

### August to December 1999

H ENRY WASN'T cowed. "I'd subpoena the Internal Revenue Service if I could," he told a newspaper reporter. "Trustees haven't ruled out legal action against the IRS; they can't tamper with us!" He claimed that improper contacts were made among the IRS by Margery Bronster and Colbert Matsumoto.

Blustering wouldn't help Henry. He had other challenges: keeping his job, overcoming criminal charges, and avoiding huge fines.

B y voluntarily resigning as a trustee, Oz made it clear that the estate's fortunes were more important than his own. The band of four didn't behave this way. They acted as if appearing on the set of *The Pirates of Penzance*. In this Gilbert and Sullivan operetta, choristers repeatedly announce their determination to do a brave thing but do nothing: "Yes, yes, we go! All right, we go! We go, we go."

The irritated model of a modern major general reminds them: "Yes, but you don't go."

Circuit Judge Weil, now with the married name of Eden Elizabeth Hifo, delivered 190 pages of facts supporting the decision she made a month earlier to remove Mrs. Lindsey permanently. In biting journalistic style, she described how Lokelani misappropriated trust assets, micromanaged the trust, ran Kamehameha Schools, and created a climate of fear and intimidation on campus. Lokelani and her lawyers appealed her decision. They wanted another trial.

Probate judge Kevin Chang temporarily ousted Peters, Wong, and Gerard Jervis and accepted Stender's voluntary resignation. He was responding to the IRS's threat to revoke the estate's tax-exempt status. Lokelani's attorneys demanded a "deal." She would step down if her resignation would not take effect until her appeal of Judge Hifo's order was decided.

Henry and Dickie were removed for a second time by Probate judge Colleen Hirai, who granted the attorney general's request, made months earlier, for interim removal of these two. She said Henry and Dickie should remain out of office at least until March 28, 2000.

Judge Hirai's ruling was more extensive than Probate judge Chang's. She said Henry and Dickie violated court orders that barred them from accumulating trust income, taking income on payments on construction of buildings, and failing to heed a court order for a management system headed by a chief executive officer. "If these issues were tried in a permanent removal suit, the attorney general's office would likely win," the judge declared.

Margery Bronster, now former attorney general, believed that trustees' behavior described in the Hirai findings would be grounds for permanent removal. A trial was yet to be scheduled over the State's suit to accomplish this. "It was a far-reaching decision because Judge Hirai agreed that trustees' serious breaches warranted their removal," Margery said.

The attorneys for Henry and Dickie considered filing a legal challenge.

Judge Hirai's interim removal order came while Judge Chang was planning to schedule an evidentiary trial to determine if there was sufficient evidence to permanently remove the Bishop Estate trustees. Reluctantly, the trustees gradually began leaving the stage.

Gerry Jervis tendered his resignation in an August 20, 1999, letter to the chairman of the estate's interim board of trustees. He stated, however, that he was doing it involuntarily. "The problems I encountered in the boardroom as a member of the minority are well established. My efforts, along with Trustee Stender, in the courts are a matter of public record. As a trustee my heart was truly touched to see our children learn and progress on our various campuses, and it saddened me deeply that we could not garner the requisite board support to implement interactive and meaningful community programs to address the educational needs of the Hawaiian community."

Dickie Wong resigned permanently on December 3, 1999.

Henry Peters resigned on December 13, 1999.

Lokelani Lindsey, the last to go, stepped down on December 16, 1999, hours before her second removal trial was to begin. Her resignation was "conditional" in that it was to take effect thirty days after the Supreme Court made a final decision on her appeal against Judge Hifo's removal order.

The State's lawyers said such a trial was moot—she had resigned. But Lokelani would not concede. One of her lawyers said they would file a motion answering the State's request to dismiss the case. "Judge Hifo's removal order raised several important issues that need to be addressed by the high court."

Even if the high court were to rule in her favor, Lokelani's resignation would still be valid. Believing she had the right to use the estate's money to pay her legal fees, she and her lawyers continued to demand court time. That trial was finally quashed.

At this juncture, I imagine a chorus continuing with lines from *The Pirates of Penzance,* urging trustees to move forward: "Go to immortality, and go to song and story."

The watching major general sighs and concludes, "At last they go. At last they really, really go!"

R etired admiral Kihune felt up to the task of negotiating with the IRS now that he could assure them the former trustees were gone. Kihune, interim board chairman, had managed a $22-billion budget while overseeing construction of all surface ships and weapons system research, development, and procurement. Interim trustees were creating history. Former police chief Keala, son-in-law of the late "Papa" Lyman, made this proclamation: "Decisions we make will help influence the future of many children in Hawai'i and at the same time ensure the survival of an outstanding institution."

Kihune promised the IRS that the interim trustees would focus on educating children rather than concentrating on business.

The IRS taxed each former trustee about $40,000 for salaries exceeding reasonable limits. It prepared a bigger surprise for Henry.

The IRS sent Henry a tax deficiency notice informing him that the trust overpaid him about $2.75 million between 1995 and 1999 and demanded a 25 percent penalty—about $687,000—on the overpayments. It added a 200 percent penalty —about $5.5 million. Henry was the only former trustee to receive this notice from the IRS.

CHAPTER 48

# A Four-Year Yo-Yo Contest

## Fall 1998 to 2002

THE FOUR YEARS of Honolulu court action by spinmasters Henry and Dickie can be described as a "yo-yo contest."[1] Their back-and-forth, round-and-round, and up-and-down activity began in early fall 1998 and continued until the string ran out in midsummer 2002.

Margery Bronster started the contest with a State grand jury looking into reports of Jeffrey Stone rewarding Dickie and Henry for arranging below-market-rate interest—2.7 percent—on the multimillion dollar land transaction discussed earlier.

State investigators made a quick "behind-the-back" move. Without Henry's permission, they searched and videotaped his new luxury condominium and brought along an appraiser to price it.

Next came "slappers." The grand jury indicted Henry for accepting a bonus from Stone. The first-degree theft charge could mean up to ten years in prison. Stone and a business partner were charged with commercial bribery and perjury and faced the same sentence.

Using a "double or nothing," a grand jury subpoenaed Dickie Wong and Nathan Aipa, head of KSBE's Legal Department.

Stone's attorney pulled a "reverse," asking Circuit Court judge Michael Town to toss out the grand jury indictment. "Attorney General Margery Bronster doesn't have authority to prosecute the criminal case," he claimed.

---

[1] Yo-yos were ubiquitous when Dickie and Henry were growing up; most everyone mastered some tricks. In one year alone (1962), the Duncan Company sold a record 45 million yo-yos in the United States, although there were only 40 million kids at that time.

"Disqualify her. She's on two teams: in her role as prosecutor and with her duties as legal guardian of the Bishop Estate."

"Stop grand jury proceedings," he asked federal judge Alan Kay.

"No," Judge Kay said. Dickie must start at the State court level before moving up.

Dickie and Henry's legal teams used a "monkey climb." They wanted to delay grand jury hearings because "Margery doesn't have the primary authority to pursue a criminal investigation and is in a conflict of interest for conducting a simultaneous civil and criminal investigation of trustees."

This play failed. Henry lost his bid to dismiss the criminal indictment. Judge Michael Town said that Margery had no conflict of interest in conducting simultaneous civil and criminal investigations of the Bishop Estate. He rejected Dickie's request to suspend the jury's investigation.

The grand jury heard the case against Dickie. Testifying were Wong's secretary, accountant, a local real estate appraiser, and a builder, along with in-house attorney Aipa. The jury indicted Dickie for first-degree theft, conspiracy, and perjury. It charged his wife, Marni Stone Wong, with conspiracy and giving a false statement, and it charged brother-in-law Jeffrey Stone with bribery. If convicted, each faced a maximum penalty of ten years in prison and up to $50,000 in fines.

The grand jury said that Dickie committed perjury by saying, "I never knew a real estate appraiser visited my home." The attorney general used an abbreviated "around the world" play to include testimony from the appraiser, then in a South Dakota federal prison for tax evasion and nonpayment of child support. He'd performed several appraisals in the complex transaction, before losing his license for fraudulent appraisals.

By then Margery Bronster was no longer in office and the attorney general's team was handicapped without its most skillful team member.

Dickie's attorney claimed that the State made an illegal play in using testimony from a local attorney who was vice president in a defunct company once owned by Stone. He was serving five years in a federal prison for laundering drug money.

Circuit judge Michael Town dismissed charges against the Wongs and Stone, saying, "The State illegally bolstered testimony for the grand jury's indictment."

Renee Yuen, Henry Peters' lawyer, asked the judge to dismiss similar kickback charges against her client. Ms. Yuen was referred to as the "Dragon Lady" by old-timers who remember Milton Caniff's comic strip *Terry and the Pirates* and enjoyed seeing Ms. Yuen in action. For decades, the Dragon Lady was the model of Asian intrigue and beauty: She smiled beautifully and seductively, her appearance was always elegant, and she sought to control every situation. She was often Terry's only chance of survival—as Ms. Yuen was for volatile Henry.

Next came a "loopy loop" from the Wongs. They said they'd sue the attorney general's office for professional misconduct. They hoped to be awarded several million dollars and wanted immunity from future prosecution.

Judge Town ruled that Henry didn't get a fair hearing and dismissed his indictment. He threw out a "sleeper" and did not rule out further criminal investigation.

State prosecutors immediately impaneled a new grand jury to seek Henry's indictment. Henry decided to "shoot the moon," letting the estate's interim board know: "I intend to return as 'rightful trustee' of Bishop Estate.

Henry Peters offers reporters the latest spin on news developments. His attorney, Renee Yuen, is to the right. Honolulu Advertiser *photo by Cory Lum.*

I plan to seek reinstatement. My temporary removal from the Bishop Estate board is the result of a conspiracy by the Governor Cayetano administration. I'm innocent; charges against me are created with smoke and mirrors, not facts." Henry said he had been contacted by the IRS's Western Region office and expected the IRS to reverse its position against him.

U.S. District judge Alan Kay rejected Henry's request for a temporary restraining order against the grand jury investigation.

Casually "walking the dog," Henry told a reporter he might seek sanctions against Governor Cayetano, who he believed masterminded the criminal case.

A grand jury indicted Henry for theft and conspiracy and indicted Jeffrey Stone for commercial bribery, conspiracy, perjury, and for being an accomplice to a theft.

Ms. Yuen said she expected the indictments as part of Governor Ben Cayetano's politically motivated plot. Another photo of her smiling inscrutably was published in local papers.

Henry asserted that the State was too deep in its criminal case to pull back without having to face millions of dollars in potential liability from his and Dickie's wrongful prosecution suits. He kept on spinning a story of complicity by political foes.

Another powerful team was ready for a matchup with Henry and Dickie —plus, this time, Lokelani. The Internal Revenue Service stepped up its criminal inquiry by issuing subpoenas for each of their tax records. This might have been related to a federal grand jury's earlier request for their banking records.

Dropping conspiracy charges against Henry and Stone, the State said it would pursue theft and commercial bribery charges.

Ms. Yuen argued that the State violated Henry's rights when it brought the estate's lawyer and acting chief operating officer, Nathan Aipa, to testify before the grand jury in July. "As the estate's lawyer, all discussions between Henry and Nathan should remain confidential."

A grand jury indicted Dickie on perjury charges, claiming he provided false testimony on ambiguous telephone messages between him and Jeffrey Stone over a three-year period. Dickie pleaded not guilty to committing perjury, as did Stone.

Circuit judge Michael Town heard arguments on Henry's motion to throw out a grand jury theft indictment. He scheduled another hearing before making a decision. He'd previously thrown out indictments against Henry and Stone but had left open the question of whether the State could reindict the two on the same charges.

Dickie lost his bid to head off a perjury trial when Judge Town ruled that settling of the civil suit did not erase the criminal charge of perjury.

Town ruled that the attorney general's office did not have a conflict of interest in bringing separate civil and criminal actions against Dickie and did not misuse the criminal process to improperly boost its civil suit to remove and recover millions of dollars.

A "gravity pull" was put into play. Judge Town dropped charges against Dickie for perjury and against Henry for theft and conspiracy because investigators with the attorney general's office provided improper testimony before a grand jury that prejudiced their rights to a fair trial. He also dismissed the perjury charge against Jeffrey Stone, saying the case relied on prejudicial testimony and lacked sufficient evidence.

Town's ruling was upheld by the State Supreme Court. Henry, Dickie, and Jeff Stone were ruled innocent of all charges.

U.S. District judge Alan Kay stated that the State's prosecution represented a "serious threat to the integrity of the judicial process."

After many agonizing courtroom appearances, Dickie and Marni Wong wait to hear themselves ultimately cleared of participating in a real estate kickback. Honolulu Star-Bulletin *photo by Craig T. Kojima.*

In the contest's final move, Judge Kay declared that Dickie could not pursue millions of dollars in damages from the attorney general's office. It was acting in its role as advocate for the State when it sought indictments against Wong and his now former wife, Marni Stone.

All courts had ruled; the string for actions had run out.

Past behavior caught up with Lokelani Lindsey. Discovering that she failed to pay taxes in 1997, the IRS placed a $230,000 lien on her Hawaiʻi properties.

The Internal Revenue Service's criminal division made a two-year investigation into Lokelani's personal dealings. A federal grand jury indicted her on charges of bankruptcy fraud, money laundering, and conspiracy.

Prosecutors said that in 1995 Lokelani's sister, who owned a hairstyling business, filed for bankruptcy, and failed to disclose to creditors she owned 100 shares of stock in a local company. According to the indictment, the sister secretly transferred her stock to Lokelani during her bankruptcy proceedings and backdated the transaction by a year to elude creditors. The sister also failed to report $136,908 on her 1995 tax return. Lokelani took $35,000 for her efforts after the stock was sold to an executive in the company for $100,000.

The trial was held in Las Vegas at Lokelani's suggestion. She said there was little chance of "fair treatment" in Honolulu.

Months earlier, her sister pleaded guilty to filing a false income tax return and was sentenced to a six-month prison term, one year of probation, and a fine. She was scheduled to testify against Lokelani.

On the day her trial was to begin, Lokelani Lindsey pleaded guilty to two felony money laundering charges. U.S. District judge David Ezra, who sentenced Lokelani in October 2002, said she was driven by a "misguided sense of greed and arrogance." Without the two sisters' plea agreements, he said he would have issued prison sentences longer than six months.

Jan Dill, president of Nā Pua a Ke Aliʻi Pauahi Inc., commented: "The schools ʻohana takes no joy in Lindsey's plight. In many ways, she served as a symbol of what was wrong with the trust's former board and its top-down management style. Rightly or wrongly, she became the poster lady of the complaints and abuses being visited on the children."

By this time, Lokelani's back tax bills were over $400,000. In efforts to collect on a $1.1 million debt, the Bank of Hawaii foreclosed on two properties. She had initiated two promissory notes—$672,000 in 1996 and $411,934 in 1997—while she was earning as much as $1 million a year as a trustee.

Lokelani was not ready to be canned. Her lawyers told the judge she was needed at home to take care of her husband who was critically ill, and she had to be with him continuously to ensure he received proper medical care. The judge granted Lokelani's request to delay the start of her prison sentence on three occasions, based on her lawyers' arguments.

People began reporting Lokelani sightings in Las Vegas. Three months after her court appearance, she was back in her favorite fun city. She made no effort to skulk around or go undercover. Eight months later she was spotted in Las Vegas, taking another break from having to care for her husband.

Scheduled to appear before an annoyed Judge Ezra, Lokelani wrote a rambling statement in which she claimed her car's brake line had been cut. In it, she asked the judge to recuse himself from her case, accusing him of federal grand jury tampering and of conspiring with others to deprive Native Hawaiians of their rights. She signed the document and dropped it in the after-hours court document box.

When she appeared in court the next day, the judge ordered her to jail immediately. Judge Ezra said she'd violated the trust of the community and the court. "I find it incredible she would have the temerity and arrogance to submit such a document in light of the steps I have taken to ensure the integrity of her family."

# PART EIGHT

# AFTERMATH

>—+—◆—O—◆—+—<

CHAPTER 49

## *Oz and I Reflect*

November 1999

O<small>N</small> M<small>ONDAY</small>, November 1, Oz picked me up at my mother's apartment in Nu'uanu Valley to accompany him to the Hawai'i Nature Center. Active with conservation organizations, he was advising Nature Center staff while they were without a managing director. I had read several of his speeches to international audiences about "finding a point between preservation of resources and land development that provides for the needs of today while preserving a portion of those resources for generations to come." I looked forward to sharing these and other views while spending the day with him.

He told me that the Bishop Estate was researching over 300 tree species in some of its forest reserves, repopulating forests with almost-vanished native Hawaiian birds, and taking care of endangered plants. "We're trying to deplete the population of rats and mongooses in our native bird forests; they eat bird eggs," he said.

I told him about being thrilled to see "extinct" sandalwood trees growing in mountain forests when I was at McCandless Ranch. "I sometimes saw native Hawaiian birds with red, yellow, green, and orange feathers, the kind used to make royal capes and feather lei."

"Our ancestors didn't waste resources," he reminded me. "To catch birds, they placed resin on tree branches, birds' feet stuck to them, Hawaiians plucked choice feathers and released the birds to grow more feathers and create more birds."

I told him how ancient chiefs kept choice areas from being overfished by putting a gourd on top of a post. These *kapu*—"keep out"—symbols remained onshore until fish schools built up again. "Anyone caught fishing in a posted area would have his head bashed in by one of the chief's warriors."

Oz declared rhetorically, "We need to preserve important forests, ecosystems, seashore, watersheds, scenic views, endangered birds, and insects. We were so isolated for so long, consequently, Hawai'i has plants found nowhere else in the world. The public needs to protect and preserve our island environments and species for the benefit of future generations.

"Doing this creates potential for ecology tourism. Open space vistas and ecosystems can be preserved. Ancient Hawai'i was Eden; the paradise we enjoyed as youths will not be lost if we take care of it. That is why I am passionate about conservation."

He continued this thought as we drove in the entrance of the Hawai'i Nature Center. "Places such as this are where we start. Young children are the most open to attitudinal change. Hawai'i Nature Center offers elementary grade school programs for public and private school children who enjoy full-day environmental field programs conducted in this forest. That style of teaching helps children to develop a personal relationship with nature. It encourages them to care for it in the long term."

We spent much of the day there. Oz worked in the office and I wandered throughout the forest recapturing youthful relationships.

A fter walking for a while, I sat under a large *wiliwili* tree (*Erythrina sandwicensis*), a leguminous tree indigenous to Hawai'i. It bears red, orange, yellow, or white flowers and grows pods containing red oblong seeds that can be strung in strands and used for leis, among other purposes.

Auntie Nona told us how the Hawaiian language communicates impressions. In the Hawaiian view, the world is alive, conscious, and able to be communicated with; all species of nature and all beings have rights and responsibilities to each other. I reflected on an example she gave: *"Ua 'ike lā'au?"* ("Do you see the tree?"). I put my hands on this tree's thick, straight trunk and "connected" with it. I leaned against it and reflected on the stories I had heard of trees like it.

*Wiliwili* wood is light and very buoyant and was used by old-time Hawaiians for outrigger canoes and surfboards.

This tree was huge and could produce many longboards (ancient Hawaiian surfboards were 16 feet long; there is an example in the Bishop Museum). In a clearing down the path were *kukui* trees—insightful planters.

Hawaiians burned *kukui* nuts to soot, making it into a dark stain to rub on a *wili-*

*wili* board. It accentuated the wood's fine grain. They rubbed the board with *kukui* oil to produce a glossy finish.

My mind filled with associations. Missionaries were horrified at seeing nearly naked natives wasting time riding boards on the surface. They turned surfboards into seats and writing desks in schools. But Merry Monarch King Kalākaua lifted the bans in 1874, and in the early twentieth century Duke Kahanamoku and other stalwarts reclaimed their right to surf at Waikīkī. The "beachboys" boards gradually came down in size to 12 feet; Duke had a 10-foot-long board and could catch a wave with two passengers on it and even surf with a woman standing on his shoulders. Surfers developed strong chests and shoulders from carrying, paddling, and swimming after these long, heavy boards weighing 150 pounds or more.

A tree such as this was the best for surfing. Some boards were made of redwood; some hollow boards were made of plywood. Balsa boards didn't have a large following until they were later combined with redwood. Technological advances made it possible to deal effectively with the water-absorption factor by combining balsa with fiberglass and resin. Now you don't need to belong to a club to store your board. You can transport it under one arm, and the board is so light that you can hook it to your foot in the water without it pulling your leg out of its socket when a wave takes it away from you.

My mind continued its wanderings as I thought of the tree's reference in the ancestral chant of Kualiʻi:

| | |
|---|---|
| Not like these is Kū: | ʻAʻole i like—Kū: |
| Not like the *wiliwili* tree, | ʻAʻole i like i ka wiliwili, |
| Of whose fruit bracelets are made, | Kona hua i kūpeʻe ia, |
| Whose trunk is gliding away, | Ka ʻōiwi ona i heʻe—a, |
| Whose body is in the sea of the | Kona kino i kai o ka |
| rollers and surf-riding, | nalu la—heʻe nalu, |
| Not like these is Kū. | ʻAʻole i like—Kū. |

My free associations and musings ended when I heard screeching mynah birds holding a court session in a clearing below me. They had formed a circle around the defendant. One bird cackled lengthily, others joined in as a chorus. The cackler hopped to the center of the ring, gave the defendant a peck, hopped back, and rejoined the circle. Another bird began to cackle, and the trial continued. The mynah bird has the ability to mimic human speech, as does the parrot, but they talk to each other in bird talk. I left them to mete out their justice, not wishing to see the end, which sometimes results in a dead bird in the middle of the circle. I walked from the forest to rejoin Oz.

His next appointment would be at the East-West Center, an internationally recognized education and research organization located on the University of Hawai'i
campus. Another of the many organizations to which Oz devotes time, it contributes
to his insights on a global economy and leadership opportunities within Hawai'i. The
island of O'ahu, known today as "the gathering place," is certainly a fine location for
exchanging ideas.

The East-West Center promotes a stable, peaceful, and prosperous Asia-Pacific
community, with the United States being a valued and leading partner. He reminds
me that "globalization"—defined as the cross-border integration of markets for capital, goods and services, labor, energy, and knowledge—has created enormous challenges for all Asia-Pacific economies.

Developed countries face the challenge of sustaining growth and prosperity as
information technology transforms all economies, as underdeveloped countries struggle to reduce poverty. The center's services include trade, investment, and technology exchange.

"What are your primary concerns now that you no longer lead the battle to save
Kamehameha Schools?" I asked Oz. He answered artfully and earnestly:

> I have heard that the time when war winds down is the time of doubts and
> rebukes. Interim trustees are working with the IRS for the schools to retain a
> tax-exempt status. They will be replaced by permanent trustees; my concerns lie
> with them.
>
> Hawaiians must protect Princess Pauahi's legacy until all Hawaiian chil-
> dren have been educated to become industrious men and women.
>
> Until Kamehameha Schools reaches out to touch each of them, some of
> these children will be lost forever. We have been missing 90 percent.
>
> The current admissions policy favors only the best and the brightest. It
> ignores most children, and many are falling through the cracks because Kame-
> hameha Schools selects applicants who demonstrate a potential for success in a
> rigorous educational program.
>
> Kamehameha's job is to take a child out of an intellectually depressed
> environment and help the child improve.
>
> About 40,000 children, many now grown to adulthood, have been denied
> a Kamehameha education solely because trustees chose to accumulate funds
> instead of furthering and expanding the trust's benefits. Then they decided to
> build new schools in areas where other schools existed.

I've always maintained that the most cost-effective way to reach great numbers of Hawaiian children is to charter public schools in neighborhoods that have the most need. While this would educate a large number of Hawaiian students, children who are not of Hawaiian ancestry also would benefit from the princess's legacy.

We need to work in partnership with public and private agencies to extend Pauahi's gifts to Hawaiians of all ages, to help them become contributing citizens and lifelong learners with a positive sense of self and culture. The inescapable fact remains that the State will never be in a position to fully fund public education and all its associated needs.

Arthur, my gravest concerns center on how we apply the money. I believe it is fallacious to build a series of schools for top-achieving students, as is mandated in the Go Forward plan. Building elitist institutions is not what Bernice Pauahi Bishop has in mind. Our focus should not be on one type of school with one type of goal for which many of her children will not qualify.

I believe in a voucher system to provide financial aid to other schools, to make scholarships available to attend schools other than those run by Kamehameha.

Nothing is more precious than the princess's will, and those who have benefited should support and protect her wishes into perpetuity. I am sure that a wealthy Kamehameha Schools will be challenged by avarice and by those coveting the opportunities she gave to her spiritual children of the Hawaiian race.

We need to give preference to our Hawaiian children until all 48,000 now and all those who come after them are touched by this legacy.

I had previously heard and shared thoughts such as these with him. He's compressed them into a peroration, giving it to me as a relay runner passes on a baton. To help move them forward, I can share them. Oz has finished running his race for Kamehameha Schools.

It had been fruitless earlier in the year to write trustees a report on classmates' career paths. Because of what Oz had just told me about diversification and education for life, I shared with him what my classmates told me:

Eighty percent of my class did not expect to go to college because they couldn't afford it. Forty-two percent of classmates were in the vocational program, 38 percent in general education, and only 20 percent prepared for college. From vocational education came one bishop, one minister, and several business owners. Two went from the general education sequence into the U.S. Coast Guard Academy and had maritime careers. College prep graduates include a federal judge, a doctor, a world-renowned entertainer, and sales and business executives.

There were but sixty-nine boys in my class; 33 percent made the mainland their home because of more opportunity there than here.

Several went directly into the service as you did, and the Korean War paid their college tuition. During their working lives, 41 percent of the young men in the class of 1949 applied the learning skills Kamehameha gave them to continue in higher education at four-year and two-year colleges, along with technical institutes. Almost everyone took some form of continuing education and additional training during their careers.

A list of men who graduated in the class of 1949 includes an aerospace engineer, aircraft mechanics, an airline captain, a bishop, business owners, a doctor, electric company officials, engineers, entertainer, a federal judge, a hotel worker, a marine engineer, a minister; several made the military their career, one became a printer, another was a police detective. Our class includes a rancher, a stock broker, teachers, telephone company officials, and a visitors bureau official.

Twenty-four percent of young women in the class of 1949 went away to college—including nursing schools. Of those, 46 percent made their home on the mainland. Their careers encompass opportunities generally available to women of their era because doors to many male-dominated professions were not yet generally open to them. The young women became corporate officers, officials in the department of education, a high-ranking legislator, nurses, teachers, and therapists.

Those not attending colleges held a variety of paid positions: airline supervisor, baker, tour bus driver, medical volunteers, office administration, and a State government information specialist. Many provide volunteer services to their communities: One has been reading to the blind for twenty-five years, another is a court mediator. One-third of the sixty-nine men and forty-one women in our class were deceased by 2005.

The next day, I was riding in my cousin Vickie Lyman's car as she drove her daughter to Assets School. Aleui, the youngest of her four children, was very bright and could succeed on beauty and charm alone. That was why her fireman father and her full-time mother sacrificed to send her to Assets, an independent school for children from five to eighteen years of age whose capability is greater than their achievement. It also provides accelerated learning and enrichment for gifted and dyslexic children. Oz, on its board of directors, told me the teacher-student ratio in elementary school is 1 to 8. "Individual attention makes it expensive, but it's also why a lot of people like the school."

Suddenly all traffic stopped on Nimitz Highway, near the school. "Wonder what this is about?" Vicki said. No whines came from Aleui in the back seat about being late for school. As the youngest of four children, she seemed to accept things as they are.

We learned later that police cars were headed to the Xerox Building next to Nimitz Highway, where an employee had shot seven fellow employees. That afternoon I read that he had driven to hide in the Hawai'i Nature Center, where I had been twenty-four hours earlier. After a six-hour standoff, he surrendered in response to a recorded message from his brother who urged him, "Please give up. The police don't want you or anyone else to get hurt."

He surrendered near the *wiliwili* tree where I was. Police confiscated his weapons: eleven handguns, five rifles, and two shotguns. Newspapers called it "the largest mass murder in Hawai'i." Reporters obviously didn't remember Pearl Harbor on December 7, 1941.

The forty-year-old Xerox shooter was "a quiet person who didn't do drugs," a neighbor said. He raised fish and worked with wood. His fish were so valuable that collectors offered as much as $700 each, the neighbor said. According to evidence at the trial, the shooter had a delusion that coworkers were conspiring against him. His inner and outer self were in conflict.

He came to work that Tuesday morning, opened fire on his coworkers and supervisor, and fled to the Nature Center. If all this had happened a day earlier, we would have met.

## CHAPTER 50

# *Classmates*

### 1999 and Retrospective

Don Ho is Hawaiʻi's most famous entertainer, raconteur, and celebrity. He is also one of my most faithful friends.

At Kamehameha Schools, he influenced everyone around him—upper classmen, his classmates, and lower classmen—by his integrity and the examples he set as an honor student, three-sport star athlete, military officer, class leader, and as a young man who appeared to do things easily but who actually worked extremely hard for perfection.

As with most graduates, even fifty years later, Don Ho remembers the influences the school gave him at an impressionable age; he feels affection for those who shared his experiences, smiling as he describes them.

We discussed this during lunch at Don Ho's Island Grill and while on the Koʻolau Golf Course—called "the most difficult course in the world." The golf course bar is named "Honey's" after Don's mother's bar, where Ho's professional music career started. We also talked a bit the next day at Aloha Market Place, during a memorial party for his recently deceased wife, Melvamay. The party was a benefit for the Arthritis Foundation, Melvamay's favorite charity.

Don proudly used to wear Melvamay Wong's "gold pin" on his school uniform; it represented the highest academic award. No one questioned him about the decorum of a boy wearing a girl's pin. You wouldn't do that with Don.

When I sat down with a tape recorder at lunch, I became careful about what I asked; although Don is my friend, people on "the other side" are close to him also. I didn't want to say anything he might construe as offensive. That would be disrespectful to someone whom I respect very much.

At a Don Ho show, you witness the master of talk story. His topic or reference in time can come out of nowhere, and what he says may at first appear to be disconnected and oblique. But he talks so convincingly and smoothly in his famous baritone that your mind catches up.

I told him I was collecting stories to support my belief that spirituality experienced on our hillside campus changed many of us for the best. "We were a ragtag bunch who left with some good character traits," I explained.

Don smiled, then answered: "If I miss a class event—such as the trips to Las Vegas—and read about it in a newsletter, I see the faces and feel as if I were with them. I never thought I was the smartest guy in my seventh-grade class, but for some reason I was chosen to go to Kamehameha."

I knew the reason: Mr. Bailey saw Ho's potential as a role model, the

Don Ho, special to all who know him. *Photo courtesy of Don Ho and Beachcomber Productions.*

kind of person he became during his second day on campus. Don retold a story I had almost forgotten.

> The first night on campus, all of us new students went to the lighted football field. This was unusual because of the blackout during World War II—although lights were never turned off at Pearl Harbor, a few miles below campus. Administrators probably wanted students to work off anxiety from all the changes.
>
> An older student threw soccer balls and runners from two teams chased them down.
>
> You and I, Arthur, were on the same team and you and I were the slowest guys in the world. Because Joe Smith and his team beat us so badly, I hit Joe Smith right in the mouth. I was from the country and that's how we established our territory.
>
> Just after I did that, Vice Principal Charlie Parrent picked me up by the back of the neck, held me up in the air, and he picked Joe Smith up in the air. I will never forget what he said: "This is your first night in school; it may be your last."
>
> I learned something important at that moment. I did not want to screw up the wonderful chance to be here that might change my life. From that moment on, I took a special pride in obeying the rules. Joe Smith became a close friend for the rest of his life.
>
> I wondered about others in the class, especially you, Arthur, because you were my eighth-grade roommate.
>
> You were a small, skinny twelve-year-old with blond hair and blue eyes. No one else at Kamehameha looked like that.
>
> I didn't think you'd last long among bigger, tougher Hawaiians. I wondered why you were there. Being curious, I asked the librarian—the attractive Mrs. Bowen whose perfume we loved—to help me with some research. I learned very quickly you are more Hawaiian than all of us.
>
> It had nothing to do with your skin color and the way you looked, it had to do with lineage. I passed the word around to our classmates who your Hawaiian ancestors were.[1]
>
> No one gave you a problem for looking different. Right?

---

[1] Don Ho's source was Fornander's *Collection of Hawaiian Folklore*. According to ancient chants on which Fornander's folklore is based, Kuali'i was born in 1555 and conquered all of the Islands except Kaua'i, which he inherited. His residence was at Kualoa, the sacred home to chiefs on O'ahu. It was out of respect to Kuali'i that Kamehameha later dipped his sails whenever he passed Kualoa. Kuali'i died in A.D. 1730 in the 175th year of his life —his long life can be contributed to his success in battle, his Hawaiian diet, and because Hawaiians weren't yet exposed to white men's diseases against which they had no immunity.

That was perfectly true. I didn't have a problem fitting into Kamehameha, despite my apparent racial difference, because I knew the language, understood the culture, and showed genuine respect for it. I did have some initial difficulties with older students until proving my grit and worth. However, classmates took me into their hearts as one of them, which, in fact, I was.

Not until this moment did I know about Don's research project that saved me from many bruises and bloody noses.

In my senior year I was inducted into Hui ʻŌiwi, the school's highly selective and prestigious Hawaiian cultural society—for "true" Hawaiians. This gave me the chance to participate in Aloha Week pageants and other special events, as did Oz and other old-time Hawaiian boys.

Don continued his story:

The school held a picnic at Hanauma Bay for the new eighth-grade students. This was a chance to define your classmates.

We watched Eugene Kaupiko surfing in on a wave that was just a ripple using a flat piece of board. All of the girls were very impressed with this Hawaiian boy who could surf on just a piece of lumber. He caught a fish with his hands and swam with it in his mouth.

Right away we could see that this boy from a little fishing village five miles from nowhere on the Big Island of Hawaiʻi was a charmer who would make you happy. His personality never changed; he was a guy who strutted out there in a lovable way. He didn't arrive with academic prowess but could quickly learn anything.

Before Kamehameha, Geno never touched a basketball or football but became a star in both sports. When the Reverend Steven Desha was allowed to read the scripture in Hawaiian at our chapel services, Geno argued technical points in Hawaiian with the Reverend Desha about what the scripture meant.

I told Don that Geno is back in Miloliʻi; he takes tourists out deep-sea fishing on his boat and looks after his mother, who speaks only Hawaiian. We both agreed he keeps her smiling.

We both just sat quietly for a while.

Don spoke up again:

These people were chosen because they were jewels. I will always remember Kui Lee at Kamehameha. He was a genius and an independent thinker even then; so sad that he died of cancer when only thirty-four.

The songs he wrote changed the substance, style, and mood of contemporary Hawaiian music. Kui's music helped me become a popular entertainer.

How lucky I was to be in that situation and to grow up with those people.

You have no control over your destiny, other than being a kid who follows the rules of society. That's how it was at Kamehameha. We had no control over anything but ourselves and following the rules and procedures of the school.

Imagine if Oswald Stender had not been a Bishop Estate trustee; there would not have been anyone inside to help the princess. The only person who came out looking good in this mess was Oswald, and where was he from? Kamehameha Schools.

We knew Oswald as a good person at school, and I agree with you—he has become the school's hero.

At Kamehameha we learned to recognize similarities, not differences, and to recognize each other's value. Even you, Arthur, who at first appeared so different and who I now think of as a brother. All of us who were there together look at each other with eyes of love.

I have never heard of anything like that.


Don Ho had delivered a parable.

Sharing lunch with Don is an adventure. He ordered *ʻopihi*—sort of like raw clams only more flavorful—barbecued ribs, poke, steamed fish, a Chinese noodle dish, a beef chop suey dish, rice, poi, and pizza with everything on it—including fresh pineapple.

He nodded when I told him I was going to talk with Tom Hugo and said that I could learn a lot from him—a classic, cryptic Don Ho sentence.

He had alerted my mind that Tom, a quiet man who kept secrets, had something more to share with me.


Classmate Tom Hugo epitomized the Hawaiian character traits of charm, warmth, and sincerity embedded in the word "aloha" when it is used as an acronym. Each letter can stand for a Hawaiian word: *akahai, lōkahi, ʻoluʻolu, haʻahaʻa, ahonui.* These words respectively mean kindness—expressed with tenderness; unity—expressed with harmony; agreeability—expressed with pleasantness; humility—expressed with modesty; and patience—expressed with perseverance.

Hearing that he had taken care of Eric Kalohelani, I phoned Tom and asked him to have lunch with me at Pauoa Chop Suey House in Nuʻuanu. Eric was one of "the jewels" Don had described. He was an honor student in the general educational program, a football and baseball star, a band member, and one of the best-liked persons in our class.

When Tom arrived and we sat down in the Chinese restaurant, I told him I was writing about Princess Pauahi's influence on her spiritual children. "Since you are one of them, please shed your *ha'aha'a* and share your experience.

He gave me a long look and answered, "I will," and he spoke of his life after Kamehameha Schools.

Tom went to the University of Denver on a football scholarship. After college he wanted to play professional football for the Los Angeles Rams, but the Alouettes in Montreal, Canada, offered him more money—$5,000—so off he went. For seven consecutive years, from the first year he played, he was an all-star player in the Canadian league. In 1958 he was voted Montreal's Professional Athlete of the Year. Tom played center on offense and linebacker on defense.

"I received many dinner invitations a week," he said. But he stayed home; he was married to the former Julie-Bethe Perkins, "his girl" from Kamehameha School for Girls, the class of 1949's best musician (organ and piano), athlete, honor student—and a beauty featured in *LIFE* magazine.

Tom returned to Hawai'i and worked for Hawaiian Telephone Company for seventeen years until Governor George Ariyoshi appointed him as the first chairperson of the Hawai'i Paroling Authority.

Tom told me this story:

Being responsible for minimum terms, for whether or not someone stayed in jail, and for how long, took a lot out of me.

Particularly when my mind said, *Keep him in there.*

So many prisoners were Hawaiians who didn't have an opportunity to go to Kamehameha as you and I did.

I reflected on that, but said nothing. By now I knew my secret; truly, if it were not for Kamehameha, I would be dead or in prison. It was the inevitable outcome for a boy who, by eleven years of age, could kill a steer with a knife, shoot a machine gun, was brutalized in a foster home, had been urged to steal, was poor, and who wouldn't back down from a fight. I said nothing; I just ate, as did Tom.

Tom drank some iced tea and resumed his story:

After a few months, I found myself drinking after each hearing. During one morning after, Julie looked at me and asked, "Is this what we're going to go through every time you have a hearing?"

I answered no and refrained from drinking.

The stress of the job began to take its toll on me; it became obvious to others that I was having an attitudinal change.

A minister who worked in the court system sensed my troubled feelings and helped me start studying the Bible. It didn't seem a strange thing to do after our experiences at Kamehameha.

I knew Eric had been a restaurant manager and in the travel business, but I hadn't seen him in a long time until, in 1984, I went to a party and Eric was there. He complained of a back ailment. This seemed unusual; Eric never used to complain about anything.

Not long after, our classmate Joe Smith said to me, "Let's look up Eric."

We went to his younger sister's home where he lived. Eric was using a walker and said again, "My back really bothers me." But he put on his shorts and we went to the beach.

We threw him in the water and he nearly drowned. He couldn't stand without his walker. He told me he had Parkinson's disease. He was fifty-four years old.

I read up on the disease and found out that although he was deteriorating, exercise could slow though not cure its progression. His sister worked; he couldn't receive the care he needed in her small apartment, and he couldn't go elsewhere because he had no insurance.

God said to take care of that boy, so I talked with Julie; we still had two kids at home and she had a job. Julie was Julie. She helped me fix a room for Eric.

By then I had retired after eight years with the Parole Administration, so Eric became my job. I registered him with the Social Security board so he would start receiving disability payments. We exercised daily. I had him lifting weights for an hour. He would walk in our swimming pool.

I prepared his meals for him, helped him on the toilet—he couldn't wipe himself. He had heavy-soled shoes that I would put on him. I kept on his ass to keep exercising, and he never stopped responding. Joe Smith came in two to three times a week to offer encouragement.

Eric had a great attitude. Once he started receiving $300 a month disability checks, he wanted to give me rent money, but I wouldn't accept it.

Eric looked forward to Sundays when our kids and their kids came to dinner. "Uncle Eric" always smiled warmly—his eyes would light up and sparkle. He loved being a member of our family and we loved him.

I took Eric everywhere I went. He had to get out and not feel isolated. We'd go to the beach, look at the girls—he never lost that; his mind was great!

We went to all Kamehameha Schools events: song contests, alumni *lū'au,* football games—he'd be in his wheelchair with an aisle seat—people waved and talked with him.

Remember his grin?

I nodded: It was fit for a travel poster.

We stymied the progression of that disease for two years. Then, in 1987, I received another gubernatorial appointment and started working again. This left Eric alone all day until we discovered a senior citizen day care center in our area for which he qualified.

I dressed Eric in the mornings and dropped him off at the day care center before going to work. Julie picked him up and took him home when she finished work.

He enjoyed the companionship at the center and everyone liked him—particularly the ladies. When I returned from work each day, we'd exercise together.

All went well for a while, but it was becoming evident that Eric was weakening, particularly after a bout with pneumonia.

His mind stayed as sharp as ever. When I made a joke, he'd give me a small grin. By this time he had no balance and his walker wasn't much help, but his eyes told us everything.

He understood what was going on around him and could give us signals, but I was the only one who could interpret his attempts to talk.

It was getting so I couldn't handle Eric by myself.

Joe Smith had died of a heart attack and although Eric made no demands, my family was experiencing stress through his disability.

After two or three months, he and I agreed that he should be placed in a home. Maybe this ought to have been done sooner, but I didn't want to give up. While all this was going on, Julie never had a word of complaint. Julie was Julie.

Throughout these times, Eric was very worried about owing more than $8,000 to doctors and about his upcoming expenses.

Don Ho said he would lend Eric the money for his bills. What Don really did was give Eric the money he needed—they both pretended it was "a loan."

The sad part was taking Eric away from our family and putting him in the home. Our young ones couldn't understand why he went away. At times we brought him back for the weekend and I would give him all the beer he wanted. I'd just hook up a catheter and a bag.

I would tell him, "You are going to die. But we are going to try to keep you from dying for as long as possible. It is so easy to die, but don't die mentally, enjoy the rest of the time you have." His eyes were filled with love.

He spent two years in the nursing home. I would have done it for any of my classmates who had nothing and needed help.

He had finished. We sat quietly and toyed with the food with our chopsticks. Taciturn Tom may never have spoken at such length.

After a while, I said, "I think the Power that told you 'to take care of that boy,'

Tom Hugo responds to football fans during a November 2001 ceremony in Montreal, Canada. Traveling with him from Honolulu were his wife Julie-Bethe and daughters Jan, Jina, and Joanne, who were born in Montreal while Tom starred for the Alouettes professional football team.

wanted Eric's story shared. Tom nodded and paid the bill. We rose, embraced as men do, and parted silently.

What Tom told me epitomizes the feeling of *'ohana* Kamehameha Schools instills, as well as a belief in a higher power. Neither Don nor Tom told others what you just read; they have *ha'aha'a*—humility—about such personal things. That's the Hawaiian way.

Years later while finishing this book, I phoned Tom to discuss a story about self-lessness after he mentioned its recent ending. Deciding to go to the source, I phoned John Colburn at 8:00 P.M. Hawaiian time; in New York, where I called from, it was 2:00 A.M.

Even though he looked more like a sumo wrestler than a youth, we always called John Colburn "Boy." He appeared formidable, and no one got in his way when he was body surfing, even though he was very Hawaiian—sweet natured, big hearted, and quick with a compliment. During football games, he'd flatten an opposing lineman, then extend his hand to help the player up. The respect Boy was accorded when he walked into a room rubbed off on anyone with him. His persona is like that of the giant healer in the movie based on Stephen King's book, *The Green Mile*.

A few days before graduation, we boys sat in a room to settle a matter. Our class advisor said none of us would graduate unless school administrators found out who burned a hole in the seat of a car belonging to a shop teacher.

Colonel Kent was serious; college plans and jobs were all at risk as the result of a prank out of control. The new, part-time shop teacher had treated shop boys poorly. A small group of them poured battery acid on the driver's seat, thinking this would give the mean guy "a hot ass." It'd be a big joke, and maybe he'd simmer down. The acid burned the seat, not his butt. He wanted vengeance. He demanded that the culprits not graduate.

It was a very solemn time. The class's greatest joker and clown and his friends were involved; we'd spent five years together and were like brothers. How could we get them and ourselves out of this?

Boy stood up and headed out of the room. "Where are you going?" some of us asked.

"I'm going to see Colonel Kent and tell him I burned the seat," Boy answered. Of course he hadn't, but he was determined to take the rap to save us all.

"It was such a *dumb idea* that he'll believe that I'm the one who did it," Boy declared, walking out with a smile.

Some of the top members of our class talked to Colonel Kent, and he agreed to let Boy walk onstage to receive a "certificate of attendance" we drew up for him. Colonel Kent kept his word—our confessed but innocent hero didn't graduate. But the audience didn't know Boy was handed a creative certificate, not a genuine Kamehameha diploma when his name was called.

Boy is one of Kamehameha's loyal alumni: The Colburns, Boy, and his wife Pua, class of 1954, put on a *lūʻau* at their ranch for classmates during their alumni week. They are regulars at our class's Las Vegas reunions.

Through urgings by his classmates and the graciousness of Dr. Michael Chun, Boy received an official diploma. It took over fifty years, but Boy Colburn has an official Kamehameha Schools diploma in addition to the one classmates created for him.

Charles Parrent, who held Don Ho by the scruff of his neck, left Kamehameha to become a hotel and resort developer. He became very wealthy doing this and turned over his substantial estate to the school. The affection of faculty for the children and their respect for the princess has been a tradition since the first graduating classes, and it undergirds this entire saga. The Parrents, as did the princess, have thought of the schoolchildren as their own.

CHAPTER 51

# Same Old, Same Old

## The Twenty-First Century Begins

RESPONDING TO the Alumni Association's request, interim trustees changed the estate's name to "Kamehameha Schools" on January 1, 2000.

Interim trustees reacted quickly to IRS directives. They agreed to spend 2.5 to 6 percent of the trust's assets yearly to educate children of Native Hawaiian ancestry—about $200 million, double recent expenditures.

Meeting the IRS's mandate, they hired a chief executive officer, effective February 1, 2000. Dr. Hamilton McCubbin, the estate's first CEO, is a 1959 graduate of Kamehameha Schools. He'd been dean of the School of Human Ecology, University of Wisconsin, heading a department with a $6 million annual budget and a fifty-person staff. An expert on early childhood development, he was a finalist for the Kamehameha Schools presidency in 1988, when the board named Dr. Michael Chun. Oz had urged interim trustees to hire an experienced business executive as CEO—not an educator, because they had Dr. Chun—but he was ignored again.

Dr. McCubbin now was Kamehameha Schools single-voice management. He told the media that the schools would restore outreach and early education programs. He said the interim board had initiated partnerships with the Department of Education and the permanent board would expand them.

"The will was intended to make industrious men and women. It didn't say college graduates. It didn't specify a single Kamehameha Schools campus. It said reach the children. That's what my business will be."

Before the Honolulu Rotary Club, in his first public appearance as CEO, Dr. McCubbin explained what would come: "We will finance technical and vocational programs and bring new resources to the trust's early childhood educational service. The Kapālama Heights campus will continue to focus on college prep curriculum. We will, however, direct Kamehameha Schools toward educating as many children of Hawaiian ancestry as possible."

He told the press interim trustees agreed to pay the Internal Revenue Service more than $72 million to settle audits of the nonprofit and for-profit operations, ending a six-year legal dispute. "Interim trustees are cleaning up the investment portfolio, writing off $50 million in bad investments."

$\text{M}$opping up after its legal battles, the attorney general's office sued former trustees for over $200 million in investment losses. It claimed that they took $17.9 to $22.9 million more than they should have and were liable for $46.6 to $54.6 million in surcharges. It wanted Dickie, Henry, and Lokelani to pay the $2 million legal bill to oust Lokelani because they'd backed her actions and defended her.

Court-appointed master attorney Robert Richards found outside firms' legal tabs for the three-year controversy was nearly $15 million and growing. He recommended the Probate Court surcharge former trustees for $5 million. "Some of the work was so egregious that the law firms should refund part of their fees," he declared.

Kamehameha Schools discontinued the service of its law firms the day after the Richards report appeared. Dr. McCubbin told one firm to disgorge more than half of the $1.3 million it billed between August 1998 and May 1999. He said the estate would conduct its own investigations.

$\text{T}$he three-year legal battle between the attorney general's office and former trustees ended shortly before a costly trial was to begin. The trust's entire $25 million insurance coverage was consumed by the deal: The attorney general's office was reimbursed for costs. The estate received over $15 million for alleged mismanagement of trust assets. The settlement didn't include legal bills for the criminal cases involving Henry and Dickie. This agreement was submitted to probate judge Kevin Chang for approval. He ruled that Kamehameha Schools was not required to pursue its former trustees for millions of dollars in legal fees because the settlement among the attorney general's office and former trustees made moot any surcharge claims.

It was *pau.*

$\text{A}$ year later, back on the mainland, I received a phone call from Cousin Vickie: "Come quickly—Hualani wants to go."

A week earlier the family had had a birthday party for my 92-year-old mother in her extended care facility. She'd seemed pleased over the Chinese food and decorations and family members had photos taken with her, but time was getting short. She was gone four hours before my plane landed.

Hualani told family members she didn't want newspapers to publish her obituary until after a modest funeral service. She was concerned that some of her former clients might read it, come to the church, and be embarrassed by stares.

This time we didn't obey.

Days before the service, newspaper stories in Honolulu papers and on the Internet described Ruth Rath as "a social worker and advocate for women's rights who fought the stigma of Hansen's disease with education and advocacy."

Hualani was the only social worker serving Hawai'i's lepers, as Hansen's disease patients once were called. A former state health education officer described her as "a real pioneer in her field and for the people of Hawai'i." Newspapers included excerpts from previous articles.

She had been on a routine clinical visit to the Hansen's disease settlement in Kalaupapa with a medical team in 1963 when their plane slid past the short runway and crashed in the ocean. She rescued the injured pilot and a fellow passenger and pushed them out of the plane and into the ocean not a moment too soon. The plane exploded 15 feet away. Although Hualani had a broken arm and cuts, she swam and brought the two injured men to shore. Rough waters off Kalaupapa are famous—the site was picked so lepers wouldn't try to escape.

The service was held in spacious Central Union Church; any of her clients would have blended in with the crowd. Hualani's remains were in an urn on the center platform, surrounded by leis.

Oz sat near an aisle in the back of the church.

I'd chosen to sing songs learned when I lived at the Salvation Army Girl's Home. After turning off the speaker's microphone, I began an unaccompanied dirge, "The King of Love my Shepherd Is." The organ joined up to tempo in the second verse. The all-male Kamehameha Alumni Chorus sang traditional Hawaiian songs, including "'Imi Au Ia 'Oe." The Lymans consider that this song has family associations because of its setting in Puna.

Nieces and nephews of all ages, including little Aleui, participated in the service. I turned the microphone back on after singing. Cousin David Lyman's voice sounded like our grandfather's as he told fond and amusing stories about Hualani, the family's matriarch.

The Reverend Chong, the minister my mother chose, was the son of her childhood neighbor in Kohala, near Parker Ranch. He said to the congregation, "I compare Hualani to a coconut tree in my backyard; it has a large hole high up in its trunk, where a heart would be if the tree were a human.

"'Cut it down,' everyone told me; 'the tree will break and fall and damage your house.' But when Hurricane 'Iniki—the fiercest hurricane in my lifetime—arrived, the wind went through the hole in the heart of the tree. Huge ironwood trees and blooming plumeria trees were blown over and uprooted, but the coconut tree endured the ferocity of the storm; it bent but would not break."

Members of the alumni choir beckoned me over to join in singing "Aloha 'Oe." The congregation completed the chorus with us and the song's final words: "Aloha 'oe . . . until . . . we meet . . . again."

We congregated at a Chinese restaurant for a meal Hualani arranged for us in lieu of a *lū'au*. Months earlier she'd given Vickie the money to pay for all sixty-five of us immediate family members. She'd looked over the menu and specified foods to be served—beef, pork, chicken, duck, fish, and many vegetable and side dishes. I placed the urn containing her ashes on the roundabout holding the side dishes.

Two days later, cousins and I went to Nu'uanu Cemetery to place her urn in a vault with her parents' and sister Maile's remains. The location is across the street and down a ways from Mauna 'Ala.

O z was pleased that new trustees were being selected by a process similar to what he and alumni had developed years earlier. As a result of announcements, over 200 persons applied as trustees; a court screening committee, including Nona Beamer and Roy Benham, selected seven final candidates. The public was given thirty days to submit written comments on the finalists. Now it was up to Judge Chang to make the selections. The Hawai'i Supreme Court had stepped out of the process.

I sat in Judge Chang's courtroom to watch the outcome. Seated not far to my left, Henry Peters looked cheerful but intent.

Judge Chang had the broad shoulders and strong torso of a football player's body and a quiet, personable demeanor. I watched as he concluded another matter before announcing the new trustees. I noticed how he explained things gently and with a kindly smile.

Now it was time. He told us that trustees' pay would be capped at $97,500 a year; the board chairperson would receive no more than $120,000. Judge Chang appointed attorney J. Douglas Ing to a two-year term of office; Hawaiian navigator Nainoa Thompson received a five-year appointment; Diane Plotts, a former Hemmeter Development Corp. executive, would serve for one year; American Savings Bank executive Constance Lau was appointed for three years; and retired admiral Robert Kihune was given a four-year appointment. Constance Lau and Admiral Kihune were members of the interim board. Each of the new trustees was eligible for reappointment.

Nainoa, son of retired trustee Pinky Thompson, enjoys notoreity, especially among young Hawaiians, for sailing by the stars to Tahiti and back from Hawaiʻi in 1978. Nainoa was the first Hawaiian to navigate a voyaging canoe in more than 600 years.

Outside the courtroom, Henry Peters offered comments to reporters surrounding him: "Every five years or less these trustees will run for office. It becomes a popularity contest. They'll make decisions in terms of what's popular. How do you plan for long term in those conditions? It's a perpetual trust, not a public office."

W hen Linda Lingle, mayor of Maui, campaigned for governor in 1998 during the height of the Bishop Estate scandal, she lost by just 1 percent of the vote. Subsequently, as chairperson of Hawaiʻi's Republican Party from 1999 to early 2002, she helped more Republicans be elected to the State Legislature than in about forty years. She was now one of the most respected women in the Islands, according to an independent poll commissioned by one of the state's leading magazines.

Congresswoman Patsy Takemoto Mink, one of Hawaiʻi's savviest politicians, had faxed the following letter to Hawaiʻi's Senate president, warning him of repercussions to be expected after Margery Bronster failed to win reappointment as attorney general:

> On May 3, I called your office and left a message, hoping that I would have an opportunity to talk to you about my feelings on the vote against the confirmation of Margery Bronster, but I did not receive a return call.
>
> Elected officeholders are expected to cast votes with which we disagree. This, however, was more than that. The ouster of Bronster constituted a failure to understand that, in the public's mind, the attorney general was and is the key litigant for and on behalf of all the people in the pursuit of justice in the matter of the Bishop Estate.
>
> To fire the state's chief lawyer in the midst of the most important case of this administration must be viewed as a deliberate, intentional interference in the swift and authoritative prosecution of this case.
>
> Every single member of the Democratic Party will have to endure the criticism emanating from this action. It is a grave setback for us.

Patsy Mink, twelve-time member of the U.S. Congress, became famous to female athletes on every high school and college campus as the "Mother of Title IX."

Mink died on September 28, 2002, of pneumonia, a complication of the chicken pox that infected her while she was campaigning for reelection. Growing up on Maui, she had played high school basketball when women were restricted to half-court games because they weren't considered strong enough for a full-court game. She was denied entry into a dozen medical schools because of her gender and discouraged as a lawyer and elected official because of her gender and her ancestry.

Her career was a series of firsts: the first woman of color elected to Congress, the first Asian-American woman to practice law in Hawai'i, and the first Asian-American woman to be elected to the Territorial House prior to statehood. She was prescient.

Linda Lingle was elected governor in November 2002, the first Republican to lead the state since 1962, when John Burns began the reign of Democratic Party control. She arrived in Hawai'i in 1975, becoming public information officer for the Hawai'i Teamsters and Hotel Workers Union. She edited a monthly newspaper for union members and then founded the *Moloka'i Free Press,* a community newspaper serving the island's 6,000 residents. As the paper's publisher, editor, reporter, photographer, and typesetter, she reported on community events and covered local government. It was during this time that she realized she could help make a difference in government.

In 1980, against a well-funded challenger, Lingle was elected to the Maui County Council. She served five two-year terms on the council—three terms representing Moloka'i and two terms as an at-large member. She became mayor of Maui County in 1990 and was reelected in 1994. She served the maximum two consecutive four-year terms by defeating the most prominent Democrats in the county—a former mayor and a forty-year veteran of the County Council. She was the youngest, the first woman, and the only non-Maui born person ever elected to the office. Throughout her term, job growth was faster on Maui than anywhere else in the state.

While the governor's race captured most attention, Henry Peters, still having reporters' interest, surfaced as a "maybe" candidate. He said many supporters in his rural district had asked him to return to run for an elected office in 2002. He wouldn't say whether he would consider a run for the State House or Senate seats in his district but confided, "There's a lot of experience in this body."

Peters was angry over Governor Ben Cayetano's plan to remove all but one trustee of the Office of Hawaiian Affairs after the U.S. Supreme Court ruled that OHA's elections were illegal. "Nothing would give me more pleasure than running against him," said Peters. But the outgoing governor wasn't running for any office. After a flurry of talk, Henry chose not to run "at this time."

As mayor, Linda Lingle was adept in achieving bipartisan cooperation. She gathered public support to counter resolute opposition. Although the Legislature remained under Democratic control when she became governor, political pundits warned that efforts to thwart her initiatives could backfire on them.

This is because Governor Lingle's election marked a new kind of Hawai'i. Many of the current generation of voters—those aged forty and under—didn't grow up under the plantation mentality, where persons automatically voted for Democratic candidates as union leaders said they should.

The Office of Hawaiian Affairs elections infuriating Henry interested Oz. He decided to run for one of the several trustee positions that Governor Cayetano declared would be available in the November 2002 election. OHA is an outgrowth of Hawaiians' struggle for land and rights that began when its kingdom was overthrown and annexed to the United States.

Oz's toughest campaigning was at home. The family had pulled together as his legal costs grew in the battle to remove Lokelani Lindsey. Oz disclosed his financial activities during his OHA campaign: He owned the business Florexotica Hawai'i jointly with his children, selling silk flowers, plants, and trees to shopping malls; and he owned 25 percent of a poi-making business called Hoae Poi (which means "soft poi"), also with his children. Having kept his real estate license from his Campbell Estate days, he now sold commercial properties.

Oz told Kuulei, "People complain about OHA but don't do anything about it. I think I can help."

A very unhappy Kuulei said, "Promise me that if you get mad at your cotrustees, you will quit. Don't sue any of them."

Oz was elected a trustee when Hawaiians were up against the ultimate challenge of preserving what they had considered their birthrights.

It began in February 2000 when the U.S. Court invalidated the State of Hawai'i's law allowing only Hawaiians to vote in Office of Hawaiian Affairs elections. A month later, a group of Hawai'i residents, led by an attorney, declared OHA "unconstitutional" because of the Supreme Court's ruling. This became the first of several lawsuits challenging OHA's creation and constitutionality.

Winning lawyers in the *Rice vs. Cayetano* case that went to the Supreme Court contended that "If it is racial discrimination to permit only Hawaiians to vote in a state election (as the Rice case held), then it is racial discrimination to admit only Hawaiians to a government-sponsored school."

This threat pertained to other programs intended to benefit the Hawaiian people: the Department of Home Lands—which made it possible for Oz's Tūtū Kāne to have a home because of his pure Hawaiian ancestry—Queen Lili'uokalani Children's Center and Trust, the Queen Emma Foundation, and all programs intended to benefit the Hawaiian people.

Turmoil began with a vague complaint from one of the U.S. Department of Education programs about Kamehameha having a race-based admissions policy. Dr. McCubbin responded by announcing that Kamehameha Schools would reject federal funds. Some of the federal grants, targeting Native Hawaiians, supported scholarships, counseling, substance abuse, and violence prevention. Other federal funds went to subsidized meals for qualified students, library equipment and materials, and student leadership.

He announced the school would drop its Reserve Officer Training Corps, the famed military program for which the government supplied weapons, training, uniforms, and a fast track on a military career.

I heard murmuring that Dr. McCubbin and trustees were reverting to former trustees' behaviors of not listening to the community's voices and not interpreting them into their decision making.

Things were slipping backward.

CHAPTER 52

# Instant Replay

2004, Retrospective

THE LAST VERSE of a song in Hawaiian often begins with the word *"haina,"* meaning "to tell." It summarizes and repeats the song's theme, sometimes including another perspective to the song's story.

*"Haina ia mai, ana ka puana"* ("This is my story, this is my song")—is how a *haina* is usually introduced.

My talk stories center on how Princess Pauahi preserved an indigenous people through education and how her spiritual children resurrected Hawaiian culture. I've told about "industrious men and women," including Oz and others who worked to keep her dream alive.

Early in the twenty-first century, judges and politicians not understanding what the princess's dream has accomplished will decide if it will be allowed to continue. There may not be the opportunity in the new Hawai'i for descendants of old Hawaiians to recover. Institutions that helped them may not be their own.

I pray that what happens is not a repeat of the past. That is all we can really do to influence our personal lives; sometimes it takes a while to want to rely solely on prayer.

It may have begun with a whim: Harold "Freddy" Rice, a fifth-generation Islander, complained to his friend, lawyer John Goemans, about having "no say" in OHA elections. Goemans arrived in Hawai'i in 1959, right out of law school. "Let's challenge the State law that only Hawaiians can vote for OHA trustees," Goemans suggested mischievously.

The lawsuit was named *Rice vs. Cayetano*—Rancher Freddy Rice versus Governor Ben Cayetano. Goemans took it all the way to the U.S. Supreme Court, and the justices invalidated a previous decision by the State of Hawai'i's Supreme Court.

Well, if it's racial discrimination to permit only Hawaiians to vote in a state election, then it is racial discrimination to admit only Hawaiians to a tax-exempt school, surmised Goemans. This would also be true of programs intended to help Hawaiians. Earlier case law allowed Hawaiians to have the same status as Native Americans and native Alaskan tribes. But in the *Rice vs. Cayetano* case, the Supreme Court failed to include Hawaiians in this special category and brought into question prior cases. The Supreme Court held that "Hawaiian" is a racial designation; therefore the State voting law restricting OHA's elections to Hawaiians was unconstitutional racial discrimination.

OHA observers at the proceedings noted that justices appeared perplexed about the definition of ethnic Hawaiians: classified as people who trace their ancestry to aboriginals who lived in the Islands before the 1778 arrival of Captain James Cook. They seemed unsure as to whether Hawaiians have political status as Native Americans even though they are not a federally recognized "tribe."

Goemans filed another lawsuit in federal court alleging racial discrimination by OHA and the Department of Home Lands. He was on a roll.

A man who hadn't held a job in twenty-five years applied for a small business loan from OHA, whose loan fund is reserved for Native Hawaiians. The application included only his name, post office box number, a request for $10,000, and a meager resume. When his application was sent back, he went to John Goemans. Because the declined applicant is white, Goemans sued the State of Hawai'i for violating his constitutional right for equal protection under the law because he is not Hawaiian. Never mind that a Hawaiian without skills or experience wouldn't have money handed him by OHA.

This lawsuit could imperil OHA's $380-million trust fund covering everything from college scholarships to home loans and cultural grants, the Department of Hawaiian Homelands' 200,000-acre land trust, and the leases of 7,000 Hawaiians currently living on that land. Its outcome will affect trust funds established by Hawaiian royalty, including services for children, old folks' homes, and cultural foundations.

John Goemans vowed to take the case all the way to the Supreme Court. He believed the outcome of the Rice case would enable him to attack State and federal programs benefiting Native Hawaiians.

Goemans also challenged the University of Hawai'i's federal funding and Kamehameha Schools federal tax-exempt status.

The conclusion could hinge on whether the court views Native Hawaiians as a racial group or as an indigenous nation having a special relationship with the U.S. government based on past mistreatment. A bill to grant such status was pending when I completed this book.

H awaiʻi's Senator Daniel Akaka introduced the bill, and it was approved by the Senate Committee on Indian Affairs. However, it was opposed by a senator who put an indefinite hold on it, preventing the bill's advancement to the Senate floor. Under the Senate's rules, a single senator, under anonymity, can block a bill's consideration by the full Senate unless sixty members vote to force it to the floor. This legislation, which would provide for federal recognition of Hawaiian sovereignty, has been made more imperative by the lawsuit challenging Kamehameha Schools' Hawaiians-only admission policy. Unless the legislation authored by Senator Akaka is enacted, the lawsuit could result in dismantlement of the schools as envisioned by Princess Bernice Pauahi Bishop.

Governor Lingle testified before a U.S. Senate committee in favor of federal recognition of Hawaiians as an indigenous people comparable to American Indian tribes. Lingle said the issue "has nothing to do with civil rights. It's about honoring a legacy and living up to someone's will. If the Akaka bill were enacted, race would not be an issue." She spoke directly about it with President Bush.

A t a time when Hawaiian cultural and land assets were being threatened and eroded by non-Hawaiians, Kamehameha *ʻohana* and Native Hawaiian people learned about a decision trustees made that could change things forever.

Dr. McCubbin and trustees ignored the courtesy of talk story. They paid no attention to Hawaiian culture and behaved as predecessor trustees. It happened at "the school Lokelani built."

Go Forward plan's first new school had been built on Maui, Lokelani Lindsey's home island. Are you surprised? She was political, bringing "pork"—money—to the home district. The speaker of the House benefited directly: His $100,000 fee as "consultant" on the school property sale in 1996 caused Attorney General Margery Bronster to question whether the estate was channeling funds indirectly to him through its real estate transactions. As House speaker, he had led opposition to a bill aimed at limiting compensation paid to trustees of the Bishop Estate and other charitable trusts. He was a longtime friend of Lokelani Lindsey, lead trustee for Kamehameha Schools education programs. That's the way a political system can work.

Oz objected to building schools in areas where public schools already existed; he wanted the estate to supply money to public schools having a high percentage of

Hawaiian students. Lokelani had her way. In August 1999, Kamehameha Schools dedicated its first neighbor island campus in Pukalani, Maui.

Built for about $26 million, it would handle 200 students from kindergarten through grade eight. After the eighth grade, students could transfer to Kamehameha High School on O'ahu and become student boarders. Administrators expected enrollment to rise to over 800.

At the dedication ceremony, interim chairman Robert Kihune credited development of the new campus to former trustee Lokelani Lindsey. Although not invited, Lokelani was there as a guest of two of her grandchildren who attend the school.

The new school began with kindergarten through grade six. The seventh grade was added in 2000, the eighth grade in 2001.

As a "feeder" for college prep matriculation, the Maui campus met Lokelani's model. Oz felt selecting only the brightest students was wrong. He had written this in memos and had said it in public: "We should help Hawaiian kids become competitive. Test scores should not be the only measure of a child's potential; many average students become great leaders."

In May 2002, Maui school administrators told trustees a non-Hawaiian was offered admission for the coming fall because its admission criteria were not met by any other Hawaiian applicants. Trustees agreed to let the boy in; he was the first non-Hawaiian in forty years to attend Kamehameha Schools—the only others were a handful of faculty children. Football coach Tom Mountain's daughter Mary graduated in 1964 as did basketball and assistant football coach John Berrington's son Robert and school president Kent's son Tom. Roberta Mountain graduated in 1965. All became industrious men and women.

Douglas Ing met with Oswald Stender before making this news public. Oz was appalled. "Rescind what you have done. Preferring Hawaiian children for admission ensures social mobility for Hawaiians as a group. You are telling Hawaiian children they are not good enough. Make a commitment not to admit another non-Hawaiian child until the education needs of Hawaiian children are met. This decision will open floodgates to future litigation. Expect to see a rise in lawsuits from non-Hawaiian students who apply and are rejected," Oz warned.

"By not consulting them on this decision, Dr. Hamilton McCubbin shows he has no clue on how to deal with the Hawaiian community."

Outraged Kamehameha 'ohana held meetings protesting trustees' action. Trustees received petitions urging them to reconsider, and trustees were asked to resign.

Henry Peters said he found it hard to believe that the estate could not find a qualified Hawaiian student to fill the opening on Maui. "While the Maui campus was in the planning stages, the trust conducted extensive demographic research that indicated there are large numbers of Hawaiian students in that district." But how many could meet the standards Lokelani demanded for her Maui school?

Trustees tried ameliorating the situation in print instead of in person. They wrote a letter to the general public and newspapers published it. In it they said:

> Princess Pauahi intended the Kamehameha Schools to serve a broad range of students. However, for the last decade, the admissions process has been heavily weighted toward academic performance, which is only one measure of talent and potential.
>
> The situation on Maui resulted from an unusually small applicant pool and brought the problems with the admissions process into sharp focus. As a result, we have pledged to work with the Hawaiian community to carefully review our admissions process so we can align our campuses and programs with the needs of the specific communities they serve.

Kamehameha Schools new charter school program would serve children of all ancestries. But this important fact did not seem to draw as much attention as the trustees' statement of "A renewed Hawaiians-only admission policy: We intend to vigorously defend our policy of giving preference to applicants of Hawaiian ancestry." They'd fallen into a trap causing adversarial lawyers to smack their lips.

Lawsuits came quickly: A U.S. district judge ordered the schools to admit another non-Hawaiian boy, pending a decision in the lawsuit filed by his mother. An earlier suit, filed by John Goemans and a Sacramento, California, law firm on behalf of an unidentified student, used inflammatory language in which Goemans evoked the 1960 American civil rights movement; he suggested Hawaiians were blocking school doors from other children.

How was the eighth-grade non-Hawaiian boy on Maui faring? Apparently he was doing well, early in his Kamehameha Schools academic career. "He's a nice boy and he's easy to get along with," said a parent whose two children attended the same school. A person whose granddaughter attended the school said, "He seems familiar with Hawaiian culture and language." The school principal said, "He is focused on learning and doing his best." The boy's father is a massage therapist, the mother a hairdresser; they live in a working-class area near the intermediate school he attended before entering Kamehameha.

D<small>r.</small> Hamilton McCubbin abruptly resigned on May 5, 2003, after Kamehameha Schools conducted two separate investigations of his inappropriate relationships with female staffers. The estate began its first investigation after Honolulu employees complained that he had a relationship with a female worker in their office.

The second went back to the University of Wisconsin involving allegations, over a three-year period, of his pursuing unwanted personal relations with a female professor while he was dean of her department. In 1999, the university paid her over $85,000 to settle her complaint. McCubbin stepped down as dean in 1999, after serving fourteen years in the position, but remained as a tenured university professor until joining Kamehameha Schools.

Dr. McCubbin, who was paid $350,000 by Kamehameha Schools, had just agreed to a new three-year contract. He accepted a $400,000 severance payment and signed a "silence" provision of not responding to allegations. He was ordered to vacate the $679,000 home owned by Kamehameha Schools in which he and his family lived.

My *haina* ends with Oz's words:

"This whole thing's like a horror movie being repeated."

# Postlude

SEEING HIM on Sundays in church, Kea commented that the anguish Dr. Michael Chun experienced appeared to increase his spiritual strength.

Her words reminded me of the meditation: "Keep me sweet and sound of heart, in spite of ingratitude, treachery, or meanness. Preserve me from minding stings or giving them. Help me to keep my heart clean, and to live so honestly and fearlessly that no outward failure can dishearten me, or take away the joy of conscious integrity."

Dr. Chun held his tongue so he could remain on campus as a quiet bulwark of faith and dignity, placing children's and teachers' needs over his own interests.

Michael Chun found a kindred soul at the girls school before leaving Kamehameha in 1961 to attend West Point. Don Ho had done similarly before going to Springfield College. Michael and Don soon returned to Hawai'i and their high school "ku'u ipo"—"sweethearts." Michael joined Bina Mossman, Kamehameha 1963, at the University of Kansas, where he earned an undergraduate degree and PhD. While there, Michael played football in the backfield with two-time All-American Gale Sayres. Don came back to Melvamay and went to the University of Hawai'i. Young Oz never left Kuulei, except to where the U.S. Marines sent him.

I understand why Michael and Don quickly returned: Mainland females can be lovely, but as an Island saying goes, "You can take the boy out of Hawai'i, but you can't take Hawai'i out of the boy." Hawaiian boys miss their culture and the mores of their *ku'u ipo,* as I found out—far too late.

In my senior year of high school, a female cousin nagged me to take professional dancing lessons. I had sat out the mandatory campus instruction after knee surgery, the result of a sports injury. My teacher was a twenty-three-year-old woman who looked like Doris Day. She taught at the Arthur Murray studio in Waikīkī. Dancing lessons were my secret. After a morning of dancing, I'd walk to the beach to bodysurf with classmates before catching the campus bus.

Senior dance time was approaching, and I needed a partner. Kamehameha School for Girls had forty-one seniors and thirty-seven juniors. I was known as "the bachelor" in our class of sixty-nine boys; I was too poor to date because "Doris Day" was costing all my money. That left nine juniors to pick from; after my whirl at Arthur Murray, I didn't want to invite any of these remaining potential partners because they'd be chest high to me. How could I use my Arthur Murray polish with a partner who is standing on her toes?

My cousin's roommate accepted my invitation. We were excited, then deflated. "Sophomores are not allowed to attend the senior ball," ruled girls school president Dr. Pauline Frederick, who was about six feet tall. I might have invited Dr. Frederick, I supposed, but was she a nimble dancer?

I thought of asking "Doris Day" from the Arthur Murray Dance Studio, but she was almost as old as some of the younger teachers at the girls school.

Tom Hugo told Julie-Bethe of my dilemma, and our class's "Miss Fixit" fixed me up. I'd worked with Julie-Bethe in joint school activities; she thought I was okay. She found a girl from another school willing to come with me; she was the sister of a day student in our class who was a song leader and cheerleader and so beautiful that I didn't dare know her.

On the night of the dance, I sat at the school entranceway, waiting for my classmate and her date to drive up with my "blind" date. Here they came!

Untangling herself from the back seat of the two-door sedan was the lankiest and loveliest female I'd ever seen. When she stood, I could look into her eyes, not onto her head.

We shook hands; I placed my seven-strand *pīkake*—jasmine—lei over her head but didn't dare kiss her. I'd ordered seven strands because it's a lucky number. I'd passed up the Hawaiian tradition of kissing someone of the opposite sex when you give them a lei.

I introduced her proudly to faculty in the receiving line. Most lingered over the conventional handshake and greeting. It wasn't because she was a classmate's sister— it was because this extraordinary person was with me!

I remember every detail of that evening. She said she could dance the hula and had been practicing ballroom dancing with her mother since receiving my invitation.

"Doris Day" taught me a dance she may have invented—"the ballroom hula."

"I have an idea to use when the band plays a waltz," I whispered to my date, without having to bend my neck.

As the band began Charles King's "Kamehameha Waltz," I said, "I'll lead you into an extension, when we are separated, move your hips in a hula motion as we close in together."

Nothing had been seen like that on the Kamehameha campus. Other dancers stopped, the faculty stared. When the music was over, I glowed, and she grinned. We hadn't done anything wrong; we had integrated the hula into ballroom dancing. Since she was a visitor, not a Kamehameha student, how could she know not to move her hips on campus?

As you might guess, I was not the same after the senior prom. I felt stunned, as if by a club in Mr. Ackerman's butcher shop. Through Tom, Julie-Bethe let me know that the faculty thought my date and I were the unofficial king and queen of the night—certainly we were the tallest—she was at least 5 feet 10.

Even though I was smitten, subsequent memories aren't as dramatic; there just wasn't enough time. She attended her sister's and my joint graduation ceremonies, bringing a crown-flower lei for me. She presented it in true Hawaiian style. I walked over to introduce myself to her mother and father, but they stayed apart from my mother and grandparents.

I had two summer jobs: an early morning one at the tuna cannery—on the days it flew a flag indicating a catch was in—and an afternoon job at the Hawaiian Pineapple Company. I needed the money to go east for college. No one was paying my way; I could earn enough for an airplane trip to New York, a railway ticket to upstate New York, new clothes—since all I have are school uniforms—and one semester of college. After that, I'd find a way to continue.

I didn't have the use of a car. Contact with my *ku'u ipo,* as I thought of her, consisted of nightly phone calls, trips to the beach, movies, and visits to her home, near a bus route. Her mother was gracious; her father was remote but polite.

I thought to myself, *Is it really a good idea to leave Hawai'i now?*

Changing my mind and going to the University of Hawai'i would have meant answering forever to my mother, who was eager for me to leave "for better opportunity." I believed she wanted me gone before I turned out "bad."

A three-minute phone call from the East Coast to Hawai'i cost about $31 back in those days—out of the question. All I could do was write letters. Almost none came to me. She was a popular high school senior, after all. I even wrote to her mother once and received a polite response: "It was nice to hear from you, good luck."

In the spring, she sent an 11 x 14-inch print of her high school portrait. The all-male student body almost wore out the floor in my dorm room coming to see "the Hawaiian goddess."

I worked for a newspaper after college; in the newsroom I saw an Associated Press photo release of her as Miss Hawai'i in the Miss America contest. She was standing by a 10-foot surfboard, and the caption described her as the tallest candidate and the winner of the swimsuit contest. She was selected as a semifinalist and was elected "Miss Congeniality" by other contestants. Years later, her photo was in an upscale magazine's article about Hawaiian living.

During my research for this book, I called her sister who lives on the mainland. She told me her father knew my father and a friend found her father's name in a book that became a television movie. "Maybe your father's name is in the book, too," she suggested. She couldn't remember the name of the book or movie—thought it was *Wild Orchid,* or something like that.

I phoned her friend in Hawai'i, who said the name of the book was *Rape in Paradise.* I moaned loudly, "Not again!"

*Rape in Paradise* is about the Massie trial named after Mrs. Massie, an alleged victim. America's famous attorney, Clarence Darrow, came to Hawai'i to defend the whites who had murdered one of the Hawaiians accused of raping the white woman. It was never proven that any Island boys raped the woman. The name of my classmate's father was in a footnote as being one of the young Hawaiians who was questioned but absolved. Junior Rath's name is not in the book—a relief.

Aunt Molly, now deceased, didn't tell me the name of the woman who died in my father's car, so back in Hawai'i, in 2000, I decided to find out. In newspaper archives, seated at a microfilm reader, I reviewed rolls of film containing images of newspapers from the early 1930s. My eyes became very tired as I advanced from frame to frame. But I kept winding the machine's handle. It was tedious work.

I made another weary turn—and the story of a fatal automobile crash came onto the screen. My father's name was in the article. Riveted, I read the victim's name and started shaking.

The article listed surviving family members, including her brother: His name was in a footnote in Theon Wright's book, *Rape in Paradise*—he was the man who was my father's friend—and he was the father of the girl whom I thought of as *ku'u ipo.*

At age sixty-nine, I now had the absolutely final piece of the puzzle to which Tom Hugo had alerted me. I was horrified.

I feel deep guilt and humiliation.

Shortly before writing this paragraph, I phoned to apologize to each of the two sisters; they were teenagers when last I talked to them. Their parents had never mentioned the name of the man involved in their aunt's fatal accident; my information was news to them.

"You didn't do anything wrong, Arthur," each assured me in a soft voice. "I hope you're over feeling sorry."

"Yeah, but. . . ."

My angst faded as I reflected on the gifts the girls' parents had given me, and I wonder if I could be as courteous to a young man who looked like the person who caused a loved-one's death? Their mother and father allowed me a joyful summer, my first flush of innocent romance, and a dance that doesn't end.

I hold those fond memories forever because *Hawaiians don't lay the problems of adults on children.*

*Aloha,*

begin the first sopranos,

*Pauahi,*

the student song leader draws the second sopranos into the canon,

*Pauahi,*

she points; first altos add their voices,

*ali'i,*

second altos start. The four parts are sung quietly; a one-measure distance between successive voices provides the aura of waves washing onto a sandy shore,

*lee-ee . . . lee-ee . . . lee-ee. . . .*

The last trilled notes float over Honolulu's Royal Mausoleum. Carried gently by a tradewind, they fade; sung words become whispers.

Standing at attention, I am transfixed.

The white-clad Kamehameha School for Girls student body recites from the Bible's *Book of Proverbs.* I believe these words pertain to me: "She opens her hand to the poor, and reaches out her hands to the needy" (Prov. 31:20) and "Her children rise up and call her blessed" (Prov. 31:29).

Along with the rest of the Kamehameha School for Boys military battalion, I pledge fidelity to Pauahi, spiritual mother. I join the combined chorus in earnestly singing Pauahi's name song, composed by Queen Lili'uokalani. At twelve years of age, my voice hasn't changed, the first tenor part seems low in places, but the high notes are thrilling; I put all of my energy into making them ring.

I study the dignified bearing of older student leaders placing fragrant maile vines and strands of flower lei on the tomb containing the princess's ashes; today, December 19, 1944, celebrates her 113th birthday.

I've learned to refer to Princess Pauahi in the present tense; we are told she lives through us.

Marching away from Founders Day ceremonies, I think mainly about emotions evoked during the "Call to Pauahi." Those feelings never leave, reminding me who and what I am.

*Aloha, Pauahi.*

Founders Day at Mauna 'Ala. The author is in the far background with "Aunt Jane" Lyman, Trustee Richard Lyman's widow. *Photo by Luryier "Pop" Diamond, reprinted with the permission of Kamehameha Schools.*

# Index

## A

Ahr, Paul, background, 269; closes extension
    programs, 171–173; seeks to enlarge
    main campus, 180
Akaka, Daniel, bill to recognize Hawaiian
    sovereignty, 352
Aipa, Nathan, fires Bobby Harmon,
    227–229; WASC report leak, 252
Anzai, Earl, describes Bronster, 223, 238;
    reappointment rejected by Senate, 298
Apaka, Richmond, flying hero and football
    star, 117; stage fright, 111–112
Armstrong, Charlotte, husband conceals
    Chinese ancestry, 48; separated from
    "dark man" by Salvation Army, 61. *See
    also* Lyman, David Belden

## B

Bailey, Allen, funds author at college, 125;
    recruits author for Kamehameha School,
    45; recruits Don Ho, 332; recruits Oz
    Stender, 71; sends George Kanahele to
    college, 123
Barnes, Homer, establishes Big Six to
    supervise behavior, 96; forced out by
    politicians, 85–87; impact on Kame-
    hameha Schools, 78–80
Barnes, Mary Frances, brings Hawaiian
    culture to classrooms, challenges
    trustee's disproval of hula, 86

Barrett, Gregory, follow-up story with Oz
    Stender, 204; interviews Lokelani Lind-
    sey, 231; writes about Auntie Nona's
    letter, 197
Beamer, Cleighton, song leader, 108; tours
    mainland with Nona Beamer's Pele
    Dancers, 126
Beamer, Edwin Mahi, classical piano, 98;
    leads band with glockenspiel, 113
Beamer, Keola, helps student overcome
    handicap, 133; slack key guitar with
    brother Kapono, 196
Beamer, Louisa Dambi, opens hula studio,
    81; "Waikiki Wedding," 83
Beamer, Winona ("Auntie Nona"), 80–84,
    127, 285; brings Charles King to meet
    Eleanor Roosevelt at Barnard College,
    83; charged as "a witch," 128; Hawaiian
    culture advocate, 80; "the letter,"
    195–199; testifies in court, 284; takes
    hula to Carnegie Hall, 126
Benham, Roy, alumni activist, 197; organiz-
    ing march, 203–205
Bishop, Bernice Pauahi, establishes school
    to save Hawaiian race, 53–55; will stipu-
    lates Supreme Court selects Bishop
    Estate trustees, 166
Bowen, Ethel, Kamehameha School librar-
    ian, 333
"Broken Trust" essay, 214–218; reactions to,
    219–222

Bronster, Margery, criticizes trustees, 274; orientation, 223–225; preliminary report, 274–275; politicians strike back, 294–299

Brown, Laura, music teacher, 107

Buck, Pearl, aids mixed-blood Chinese children, 126

Burns, John, and Hawai'i's second revolution rewards, 129–130

## C

Campbell Estate, challenges management and Oz Stender builds executive career, 137; trusteeship open to Oz Stender, 138

Carlson, Douglas, reaction to Judge Patrick Yim's fact finding, 240; serving as Lokelani Lindsey's publicist, 231

Cayetano, Benjamin, praises Colbert Matsumoto's integrity, 184; says budget constraints won't halt Bishop Estate investigation, 260

Chang, Kevin, forces lawyers to deliver documents, 275; orders four trustees to resign, 312

Ching, Hung Wo, becomes Bishop Estate trustee, 129

Chun, Michael, cheered by students, 188; delivers a diploma over 50 years later, 341; targeted by Lokelani Lindsey, 155

Clark, Charles, faculty father figure for orphan Oz Stender, 120

Colburn, John "Boy," takes blame so classmates will graduate, 340

Colburn, Pua, hospitality for classmates, 341

Cornuelle, Herbert, president of Hawaiian Pineapple, taught Oz Stender to "close circles," 137; talks Oz Stender out of quitting Bishop Estate post, 150

Court Master's report on Bishop Estate, trustee performance and audit, 266–271

## D

Dawson, Beadie, says Supreme Court's foot-dragging is scary, 261; volunteers as Nā Pua Ke Ali'i Pauahi's lawyer, 210

Diamond, Luryier, compassion for students, 361; helps author buy camera, 101

Dill, Jan, compassion for Lokelani Lindsey, 322; interprets Princess Pauahi's wishes, 263–264

## E

Eagles, Anna, conducts new type of singing, 107–108

Emory, Kenneth, ethnologist, teaches U.S. fliers to survive on "millionaire salads" if marooned on Pacific islands, 92–93

## F

Fernandez, William, alumnus and judge, frustrated by Bishop Estate representative, 9–10; loans barbells to author, 102

Fong, Randie, 187–189; harassed by Lokelani Lindsey, 187; ready to leave school, 200

Freitas, Rockne ("Rocky"), Lokelani Lindsey wants him "on top," 155

Fukunaga, Emily, daughter of Margery Bronster and Mark Fukunaga, benefits from inspired educators, 225

Fukanaga, Mark, encourages wife, Margery Bronster, to achieve her goals, 224

## G

Gandall, Patrick, helps create plan to stimulate Hawaiian political activity, 9; thoughts on what makes Oz Stender likeable, 97

Goemans, John, lawyer, challenges Hawaiians' rights in *Rice vs. Cayetano* case, 350–351

Goldman Sachs, Bishop Estate insures Robert Rubin's stake in, 278; provides most of Bishop Estate's revenue, 267

## H

Hannabusa, Colleen, survives Bronster political fallout, 297

Hannahs, Neil, publicly scolded by Lokelani Lindsey, 158

Harmon, Bobby, 226–229; on ethical colli-
sion course with Aipa and Peters,
226–228; loses job, 229

Hifo, Elizabeth Eden. *See* Weil, Judge
Bambi

Hirai, Coleen, decides if trustees are personally liable for Bishop Estate performance, 238; orders Colbert Matsumoto to
consolidate reports, 266

Ho, Don, class leader, 109; eyes of love,
331–335

Holt, Milton, overwhelmed by "allurements," 306–307

Holzclaw, "Mother and Daddy," 23–27

Hokoana, William, Hawai'i's Saipan battle
hero, 94–95

Hualani (Ruth Hualani Lyman, Ruth
Lyman Rath), author's mother, 23;
as a young woman, 15; isolates author
because of father's sins, 46; lives in
Salvation Army Girls Home as do prostitutes, 21–22; ranch life toughens
author without her knowledge, 36–39;
silent about author's father, 14

Hudson, Loring, helps Kamehameha Boys
help U.S. servicemen survive, 93

Hugo, Tom, Jr, 339; his girl, Julie-Bethe,
117; Hugos' and the princess's flowers,
124; secret keeper, 14; and story of Eric
Kalohelani, 335–339

Hugo, Tom, Sr, story unfolds, 14; "would be
proud," 5

Hung, Chun, Chinese connection revealed,
48–52; "houris" wail, 57

I

Ing, Douglas, attorney, closes case against
Lokelani Lindsey, 300–302

Internal Revenue Service, vs. Bishop Estate
trustees, 309–313

Iungerich, Zoe, helps chicken-pox victim
look Hawaiian, 121

J

Jennings, Pauline K. Lee. *See* Kea

Jervis, Gerard ("Gerry"), 212; episode in
men's room, 289–290; investigates Oz
Stender, 211; justices ignore will in
appointment as trustee, 165; prayers and
sadness, 290

K

Kalākaua, King David, music influenced by
German tunes, 105; refuses to surrender
Pearl Harbor, 52

Kalohelani, Eric, football running back and
flower star, 117; "my brother's keeper,"
335–339

Kamehameha Schools, brief history of,
75–79

Kanahele, George, author's ninth-grade
roommate, 123; leader in Hawaiian
cultural renaissance, 168

Kauihilo, Ann, teaches student to be
careful what he says in Hawaiian, 103;
whets Arthur Godfrey's appetite for
hula, 103

Kaupiko, Eugene, boy from Miloli'i can
accomplish anything, 334

Kawananakoa, Abigail Wahi'ika'ahu'ula
("Princess David"), funeral awakens
students awareness of Hawaiian culture,
104

Kea (Pauline K. Lee Jennings), hidden
secret revealed to her, 11–16; sends
author draft of Nona Beamer's letter,
197

Keahi, Sarah, calls for Aunty Nona
Beamer's help, 195; resists Lokelani
Lindsey's edict on Hawaiian language,
170–171

Kent, Harold W., assists Kamehameha
School band's redemption, 113; brings
Hawaiian culture to Kamehameha
School's campus, 119

King, Charles, describes tradition of choral
singing, 105–106; member of Kamehameha School for Boys first graduating
class, 76

King, Samuel, tells CBS *60 Minutes* why
Kamehameha Schools family marched,
204

Kinimaka, Pii Ellis, insights into Kamehameha School for Girls, 117–119

Kualaau, Kamani, interrogated by Lokelani, 192–193

Kuali'i, author's ancestor, death at age of 175 years, 333; disguised champion and fabled warrior-king before Kamehameha I, 183

# L

Lili'uokalani, Queen, gold coins for West Point cadets, 59–60; palace prisoner, 206

Lindsey, Lokelani, 312; appointed Bishop Estate trustee, 153–154; damage control, 239–244; impact on Kamehameha Schools' reputation, 248; jail the outcome, 323; petty larceny grows, 155; trial, 283–291

Lyman, David Belden, called "Hallelujah" by Salvation Army founder, 61; foiling critics, 114; "grass ceiling" for Hawaiian men, 59

Lyman, Richard, Jr. ("Papa"), tantalizing students, 271

Lyman, Ruth Hualani. See Hualani

Lyman, Victoria, helps author find confidence amidst nature and the unnatural, 18–19

# M

Markham, Emma, entertains Arthur Godfrey, 103–104

Matsumoto, Colbert, 184–186, 237; family pride enculturation, 185; reports on Bishop Estate's abysmal financial performance, 266–271

McConoghy, Mark, financial rewards for trustees, 279

McCorriston, William, intimidator, 258; striking at Margery Bronster, 311

McCubbin, Hamilton, a "single voice," 342; preemptive leadership, un-Hawaiian style, 352

Midkiff, Frank, emphasis on work skills for students, takes pride in their achievements, 77

Moon, Ronald, mum about trustee recycling, 162; opens his mind to the public, 220

Moore, Paulette and Robert, describe march to Kawaiha'o Plaza, 206–209

Moses, a Christmas gift, 17; diminutive cowboy who shepherded the author and made him unafraid of challenges, 40–45

Mountain, Thomas, football coach, 116

Mulholland, John, chaplain, 99

# N

Nakagawa, Kenneth, consoles lonely author, 30

Nā Kumu O Kamehameha ("The Teachers of Kamehameha"), 203, 204, 209, 210

Nā Pua Ke Ali'i Pauahi ("The Flowers of Pauahi"), 202, 210, 211, 213, 263–264, 288

# P

Parker, Edmund, boyhood martial arts expert, 102; track iron man, 117

Parrent, Charles, auto shop teacher and administrator, sets Don Ho straight, 333; legacy for "Pauahi's flowers," 341

Perkins, Julie-Bethe, arranges prom date for author, 357; May Day Queen, 117

Peters, Henry, destined for greatness, 140; remains unflappable, 319–320; vanity prevails, 237

"Princess David." See Kawananakoa, Abigail Wahi'ika'ahu'ula

Prossner, Charles, halts Barnes' achievements, 86; hinders progress for dark-skinned youngsters, 77

# R

Rath, James Arthur and Ragna, author's grandparents, Palama Settlement founders, 13

Rath, James Arthur, Jr., author's missing father, 12–13

Rath, Ruth Lyman. See Hualani

Richards, Theodore, music teacher and principal, 105–106

Richardson, William, inner circle of Hawai'i's Second Revolution, 129

Roth, Randall ("Randy"), caustic observer of

loose money practices at Bishop Estate, 282; essay galvanizing public opinion, 215

## S

Sequeiras, Kuulei, honor student, 123; marries Oz Stender, 128

Stender, Oswald, 313; becomes Bishop Estate trustee, 139–147; boyhood, 64–74; guerilla warfare, 182–183; making Kamehameha Schools the world's greatest, 151; "lost generations" explained, 225; pursuing educational excellence, 180

## T

Takabuki, Matsuo, confidant to Governor Burns becomes Bishop Estate trustee, 129

Thompson, Myron ("Pinky"), gains world-wide prestige for Kamehameha Schools, 149; social worker and Governor Burns' right-hand man, 141

Trask, David, rejects Barnes' programs to improve Kamehameha Schools, 85

## V

Van Dyke, Robert, sale of book collection to Kamehameha Schools, 175–176

Veary, Emma, story of Hawai'i's virtuoso, 109–110

Vierra, Rowena, led the "invincibles," Kamehameha Girls School class of 1947 singers, 107–108

## W

Waihee, John, life after political office, 281

Webster, Ernest, toughened Kamehameha School for Boys curriculum, 76; started tradition of school song contests, 107

Wong, Richard ("Dickie"), 321; appointed Bishop Estate trustee, 153–154; dealing within the family, 292–293; offers excuses for Lokelani Lindsey, 287; "stew and rice" for Hawaiians' support, 203

Wong, James Kaupena, becomes master chanter, 104

Wong, Melva Mae, pins down Don Ho, 331

## Y

Yadao, Elisa, communicator under pressure from Lokelani Lindsey, 156, 168, 169

Yim, Judge Patrick, releases report, 230–233; shocks Lokelani Lindsey, 230

## Z

Zane, Patty, a teenager looking out for a young neighbor, 31, 33

# About the Author

J. ARTHUR RATH is a Kamehameha Schools graduate, author of several books, a retired public relations executive, and a former university adjunct professor. He is an inductee in the Kamehameha Schools Hall of Fame.

Production Notes RATH / LOST GENERATIONS

Cover and interior designed by Trina Stahl Design
in New Caledonia with display text in Fairbank MT

Composition by Josie Herr

Printing and binding by The Maple-Vail Book
Manufacturing Group.

Printed on 60# Sebago Eggshell, 420 ppi